About the authors

Rod Hill grew up in Ontario, was educated at the University of Toronto, the University of Stockholm and the University of Western Ontario, where he obtained a PhD in economics. He has taught at the University of Windsor, the University of Regina and the University of New Brunswick, where he has been a professor of economics since 2003. His research interests have included international trade policy, taxation and the underground economy, and (as a result of growing dissatisfaction) the content of the introductory textbooks. He is a research associate with the Canadian Centre for Policy Alternatives and a member of Economists for Peace and Security and the Progressive Economics Forum.

Tony Myatt received his PhD from McMaster University with distinction in theory. He has taught at McMaster University, the University of Western Ontario, the University of Toronto and the University of New Brunswick, where he has been professor of economics since 1992. His research interests have included the supply-side effects of interest rates, labour market discrimination, unemployment rate disparities, and the methods and content of economic education. He has developed several different introductory courses as well as for teaching principles of econ of everyday life', 'Economics in nomics through film'. Professo UNB's Arts Faculty Award for E. 2008.

The economics anti-textbook

A critical thinker's guide to microeconomics

Rod Hill and Tony Myatt

Fernwood Publishing
HALIFAX | WINNIPEG

Zed Books
LONDON | NEW YORK

The Economics Anti-textbook: A critical thinker's guide to microeconomics was first published in 2010

Published in Canada by Fernwood Publishing Ltd, 32 Oceanvista Lane, Black Point, Nova Scotia BOJ 1BO

<www.fernwoodpublishing.ca>

Published in the rest of the world by Zed Books Ltd, 7 Cynthia Street, London N1 9JF, UK and Room 400, 175 Fifth Avenue, New York, NY 10010, USA

<www.zedbooks.co.uk>

Copyright © Rod Hill and Tony Myatt 2010

The rights of Rod Hill and Tony Myatt to be identified as the authors of this work have been asserted by them in accordance with the Copyright, Designs and Patents Act, 1988

Designed and set by Ewan Smith, London <e-smith@dircon.co.uk>
Index <ed.emery@thefreeuniversity.net>
Cover designed by David Bradshaw

A catalogue record for this book is available from the British Library
Library of Congress Cataloging in Publication Data available

Library and Archives Canada Cataloguing in Publication:
Hill, Roderick
   The economics anti-textbook : a guide to critical thinking / Rod Hill and Tony Myatt.
ISBN 978-1-55266-360-8
   1. Economics. 2. Critical thinking. I. Myatt, Anthony II. Title.
HB171.H637 2010   330
C2010-900699-2

ISBN 978 1 84277 938 5 hb (Zed Books)
ISBN 978 1 84277 939 2 pb (Zed Books)
ISBN 978 1 84813 548 2 eb (Zed Books)
ISBN 978 1 55266 360 8 (Fernwood Publishing)

Contents

Tables and figures

Acknowledgements

We would like to thank Walid Hejazi, Michael Krashinsky and Jack Parkinson of the University of Toronto, participants in a seminar at the University of New Brunswick, and a variety of anonymous referees who provided helpful comments on the initial outline of the book. Many colleagues also helped in selecting a title: Abdella Abdou (Brandon University), Hafiz Akhand (University of Regina), Marilyn Gerriets (St Francis Xavier University), John Janmaat (University of British Columbia, Okanagan), Harvey King (University of Regina), Rob Moir (University of New Brunswick), Saeed Moshiri (University of Saskatchewan), Michael Rushton (University of Indiana, Bloomington), Jim Sentance (University of Prince Edward Island), Calin Valsin (Bishop's University) and Fattaneh Zehtab-Jadid (Brandon University).

Special thanks to: Michael Bradfield of Dalhousie University, who commented on initial drafts of some chapters; our two editors at Zed Books, Ellen Hallsworth and Ken Barlow, for their guidance and their patience with our missed deadlines; and to two anonymous referees who read the first draft.

None of the above should in any way be held responsible for the views expressed here.

Finally, thanks to our respective wives – Virginia and Muriel – for putting up with us through the writing of this book.

We dedicate this book to our respective children, Rose and Thomas Myatt, and Joan-Maki Motapanyane, and grandchildren, Maia and Terence Motapanyane, and to all inquisitive economics students who want to think for themselves and not just believe what they're told.

Introduction: our goals, audience and principal themes

'I am so displeased at the way undergraduate economics is taught. Undergraduate economics is a joke ... they teach this stuff that you know is not true ...' Herb Gintis, Emeritus Professor of Economics, University of Massachusetts (from Colander et al. 2004: 92)

'It is true that we cannot, in the time available, teach everything that we would like. But why do we pick out for treatment just that selection of topics that is least likely to raise any questions of fundamental importance?' Joan Robinson of Cambridge University (1965: 3)

In brief

The typical introductory economics textbook teaches that economics is a value-free science; that economists have an agreed-upon methodology; and they know which models are best to apply to any given problem. They give the impression that markets generally are sufficiently competitive that (for the most part) they lead to efficient outcomes; that minimum wages and unions are harmful to workers themselves; and that government regulation is either ineffective or harmful.

This *Anti-Textbook* points out that all this is a myth. Value judgements pervade economics and economic textbooks. These value judgements reflect a social and political philosophy and can be called an ideology or world-view. It is one that textbook writers are implicitly attempting to persuade the reader to accept. The *Anti-Textbook* makes this ideology, and the value-judgements behind it, explicit. The point is not so much to claim that this ideology is wrong, but simply to point out that it exists, and that there are always alternative views that one ought to consider.

Our aim is not to debunk mainstream (neoclassical) economics – just the textbook presentation of it. Partly, this is because the neoclassical paradigm is remarkably malleable. It is capable of transforming itself, of shedding many an unappealing feature.[1] Partly, it is because the boundaries of mainstream neoclassical economics are blurry. It is not clear, for example, whether recent work on 'limited rationality' lies within the neoclassical paradigm or is a direct assault upon it. In any event, the recent work on imperfect information by Joseph Stiglitz overthrows many of the neoclassical presumptions about efficiency and

I

the harmfulness of government intervention, and we see his work as being squarely within the neoclassical paradigm.[2] Though we are sympathetic to alternative paradigms and to heterodox views (one of us thinks of himself as a 'post-Keynesian' and the other as a 'European-style social democrat'), the *Anti-Textbook* is not a presentation of alternative paradigms.

This book is not 'anti' economics, or even 'anti' mainstream economics. It is 'anti' mainstream textbook economics. This is a much easier target to attack. The evidence is palpable. The books exist. You can see them, touch them and read them yourself. And should you do so, you would find that the mainstream textbooks are remarkably uniform and reflect a narrow range of world-views – indeed, a much narrower range of world-views than those held even by mainstream economists.

Of course, there are a few non-traditional textbooks – we name several in our suggestions for further reading at the end of this chapter – but they comprise a very small share of the market in the English-speaking world. Unfortunately, the vast majority of first-year economics students are subjected to the standard mainstream textbook. It is for them, and their suffering professors, as well as the intelligent layperson, that we have written this book.

We hope that our book, by citing the views of many prominent economists from a variety of schools of thought, both mainstream and heterodox, will help students to understand that economics is much more diverse (and interesting!) than what they see in their mainstream introductory text.

The structure

Our *Anti-Textbook* follows the structure of the typical microeconomics textbook and can be read in conjunction with any standard text. Alternatively, since each chapter of the *Anti-Textbook* begins with a concise exposition of the conventional textbook material before beginning our critical examination, it can even be read on its own. As such, we hope it will prove useful to students, to those professors who feel even slight discomfort with the hegemony of the conventional text, and to everyone else interested in understanding more about contemporary economics.

To help stoke the fires of revolution, each chapter contains 'questions for your professor'. These are aimed at the weak points of the texts' exposition. The aim is not so much to embarrass your professor, as to bring a deeper understanding of economics into the classroom.

Our thesis

Textbooks are necessarily selective. They must include and emphasize some things and exclude or downplay others. They ask certain questions and not others. They place some topics and questions in the forefront, and put others in the background or leave them out entirely. Those decisions usually reflect implicit, not explicit, value judgements about what is interesting and important. No 'objective' account is possible. For most people – including many economists – this is not a controversial claim.

Yet the textbooks cloak themselves in an aura of objectivity. They portray economics as a science dealing with facts and theories that make predictions. Economists are the technicians wearing white lab coats objectively comparing one theory with another, coming up with policy prescriptions supported by a consensus of professional opinion.

The *Anti-Textbook* argues that this is a myth – one which is not only dangerously misleading but also bland and boring. Value judgements arise on the first page, where the textbook writers ask 'what is economics?' and attempt to define the subject and the main problems that it addresses. A variety of possible definitions exists, and each one would give rise to different lines of enquiry. One definition might stress the importance of using society's scarce resources to make total income and production as large as possible; another might stress the importance of eliminating poverty and deprivation so that everyone's basic needs are met. When an author gives one view and ignores alternative possibilities, a value judgement has been made.

Moreover, the hope that economics would one day become a positive science relying on the evidence to confirm or to refute theories has, up to this point, been in vain. There are long-standing disputes about the effects of relatively simple policy changes. For example, does an increase in the minimum wage increase unemployment? What could be simpler than that? Many texts claim that economists have a consensus answer to this question supported by a clear body of empirical evidence. But nothing could be farther from the truth. Contradictory evidence abounds; the dispute is sometimes heated and, as we show in Chapter 2, consensus among economists has broken down beginning in the 1990s. Because competing teams of researchers consistently find opposing evidence, one journal editor (Levine 2001: 161) talked openly about 'conscious or unconscious biases' in finding a 'robust equation'. Some (such as Arnott 1995: 117) acknowledge that such disputes are a 'battleground for those who believe in free markets and those who do not'.

Furthermore, the notion that an appeal to evidence could resolve all theoretical disputes is – to put it mildly – methodologically naive. As Einstein (1926) said: 'Whether you can observe a thing or not depends on the theory which you use. It is the theory which decides what can be observed.' And as a philosopher of science, Imre Lakatos (1978), explained, the central propositions of any theoretical framework are surrounded by a 'protective belt' of 'auxiliary assumptions' that prevent them from being refuted. These issues are explored in detail in Chapter 2.

Economics is inevitably a battleground between opposing ideologies. This isn't necessarily a bad thing. Recognizing this reality puts the controversy and excitement back into economics, and reveals a fascinating and vibrant field of study – one which is more an 'art of persuasion' than it is a science.

One of the major aims of our book is to point out where ideological issues arise, and where the textbooks make implicit value judgements that you may not share. One major area where such value judgements crop up is the decision as to what to leave out of the text. Alternative perspectives may not be discussed, inconvenient questions may not be asked and contrary empirical evidence may be omitted.

We offer the readers of *The Economics Anti-Textbook* examples of such omissions in the hope that they will get into the habit of thinking about what is *not* in the text as well as what is. After all, the textbooks are not only trying to teach you how to think ('like an economist'), they are also trying to tell you what to think about.

We stress that our aim is not to trash the textbooks, nor are we portraying textbook writers (or economists generally) as propagandists or ideological hacks. All too often, the word 'ideology' is used as a term of abuse: one group that claims to be 'non-ideological' accuses others of being 'ideological'. Like anyone else, we have our own ideology or world-view that is reflected in the topics we choose to raise for attention.

Our point is not so much to claim that the ideology of the textbooks is wrong, although admittedly we do not share it. Rather, we want to remind readers that it exists. Students should be consciously aware of it – and that there are alternatives on offer.

The world-view of mainstream textbooks

So what is the world-view of the introductory texts? Harvard professor Dani Rodrik (2009) put it well in a recent commentary:

> Non-economists tend to think of economics as a discipline that idolizes markets and a narrow concept of (allocative) efficiency. If the only economics course you take is the typical introductory survey ... that is indeed what you will encounter. But take a few more economics courses, or spend some time in advanced seminar rooms, and you will get a different picture.

We agree that the typical text offers a view that 'idolizes markets' – usually not in a crude way, but in a subtle way through its choice of themes, and through its emphasis on demand and supply (also called the model of perfect competition) as the central theoretical structure. Most of the standard textbook is spent developing and applying that structure. It describes a world of perfect markets in which given resources are allocated as if by an invisible hand in a way that maximizes the value of total production. The belief that this model approximates how markets operate in the real world is often referred to as 'market fundamentalism'.[3]

According to Prasch (2008: 3): 'market fundamentalism remains the perspective of virtually every introductory economics textbook'. To further clarify the policy implications of emphasizing the perfectly competitive view of the world, Prasch (ibid.: 5) says:

> Minimum wage laws, usury laws, truth-in-advertising laws, laws to regulate fraud, health-and-safety codes, anti-discrimination laws, building inspection codes, environmental laws, investor protection rules, and many other rules and regulations have each and severally been breezily, even haughtily, dismissed by market fundamentalists and the many columnists and politicians who invoke their arguments.

It's quite true that many qualifications to market fundamentalism can be found in the mainstream texts, but they are made in such a way that they appear of secondary, rather than primary, importance. The theory of perfect markets is all too often applied reflexively to policy questions, without any discussion of whether it is relevant or appropriate. As Dani Rodrik explains, 'one's skill as an economist depends on the ability to pick and choose the right model for the situation'. Instead, the texts offer a one-size-fits-all model – the theory of perfect markets – and apply it to any and every situation. It is this deeply ingrained training which leads even professional economists to reach for that theory when offering 'a quick opinion on a policy issue', as Rodrik observes.

What's wrong with this world-view?

Market fundamentalism – the analysis that dominates the mainstream textbooks – assumes *perfect and costless information*. Much research in recent decades has explored the implications of relaxing this extreme assumption and considering what happens in a setting of imperfect information, where some people know more than others (termed 'asymmetric' information). The *Anti-Textbook* highlights the many places where this more realistic approach is relevant. With pervasive informational problems, the market economy systematically fails to produce the efficient allocation of resources that is the centrepiece of the textbook story.

Furthermore, the perfect markets of the texts are populated by large numbers of small firms, producing identical products, with no power to set their own product price. Does it matter that very few actual markets resemble this? Many economists think it does. In recent decades, a great deal of research has been devoted to markets in which there are a few large firms, or in which firms produce different products. Theories of international trade are now dominated by such approaches. The efficient allocation of resources that occurs in the perfect markets story does not happen in these more realistic approaches.

The focus on 'efficiency' that runs through the texts comes at the cost of neglecting issues of the distribution of income and wealth and of economic justice, which get short shrift in virtually all texts. In Chapter 9, we examine the textbook claim that income redistribution and greater social spending are a costly exercise that reduces economic growth; we argue that the evidence does not support this view.

Another neglected topic is the problem of *externalities*. Even when people make their decisions with perfect information, they can still choose not to take into account the effects of their actions on others. Every kind of pollution, from the local to the global, is an example of this. We show in Chapter 7 that externalities are not the afterthought that the textbooks suggest, but are a pervasive problem that render the invisible hand story irrelevant as a description of the world we live in.

Questions of *power* are absent from the texts. Yet in reality sellers try to shape and to influence the preferences of consumers, while consumers may try to exert their power to get producers to produce products in more ethical or environmentally sustainable ways. Managers exert power over workers if business organizations are authoritarian and hierarchical, as is typically the case. Corporations, labour unions, citizens' groups and non-governmental organizations may struggle to influence the 'rules of the economic game' – tax law, regulation, government programmes and so on. A similar struggle takes place at the international level. Yet, as we argue, particularly in Chapters 4, 5 and 10, power of this kind, while important in the understanding of actual economic life, is virtually absent from textbook economics.

Economics textbooks often present hypotheses and policy prescriptions with surprisingly little or no supporting evidence, or (worse) they ignore inconvenient contrary evidence. Indeed, the textbooks contain very few references to the professional literature. Another goal of this book is, where relevant, to ask for the evidence and to show the student the way to the evidence that the texts omit. It is remarkable, for example, that the texts present no evidence at all about what determines individuals' well-being. Lurking between the lines is the materialist assumption that people are better off if they have more stuff. Yet the evidence we consider in Chapter 4 offers little or no support for the materialist position.

Finally, the whole textbook structure is built on a view of human beings as rational calculators – a view that is increasingly being challenged. It is being replaced with a view of human beings as having limited rationality, and capable of irrational exuberance and exaggerated herd-like reactions to economic events.

Many of these neglected topics are needed to understand the recent global financial meltdown. Despite the existence of competition in credit markets and despite the existence of theories telling us that stock markets are efficient, we have seen a huge financial and real estate bubble burst and threaten to plunge the world economy into another Great Depression. This would be hard to explain using the textbook model of rational economic actors operating in perfectly competitive markets where there is perfect information. Indeed, as we argue in the Postscript, a full explanation involves precisely all those aspects of reality that mainstream textbooks downplay – imperfect and asymmetric information, externalities, power and limited rationality.

The shortcomings of the mainstream textbooks' world-view have not escaped all students. In 2000, a group of economics students in France circulated an open letter to their professors declaring 'We wish to escape from imaginary worlds!' and deploring the 'disregard for concrete realities' in their teaching. They asked for less dogmatism and more pluralism of approaches. Since then, petitions and open letters have appeared in the United Kingdom and in the United States. (For details, see www.paecon.net.)

The textbooks and the *Anti-Textbook*

The Economics Anti-Textbook presents a different picture of economics and a different vision of the economy – it's one that many economists see, but it has been filtered out of the mainstream introductory textbooks. It is not based on the ideas of an obscure fringe of the economics profession. We draw on the writings of many prominent economists – many winners of the Nobel Prize in economics, including even the authors of prominent introductory textbooks.[4]

We echo Akerlof and Shiller (2009: 173) when they say: 'There is then a fundamental reason why we differ from those who think that the economy should just be a free-for-all, that the least government is the best government, and that the government should play only the most minimal role in setting the rules. We differ because we have a different vision of the economy.'

Suggestions for further reading

There are quite a few non-traditional alternative texts. The Union for Radical Political Economics has a list of texts it recommends, to be found at www.urpe. org/res/text.html. Goodwin et al.'s *Microeconomics in Context* (2008) includes traditional topics, but takes ideology seriously and teaches a variety of approaches within a broader, more holistic perspective. The book by Hunt and Sherman (2008) is now in its seventh edition and has been in print for over thirty-five years. Finally, there is the long-awaited book *The Economic Conversation* by Klamer et al. (2010), which attempts to teach the diversity in economics and expose its persuasive roots. (See Bibliography.)

We will keep a blog for this book, www.economics-antitextbook.com, where we will provide updated suggestions for further reading. Readers are invited to send us suggestions as well as comments about the book itself and questions to which we'll respond on our blog. Our email address is rodntony@gmail.com.

1 | What is economics? Where you start influences where you go

'The purpose of studying economics is not to acquire a set of ready-made answers to economic questions, but to learn how to avoid being deceived by economists.' Joan Robinson[1]

'The enterprise of economics is better characterized by the content of elementary texts than by what goes on at the frontiers of economic theory.' Stephen Marglin (2008)

1 THE STANDARD TEXT

1.1 Economics is the science of choice

It seems obvious that economics is about the economy; so a commonsense definition of economics might be that it concerns itself with money, markets, business and how people make a living. But this definition is too narrow. Economics is not just the study of money and markets. It studies families, criminal behaviour and governments' policy choices. It includes the study of population growth, standards of living and voting patterns. It can also have a shot at explaining human behaviours in relation to dating and marriage.

The fact that economics can examine subjects traditionally studied by other social sciences suggests that *content* does not define the *discipline*. As long as a topic has a social dimension, we can look at it from the perspective of any social science.

Most textbooks define economics as the science of choice. It's about how individuals and society make choices, and how those choices are affected by incentives. This definition includes all aspects of life: a couple's choice to have a child, or a political party's choice of its platform. Its drawback is that it doesn't help to differentiate economics from the other social sciences, since they too look at how we make choices.

What distinguishes economics from other social sciences is its commitment to *rational choice theory*. This assumes that individuals are rational, self-interested, have a stable set of internally consistent preferences, and wish to maximize their own happiness (or 'utility'), given their constraints – such as the amount of time or money that they have. Social situations and collective behaviours are analysed as resulting from freely chosen individual actions. Just as science attempts to understand the properties of metals by understanding the atoms that comprise them, so economics attempts to understand society by analysing the behaviour of the individuals who comprise it.

1.2 Scarcity

Why is choice necessary? Textbooks emphasize that people have unlimited wants. Therefore, no matter how abundant resources may be, they will always be scarce in the face of these unlimited wants.

The fundamental question in economics has always been how do we maximize happiness? Economists maintain that while we must allow people to decide for themselves what makes them happy, we know that people always want more. Therefore, society needs to use its resources as efficiently as possible to produce as much as possible; and society needs to expand what it can produce as quickly as possible. This explains why economists emphasize the goals of efficiency and growth.

But does the concept of unlimited wants mean that someone will want an unlimited number of new coats, or an unlimited number of pairs of shoes? No, it doesn't. Along with unlimited wants, economists normally assume that the more you have of something, the less you value one more unit of it. So, unlimited wants does not mean we want an unlimited amount of a specific thing. Rather, it means that there will always be something that we will desire. There will always be new desires. Our desires and wants are fundamentally unlimited.

1.3 Opportunity cost

Since resources are scarce, if we choose to use them in one way, we can't use them in another. Choosing more of one thing implies less of another thing. In other words, everything has a cost, and the real cost of something is what must be given up to get it. This is its opportunity cost – the value of the next best alternative forgone.

It's a cliché that *there's no such thing as a free lunch* – there is always an opportunity cost. Even if someone else buys you lunch, there is still a cost. There is a cost to society for all the resources used to grow the food, ship it to the restaurant and have it prepared. Your free lunch even costs you something: it uses up some of your scarce time that you could have used to do something else.

1.4 Marginal thinking: costs and benefits

You are familiar with the margin on a page – it lies at the edge. And when someone describes a soccer player as being *marginal* they mean he is a fringe player, on the edge of inclusion. Economists use the word marginal in a similar way. Marginal cost is the cost at the margin – or to be more precise, the cost of an additional unit of output or consumption. Thus, the marginal cost of wheat is the additional cost of one more unit of wheat. Similarly, marginal benefit is just the benefit someone gets from having one more unit of something. We might

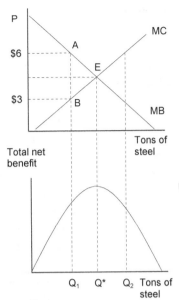

FIGURE 1.1 Marginal thinking

measure benefit in hypothetical *utils of satisfaction*; or in dollar terms – the maximum willingness to pay for one more unit. As the science of choice, the core economic framework is remarkably simple: *all activities are undertaken to the point where marginal cost equals marginal benefit*. Why? Because at this point total net benefit is maximized. An example will help.

Imagine we are old-style Soviet planners, trying to determine the quantity of steel to produce. Let's assume that the marginal cost of producing a ton of steel increases the more we produce – so we draw it as the upward-sloping line in the upper diagram of Figure 1.1. Further assume that the more steel is produced, the less one more ton is valued – so the marginal benefit line slopes down. How many tons should we produce? If we produce only Q_1 units, the marginal benefit of one more ton is $6, but the marginal cost is only $3. This means that the extra benefit of one more unit is greater than the extra cost of producing it. Therefore, we can improve society's well-being by producing one more ton. This remains true as we increase production to Q*. But we should not produce more than Q*. Beyond that point marginal cost exceeds marginal benefit, reducing total net benefit from steel production. Total net benefit is shown in the lower diagram of Figure 1.1. Clearly, this is maximized at an output of Q*.

This marginal-cost/marginal-benefit framework can be applied to everything we do, buy, hire or produce. If I want to maximize my satisfaction from studying economics, I should study until the marginal cost of one more hour of study just equals the marginal benefit. If I want to maximize my satisfaction from buying oranges, I equate marginal cost to the marginal benefit of one more orange.

When textbooks claim '*rational people think at the margin*' it is this framework they have in mind. But are people rational?

1.5 Rational and self-interested individuals

Critics claim the foundations of economics are shaky – people are not rational, they say, nor solely self-interested. But rationality in economics means something quite different from its colloquial and philosophical meaning. All it means in an economic context is that individuals are goal oriented and have internally consistent preferences (or tastes).

Economists assume everyone has the same fundamental goal: to be as happy as possible, or (to use economic lingo) to maximize their utility (or satisfaction). But different things bring happiness to different people. One person prefers to give their money to charity and live a simple ascetic life. Another prefers to spend their money on the fast life – W. C. Fields famously quipped, 'I spent 99% of my money on wine, women and song. The remainder I squandered!' Economists do not judge the things that bring utility to people. To be 'rational' in economics simply means that given your preferences, you choose to allocate your time and money to maximize your utility.

Further, individuals are not assumed to think only of themselves. Someone's utility may depend on the well-being of others. The altruist is viewed as no better or worse than the miser, since they are both trying to be as happy as possible. Selfish and selfless, virtue and vice, have no meaning in economics – they're just different preferences.

To give an idea of how broad and encompassing is the economist's notion of rational behaviour, consider this: rational behaviour and utility are often defined in a tautological or circular way. Thus, rational behaviour is: *behaviour that maximizes a person's utility*. And utility is: *what rational people maximize*. This isn't damning criticism. After all, our numbering system that defines two plus two as equalling four is also a tautology, and we find this quite useful. But the point is that such an open-ended definition of 'rational' makes it hard to find examples of irrational behaviour. In fact, we challenge our students to find examples of irrational be-haviour remembering: first, not to judge someone's preferences; second, to make allowance for less than perfect information; and finally, to make allowance for habit formation. It's not that easy. We say more on this shortly, in Section 2.

If individuals are rational, they respond to incentives in predictable ways. Thus, if we wish to encourage people to give blood we could pay them for their time. Or, if we wish to encourage people to recycle bottles, we could make them pay a bottle deposit that is refunded upon return.

1.6 Markets are usually a good way to organize economic activity

We don't need economic planners – as long as we have competitive markets they organize the economy in a way that maximizes the value of total production. This is better than the perfect planner for two reasons: first, it doesn't require an expensive planning bureaucracy; second, it doesn't require that anyone be altruistically motivated.

Most textbooks develop the argument over several chapters, but since you're reading an *anti*-textbook let's have a quick synopsis right now. Here it is in three sentences:

In competitive markets, prices and quantities are determined by demand and supply. But demand is nothing other than marginal benefit, and supply is nothing other than marginal cost. So, competitive markets guarantee that the right quantities are produced and society's net benefit is maximized.

This is the technical argument for laissez-faire, the view that governments should leave the economy alone. But textbooks seek to persuade. So, most textbooks selectively paraphrase the argument developed by Adam Smith in *The Wealth of Nations*, published in 1776. In an analogy that has become iconic, Smith compares competitive market forces to an *invisible hand* that guides self-interest into socially useful activities. In a famous passage he says: '*It is not through the benevolence of the butcher, the brewer or the baker, that we expect our dinner, but from their regard to their own interest.*' The novel twist in Smith's argument is that he turns selfishness into a virtue. Government intervention is not needed because a competitive market system naturally leads to a *harmony of interests*. In Smith's example, it leads to the optimal quantities and lowest possible prices for meat, beer and bread. In other words, it leads to an efficient outcome.

1.7 Governments can sometimes improve market outcomes

The central textbook message is this: if *all* markets were competitive (including markets that don't currently exist!), laissez-faire would produce an efficient outcome in three key aspects: it would produce the optimal quantity of each good; it would produce these quantities at the lowest possible cost; and it would distribute the output to those who 'value' it most. This ideal situation is called Pareto optimal, and it has the property that it is not possible to make anyone better off without making at least one person worse off – in other words, there would be no waste anywhere in the economy.

The condition that *all* markets must be competitive can be violated in two ways, however. First, *existing* markets may be *non-competitive*, as in the case of monopoly (a single seller). Second, many markets required for efficiency *may not exist*, such as the market for unpolluted air. Both cases lead to 'market failure'. In such situations, government intervention can (in theory) improve upon the inefficiency produced under laissez-faire. Thus, the role of the government is critically dependent on two factors: first, how competitive existing markets are; and second, upon how many markets don't exist.

1.8 Another government role: providing equity

In the special situation of complete and competitive markets, laissez-faire leads to a Pareto-optimal situation – an ideal situation in an efficiency sense. But that doesn't mean that the outcome would be fair or humane. It might be a situation where widows and orphans are starving while everyone else has three homes and a luxury yacht. So the government has another role in the economy: to redistribute income to make market outcomes more equitable. Textbooks emphasize that redistributing income necessarily creates inefficiencies, and this creates a trade-off between efficiency and equity.

1.9 The efficiency–equity trade-off

Trade-offs follow from scarcity and opportunity cost: we are always trading off more of one thing for less of another. While this kind of trade-off is mundane, textbooks also emphasize a more abstract trade-off: that more equity always comes at a cost of less efficiency. This view is encapsulated in Arthur Okun's (1975) leaky bucket metaphor: redistributing income is like carrying water from the rich to the poor using a leaky bucket – the result may be more equitable, but comes at a cost of water wasted on the ground.

The textbook argument hinges on two kinds of adverse incentive effects – direct and indirect. The direct effect is this: the more the government helps people, the less incentive they have to help themselves. For example, the so-called 'social safety net' comprises things like unemployment insurance benefits and old-age pensions. The first of these state-provided benefits is said to reduce the incentive to work and the second reduces the incentive to save (and hence to work). Therefore, they reduce efficiency by distorting people's incentives.

The indirect effect operates via the necessity to pay for the social safety net: this necessitates various forms of taxation, which also cause inefficiencies. For example, conventional textbooks claim that income taxes reduce incentives to work. Sales taxes increase prices so buyers demand less of the good, leading to a decrease in production. If an optimal amount was previously being produced, sales taxes lead to a sub-optimal or inefficient situation. Textbooks emphasize that the 'best' location on the efficiency–equity trade-off is a political issue, about which economics can add little. That is because it is a *normative* question – it depends on people's values and priorities. Instead of proposing the 'best' location on any given trade-off, the job of the economist (they say) is to explain why there is a trade-off, and to suggest ways of improving the nature of the trade-off by shifting it in such a way that society could enjoy both more efficiency and more equity.

1.10 A word on methodology

Textbooks claim that economics is a social science that avoids making value judgements. It deals with facts and concerns itself with explaining and predicting the world as it is. Questions about moral values lie outside the scope of economics. Economics cannot say how much fairness (or equity) there ought to be. Such moral questions are ultimately resolved by political decisions. All economists can do is give advice on how to achieve society's goals as efficiently as possible. The science of economics is value free.

2 THE ANTI-TEXT

2.1 The inherent tension with macroeconomics

As we mentioned the first seminal book in economics, Adam Smith's *The Wealth of Nations*, it behoves us to mention another, John Maynard Keynes's *The General Theory of Employment, Interest and Money*. Published in 1936 during the Great Depression, it attempted to explain how unemployment could persist, and what ameliorating actions governments could take. In the process of doing this, Keynes became the founding father of macroeconomics. This is the study of large aggregates, and explains such things as unemployment, inflation, exchange rates and interest rates; whereas microeconomics deals with smaller chunks of reality, such as individual markets.[2]

Keynes's message is the opposite of Smith's. Whereas Smith emphasized that a capitalist market economy can be self-regulating and efficient, Keynes emphasized that it was inherently prone to cycles of boom and bust – and those periods of bust are terribly inefficient. Whereas Smith emphasized that rational decision-making leads to an efficient outcome, Keynes emphasized that people's 'animal spirits' are driven by waves of spontaneous optimism and pessimism and (implicitly) fuelled by greed, fear and the herd instinct.

When it comes to macroeconomics, Keynes's thinking still dominates. It is generally accepted that the government must intervene in the economy to prevent both recessions and overblown expansions, and that it must regulate some sectors. Yet, when it comes to microeconomics, the thinking of Adam Smith dominates. It's an uneasy coexistence.

```
Question for your professor: Keynes emphasized the importance
of animal spirits - waves of optimism and pessimism. If the
economic actors in microeconomics were as Keynes envisaged
them, would competitive markets still be efficient?
```

2.2 Scarcity and unlimited wants

Economists in the 'post-Keynesian' school reject scarcity as a fundamental truth. Their focus is the economy in deep recession, and they argue that it is difficult to maintain the idea of scarcity when there is an 'army' of unemployed workers wanting to work, factories where they could work (but which are closed), which would produce goods that people need (but which they can't afford without a job).[3] If people could be put back to work, more of everything could be produced. We could have our cake and eat it too; there would be no opportunity cost. This gives post-Keynesians a completely different view of markets. Markets are not seen as places where scarce resources are allocated among competing ends, but rather as places where funds required for investment and expansion are realized.

> Question for your professor: Would there be an opportunity cost to putting people back to work (and producing more goods) even in a deep recession? If not, then does scarcity depend on full employment?

Post-Keynesians aren't the only ones who reject scarcity as a basic economic condition. For example, Emily Northrop (2000) questions whether the fundamental cause of scarcity – unlimited wants – is really innate, and argues that it may be merely constructed. She notes that some people manage to resist consumerism and choose different lifestyles embodying simplicity, balance or connection (to the earth and to others). The fact that some are able to do this suggests unlimited wants aren't innate. In arguing that our wants are constructed, she emphasizes the power of social norms and the power of advertising: some of society's cleverest people and billions of dollars a year are spent creating and maintaining our wants.

Northrop also points out that the notion of unlimited wants puts all wants on an equal footing: one person's want for a subsistence diet is no more important than a millionaire's want for precious jewellery. This equality of wants reflects the market value system that no goods are intrinsically more worthy than others – just as no preferences are more worthy than others. This is clearly a value judgement and one that many people reject. Yet economics, which unquestioningly adopts this approach, claims to be an objective social science that avoids making value judgements!

It is noteworthy that Keynes disagreed that 'all wants have equal merit'. Rather than identify the economic problem with scarcity, he identified it with the satisfaction of what he called absolute needs: food, clothing, shelter and healthcare (Keynes 1963 [1931]: 365). This definition of the economic problem puts equity and the distribution of income front and centre. It contrasts with the textbook approach of treating equity as a political issue outside the scope of economic analysis.

Another economist who rejects the 'innate unlimited wants' idea is Stephen Marglin (2008). Unlike Northrop, he doesn't blame advertising or social norms. Rather, he sees the fundamental cause to be the destruction of community ties, which creates an existential vacuum: all that's left is stuff. Goods and services substitute for meaningful relationships with family, friends and community. His conclusion: as long as goods are a primary means of solving existential problems, we will always want more. But what or who is responsible for undermining community ties and bonds? Marglin argues that the assumptions of

© Andy Singer

textbook economics, and the resulting policy recommendations of economists, undermine community. Let's consider how this works.

2.3 The individual versus the community

According to Marglin, the textbook focus on individuals makes the community invisible to economists' eyes. But it is our friendships and deep connections with others which give our lives meaning. So community ties, built on mutual trust and common purpose, have a value – a value that economists ignore when recommending policy.

Furthermore, Marglin argues that rational choice theory – emphasized in the mainstream textbooks – reduces ethical judgements and values to mere preferences. Are you working for the benefit of your community? That's your preference. Are you cooking the books to get rich quick and devil take the hindmost? That's your preference. Being selfish is no worse than being altruistic, they are just different preferences.

Indeed, according to mainstream textbook economics it is smart to be selfish. It not only maximizes your own material well-being, but through the invisible hand of the market it also produces the greatest good for the greatest possible number. This view influences the cultural norms of society and indirectly erodes community. This influence of economics on attitudes isn't mere speculation. Marwell and Ames (1981) document that exposure to economics generates less cooperative, less other-regarding, behaviour. Frank et al. (1993) show that uncooperative behaviour increases the more individuals are exposed to economics.

Marglin's key point concerns the uneasy relationship between markets and communities. Textbook economics praises the efficiency of markets, and economists generally favour expanding the reach of the market.[4] For example, economists favour free trade agreements because they expand markets. But free trade creates winners and losers and sometimes the losers are concentrated in geographical areas. Sometimes whole communities are wiped out. Still, economists argue that free trade is beneficial because the gains outweigh the losses. But this accounting ignores the cost of community destruction. Marglin notes (2008: 10): '[I]n practice compensation is not forthcoming. And how do you compensate somebody for the destruction of the community in which she grew up, is raising a family, and hopes one day to retire and look after her grandchildren?'

Marglin is not against markets. They can promote economic growth and raise material standards of living. But he argues that economists fail to do an appropriate cost–benefit analysis on whether extending the influence of markets is a good idea. They see the benefits, but since the community is invisible, they don't see the costs. As a result, they fail to address the question: What limits should be placed on markets for the sake of community?

> Question for your professor: Since it is our friendships and deep connections with others which give our lives meaning, why does cost-benefit analysis always give a *zero* value to community ties?

2.4 The individual versus the corporation

Marglin argues that the textbook focus on individuals is problematic. John Kenneth Galbraith went farther. He thought the textbook focus on individuals was a source of grave error and bias because in the real world the individual is not the agent that matters most. The corporation is. By having the wrong focus, economics is able to deny the importance of power and political interests.

Textbooks assume that rational individuals with a stable set of preferences allocate their spending to maximize their own happiness. This suggests that individuals exercise ultimate control over the economy – both what is produced and how – through their spending. Of course, entrepreneurs and corporations actually make those decisions. But (so the conventional argument goes) they are governed by their anticipations of market response – they cannot survive if customers don't buy. So individuals ultimately exercise control over the economy through their spending.

Further, textbooks assume that the state is subordinate to individuals through the ballot box. At the very least, government is assumed to be neutral, intervening to correct market failure as best it can, and to redistribute income so as to make market outcomes more equitable.

But this idealized world is so far removed from the real world that it is little more than a myth, or 'perhaps even a fraud' (John K. Galbraith 2004). The power of the largest corporations rivals that of the state; indeed, they often hijack the state's power for their own purposes. In reality, we see the management of the consumer by corporations; and we see the subordination of the state to corporate interest.

Galbraith saw economic life as a bipolar phenomenon. In one part of the economy there are vast numbers of small-scale businesses, the market is paramount and the state is remote. This is the part featured in economic instruction and in political speeches, even as it fast disappears. 'For the small retailer, Wal-Mart awaits. For the family farm, there are the massive grain and fruit enterprises and the modern large-scale meat producers' (ibid.: 25).

The other part of the economy consists of a few hundred enormously powerful corporations. What they need in research and development, or environmental policy, or public works, or emergency financial support, becomes public policy. Government policy is influenced in widely accepted ways. 'Between public and private bureaucracies – between GM and the Department of Transportation, General Dynamics and the Pentagon – there is a deeply symbiotic relationship. Each of these organizations can do much for the other. There is even, between them, a large and continuous interchange of executive personnel' (John K. Galbraith 1973a: 5).

In the United States, a prime example of how corporate interest takes over public interest is provided by the 'military-industrial complex'. President Dwight D. Eisenhower coined this term in 1961 in his last address to the nation as he warned about the dangers of a takeover of military policy, and even foreign policy, by the weapons industry. This industry provides employment in its political constituency and funds for politicians. 'The gratitude and the promise of political help go to Washington and to the defence budget, on to the Pentagon need and decision. And to foreign policy or, as recently in Vietnam and Iraq, to war. That the private sector moves to a dominant public sector role is apparent' (John K. Galbraith 2004: 35).

Galbraith argues that the biggest corporations have power over markets,

Questions for your professor: What the biggest corporations need in environmental policy, or public works, or emergency financial support, they usually get. But textbooks emphasize demand and supply, which omits the power of large corporations. Doesn't this stop us from seeing how we are really governed? Aren't textbooks part of the problem?

power in the community, power over the state, and power over belief. As such, the corporation is a political instrument, different in form and degree but not in kind from the state itself. Textbook economics, in denying that power, is part of the problem. It stops us from seeing how we are governed. As such it becomes an 'ally of those whose exercise of power depends on an acquiescent public' (John K. Galbraith 1973a: 11).

2.5 The trade-off between efficiency and equity reconsidered

The textbook argument for an efficiency–equity trade-off revolves around the disincentive effects from having a social safety net, and the inefficiencies created from the taxation necessary to pay for it. But taxes are not necessarily inefficient. And there are beneficial incentive effects from living in a more equitable society.

Taxes need not cause inefficiencies When it comes to pollution we actually want to create disincentives. As we see in Chapter 7, a tax on emissions of pollutants can improve economic efficiency and give society a double dividend: not only does the tax reduce a harmful activity, but society also gains the additional government spending financed by the tax. In general, we should first be taxing things that society doesn't want, such as pollution, before taxing things that society wants, such as incomes and useful commodities.

Inequality might be bad for efficiency Inequality might be bad for efficiency for many reasons. Let's begin by considering two obvious reasons. First, a high degree of inequality leads to high crime rates, which increases the social costs associated with law enforcement, the judicial process and individuals' efforts to protect themselves and their property. This reduces the resources available for other things. Second, inequality and poverty are associated with the lack of educational opportunities for the poor and worse health outcomes for everyone. A better-educated and healthier workforce is more productive than a less-educated one.

Inequality has numerous more subtle effects. Recent work, summarized by Jeff Dayton-Johnson (2001), emphasizes the importance of 'social cohesion' and the economic pay-off from trust and cooperation. These are part of a society's 'social capital' and play an important role in promoting growth. Equity promotes social cohesion and trust, whereas inequality weakens people's sense of reciprocity, and increases the sense of 'us' versus 'them'. For example, Knack and Keefer (1997) found that greater inequality significantly reduces expressed levels of trust. Lower levels of trust are, in turn, associated with lower levels of average individual well-being (Helliwell 2003).

Trust and cooperation matter to efficiency and growth for many reasons. Whereas trust between workers and management facilitates the adoption of new and more productive techniques, polarized groups engage in wasteful conflict that brings production to a standstill. Where there is trust, parties can reach handshake agreements; without trust, elaborate contracts are required. In general, the importance of trust and mutual cooperation is demonstrated by the fact that when workers 'work to rule' (and do nothing except what they are contractually obliged to do) output falls and delays increase. Clearly, workers normally do much more than they are contractually obliged to do.

Greater social cohesion also has political advantages. In *Making Democracy Work* (1993), Robert Putnam shows that engaged citizens have better government. Social cohesion leads to more political participation and better monitoring of government, which increases governmental efficiency and reduces corruption. The economic benefits take the form of better roads and sewerage systems, better regulation of business, more effective enforcement of contracts, and overall a better quality of life.

An empirically significant effect The experiences of many countries show that greater income inequality is associated with significantly lower rates of economic growth. For example, Persson and Tabellini (1994) find such a relationship in a large cross-section of countries while controlling for a wide array of other things that could also influence growth rates. Alesina and Rodrik (1994) corroborate this result using a different set of countries, different control variables and a different measure of inequality.[5]

These results help substantiate the view that equity might be good for growth – but what about efficiency? Conceptually a country might be efficient, but still choose a low rate of growth. It would be more difficult, however, for an inefficient country to grow rapidly. On balance, it is hard to imagine how equity could be bad for efficiency when it is good for growth.

> Questions for your professor: Aren't there good reasons to think that equity might enhance efficiency, for example, improved trust, less crime and violence, less waste of human potential, better health, better governance? Why does the text mention only how efficiency might be reduced?

2.6 Reconsidering the assumption of rationality

Are people really rational? We like to challenge our students to find examples of irrational behaviour. In response, students often point out that we live in an irrational society – one that's on the brink of destroying itself. But we must beware of the fallacy of composition, which states: *what's true for a part need not be true for the whole.* Individuals may be rational even when the combined outcome of their actions is something no one wants. (See Chapter 7 dealing with *externalities*.)

The next most common student suggestion is addictive behaviour. It is hard to reconcile rational choice theory with addictive behaviour – with someone destroying their own life and the lives of those they love. But mainstream economists are reluctant to abandon the attempt: if they did, where would they stop? The next step would be to recognize that people can become 'addicted' to almost anything: work, eating, television, casual sex, religion and many other activities. Ruling out all addictive behaviour rules out a huge slice of human activity.

How can rational choice theory explain addictive behaviour? Addiction to soft drugs like tobacco is somewhat amenable to explanation. Both the amount smoked and the decision to quit respond in systematic ways to the abolition of advertising, to health warnings, to rules governing smoking in public places, and to the price of cigarettes. All this conforms to the predictions of rational choice theory. But can it explain getting addicted in the first place? And what about addiction to hard drugs that destroy people's lives relatively quickly? Research suggests (see Badger et al. 2007) that the key element is inadequate understanding and inadequate information – people systematically underestimate the power of the addictive craving. Not only is this underestimated by those who have never experienced such craving. The power of future craving is underestimated by addicts as soon as they have a fix.

As even rational people make mistakes, one could argue that addictive behaviour is not necessarily irrational. But once we allow for *systematic* mistakes in evaluating self-interest, where do we stop? If this idea were extended beyond the realm of addictive behaviour, what would be left of rational choice theory? If individuals are not the best judges of their own self-interest – because they make systematic mistakes – then Adam Smith's invisible hand is not only invisible, but non-existent. So, the question of systematic mistakes is an important issue, one that has been explored by Daniel Kahneman – who, despite being a psychologist by training, received the 2002 Nobel Prize in economics.

Systematic mistakes It is generally accepted in psychology that the mind works in two quite distinct ways. *System one* is best described as a system of short cuts (or *heuristics*) that allow the mind to jump to intuitive conclusions relatively easily. Its advantage is its speed; it is also associative, uncontrolled and essentially automatic, and these constitute its areas of vulnerability. On the other hand, *system two* is systematic, logical and rule bound; it is controlled and deliberate. It is system two which is rational in a calculating sense. But most of the time we operate on the software of system one – usually with remarkable success and accuracy. Unfortunately, it is prone to making systematic errors, even with very simple mathematical questions.

For example, suppose a bat and a ball cost $1.10 in total. The bat costs $1 more than the ball. *How much does the ball cost?* What do you say?

According to Kahneman (2002) most people answer 10 cents, including 50 per cent of Princeton students! Even actuaries and researchers make similar errors. (The right answer: the ball costs 5 cents since $0.05 + $1.05 = $1.10.) We are poor at calculating some things, especially probabilities, and our intuitive answers are systematically biased: we underestimate the likelihood of mundane things happening, even as we overestimate the likelihood of frightening or exciting things happening. We are overly influenced by the decisions of others – to the point of sitting quietly in a room filling up with smoke, as long as there are others in the room doing likewise (Darley and Latane 1968). We give undue weight to the most recent past, and when making life decisions we systematically underestimate the importance of the distant future. Nevertheless, we are confident – overconfident in fact – of our ability to make judgements.

One of Kahneman's most interesting findings is that our preferences depend on inconsequential differences in the way choices are *framed*. Take two mathematically identical options and dress one up as a loss, and the other as a gain, and we choose the one dressed up as a gain. For example, if the risk associated with a medical procedure is expressed as a 10 per cent risk of dying, fewer people will accept the procedure than when the risk is expressed as a 90 per cent chance of living (Redelmeier et al. 1993).

2.7 Behavioural economics

Work such as Kahneman's has inspired an entirely new area of economics, called behavioural economics, which investigates what happens in markets in which some people display human limitations and complications. Unlike rational choice theory, behavioural economics allows human nature to be bounded in three ways: bounded (or limited) rationality, bounded willpower and bounded selfishness.

With regard to bounded rationality, it is surprising that economists are just now catching on to the importance of framing – advertisers have understood this concept for years. They understand that choice depends on how the decision-maker describes the object to himself and what associations can be given to it. Advertising attempts to frame the choice in a way that skews the buyer's decision in favour of the seller. If the seller is successful, the buyer may no longer be acting entirely in his own best interest. Instead of the presumption that markets will make everyone as well off as they can be, now all bets are off.

With regard to bounded willpower, behavioural economics recognizes that once we make a choice, we often fail to follow through. We want to lose weight and exercise more. But it's tempting to do all that tomorrow, not today. An important example of this procrastination is saving behaviour. It is generally accepted that Americans should save more, and apparently they want to. But they don't. It has proved an intractable problem. But through a better understanding of our psychology, the behavioural economist Richard Thaler (Thaler and Bernartzi 2004) came up with a solution: the Save More Tomorrow programme. The idea is that people commit a portion of their *future* salary *increases* into a retirement savings account. Brilliant! There is no sacrifice today; we do our savings tomorrow as we would prefer. When this plan was offered in several firms, a high proportion (78 per cent) joined. Those enrolled increased their saving rates from an average of 3.5 per cent to 13.6 per cent.

As to our bounded selfishness, most of us want to 'do the right thing'. This means that financial incentives can crowd out altruistic behaviour, leading to perverse effects. For example, Richard Titmuss (1970) showed that paying blood donors in the USA not only reduced the quantity of donated blood, but it also reduced its quality. As a result of his work, the World Health Organization in 1975 urged its member states to 'promote the development of national blood services based on voluntary non-remunerated donation of blood' (Dawnay and Shah 2005: 6).

Gneezy and Rustichini (2000) note that the introduction of small fines for parents who arrive late to collect their children from a nursery school causes parents to arrive late more often than before. The payment reduces the guilt about arriving late, and parents treat the situation as if they are paying for a service.

Given these results, should we pay households for recycling waste? Should we give tax relief to those who buy greener cars? The issues aren't trivial. Financial incentives can backfire.

Another interesting aspect of our bounded selfishness is that besides having a social conscience and altruistic motivations, we exhibit consideration for total strangers – and expect it in return. Giving tips in restaurants we will never again visit is one example. But systematic evidence has been provided by the *ultimatum game*: player A is given a sum of money to split with player B; if B accepts A's offer, they divide the money accordingly; but if B rejects A's offer, both players get nothing. Textbook economics says that player B should accept any offer greater than zero. Yet in thousands of trials around the world, with different stakes, people generally reject offers of 30 per cent (or less) of the total sum. The results hold even when the players are anonymous and when the sum involved is up to three months' income (Lunn and Harford 2008: 2).

This has applications to all areas in economics. An individual's willingness to pay for an object is influenced by knowing what the workers who made it were paid. A union may be prepared to jeopardize the future of the whole enterprise if it decides that the offered wages are too unfair. And empirically we find that unskilled workers in more profitable sectors or companies are paid more than identical unskilled workers elsewhere. When textbook economics ignores our instinct for fair shares, it misses a critical element of many economic interactions.

Question for your professor: Behavioural economists have
shown that financial incentives can crowd out altruistic
behaviour, and produce perverse results (examples: blood
donors, late fines at day care centres). How do we know when to
use financial incentives, and when not to?

The impact of behavioural economics on the mainstream What impact has this research had on mainstream economics? The answer is: not much. Nowadays, most textbooks contain a box somewhere mentioning behavioural economics and describing a few 'anomalies' – but they are treated as exceptions that prove the rule. Take, for example, bounded selfishness: individuals have a desire to do the right thing. Mainstream economists argue that this desire can't be that strong or there would be no pollution problem and no overfishing. Or take bounded rationality: mainstream economists argue that these cases are of limited relevance and that market outcomes will be less sensitive to these anomalies than is suggested by the behaviour of a few students in a laboratory.

In a detailed analysis of twenty-five principles and intermediate-level microeconomic textbooks used at thirty of the world's most prestigious universities, Lombardini-Riipinen and Autio (2007) found that ten made no reference at all to behavioural economics, while six dedicated less than 1 per cent of total pages to it, and another six between 1 and 2.6 per cent. They conclude that the analysed textbooks appear to share the opinion of Krugman and Wells (2005: 244), who state: 'But it's hard to find a behavioral economist who thinks that her field should replace the analysis of utility maximization. The theory of the rational consumer remains the main way that economists analyze consumer behavior.'

Of course, it's not hard to find behavioural economists who disagree with this assessment. (See the interesting debate between Pete Lunn, a behavioural economist, and Tim Harford, a mainstream economist, in *Prospect* magazine, September 2008.) Marglin feels that 'if the research agenda of behavioural economics were to be carried through unflinchingly, the results might well be devastating for the self-interested, utility-maximizing individual who has had the leading role in economics since its emergence as a separate discipline' (2008: 5).

Whether this new psychological realism will revolutionize the subject remains to be seen. Either way, it certainly provides a nice segue into our next chapter on methodology.

2.8 Concluding comment

Note how often the notion of community ties comes up in our commentary. It features in the critiques of unlimited wants, efficiency–equity trade-offs and unbounded selfishness. Starting with a view of the world that portrays society as a bunch of individual atoms each caring only about their own little universe has created a bias in economic thinking.[6] Marglin quotes the first-century Jewish sage Hillel, who asked, 'If I am not for me, who will be? And if I am only for myself, what am I?' His point is that economics has lost the balance and the tension expressed by Hillel. Rather than seeing individuals as atoms, Marglin suggests that we see individuals as subatomic particles that exist only in relation to other particles.

Suggestions for further reading

For a focused discussion of social cohesion and its economic benefits, see Dayton-Johnson (2001); for an interesting discussion of why and how economics has ignored community and the consequences of this neglect, see Marglin (2008) *The Dismal Science: How thinking like an economist undermines community.*

2 | Introducing economic models

'Whether you can observe a thing or not depends on the theory
which you use. It is the theory which decides what can be observed.' Albert Einstein[1]

'Economics is the science of thinking in terms of models joined
to the art of choosing models which are relevant to the contemporary world.' John Maynard Keynes[2]

1 THE STANDARD TEXT

1.1 Model building and model testing

Science is a method – a process of forming hypotheses, making predictions and
testing the predictions against the facts. Sometimes a hypothesis will emerge from
inference: looking at the world and making a generalization about it. Sometimes it
will emerge from a process of deduction: thinking about the world in a systematic
way. Usually deduction involves trying to separate what is essential about a
problem from its irrelevant details. When we do this, we have created a simplified
version of reality, or a *model* of reality. Thus, building models necessarily entails
making assumptions that are *unrealistic* – otherwise they wouldn't be *simplifying*.

The point is that if a model makes good predictions, then that aspect of reality
which is ignored (or simplified away) did not significantly affect the outcome.
Therefore, it is inappropriate to judge the usefulness of a model by the realism of
its assumptions; the only relevant test is the accuracy of the model's predictions.

Having established this, most texts then illustrate the notion of model
building by presenting several different models – one of which is invariably the
production possibility frontier.

1.2 Examples of economic models

The production possibility frontier (PPF) The production possibility frontier model
has several uses. Besides providing a visual illustration of the contrast between
efficiency and inefficiency, it also illustrates opportunity cost and the inevitability
of trade-offs. Many textbooks begin their presentation with a Robinson Crusoe
situation: Crusoe on his desert island has to divide his time between two
activities, fishing and gathering coconuts. Devoting more time to fishing implies
less time for coconuts; the opportunity cost of one more fish is the number of
coconuts forgone.

Next, Crusoe meets Man Friday, who also fishes and gathers coconuts. Man Friday is less productive at both tasks, but especially at gathering coconuts; when it comes to fishing he is only slightly worse than Crusoe. Having met, should they continue to work in isolation? Since Crusoe is more efficient in everything, could it be in his best interests to continue to go it alone?

It turns out that specialization and exchange (trade) can benefit them both. It doesn't matter that Crusoe is more efficient (or has an 'absolute advantage') in producing both fish and coconuts. Crusoe should spend more time gathering coconuts (at which he is much better), and Man Friday should spend more time fishing (at which he is only a little worse). Such an arrangement will increase their total production of fish and coconuts.

Having established the benefits of trade in this context, individuals are replaced with countries. In this way the gain from international trade is put on the same footing as the gain from interpersonal trade. Since the latter must be beneficial as long as both individuals engage in trade voluntarily, we may be lulled into thinking that trade between nations is similarly unproblematic.

We take up the story at this point assuming two countries (England and Canada), two industries (wheat and cloth) and one factor of production, labour. This parallels the demonstration of comparative advantage by David Ricardo in 1817, and for that reason is often called the Ricardian model of trade.

Comparative advantage and the gains from trade Suppose that one unit of labour can produce 5 bushels of wheat or 10 yards of cloth in England; whereas one unit of labour can produce 100 bushels of wheat or 50 yards of cloth in Canada. These data are shown in Table 2.1 below.

TABLE 2.1 Labour's productivity in England and Canada

| | One unit of labour can produce: | | Opportunity cost of 1 yard of cloth |
	Wheat (bushels)	Cloth (yards)	
England	5	10	½ a bushel of wheat
Canada	100	50	2 bushels of wheat

Clearly, Canadian labour is more efficient in both industries; so Canada has an absolute advantage in both. But England has a comparative advantage in the production of cloth. This simply means that the opportunity cost of producing cloth is lower in England than in Canada.

In particular, it takes one tenth of a unit of labour to produce 1 yard of cloth in England. But one tenth of a unit of labour could have produced half a bushel of wheat in England. Thus, the opportunity cost of a yard of cloth is half a bushel of wheat in England. Following the same logic, the opportunity cost of 1 yard of cloth in Canada is 2 bushels of wheat.

England's lower opportunity cost of cloth means that it has a *comparative advantage* in cloth. Both countries will benefit by specializing according to their comparative advantage. This can be demonstrated using production possibility frontiers.

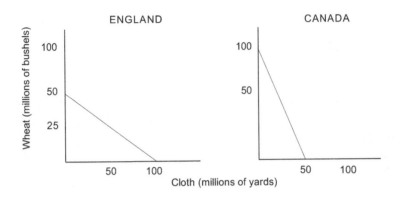

FIGURE 2.1 Wheat and cloth production in England and Canada

Suppose that England has 10 million units of labour. Devoting all its labour to wheat production, it could produce 50 million bushels. Alternatively, if it devoted all its labour to cloth production it could produce 100 million yards of cloth. We plot these two extremes in the left-hand panel of Figure 2.1 and connect the two points with a solid straight line to show England's current production possibility frontier (PPF). As we assume constant output per unit of labour input, the PPF is linear. England could choose to produce anywhere along it.

Assume that Canada has 1 million units of labour available for production per month. Referring back to Table 2.1, Canada could produce 100 million bushels of wheat and no cloth, or 50 million yards of cloth and no wheat. Joining these points yields Canada's production possibility frontier, shown in the right-hand panel of Figure 2.1. If each country specializes a little more in the commodity in which it has a comparative advantage, then total world output of both goods will be increased. Let's see how.

Suppose that in England international trade causes 100 units of labour to move out of wheat and into cloth production. From Table 2.1, English wheat output falls by 500 bushels and English cloth output increases by 1,000 yards per month. In Canada, let's suppose that international trade causes ten units of labour to move out of cloth and into wheat production. As a result, Canadian cloth output decreases by 500 yards, and Canadian wheat output increases by 1,000 bushels per month. Table 2.2 summarizes the result.

TABLE 2.2 Changes in world output

	Wheat (bushels)	Cloth (yards)
England	- 500	+ 1,000
Canada	+ 1,000	- 500
WORLD	+ 500	+ 500

World output increases as a result of each country specializing a little more in that commodity in which it has a comparative advantage. Since world output increases, it is clear that mutually beneficial trade is possible.

Could one country seize most of the benefits for itself? It is possible, depending on the terms at which they trade. Since England is exporting cloth, the higher the price of cloth (in terms of wheat) the more England benefits (and the less Canada benefits). But as long as trade is voluntary, both countries must gain something to induce them to trade at all.

Before trade, the price of each good is determined by its opportunity cost. So, in England the price of a yard of cloth is half a bushel of wheat. It will export cloth providing it can get a better price than that. In Canada the price of a yard of cloth is 2 bushels of wheat. It will import English cloth if it can pay less than 2 bushels of wheat per yard of cloth. For illustrative purposes, suppose they settle on a price halfway between the two extremes, a price where they both benefit equally: a price of 1 yard of cloth for 1 bushel of wheat.

Without trade, consumption possibilities are limited to what each nation can produce for itself. Trade expands the consumption possibilities, however, out to the dotted lines in Figure 2.2. Since both nations have expanded their consumption possibilities, both nations are better off as a result of trade, or so it is claimed.

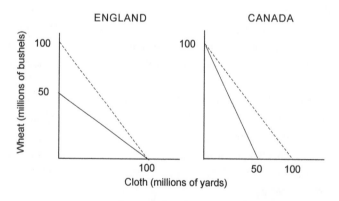

FIGURE 2.2 Expanded consumption possibilities

1.3 Positive and normative economics

Having illustrated several important concepts through the use of models, the typical textbook now emphasizes that models can be used only to shed light on questions of fact. This is the subject matter of *positive economics*, which focuses on the way the world actually works; it can help us to determine whether positive statements, or statements about fact, are true or false. For example, 'an increase in the minimum wage will increase unemployment for young and unskilled workers' is a positive statement. It may not be true, but it is still a positive statement in so far as it can be refuted or confirmed by appealing to the empirical evidence.

On the other hand, economic models can't be used to shed light on how the world *ought* to be. This involves making value judgements, often involving questions of fairness or equity, and is the subject matter of *normative economics*. For example, the statement 'there should be no homeless people in rich developed countries' is a normative statement based on values – it cannot be tested by appealing to empirical evidence.

Textbooks use this distinction to help explain why there is a public perception of widespread disagreement among economists. Economists, like other citizens, have different values; therefore they often disagree over normative issues. But on positive issues decided by statistics and economic analysis, textbooks claim there is widespread consensus. For example, many textbooks cite the survey by Alston et al. (1992) which finds that 93 per cent of economists agree with the statement: *tariffs and import quotas usually reduce general economic welfare.* A similar percentage agree that *a ceiling on rents reduces the quantity and quality of housing available*; and more than 80 per cent of economists agree with the statement *minimum wages increase unemployment among young and unskilled workers.* This shows, textbooks argue, that there is a great deal of consensus among economists on questions of fact – on positive issues.

Positive economics occupies most of the time and effort of the economics profession. Textbooks claim normative issues lie outside the scope of economics. Economics cannot say how much fairness (or equity) there ought to be. That is ultimately a political decision.

2 THE ANTI-TEXT

2.1 Textbooks fudge their own methodology

Textbooks emphasize that models cannot be judged by the realism of their assumptions, but only by the accuracy of their predictions. Yet in this chapter of the typical mainstream textbook several models are presented and their predictions are *not* tested against the facts. Instead, predictions about the benefits of specialization and trade (for example) are stated as if they have been *demonstrated* by the model. This lack of testing can perhaps be forgiven in such an early chapter of a textbook. But this same omission continues throughout subsequent chapters. Rarely is any evidence presented to back up a model's predictions, let alone a systematic consideration of evidence.

Further, the textbooks fail to clarify the comparative nature of model testing. The real issue is always how well a model performs relative to an alternative model; how well one set of assumptions performs relative to an alternative set of assumptions. In practice, a poorly performing model will not be abandoned unless we have an alternative that can do better. Textbooks don't mention difficulties associated with model selection.

Why don't the textbooks consistently apply the test of predictive power to the models they present? One possible answer is that predictive power isn't all it's cracked up to be. Predictive power may be fine in the natural sciences, such as physics or chemistry, but in a social science like economics, where there are so many variables that are impossible to control, it simply doesn't give us conclusive answers. Consequently, if we restrict ourselves to talking about things that we can statistically test, then we'd have nothing (or very little) to say.

This is the view taken by McCloskey and her associates in many papers and books spanning twenty-five years.[3] Her key point is that the textbook methodology does not actually describe how economists go about doing economics. For McCloskey, economics isn't really a science; it's more a rhetorical art, an art of persuasion. And one of the techniques used in persuading people is to cloak economics in an aura of science. Economics textbooks talk about 'testing hypotheses' – it makes economists seem impartial and gives them authority. But because the story is a fiction, textbooks quickly forget about predictions and hypothesis testing, and get back to their main business, telling persuasive parables. Let's look at this in more depth. We begin by investigating the limits of predictive power and hypothesis testing in economics.

> Question for your professor: In this course, are we going to decide which models to use by the relative accuracy of their predictions?

2.2 Predictive power isn't all it is cracked up to be

Nearly all textbooks claim widespread agreement among economists about non-normative economic questions. Many cite a 1992 survey for support. For example, Parkin and Bade (2006: 14) claim that 'at least 7 out of every 10 economists broadly agree' that: *a minimum wage increases unemployment among young workers and low-skilled workers*. Mankiw et al. (2002: 32) claim that this proposition was endorsed by 79 per cent of economists – a number they call 'an overwhelming majority'. Let's consider this purported consensus. There have been three surveys published, the results of which are contained in Table 2.3.

TABLE 2.3 Percent in agreement with the proposition: 'minimum wages increase unemployment among young and unskilled workers'

	1979*	1992†	2003‡
Generally agreed	68	56.5	45.6
Agreed with provisos	22	22.4	27.9
Disagreed	10	20.5	26.5

Note: * Kearl et al. 1979; † Alston et al. 1992; ‡ Fuller and Geide-Stevenson 2003

From Table 2.3 we see that to get 79 per cent agreeing with the minimum wage proposition on the 1992 survey, one must add the 'generally agree' category to the 'agree with provisos' category. This is a bit of a liberty, isn't it? What if the proviso is related to the size of the minimum wage increase? For example, a doubling of the minimum wage would increase youth unemployment, but a 20 per cent increase would not. If that were the proviso then the economists who 'agreed with provisos' would hold 'heretical' beliefs. They are not singing from the same hymn book as the textbooks because (as we will see in the next chapter) the textbook prediction is that any increase in minimum wages would increase unemployment. Since we really don't know what the provisos are, we simply shouldn't group the two categories.

Comparing the results of the three surveys, we see a clear trend: a decline in the percentage of those who generally agreed and a rise in the percentage of those who disagreed. If these three surveys show anything at all, they show the breakdown of consensus with regard to the minimum wage proposition.

This breakdown of consensus almost certainly reflects the work of Card, Katz, Krueger and others, much of it published in the early 1990s, which apparently showed that minimum wage increases often have a zero or positive impact on employment. These results have been the subject of a 'lively' debate, discussed in Card and Krueger's 1995 book *Myth and Measurement*.[4]

Some idea of the tone of the debate can be had by noting that Valentine (1996) accused Card and Krueger (1994) of practising 'politically correct' economics, and of deliberately using suspect data in one of their studies. For their part, Card and Krueger present evidence of 'publication bias' against results contrary to textbook conventional wisdom (1995: 186).

A feature of the debate, key for our discussion of methodology, is that one team of authors would consistently find results different from another team. David Levine, editor of the Berkeley journal *Industrial Relations*, attributed this phenomenon to 'author biases', which he diplomatically defined as 'conscious or unconscious biases in searching for a robust equation' (2001: 161).

What does searching for a 'robust' equation mean? The point is that testing hypotheses is not an easy matter. For the minimum wage proposition, other things besides minimum wages affect the unemployment of young and un-skilled workers, and these other influences need to be 'controlled' for, taken into account. For example, we need to control for the number of school leavers entering the labour market searching for jobs, and for the overall state of the economy, whether we are in a recession or boom. And so on, and so on. A full set of such controls needs choosing, defining and measuring, and the choices we make may influence the result.

On top of this, there are well-known statistical pitfalls to avoid. If the data don't have certain statistical properties, it is possible to erroneously find sig-nificant evidence where there is none in reality. To add to the difficulty, there may be more than one way to avoid such pitfalls, and the choice of method may influence the result.

Finally, a statistical result may be dependent on a very particular time period. It may be that addition or deletion of observations changes the result.

These are examples of non-robustness. To recapitulate, results may not be robust to: slightly different choices of control variables; or seemingly trivial dif-ferences in how any given control variable is measured; or seemingly equivalent ways of correcting for statistical pitfalls; or slight changes in the data period.[5] Indeed, in the case of the minimum wage proposition, all these small decisions evidently did affect results to such an extent that different teams consistently found different results, leading to apparently serious economists being reduced to name-calling.[6]

It's not just differences in research design which can lead to different results. Dewald et al. (1986) had great difficulty *replicating* published results – that is, using exactly the same data, exactly the same definitions and exactly the same statistical procedures, they could not arrive at the same results as those published. Replication is an essential component of scientific methodology, and is the only way to create a defensible, coherent body of knowledge. Yet seldom are results replicated. They note: 'It is widely recognised that errors occur in empirical eco-nomic research and appear in published empirical articles. Our results ... suggest that such errors may be quite common' (ibid.: 600).[7] McCullough et al. (2006) and McCullough and Vinod (2003) suggest that things have not improved.

The point is that in practice hypothesis testing is problematic. It relies on a combination of economic theory and statistics known as econometrics and 'econometrics ... has not been able to deliver as a tool for falsification of theories' (Hahn 1987: 110). We have illustrated this point using the minimum wage controversy, but there are many, many more.[8]

The minimum wage debate became surprisingly heated given how little is at stake – a prediction of the standard textbook competitive model of the labour market, which, as we'll see in the next chapter, requires many highly unrealis-tic assumptions. It is astonishing that so many economists are so committed to believing in the empirical relevance of this model that they feel extreme discomfort when its predictions are challenged. Indeed, textbook writers (or the economics professors who adopt the textbooks) apparently feel so much discomfort that they continue to assert that a *consensus* exists about the effect of minimum wages! It is almost as if the minimum wage proposition is believed as an article of faith and is incapable of refutation.

But wait ... should we really be surprised by this? Many years ago Imre Lakatos (1978) explained that we should expect this to be the case – at least the 'incapable of refutation' part.

> Question for your professor: How can we have confidence in econometric test results when economists can't even replicate each other's results [see Dewald et al. (1986); McCullough and Vinod (2003); McCullough et al. (2006)]?

2.3 Core propositions are incapable of refutation

According to Lakatos the central propositions of any theoretical framework are surrounded by what he termed a 'protective belt' of 'auxiliary assumptions' that prevent them from being refuted. For example, in the minimum wage case the central proposition that is being tested is that the standard textbook competitive model has empirical validity – that it is an empirically accurate portrayal of how actual markets function. This proposition gives rise to testable predictions; one is the minimum wage prediction. The auxiliary assumptions involved in testing this prediction include: that the correct control variables are selected; that they are measured in the correct way; that statistical pitfalls are properly corrected; and that there are no errors in the computations.

The auxiliary assumptions provide a protective belt because negative evidence can be discounted by the true believer on the grounds that the auxiliary assumptions didn't hold: the authors of some particularly damning piece of empirical research must have made poor decisions or errors that led them to fail to identify the true minimum wage effects that are surely latent, waiting to be discovered. A true believer taking that view would be consoled by the occasional appearance of a paper that seems to uncover such evidence.

The minimum wage prediction isn't even a particularly difficult prediction to test. Blinder et al. (1998) faced an altogether more challenging task – trying to evaluate the relative merits of models offering different explanations for why prices aren't instantaneously determined by supply and demand (a phenomenon known as price stickiness). They say:

> If a theory makes no prediction other than that prices move less rapidly than [competitively determined] prices, econometric testing is almost (but not quite)

out of the question. To conduct a test, a complete model of supply, demand, and price adjustment must be specified, estimated, and used to derive a quantitative measure of the speed at which the market-clearing price moves. Then actual price movements can be compared to this norm. This ... is one of the ways that econometricians have demonstrated that prices and wages are sticky. But, of course, any such demonstration is conditional on the validity of the many maintained hypotheses used as the framework for estimation. So any such finding is open to dispute. (Ibid.: 7)

McCloskey (1983) agrees that any hypothesis 'is insulated by the ancillary hypotheses necessary to bring it to a test'. (Treat 'ancillary' and 'auxiliary' as synonyms.) She goes on to say:

This is no mere possibility but the substance of most scientific disagreement: 'Your experiment was not properly controlled'; 'you have not solved the identification problem'; 'you have used an equilibrium model when a disequilibrium (monopolistic, 500 equation) model is relevant'. And even if the one hypothesis in question could be isolated, the probabilistic nature of hypotheses, most especially in economics, makes crucial experiments non-crucial: chance is the ever present alternative ... that spoils falsificationism. (Ibid.: 487)

(McCloskey uses the word 'falsificationism' to refer to the belief that false hypotheses will be rejected through econometric – or statistical – methods. At a deeper level it is the notion that an appeal to evidence could resolve all theoretical disputes.)

> Question for your professor: Since any negative result could always be blamed on the way a hypothesis was framed, can a hypothesis ever be categorically rejected?

2.4 Economics is the art of rhetoric

McCloskey is only one of many who have pointed out the limitations of hypothesis testing (and predictive power) as criteria for model selection. Where she is unique is in labelling this methodological approach the official or explicit methodology and in claiming that economists have another methodology, an unofficial or implicit one, that is far more effective. Furthermore, the chief difficulty with economics in her view is that economists haven't abandoned their official methodology. She thinks economists need to consciously embrace their implicit (unofficial) methodology. McCloskey calls this unofficial methodology 'the art of rhetoric'.

Rhetoric literally means effective communication. So, McCloskey means something very broad and encompassing by the art of rhetoric: she means any form of reasoned argument. It is 'the art of probing what men believe they ought to believe; the art of discovering good reasons, finding what really warrants assent' (ibid.: 484). Recently, she put it like this: 'all it means is it's argued and that the proofs or evidence are not slam dunks every time' (Klamer et al. 2010: ch. 1).

Of course, in engaging in this gentle art of persuasion economists use the full range of rhetorical devices. They use analogies (or metaphors), thought experiments, natural experiments, historical precedents and appeals to authority. Moreover, McCloskey argues that the official methodology – predictive power and hypothesis testing – is also rhetorical. Such tests are ornamental, designed to give an argument more authority. Relying solely on such tests, however, would be sterile and antiquated.

McCloskey's critics universally agree that she has successfully described the unofficial methodology that economists actually use – that economists are persuaders, not hard-nosed scientists. For example, Hahn says: 'McCloskey has no difficulty in showing that economic discourse is primarily rhetorical and not scientific. For instance [s]he gives convincing demonstration of the use of "literary devices" in what appear to be formal arguments by Samuelson, [s]he documents the metaphorical nature of well known propositions, and [s]he has a masterly chapter on the rhetoric of significance tests' (1987: 110).[9]

Similarly, Robert Heilbroner praises aspects of McCloskey's work:

> What McCloskey wants economists to understand is that the language of formalism and mathematics is still a language, and therefore inescapably 'rhetorical'. Moreover, it is a dangerous language in that it conceals the elements of judgment and moral valuation that are an intrinsic part of economics. (1998: 39)

In other words, Heilbroner agrees with McCloskey that so-called positive economics – even when it's phrased in mathematical terms – contains a normative base. This is a point we'll come back to later in the chapter.

While praising different aspects of McCloskey's work, the critics unanimously disagree with her on a key issue: McCloskey feels that the unofficial methodology is appropriate and fruitful, whereas her critics do not. For example, Hahn worries that '... without rules a chasm opens up in which cranks and madmen will frolic. McCloskey ... invites us to engage in honest and open-minded conversation but on the grammar of this conversation [s]he has little to say' (1987: 111).

Similarly, Heilbroner disagrees with McCloskey that the chief difficulty with economics is that economists haven't abandoned their official methodology. He says: 'The deepest failure of economics is not its failure to shake off an obsolete and damaging rhetoric, but its failure to recognize the inescapably ideological character of its thought' (1998: 42).

But what is wrong with the unofficial methodology that McCloskey wants economists to embrace? Let's consider her list of rhetorical devices in more detail.

Analogies and metaphors ... are mere literary devices. They shouldn't convince anyone of anything. But McCloskey is right when she says that they do. They can exert a powerful influence over the imagination. For example, consider the fundamental model used to explain individual choice. In Chapter 1 we explained that all activities should be undertaken up to the point where marginal cost equals marginal benefit. Why don't we test this model by going out and asking people whether that's how they make their decisions? Of course, few would even understand the concepts, let alone affirm that they operate like that. But not to worry; we have an analogy – originated by Milton Friedman (1953: 21) – that explains the problem away. This is the pool-player analogy.

Consider the world champion pool player. He intuitively makes excellent use of the laws of physics concerning angles, rotation of spheres and friction, without understanding them intellectually. On the pool table, he acts *as if* he understands the laws of physics. We could probably write a computer program utilizing all these laws of physics that might do an excellent job of predicting the pool player's next shot. But if you ask the pool player, you would find he didn't understand those laws. Yet this doesn't affect the predictive power of our computer model.

Of course, there are other difficulties with surveying people: responses may be sensitive to the precise wording of the question; and people may have no incentive to respond truthfully. But the pool-player analogy – he acts *as if* he understood the laws of physics without realizing that he does – has exerted a powerful influence over the imagination of economists and helps to explain their extreme scepticism that anything can be learnt about economic behaviour by asking people.

What about thought experiments? This is just a folksy way of talking about model building and deductive thinking. This is nothing new. As we know, model building can be useful – providing the predictions can be tested against the evidence. If they are not tested, or if they can't be tested, we end up with the situation described by Wassily Leontief: 'Page after page of professional economic journals are filled with mathematical formulas leading the reader from sets of more or less plausible but entirely arbitrary assumptions to precisely stated but irrelevant theoretical conclusions' (1983: viii).

If economists could start their theorizing process from axioms – from assumptions that are self-evidently true – then we would hardly need to test the predictions of theory. As long as we make no errors of deduction, the conclusions are as sound as the axioms they are based on. But unfortunately, we don't have axioms. Instead, as Alan Musgrave (1981) explains, there are really only two types of assumptions in economics: 'negligibility' assumptions – which ignore irrelevant minor details that clutter up our thinking; and 'domain' assumptions – which determine the range of applicability of a given theory. Musgrave makes a convincing case that economists often confuse the two types. The trouble with Musgrave's distinction is there is no *objective* criterion to distinguish the two types.

What about natural experiments? McCloskey (Klamer et al. 2010) believes natural experiments are often the most persuasive arguments economists have. She talks about the 1911 influenza pandemic in India that eliminated 10 per cent of the labour force. This caused a decrease in the supply of labour, which the textbook competitive model predicts would lead to increased wages. According to McCloskey the prediction is borne out.

This sounds impressive. But before we get carried away, consider McCloskey's other example of a natural experiment: in the early 1990s the state of New Jersey raised its minimum wage relative to neighbouring Pennsylvania. This is a potentially attractive natural experiment since both states had similar economic and social structures – *especially either side of the state boundaries*. This natural experiment is precisely what Card and Krueger's 1994 article was about – and this article turned out to be very controversial. In particular, the critics of Card and Krueger (1994) contend there *were* important differences in the operating environment of firms on different sides of state boundaries: in taxes, for example, and in the way in which wages were reported and therefore measured.

As the controversy surrounding this article shows, natural experiments do not eliminate the need to choose and measure the relevant set of control variables, nor do they eliminate the need to avoid statistical pitfalls. So, it is not at all clear what advantage natural experiments have over everyday econometric hypothesis testing.

Then what about historical precedents? These are unique historical events such as the transition to a market economy in former communist countries. But these are the most problematic of all. Is China progressing so well because it embraced markets, or because it gave them so tight a rein? Were the problems with the Russian transition from communism in the 1990s because it moved too quickly to a market system or too slowly, or something else altogether? Evaluating such questions is really an art, requiring in-depth study and amassing a ton of evidence. And in the end the conclusions could be situation specific.

What about appeals to authority? Yes, economists do this all the time to sound more persuasive. In this *Anti-Textbook* we quote economists more celebrated than ourselves to bolster our arguments. We mention approvingly when Nobel

Prize winners in economics support the points we make. In this, we are no different from medieval astronomers justifying their earth-centred view of the universe by appealing to the authority of Aristotle or the Holy Scriptures. Thankfully, those appeals didn't impede the march of scientific progress. We hope ours won't either. In other words, readers should take appeals to authority with a pinch of salt. The reason we do it is to show you that we're not making this up.

What else is left? We discussed surveys in the context of the pool-player analogy, and we discussed the use of controlled experiments in Chapter 1. We saw how the experiments of the behavioural economists have had a limited impact on the mainstream. The majority view continues to be that we should observe what people actually do in markets (not what they say they do, or what they do in laboratories); then we should model that behaviour theoretically, and test the model econometrically.

McCloskey in a nutshell The problem with McCloskey's unofficial methodology is that it offers nothing new that is useful. In particular it offers no solution to the difficulties of doing so-called positive economics. The only difference is that McCloskey is more honest about the tricks of the trade, and the rhetorical devices used to persuade. As Heilbroner points out, she fails to recognize the inescapably ideological character of economic thought.

Question for your professor: If we can't rely on econometrics, how can we determine which hypotheses are right and which are wrong?

2.5 Paradigms and ideology

While the word *paradigm* doesn't appear in most economics textbooks, it is a simple and important concept: it is the *world-view* shared by members of a scientific community. It defines what is to be investigated and the methods and abstractions that are regarded as legitimate. In a nutshell, a paradigm refers to a coherent 'school of thought'.

One reason mainstream textbooks don't mention the word 'paradigm' is that they don't mention alternative schools of thought. They teach exclusively within the dominant paradigm called neoclassical economics. But it's not the only one. Perhaps you could ask your professor about alternative economic paradigms and how their view of the world differs from the textbook view.[10]

Thomas Kuhn (1962), who gave the word 'paradigm' its contemporary meaning, argues that paradigms are a kind of necessary indoctrination – necessary

In the figure on the left, do you see the young woman looking over her right shoulder? Or do you see the older woman looking down towards the left? In the figure on the right, viewed one way, one sees the old hag; viewed upside down, one sees the beautiful princess. In a way, paradigms operate just like this. Confronted with the same reality, some perceive the benefits of a free-market capitalist economy; while others see the opposite and predominantly perceive the costs.

FIGURE 2.3 Different perceptions of reality

because research needs rules. It is difficult enough to push forward the frontiers of science without always questioning the fundamental assumptions upon which it is based. While this provides an advantage, there is an obvious drawback: scientists trained to think in a specific paradigm have difficulty thinking 'outside the box'. This is what Keynes had to say about the difficulties he encountered writing *The General Theory* – his macroeconomic explanation for the Great Depression of the 1930s:

> The composition of this book has been ... a long struggle of escape ... from habitual modes of thought and expression. The ideas which are here expressed so laboriously are extremely simple and should be obvious. The difficulty lies, not in the new ideas, but in escaping the old ones, which ramify ... into every corner of our minds. (Keynes 1936: viii)

What we are trained to see influences what we actually do see. And reality can be perceived in many different ways, as Figure 2.3 illustrates. Furthermore, no paradigm – especially in the social sciences – can be value free. While mainstream textbook economics claims to be a 'positive' subject, and claims to avoid value judgements, the claim hardly stands up to the most casual scrutiny. Values inevitably creep into so-called positive economics, since our values determine the questions we ask, the data we use, and the way we conceive the problem.

Think back to Chapter 1, to the fundamental building blocks of textbook economics. There we see how values creep in the moment we focus on individuals as the most important economic agent, rather than the corporation or the community. They creep in the moment we define all wants as equal – the want for a subsistence diet and the want for a larger luxury yacht. They creep in the moment we reduce ethical judgements and values to mere preferences. And in this chapter we have seen how the values of researchers 'consciously or unconsciously' affect their research results.

If values necessarily pervade any paradigm in the social sciences, how does a paradigm differ from an ideology? The answer is that it doesn't differ much. An ideology is a view of the way the world works, especially as applied to politics. It embodies a view of human nature and the possibilities for change. It embodies value judgements about what's good and bad. Different political ideologies give rise to different schools of thought in the social sciences. So, one might argue that an ideology is more fundamental than the paradigm it gives rise to. But the point is that any paradigm is necessarily infused with an ideological perspective.

What is the ideological perspective with which neoclassical economics is infused? Well, that's what this book is about. We argue that it is possible to infer the values of neoclassical economics from the textbook presentation of the subject: from the emphasis given to certain topics and the lack of emphasis given to others, from the unsupported claims, from the questions that are never asked, and from the propositions that are believed as articles of faith and can never be refuted.

It's not the only possible approach. We could have taken an approach that traces the intellectual history of ideas and pointed out that the roots of neoclassical economics go back through Adam Smith to the classical liberals – to John Locke and then later to John Stuart Mill – and their fundamental values of individual responsibility, freedom of choice, the sanctity of private property, and minimal government interference. In other words, neoclassical economics is aligned with a political philosophy that in the eighteenth and nineteenth centuries was called classical liberalism and today would be called conservative.

Yet another approach is taken by David George (1996). He analyses carefully the language used in textbooks. He says: 'it is the rhetorical practices of introductory texts more than it is the "received theory" that convey a conservative (or "classical liberal") world-view' (ibid.: 28). For example, some textbooks emphasize the opportunity cost associated with public spending, but private

---

Question for your professor: It is generally accepted that all paradigms reflect a particular world-view or ideological perspective. What is the ideological perspective of neoclassical economics?

expenditures would never be characterized as a diversion of real resources from the public sector (ibid.: 30). Some talk about the resources 'used up' by the government, as if the citizens get no benefit from them, and about the government 'imposing' taxes, which suggests an authoritarian government going against the popular will.

2.6 Evaluating comparative advantage

To illustrate their methodological approach in their introductory chapter the textbooks present the theory of comparative advantage and *demonstrate* the benefits of specialization and trade. We suggest you treat the model as a rhetorical device, since no evidence is presented to support it. Moreover, the assumptions it uses restrict the domain of its applicability to an era long since past.

In his intermediate trade textbook, Thomas Pugel (2007) draws out some testable predictions from the theory of comparative advantage. He argues that since the industrialized nations are so similar – similar economic structures, resources and technology – they likely have similar opportunity costs in production. Thus, they would not be expected to trade much with one another. But in fact industrialized countries trade extensively with one another. He says: 'Over 70 per cent of the exports of industrialized countries go to other industrialized countries ... These facts appear to be inconsistent with comparative advantage theory' (ibid.: 88).

Pugel argues that trade between industrialized countries is best explained by two ideas: on the demand side, consumers seek variety in the products they buy; and on the supply side, average costs of production decrease as output expands (a situation known as increasing returns, examined in Chapter 5). It is the latter factor which makes history so important: the larger the output, the lower the costs of production. Getting a head start in these industries can also confer a permanent advantage from 'learning-by-doing', the idea that you get better at doing something the more experience you've had doing it. Of course, history doesn't matter at all in the theory of comparative advantage.

With regard to the larger claim that trade makes both countries better off, it is hard to know how to test such a proposition empirically. Early in the Industrial Revolution, Britain used brute force to capture colonial markets and to guarantee a supply of raw materials. Such trade wasn't voluntary, but it set a blueprint for 'voluntary' trading patterns that lasted long after colonialism disappeared. Then in the nineteenth century, countries like the United States, Canada and Germany erected high tariff walls to protect their fledgling industries against British competition. Few would deny that this speeded up the process of industrialization of these countries.

Judging the theory on its own terms it is clear that trade produces winners and losers. English wheat producers will be worse off as a result of the cheap foreign competition, as will Canadian cloth producers. There will be unemployment in these industries. In reality, as Marglin (2008: 280) points out, the unemployment could be concentrated geographically and whole communities in both countries could become economically non-viable. Textbook economics treats such losses as transitional costs and assumes that the permanent gains from trade must necessarily outweigh temporary losses. But this is an empirical question, and up to this point empirical studies have not counted as costs the destruction of community ties.

But our comparative advantage model suggests that trade leads to an increase in total world output of all goods. This means that whoever is winning must have enough to compensate the losers and still be better off. But if the compensation isn't actually paid, then the result of trade can be a more unequal distribution of income. This isn't a transitional cost, it's permanent. What weight should we give this factor? In arguing that free trade is necessarily good, textbooks don't give it any.

Further, the theory makes its case by assuming that England and Canada barter wheat for cloth. In reality, they will trade using money and they will need to convert English pounds and Canadian dollars at the going exchange rate. What's to say that the exchange rate will be at the appropriate level such that England's exports of cloth will just pay for its imports of wheat?

Exchange rates are influenced by many things. One of the most important is international flows of capital. When the principle of comparative advantage was discovered by David Ricardo in 1817, these flows of capital were of negligible importance. Now they are a dominant factor. They allow a country like the United States to run increasingly large trade deficits for decades. Beginning at around $200 billion in 1997, these trade deficits ballooned to nearly $1 trillion in 2006.[11] That is a lot more imports than exports. No wonder there are persistent complaints in the United States about job loss to Mexico, China and India.

Finally, free trade in the modern world is not so much about the free movement of goods as it is about the free movement of capital – only now we're not talking just about financial capital, we're talking about real capital: factories relocating abroad. One common term used to describe this phenomenon is offshoring. The neoclassical consensus – until recently – was that this did not disturb the 'result' that free trade was beneficial to all. But that consensus has been disturbed by recent arguments by Gomory and Baumol (2000) and Paul Samuelson (2004) that offshoring could produce net economic losses.

This created quite a stir, because Paul Samuelson is not your average economist. Winner of the Nobel Prize in economics in 1970, he wrote much of the canon of neoclassical theory.

Samuelson called the view that *the long-run gains from all forms of international trade must more than offset the losses* a 'popular polemical untruth'. He said that this theory 'can only be an innuendo. For it is dead wrong about necessary surplus of winnings over losings' (ibid.: 136).

We'll have much more to say about trade in Chapter 10.

Questions for your professor:

1 How would we test the theory of comparative advantage?
2 Do the mutual gains from trade depend on resources from the import-competing sector moving into the export sector? What would happen if they just remained unemployed?
3 Didn't the United States, Canada and Germany industrialize behind high tariff walls? Isn't it a little hypocritical to now oppose other countries doing the same?
4 Must the long-run gains from all forms of international trade more than offset the losses? Paul Samuelson recently described this view as a 'popular polemical untruth'. Why?

Suggestions for further reading

Take a look at 'Appendix A: The limits of dissent' in Marglin (2008, pp. 265–98). This has an especially good section on whether comparative advantage justifies free trade (pp. 274–82).

On methodology and the minimum wage controversy, a very good source is Card and Krueger's 1995 book, *Myth and Measurement: The new economics of the minimum wage*. Focus on Chapter 1 ('Introduction and overview', pp. 1–20) and on Chapter 12 ('Conclusions and implications', pp. 387–401).

Also highly recommended is George's (1990) analysis of the rhetorical subtext in economics textbooks.

3 | How markets work (in an imaginary world)

'The supply and demand model, which we introduced in Chapter 3 and have used repeatedly since then, is a model of a perfectly competitive market.' Krugman and Wells (2005: 207)

'Perfect competition is rarely, if ever, found in practice.' Baumol and Blinder (2006: 194)

I THE STANDARD TEXT

I.I What is a competitive market?

There is no 'competing' behaviour in a competitive market – no advertising, no price-setting strategies, no rivalry. This is because all buyers and sellers are *price-takers*. This requires large numbers of buyers and sellers, with no one buyer or seller having a significant market share, and all firms producing an identical (or homogeneous) good or service.

I.2 The demand curve

An individual's demand curve describes the relationship between the quantity demanded and the good's own price *ceteris paribus* (holding all other influences constant). These other influences include the individual's preferences, income and the prices of related consumption goods. These may be either complements (such as DVDs and DVD players) or substitutes (such as chicken or beef). Expected future prices may also be important in determining how much is bought currently.

An individual's demand curve is a frontier – it tells us the maximum price he or she is willing to pay to obtain any given quantity. If any of the other influences change, the demand curve *shifts*. To obtain the market demand, we sum the amounts every individual wishes to buy at any given price. Thus the size of the population influences demand.

The shape of the market demand curve shows the responsiveness of quantity demanded to price changes. Normally, as the price increases, quantity demanded decreases, as seen in Figure 3.1.

The responsiveness of quantity demanded to a change in price is measured by the *price elasticity of demand*. It is defined as:

$$e_d = \frac{\% \text{ change in quantity demanded}}{\% \text{ change in price}}$$

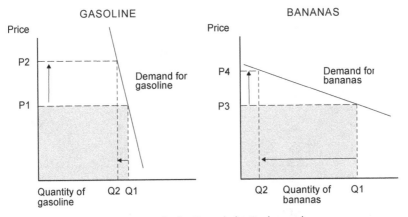

FIGURE 3.1 Inelastic and elastic demand

Suppose a 10 per cent increase in the price of gasoline leads to a 1 per cent decrease in the quantity demanded. The price elasticity of demand for gasoline is 0.1 (1 per cent divided by 10 per cent). In contrast, suppose a 10 per cent increase in the price of bananas leads to a 70 per cent decrease in the quantity demanded. The price elasticity for bananas is 7. Elasticities depend on the availability of substitutes among other things. There are many substitutes for bananas (other fruit), but few substitutes for gasoline (petrol), at least over a short time period.

Total revenue is price multiplied by quantity. Elasticity of demand determines how total revenue changes when price changes. For example, when the price of gasoline is P1, total revenue equals the shaded box in the left-hand diagram of Figure 3.1. When the price goes up to P2 the height of the total revenue box increases by 10 per cent, and its width decreases by 1 per cent. It is clear that the new total revenue box is bigger than before.

Similarly, when the price of bananas is P3, total revenue equals the shaded box in the right-hand diagram in Figure 3.1. When the price goes up to P4 the height of the total revenue box increases by 10 per cent while its width decreases by 70 per cent. Clearly, the new total revenue box is smaller than before.

As an application, suppose the London tube system is losing money. If the objective is solely to increase total revenue, should the tube authority increase or decrease fares? If the demand for tube rides is inelastic, they should increase fares; if it is elastic they should decrease fares. If the elasticity is equal to one (a so-called 'unit-elastic' demand curve) then a fare change would have no effect on total revenue.

1.3 The supply curve

The supply curve describes the relationship between the quantity of a good supplied and its own price, *ceteris paribus*. It too is a frontier, showing the *minimum* price that sellers are willing to accept for any given quantity. Generally speaking, as the price of a product increases, the quantity supplied goes up. The

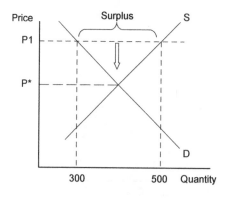 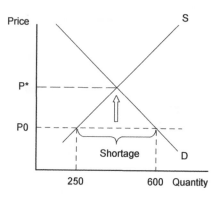

FIGURE 3.2 Movement towards equilibrium

responsiveness of quantity supplied to a change in price is measured by the *price elasticity of supply*.

$$e_s = \frac{\%\ \text{change in quantity supply}}{\%\ \text{change in price}}$$

The six key shift factors on the supply side are: the weather (especially important for agricultural products); changes in the prices of goods related in production; changes in input prices (or prices of 'factors of production'); changes in technology; changes in the number (and size) of firms in the industry; and changes in expectations about future prices.

Comparing the demand shift factors with the supply shift factors we see only one identical item: expectations of future prices.

I.4 Market equilibrium

When prices are free to fluctuate, market forces move the actual price (and quantity) towards the equilibrium price (and quantity). The left-hand diagram of Figure 3.2 shows that at a price P1, which is above the equilibrium price, P*, there is an excess supply (or surplus) equal to 200 units per period. This creates downward pressure on the price, causing it to fall until equilibrium is restored at P*. The right-hand diagram shows that when the price is below equilibrium there is an excess demand (or shortage). This creates upward pressure on the price, causing the price to increase until equilibrium is restored at P*.

I.5 Comparative static analysis

We simulate change by considering how an exogenous shock would affect the equilibrium position. 'Comparative statics' compares one static equilibrium position with another. The analysis is timeless (we don't know how long anything takes) and ahistorical (it doesn't matter in what order things happen).

In the left-hand diagram of Figure 3.3 we show the effect of an increase in the

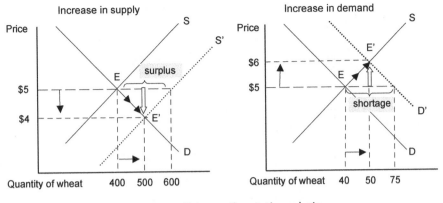

FIGURE 3.3 Comparative static analysis

supply of wheat from S to S' – perhaps caused by a fall in the price of fertilizer. At the original price of $5 there is now a surplus of wheat. This causes the price to fall to $4, eliminating the surplus. In the right-hand diagram of Figure 3.3 we show the effect of an increase in the demand for wheat – perhaps caused by an increase in incomes. The original demand line *shifts rightwards* to D', causing a shortage at the original equilibrium price of $5. This causes the price to increase to $6, at which point the shortage is eliminated.

Note that an expectation of a future price increase causes supply to shift left and demand to shift right. Both these shifts cause prices to increase now: an example of a self-fulfilling prophecy.

1.6 A government-regulated price ceiling: rent controls

Governments often try to control market prices using price ceilings and price floors. Rent control (an example of a price ceiling) is an attempt to help low-income families afford the cost of accommodation. Textbooks emphasize that attempts to overrule market forces always lead to unintended effects that usually hurt the very group the government is intending to help.

Figure 3.4 shows the market for apartments in Montreal assuming all apartments are identical. The going rent is $1,000 a month and 2 million units are rented. When the government imposes a rent ceiling of $800, fewer apartments are offered for rent and more demanded, causing a shortage of 400,000 rental units. The shortage is likely to get worse the longer the rent control is in effect, as apartment buildings are knocked down or converted to condominiums.

Shortages induced by price controls in competitive markets lead to *inefficiency*: missed opportunities to make some people better off at no cost to anyone else.

The first inefficiency is an inappropriate distribution of apartments among renters. For example, 'empty-nesters' want to downsize, while households with new children want something bigger. These moves benefit both parties, but are hampered by the shortage created by the rent control.

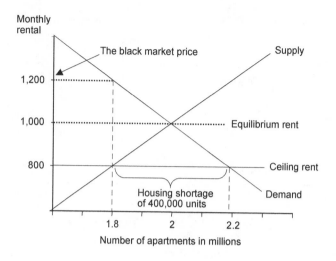

FIGURE 3.4 The effect of rent control

A second inefficiency is the wasted time, energy and money spent searching for an apartment.

A third inefficiency is that the quality of apartments will become undesirably low. Some tenants would be happy to pay for better conditions, and landlords would be happy to provide them for increased rent. This is a missed opportunity.

Finally, price ceilings encourage *illegal activities*, specifically the emergence of black markets – side payments (or bribes) to obtain an apartment. Given the shortage of apartments under rent controls, Figure 3.4 indicates that buyers are willing to pay up to $1,200 a month – $400 more than the legal ceiling. So, we can expect side payments as high as $400 a month.

Our analysis contains five predictions that we will state generically (not tailored to the market for apartments). First, price controls in competitive markets lead to shortages that get worse the longer they are in effect (prediction 1). Next, the fundamental reason shortages are bad is that they are inefficient, and this inefficiency manifests itself in three distinct ways: an inefficient distribution of the good among buyers (prediction 2); wasted resources trying to buy the good (prediction 3); and an inefficiently low quality of the good (prediction 4). Finally, whenever there are unsatisfied wants because of legal restrictions, crime will always arise to profit from them (prediction 5).

I.7 A government-regulated price floor: minimum wages

Figure 3.5 depicts a competitive market for unskilled workers. The equilibrium wage is $9 an hour, and total employment is 15 million workers. Suppose the government decides that $9 an hour is not a living wage, and imposes a minimum wage of $12 an hour. The impact is 3 million fewer jobs, 3 million more people willing to work and unemployment (or a surplus of labour) of 6 million workers.

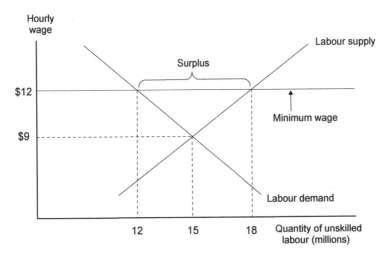

FIGURE 3.5 The effect of a minimum wage

Any minimum wage above the equilibrium has the same qualitative effect; but the higher the minimum wage, the worse it is.

The surplus caused by a price floor creates inefficiencies – missed opportunities – that resemble those created by price ceilings. First, there is an *inefficient allocation* of sales among sellers. With a minimum wage there may be some job seekers who really want to work but cannot find a job, and others who have a job but are almost indifferent as to whether they work or not. Second, sellers (job seekers) waste time and effort searching for a buyer (an employer). Third, suppliers offer an inefficiently high quality to try to attract buyers, who might have preferred the original quality at a lower price. Finally, price ceilings provide an incentive for *illegal activity* – only in this case it is sellers (job seekers) bribing buyers (employers), or employment arrangements out of sight of the law.

1.8 Who bears the cost of sales taxes?

Contrary to popular belief, the person who ends up 'paying' a sales (or excise) tax is not the same person on whom the tax is levied. Rather, the incidence of the tax depends on the relative size of the price elasticities of demand and supply. The texts demonstrate this proposition using demand and supply diagrams.

The left-hand diagram of Figure 3.6 shows supply and demand for parking spaces. We assume the government collects the sales tax from producers of parking spaces. This adds to producers' costs, so a $4 per unit sales tax shifts the supply curve upwards by $4 per unit for each level of output. According to the diagram, the effect is to raise the equilibrium price from $6 to $7. Effectively $1 of the tax has been passed on to consumers in higher prices. The remainder, $3 per unit, is paid by producers. Finally, the tax raises $1,600 in revenue for the government ($4 x 400 units).

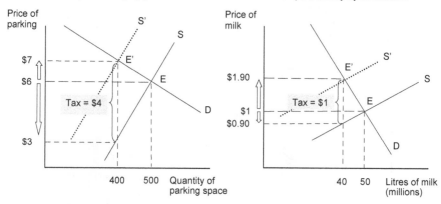

FIGURE 3.6 The incidence of taxation

In the right-hand diagram, we have supply and demand for milk. A sales tax of $1 per litre of milk shifts the supply curve up by $1 per litre. According to the diagram, the tax raises $40 million in government revenue ($1 x 40 million litres), and raises the equilibrium price by 90 cents. In contrast to the previous example, where producers paid most of the tax, here most of the tax is passed on to consumers, and only 10 cents per litre is paid by producers. What causes this difference in who bears the burden of the tax?

It turns out that the incidence of the tax depends on the relative size of the price elasticities of demand and supply at the equilibrium prices and quantities. The actual formula (almost never revealed by textbooks) is:

Formula 1: proportion of sales tax borne by consumers $= \dfrac{e_s}{e_s + e_d}$

Formula 2: proportion of sales tax borne by producers $= \dfrac{e_d}{e_s + e_d}$

where e_s and e_d are the elasticities of supply and demand in equilibrium. Note that the proportions sum to one – the total tax is split between buyers and sellers.

Formula 1 shows that the greater the price elasticity of supply, and the smaller the price elasticity of demand, the more the tax is paid by consumers. If we understand elasticity to mean 'responsiveness', this amounts to a claim that if producers are responsive (or flexible, or elastic) to price changes, while consumers are unresponsive (or inflexible or inelastic), the more the tax burden falls on consumers. As in the martial art of t'ai chi, the flexible opponent will always beat the inflexible one. In this case, the more flexible side of the market avoids the larger part of the sales tax, while the inflexible one pays it.

1.9 The costs of taxation

In Figure 3.6 the tax on milk reduced consumption by 10 million litres. This is milk that would have been consumed in the absence of the tax, to the mutual benefit of both producers and consumers. Nobody would have been worse off. So, an excise tax creates inefficiency. This represents a cost of the tax over and above the money paid to the government in taxes. This extra cost is referred to as the excess burden or deadweight loss of the tax. Economists say that the real cost of a tax is not what people pay but what they don't pay – meaning the mutually beneficial trades that no longer occur because of a tax.

2 THE ANTI-TEXT

2.1 The demand and supply model is sold as a generic tool

The material summarized in the previous section is often called 'How markets work', the terminology of Parkin and Bade (2006) and Mankiw et al. (2006). It follows a discussion of models and methodology that emphasizes the overriding importance of predictive power, and it contains applications to a broad range of labour and product markets. The range of these applications, the position of these chapters near the front of the text, and the immediately preceding methodological discussion that plays down realism of assumptions, *all suggest that the supply and demand framework is a generic tool that can be applied to all markets*. Colander et al. (2006: 72) are explicit here, saying supply and demand provides 'a good off-the-cuff answer for any economic question'.

But the supply and demand framework is actually a simplified representation of a perfectly competitive market structure, one which (according to some textbooks) is so rare as to be hardly ever found in practice. Many textbooks are quite explicit about this, but only much later in the texts, when they discuss perfect competition. For example, Krugman and Wells state in their Chapter 9: 'The supply and demand model, which we introduced in Chapter 3 and have used repeatedly since then, is a model of a perfectly competitive market' (2005: 207).[1]

We can demonstrate the equivalence between supply and demand and perfect competition by showing that perfect competition is the *only* market structure where a supply curve exists. While this demonstration is delayed until Chapter 6, the intuition is straightforward. Unlike the competitive firm, which is a price taker, the non-competitive firm faces a downward-sloping demand curve and has to decide on its best price–output combination. But the best price depends on the position of the demand curve; as a result, there is no unique relationship between price and the quantity supplied, and hence no supply curve.

Since supply curves exist only in perfectly competitive markets, we need to know: first, how many markets are perfectly competitive in the real world? And second, even though the competitive model is not (strictly speaking) applicable to non-competitive markets, can it be usefully applied as an approximation? We address those questions next.

Question for your professor: If an industry is not perfectly
competitive, can we still draw the industry supply curve?
(Right answer: No.)

2.2 How many markets are perfectly competitive?

To this point we've talked vaguely about 'non-competitive' markets. Let's be more precise. Textbooks categorize markets according to the number of producers and the type of product, as shown in Table 3.1.

Non-competitive markets fall into three types: monopolistic competition, oligopoly and monopoly. Firms in all three non-competitive markets have 'market power', which means they face a downward-sloping demand curve, and so can choose the price of their product rather than simply accept a 'market price' like the perfectly competitive firm. Market power derives either from the firm being large relative to the industry (monopoly), or from having a product that is unique (or differentiated) in some way (monopolistic competition), or for both reasons (oligopoly). The question is: how prevalent is perfect competition relative to the other market structures?

The key requirement for perfect competition is price-taking behaviour. All texts agree that this requires large numbers of buyers and sellers and an identical product. But two other assumptions are often included: perfect information and easy entry by firms into (and exit from) the industry. This last assumption is necessary to show the long-run optimality qualities of perfect competition (discussed in Chapter 6). Easy entry (and exit) is not necessary for price-taking behaviour.[2]

Concerning the information requirements, four of eleven leading US textbooks state that perfect information is required for perfect competition (Beaulier and Mounts 2008).[3] Of the remainder, several state that market participants just need to be 'well informed'. An extreme position is that of Mankiw (2004) – one of the leading US textbooks – who chooses not to mention any information requirements for perfect competition at all.

TABLE 3.1 Types of market structure

How many producers are there?	Are products differentiated?	
	NO	YES
Many	Perfect competition	Monopolistic competition
Few	Oligopoly	Oligopoly
One	Monopoly	Monopoly

Given the amount of research on the effects of imperfect information, this difference of opinion among the textbooks is odd. Joseph Stiglitz received the Nobel Prize for his work on information economics in 2001. In his acceptance speech, published the following year in the flagship journal of the American Economic Association, he explains:

> For more than 100 years, formal modeling in economics has focused on models in which information was assumed to be perfect. Of course, everyone recognized that information was in fact imperfect, but the hope ... was that economies in which information was not too imperfect would look very much like economies in which information was perfect. One of the main results of our research was to show that this was not true; that even a small amount of information imperfection could have a profound effect on the nature of the equilibrium. (2002: 461)

Why could even a small amount of imperfect information have a profound effect? Stiglitz gives the following example:

> Assume for example, as in the standard theory, that all firms were charging the competitive price, but there were an epsilon cost of searching, of going to another store. Then any firm which charged half an epsilon more would lose no customers and thus would choose to increase its price. Similarly, it would pay all other firms to increase their prices. But at the higher price, it would again pay each to increase price, and so on until the price charged at every firm is the monopoly price, even though search costs are small. (Ibid.: 477)

In the above quote, 'epsilon' stands for an arbitrarily small quantity. Just an epsilon of costs of acquiring information could lead otherwise competitive firms to charge the monopoly price. The point is that even slight departures from free, and hence perfect, information have large consequences. Depending on the market, other consequences could be an equilibrium where the market does not clear (the quantity demanded differs from the quantity supplied *in equilibrium*), or even multiple equilibria.

If imperfect information undermines the competitive model, is there a better alternative? Stiglitz explains: 'a central consequence of imperfect information is that ... product markets are more aptly described by models of imperfect competition, where ... [firms] perceive themselves facing downward sloping demand schedules' (1985: 34).

Apparently, the prevalence of competition depends on the likelihood of having perfect information. To appreciate how implausible the assumption of perfect information is, it helps to realize that many information asymmetries (some people knowing more than others) are inevitable. Job applicants know more about their ability than prospective employers; workers know more about their work effort than management; management knows more about their firms than potential investors; borrowers know more about their likelihood of default than lenders; people buying insurance know more about their efforts to avoid risk than insurers. According to Stiglitz, information imperfections are so pervasive 'it is hard to imagine what a world with perfect information would be like' (2002: 469).

Given the prevalence of imperfect information, Stiglitz's argument seems to leave little room to apply the competitive model. This leads him to ask why the competitive paradigm persisted for so long. He says:

> Despite its deficiencies, the competitive paradigm did provide insights into many economic phenomena. There are some markets in which the issues which we have discussed are not important – the market for wheat or corn – though even there, pervasive government interventions make the reigning competitive paradigm of limited relevance. (Ibid.: 488)

So, if not for government interventions, the competitive model would be good enough to describe the markets for wheat and corn. Are there other markets where information is close enough to perfect that the competitive model can be applied? What do the textbooks themselves say on this question?

Opinions differ as to whether perfect competition actually describes many real-world markets. Those textbooks that include *perfect* information as a requirement state that perfect competition has very limited applicability. For example, Baumol and Blinder say that perfect competition is 'rarely, if ever, found in practice' (2006: 194). Those that don't insist on perfect information make stronger claims for the existence of perfectly competitive markets. For instance, Krugman and Wells state: 'important parts of the economy are fairly well described by perfect competition' (2005: 383). The stronger claim was also made by Ragan and Lipsey, who provide examples of perfectly competitive industries. They state (2005: 259): 'Forest and fish products provide many examples. Agriculture also fits fairly well in most ways since individual farmers are clearly price takers. Many basic raw materials, such as iron ore, tin, and copper, are sold on world markets where most individual firms lack significant market power.'

But not all agricultural and raw material products are perfectly competitive. The existence of market power in markets for diamonds, aluminium and oil are well known.[4] Perhaps less well appreciated is the existence of market power in agricultural markets. At least in North America, many farmers and fishers are increasingly squeezed by the market power of the few firms that supply their inputs and the few buyers of their outputs – especially supermarket chains and the fast food industry (Phillips 2003; Lawrence 2004; Schlosser 2001).[5]

But even assuming that the whole of agriculture, forestry, fishing and hunting were perfectly competitive, their combined output is only a very small fraction of total production in the industrialized economies. (It's about 2 per cent of production in Canada in 2006.)[6]

Evidence that price-taking behaviour is rare outside of agriculture is provided by Blinder et al. (1998). They survey 200 representative firms in the United States, excluding agriculture. They say: 'First of all, we took it for granted that almost all firms in our economy are price-makers rather than price-takers – an assumption amply justified by the survey responses' (ibid.: 12). They find that prices are 'sticky' – set by firms and periodically reviewed; they are not determined instantaneously by supply and demand. They say:

> First, the evidence gathered in this study emphatically supports the mainstream view that sticky prices are the rule, not the exception, in American industry. According to our respondents, the median number of price changes for a typical product in a typical year is just 1.4, and almost half of all prices change no more often than annually. Among firms reporting regular price reviews, annual reviews are by far the most common. At the other end of the spectrum, only about 10 percent of all prices change as often as once a week, and about 7 percent of all firms schedule price reviews at least weekly. (Ibid.: 298)

Competitive firms are price-takers. They never need to review their price schedules. Their prices change continually with shifts in demand and supply. *None* of the firms surveyed by Blinder et al. fell into that category.

Questions for your professor:
1 In the demand and supply model no one is a price-setter. So, who determines what the price will be?
2 Most firms in the real world set their own prices; does the model apply to them?

2.3 Is the competitive model a useful approximation?

No two hairstylists are equally skilled. They sell a differentiated product. Each stylist faces a downward-sloping demand curve, implying that the supply curve for haircuts does not exist, as stated earlier. Furthermore, there is no unique price for haircuts, but instead a range of prices – each price *set* by the hairstylist – depending on the stylist's quality, reputation, location and clientele. This is a non-competitive market.

Nevertheless (we ask, as the devil's advocate), can the competitive model be applied to this market as an *approximation*? Assume away all the complications. Assume all hairstylists are identical. Assume perfect information. Won't the competitive model give us insights into the determinants of the average price of haircuts? Won't the things that cause supply curves to shift left – an increase in the costs of production (shampoo prices go up), or a decrease in the number of firms (hairstylists) – increase the average price of a haircut? If so, the competitive model provides a *useful approximation* even to this non-competitive market.

If this were generally true, the textbook emphasis on competitive markets as a generic tool would be justified. Maybe it's like the law of gravity: strictly speaking it holds only in a vacuum; but it can be usefully applied in everyday life.

This is the position taken by Krugman and Wells, who, after noting that oligopoly is by far the most common market structure, ask, 'Given the prevalence of oligopoly, then, is the analysis ... based on perfect competition still useful?' They argue that it is because '[i]t is also true that predictions from supply and demand analysis are often valid for oligopolies'. Given the complexity of oligopoly models, 'in situations where they do not expect the complications associated with oligopoly to be crucial, economists prefer to adopt the working assumption of perfectly competitive markets' (2005: 383). In other words, the competitive model is simpler and can be applied even to non-competitive markets, because it gives us accurate predictions.[7]

Let us, then, consider the predictive power of the competitive model, focusing on the core applications emphasized in introductory textbooks.

Predictions concerning minimum wages Does the evidence support the predictions of the supply and demand framework concerning the effects of minimum wages? We addressed this question in detail in Chapter 2. In brief, the empirical studies conflict to such an extent that we used it as a case study to illustrate the limitations of hypothesis testing and predictive power as criteria for model selection. The consensus concerning the effects of minimum wages has broken down – though this is not generally reported in the textbooks.

What we have yet to explain is why moderate increases in the minimum wage might *not* reduce employment of low-wage, low-skilled workers. There are several possible explanations, all of which depend on 'frictions' – imperfect information or mobility costs.

One category of explanation is the 'efficiency wage' thesis. If work effort is hard to monitor, workers may shirk. Wage increases make the job more desirable and provide an incentive not to get caught shirking (which might result in getting fired). As a result, workers shirk less and productivity increases. In addition, increased worker morale may reduce labour turnover, which reduces hiring and training costs for the firm. Either way, the higher wages pay for themselves without causing job losses.

An alternative category of explanation is the dynamic monopsony thesis. Here employers are not simply wage-takers: they have some short-run (or temporary or dynamic) power to set wages lower than other firms without losing all their workers. This power may derive from the time and resources necessary for a worker to find a new job, or because taking another job might entail moving home or increased costs of commuting. Either way, moderate minimum wage increases may offset the market power of employers without causing job losses – indeed, they may even cause job gains (as we explain more fully in Chapter 8).

The minimum wage application is precisely about whether frictions in the labour market are significant. The easiest way to account for the array of mixed evidence is to concede that frictions are important in certain cases. So, when discussing the effects of minimum wages it is important to contrast the predictions of the competitive model with those from non-competitive models.

A small minority of textbooks do compare the predictions. For example, Ragan and Lipsey (2008: 99) alert the reader that the minimum wage is re-examined in a later chapter on labour markets using a monopsonistic framework.

But the average textbook continues to apply the competitive model *as if it were the only model* relevant to the minimum wage question. Some of these mention the empirical controversy in passing. Others mention the controversy, but dismiss results contrary to the competitive model as wrong (Parkin and Bade 2006: 131). And others pretend there is no empirical controversy and continue to cite results from 'the typical study', which finds that 'a 10 percent increase in the minimum wage depresses teenage employment between 1 and 3 percent' (Mankiw et al. 2006: 125). Krueger (2001: 247) tracks down this 'typical' study to an influential survey paper published in 1982!

A third option is to omit the minimum wage application completely (e.g. Frank et al. 2005; McConnell et al. 2007). Krueger believes this reaction is unfortunate:

> Did astronomy classes stop teaching Newtonian principles once quantum mechanics was discovered? Did physics classes drop lectures on the atom once quarks were discovered? No. Instead, these disciplines explain the limitations of their models, teach the research methods and findings that have been used to establish (and reject) their core principles, and seek to provide students with an understanding of which models work best in which circumstances and why. (2001: 243)

```
Question for your professor: Does the empirical evidence
support the predictions of the supply and demand framework
concerning the effects of minimum wages? (Right answer: It's
very mixed. )
```

Predictions concerning rent controls The main prediction of the competitive model – shortages that get worse the longer the rent control is in effect – depends on the rent ceiling remaining below the equilibrium level: it must be *binding*. If the extent to which it is binding lessens – if the ceiling rent moves towards the equilibrium rent – then we would not expect shortages to worsen. On the contrary, we'd expect them to moderate. But knowing the extent to which the ceiling rent is binding over time is very tricky. It's complicated by the fact that we cannot observe the equilibrium rent.

A second complication is that the type of rent control prevalent nowadays is very different from the type assumed in textbooks – a rigid rent freeze. Controls of this sort were introduced in major US cities during the Second World War, but every city (apart from New York) had abandoned this 'first-generation' rent control by the early 1950s. 'Second-generation' rent control, first introduced in the 1970s, is significantly more flexible. For example, it commonly allows automatic rent increases geared to increasing costs, excludes luxury high-rent buildings and new buildings, restricts conversions, decontrols between tenants, and provides incentives for landlords to maintain or improve quality.

A third complication is that housing units are assets, the desirability of which is impacted by many other factors besides rent control: interest rates, inflation, profit opportunities elsewhere, the local real estate cycle, government housing and tax policies, and current and expected future changes in all relevant variables.

In reviewing the empirical evidence on rent control, Arnott says: 'The impact of these other factors is likely to be significantly greater than any effect due to controls. Trying to discern the effects of rent control in such a situation is akin to trying to hear a whispered conversation across a street of roaring traffic' (1995: 112). He suggests that with the exception of New York City (which retained its first-generation controls) and perhaps Toronto (which had poorly designed second-generation controls) the effects of rent control in North America have been almost imperceptible. This is a dramatic contrast to the treatment in the textbooks. By assuming that the rental housing market is perfectly competitive, and by considering a crude form of price ceiling, most texts suggest that rent controls necessarily have destructive effects.

Why are most textbooks (and most North American economists for that matter) so negative on rent controls? Arnott suggests two reasons: 'The first is ideological. The debate over rent control has been a battleground between those who believe in the free market and those who do not. The echoes of the debate carry over to other policy arenas where its resolution has far more quantitative import. The second is methodological' (ibid.: 117).

The methodological battle is about whether the competitive model is good enough as a generic approximation to most markets. The housing market has many non-competitive elements: apartments are heterogeneous and tastes idiosyncratic, which renders the market thin; search costs are substantial (as evidenced by agents' fees), as are moving costs; and there is a lack of information about who's a good landlord and who's a good tenant. Are these merely details that can be ignored as irrelevant? Most housing economists believe that these are too important to be ignored in practice. Since the mid-1980s most of them have turned their attention to non-competitive models – models that emphasize search costs and the importance of contracts.

Because of this different methodological perspective, they are much less critical of rent control. Arnott conjectures: 'Perhaps a majority, at least among the younger generation, would agree with the statement that a well-designed rent control program can be beneficial' (ibid.: 99) Yet this research seems to have had no impact on the principles textbooks.[8]

> Question for your professor: Would rent controls necessarily cause shortages if the rental housing market were only imperfectly competitive? (Right answer: No.)

Predictions concerning the incidence of taxation If the evidence presented for the effects of minimum wages and for rent controls is weak, things are even worse when it comes to the incidence of sales taxes: the textbooks present no evidence at all.

This is very strange because the competitive model makes clear predictions: the proportionate burden of a sales tax is determined by the relative elasticities of supply and demand. The texts illustrate this idea using relative slopes of supply and demand in a wide variety of markets. Table 3.2 shows the examples used by ten leading US and Canadian texts. The favourite example is cigarettes (seven cases) – a *highly* oligopolistic industry composed of six US producers; next comes gasoline (five cases) – another non-competitive industry (oligopolistic at the production level, oligopolistic or monopolistically competitive at the retail level); and finally, luxury boats (three cases) – an industry with many sellers but highly differentiated products. None of the examples remotely resembles

TABLE 3.2 Tax incidence applications used in ten major North American textbooks

Text	Example used
Colander (2004, pp. 163–5)	Luxury boats
Gwartney et al. (2006, pp. 94–9)	Gasoline and luxury boats
McConnell and Brue (2005, pp. 589–90)	'A certain domestic wine'
Miller (2004, pp. 125–7, 485–6)	Gasoline and cigarettes
O'Sullivan and Sheffrin (2003, pp. 334–40)	Apartments, cigarettes and luxury boats
Ragan and Lipsey (2008, pp. 84–7)	Cigarettes
Samuelson and Nordhaus (1992, pp. 74–5)	Gasoline, cigarettes; imports; factor inputs
Stiglitz and Walsh (2002, pp. 206–7)	Cigarettes and cheddar cheese
Taylor (2004, pp. 174–6, 348–54)	Gasoline and salt
Tucker (2005, pp. 123–5)	Gasoline, cigarettes and alcoholic beverages

a competitive market. And this explains the complete absence of empirical evidence: while the elasticity of demand could be measured, we cannot measure the elasticity of supply when the supply curve doesn't exist.

Put it this way: it is one thing to generate predictions using hypothetical shifts of a hypothetical supply curve – if it yields accurate predictions this could be a useful approximation. But it is altogether another to test the accuracy of those predictions by *measuring* something that doesn't exist in reality. We suggest this is why *no text* presents *any* corroborating empirical evidence on the ability of the competitive model to predict the incidence of taxation.

> Question for your professor: Can the demand and supply model predict the incidence of taxation in imperfectly competitive markets?

2.4 But don't price floors cause surpluses and price ceilings shortages?

Price ceilings Price ceilings have been imposed on different commodities, in different countries, in different times. During the Second World War, there were price ceilings on many commodities in Britain, Canada and the USA – commodities such as meat, milk, eggs, sugar and gasoline. In every case, shortages developed. Doesn't this confirm the usefulness of the competitive model?

Not really. In Chapter 6 we show that the textbook model of monopoly contains the same prediction: if price ceilings are sufficiently low there will be shortages. Similarly, shortages are also a likely outcome in textbook models of oligopoly and monopolistic competition. The fact that shortages develop in response to price ceilings doesn't demonstrate the superiority of the competitive model.

We quote Krugman and Wells as preferring the competitive model because models of oligopoly (where strategic interaction is the key) are so complex. But the monopoly model is simple – just as simple as the competitive model. Why not use that? Why not champion the usefulness of the monopoly model as a generic tool?

The reason is that such an analysis would tell the wrong 'story'. For all the qualifications that are later tacked on to it, the central textbook story is how the market economy works like an invisible hand, efficiently allocating resources among alternative uses. As we'll see, an economy populated with firms that have market power does not allow a clear-cut story – hence the necessity to study an imaginary economy rather than something resembling the real one.

So, we're not arguing that price ceilings do not cause shortages. The issue is whether a competitive veneer can be smeared over every market as a decent enough approximation. If we accept the official methodology, of hypothesis testing and predictive power, then in each application, in each approximation, we need to ask which works better: the competitive model or a non-competitive model.

> Questions for your professor: If price ceilings were low enough, would they cause shortages in non-competitive markets too? (Answer: Yes.) So, if price ceilings caused shortages in the Second World War, that can't be taken as empirical support for the demand and supply model, can it?

Price floors Similarly, we are not arguing that price floors don't cause surpluses. All economists would agree that if the minimum wage were raised high enough, a surplus of labour would be created. Where the minimum wage controversy begins is when we ask whether moderate increases have the same effect. As we've explained, the issue revolves around whether labour markets are *perfectly* competitive, or whether there are significant imperfections.

Perhaps one reason for the popularity of the minimum wage application is that there aren't a lot of examples of price floors where governments do not buy up the resulting surplus production. The combination of price floors and a 'government buyer of last resort' has resulted in butter and grain 'mountains' and milk 'lakes' in the European Community. This arrangement most certainly produces surpluses. But there are very few examples of a government imposing a price floor and not buying up the surplus production – besides minimum wages.

Krugman and Wells (2005: 93) use the example of transatlantic airfares. Prior to deregulation of airlines in 1978, airfares were set artificially high by international treaty. Certainly this restricted the quantity demanded, and since airlines couldn't compete in the price dimension, it led to them competing for customers by providing expensive (often unwanted) services. Krugman and Wells argue that it also resulted in surplus production, which manifested itself in empty seats on flights.

But this anecdotal evidence is hardly convincing. There are often empty seats on flights, even without price floors. And with price regulation we would expect airlines to reduce the number of flights to match the limited demand for travel; we would not expect them to increase the number of flights. Yet that's exactly

> Question for your professor: The demand and supply model suggests that suppliers will increase supply when binding price floors are imposed, despite observable surpluses. Isn't this irrational?

what an upward-sloping supply curve says firms would do in the face of a price increase. This is one aspect of a general problem: the competitive framework is based on assumptions that are violated in the context of disequilibrium. We develop this point in the next section.

2.5 What the texts don't tell you about the competitive model

The competitive model is internally inconsistent when not in equilibrium The perfectly competitive demand and supply model seems to make sense in equilibrium. Everyone takes prices as given, which is fine since everyone trades the amount they want, and no one has any incentive to change. But when something happens to disturb equilibrium the story starts to unravel.

Let's go back to the comparative static analysis, explained earlier using Figure 3.3. In the left-hand diagram we assumed a fall in the price of fertilizer shifted the supply curve of wheat to the right. This caused a surplus of wheat at the original equilibrium price. As a result, we are told prices fall. But since no one sets prices, how do they fall?

The lack of an explanation for price movements in the demand and supply model is known as Arrow's Paradox, after the issue raised by Kenneth Arrow (1959): all individuals and firms are assumed to be 'price-takers' and to have no influence over the market price, yet somehow the market price adjusts and reaches the equilibrium value. One 'solution' to this conundrum is to invent an auctioneer, who is 'the visible, if imaginary, embodiment of the invisible hand. He has no economic involvement in the market: no mention is made of his objectives or constraints' (Dixon 1990: 361–2). This fictitious character fills the glaring gap in the demand and supply model to adjust prices in response to excess supply and demand.

If having to invent an auctioneer is bad enough, what's worse is that the auctioneer can't allow any trades to occur until he finds the equilibrium solution. This is because the auctioneer needs eventually to end up at the intersection of the demand and supply curves. If we allow trades before equilibrium is reached, people will have spent some of their budget. As a result, they would not be able to buy what they otherwise would have bought at what would have been the new equilibrium price.

The demand and supply curves are derived assuming market participants can buy or sell all that they wish at the going market price. But they can't do that when there are shortages or surpluses. Out of equilibrium these curves are only 'notional'. They don't tell us how much buyers would try to buy, or sellers would try to sell, if there were a surplus or shortage.

For example, suppose there is a surplus. Do firms ignore this and continue to supply *as if* they could sell all that they wished? If so, the competitive supply curve would tell us what it purports to tell us: the quantity supplied at any given price. But surely it's more likely that firms would notice the surplus and reduce their production. But if they do, the market supply curve no longer describes the quantity supplied at any given price.

Being unable to sell all they would like at any given price has ramifications for factor markets. Patinkin (1965) argued that excess supply in the goods market 'spills over' to constrain the demand for labour. Instead of the usual labour demand function (where the quantity of labour demanded increases as the wage decreases), sales-constrained firms demand just enough labour to produce the goods they can sell – regardless of how low wages might fall.

Problems also arise with shortages. When demand exceeds supply individual firms can raise their prices without losing all their sales since competitors cannot saturate the market more than they already do. The competitive model assumes that firms pass up this opportunity to exploit their market power.

In sum, when the market is not in equilibrium, the competitive model assumes that market participants continue to act as if it is; they do not exploit all their market opportunities; they do not maximize their profit or utility. This problem becomes more serious the longer the disequilibrium persists. But the model is silent on how fast prices adjust towards equilibrium. The competitive model offers no theory of how prices adjust out of equilibrium. Indeed, there is no theory of price setting in perfect competition at all.

> Question for your professor: If everyone is a price-taker in the competitive demand and supply model, who makes prices fall when there is a surplus?

The requirements for perfect competition are mutually incompatible In 1926, Piero Sraffa, a young Italian economist at Cambridge, made some very inconvenient observations about the supply and demand theory of perfect competition. In particular he argued that the conditions necessary for independence between the supply and demand curves are incompatible with the conditions necessary for large numbers of firms in the industry.

Consider a movement to the right along an industry supply curve. As the industry's output increases, it uses more factors of production. Suppose that this increased usage of factors drives up the price for at least one factor of production – say Factor X. If substitute goods (or complementary goods) also use Factor X, their costs rise and so do their prices. But an increase in the price of a substitute good shifts the demand for the original good (to the right). Thus a movement along the industry supply curve causes a shift in the industry demand curve. Supply and demand would not be independent of each other, and yet they must be if the framework is to provide a clear and determinate result.

We can fix this problem by assuming that perfectly competitive industries do not influence the prices of any of the inputs they use. This guarantees independence of supply and demand. But this solution opens up a different problem: what is going to limit the size of the firm? If all factors are available at a constant price, why can't firms duplicate plants and grow without limit? If they can, there is nothing to guarantee that there will be large numbers of small-sized firms in the industry – a requirement of perfect competition.

Sraffa's critique led to the development of the model of imperfect competition: many firms, each selling a differentiated product. What limits the size of the firm in this context is that each faces a downward-sloping demand curve.

Question for your professor: What's your take on Sraffa's (1926) critique of the competitive model?

Multiple equilibria Nothing guarantees that the demand and supply curves are linear. They might have backward-bending regions, giving rise to multiple intersection points. For example, Prasch (2008: 88) argues that when needs are an important consideration, the labour supply curve could look like that shown in the left-hand diagram of Figure 3.7.

The standard story (often found in textbooks) describes the section of the curve above W_s. As wages rise, the opportunity cost of leisure increases, causing people to substitute leisure for more work. This is the effect that initially dominates between W_s and W_L. On the other hand, since leisure is a normal good, people want to 'buy' more leisure as their incomes rise. When wages get high enough, this income effect dominates, leading to a backward-bending section above W_L.

Prasch supplements this standard story by considering what happens when

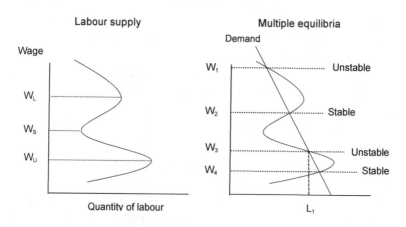

FIGURE 3.7 Multiple equilibria in the labour market

66

wages fall towards (and even go below) subsistence levels. He argues that when wages go below the level necessary to maintain minimum living standards with normal working hours, households increase their labour supply to abnormal levels. They might hold two jobs or work fourteen-hour shifts. So, below the subsistence wage, which we assume to be W_S, labour supply increases, accounting for another bend in the labour supply curve at W_S.

As wages continue to fall, they will eventually reach the point where the total hours of work required to maintain a socially acceptable standard of living are too long to be sustainable. Below the unsustainable wage, W_U, working hours fall precipitously. Prasch says (ibid.: 88): 'the primary worker and his or her family will be forced by exhaustion, disease, despair, and disrepair to abandon their effort to maintain a standard of living consistent with effective membership in the labour force and, consequently, civil society. They become homeless, petty thieves, or beggars, with strong prospects for a relatively short and miserable life.' This explains the third bend occurring at W_U.

When we confront this labour supply function with a standard downward-sloping labour demand function, we get four possible equilibrium points, as shown in the right-hand diagram of Figure 3.7. Of these, both W_1 and W_3 are unstable. (At a wage slightly below either of these levels, supply exceeds demand, causing wages to continue to fall; similarly, at a wage slightly above either of these wage levels, demand exceeds supply, causing wages to continue to increase.) This leaves two stable equilibria – one of which offers wages quite a bit higher than the subsistence level, W_2; while the other is a poverty trap where wages are substantially below subsistence, W_4.

Prasch uses this construction to show the potential usefulness of minimum wage laws and maximum hours provisions. Either a minimum wage set above W_3, or maximum hours restriction set below L_1, would preclude the poverty trap equilibrium. Interestingly, in this model the legislation pushes the economy to a desirable equilibrium, but once at this equilibrium neither restriction appears 'binding'. That is to say, the equilibrium wage would be above the legal minimum wage and the offered hours would be less than the legal maximum. Prasch notes that this is 'a nice illustration of how market forces can interact with legislation to bring about results that are not immediately evident or expected' (ibid.: 93).

As we shall explain in Chapter 8, there are reasons to think that the demand for labour could also have points where it switches its slope.

Multiple equilibria might also arise out of imperfect information. Stiglitz (2002) argues that if there is a lack of information about quality differences between workers (or goods), then all those workers (or goods) will be lumped into a general category and sell for a wage (or price) that reflects the average quality. Clearly, those selling the better quality have an incentive to try to demonstrate this – to get the information out there – so they can command a premium price.

Conversely, those selling the inferior quality have an incentive to impede the flow of information, to sow confusion and doubt. This leads to the possibility of multiple equilibria, 'one in which information was fully revealed (the market identified the high and low ability people) and another in which it was not (called a pooling equilibrium)' (ibid.: 471).

Self-fulfilling prophecies Yet another source of non-uniqueness arises from self-fulfilling prophecies as illustrated in Figure 3.8. Expected future prices influence both the demand and supply curves. Suppose both consumers and producers expect future prices to increase by 10 per cent. Consumers will try to buy more now before prices increase, thus shifting up the demand curve from D1 to D2. Producers will withhold sales now in the expectation of getting higher prices in the future, thus shifting the supply curve left from S1 to S2. It is possible that these shifts will increase the price from P1 to P2 by precisely 10 per cent. If so, there has been a self-fulfilling prophecy: the price is what it is because that's the price we expect. If we had expected a price 40 per cent lower, the price would be 40 per cent lower. Models that embody self-fulfilling prophecies have been used predominantly in macroeconomics to explain instability in aggregate economic activity (Farmer 1993).

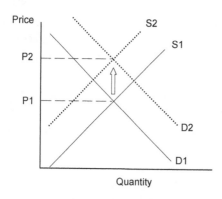

FIGURE 3.8 Self-fulfilling prophecies

© Andy Singer

Destabilizing speculation and bubbles We've had the Japanese property and stock market bubble (which burst in 1990), the technology stock bubble (which burst in 2001), the Chinese stock market bubble (which burst in 2008) and housing price bubbles in numerous countries which precipitated the financial collapses that began in 2008. Imperfect information is an understatement when it comes to thinking about the future. Yet the textbooks scarcely mention issues of time and uncertainty, the role of speculators or the possibility of price bubbles (i.e. unsustainable price increases driven by expectations that end in a price collapse).

Perhaps some of these issues are beyond the scope of first-year textbooks, but the role of speculators is important enough to warrant consideration. Suppose there are ongoing price fluctuations – for instance, a cycle of boom and bust in commodity prices; what role do the speculators play? Do they make things better or worse? The traditional textbook answer is that if speculators make money, they must buy low and sell high. This extra buying when prices are low, and extra selling when prices are high, implies their activity must act to smooth price fluctuations. Hence, speculators add to the efficiency of markets.

But Mullainathan and Thaler (2004) explain that economists now realize that there are important limits to this argument. First, in the face of irrational traders, the speculator may privately benefit more from trading that helps push prices in the wrong direction than from trading that pushes prices in the right direction. Put another way, it may often pay 'smart money' to follow 'dumb money' rather than to lean against it (Russell and Thaler 1985). For example, if speculators buy when prices are rising, and sell when prices are falling, they could still make money but would add to the amplitude of the price fluctuation.

So, markets per se cannot be relied upon to make rational economic decisions – not even when they are competitively structured.

Scandals Numerous examples of corporate misbehaviour have been documented, from the accounting scandals at Enron in 2001 and Worldcom in 2002 to the unsupervised creation and trading of financial assets (consisting in part of the now-notorious sub-prime mortgages) so complex that no one really knew what they ultimately consisted of or what they were really worth.

These problems arise where there is imperfect and asymmetric information. Using the competitive model as a generic tool for all markets obscures the importance of information imperfections and the legal and regulatory framework that's necessary to oversee markets and make sure they work as we want them to. More on this in Chapters 6 and 8.

> Question for your professor: The world price of oil hit an all-time high of $147 in July 2008. Many believed that this was in part driven by speculators. How does speculation fit into the demand and supply model?

The legal framework: eviction protection legislation The standard textbook world is implicitly one of perfect information and contracts that are costless to negotiate and enforce. The legal framework within which markets operate gets scarcely a passing mention. These assumptions certainly simplify the discussion, but they also impart a subtle laissez-faire message hiding between the lines of the text itself. It implicitly says that the legal and regulatory framework is (at most) of secondary importance.

The nature of the legal and regulatory framework is crucially important for the efficient functioning of markets, as we'll see repeatedly throughout this *Anti-Textbook*. An example relevant to the rental housing market is the nature of eviction protection legislation. Should tenants be liable for eviction after failing to pay one month's rent? If not, after how many? Should the rule be modified in the depths of winter? Does it matter how high the general level of unemployment is? The wrong balance in eviction protection legislation can create an imbalance in the rental housing market as severe as the first-generation rent freeze did in New York City. The case study here is Paris.

During the severe recession of the early 1980s, many people lost their jobs and became unable to pay their rent. People were being thrown out on to the streets. To prevent that, legislation was passed that gave tenants increased eviction protection that shifted the balance of power between landlord and tenant so much in favour of the tenant that it resulted in only about 70 per cent of all rents being paid.[9] Landlords had to embark upon months and sometimes years of legal wrangling to evict tenants who defaulted on their rent.

The consequences were in many ways similar to a binding rent freeze: an increase in the quantity of units demanded, a decrease in the quantity supplied, and an excess demand for units. The one difference was that since better-quality tenants were less liable to default on their rent, landlords did have an incentive to upgrade their units (Myatt 2004). Clearly, Paris had the balance wrong in its eviction protection legislation. But what is the right balance?

Questions for your professor: Is the legal framework within which markets operate important in determining the efficiency of markets? Is this ever going to be discussed?

2.6 Summing up

Using the competitive model as a generic tool applicable to a broad range of markets irrespective of the number of producers, heterogeneity of the product or information imperfections creates an inbuilt bias against government market intervention. It loads the dice against rent controls and minimum wages.

The textbooks justify the generic application of the competitive model because it supposedly gives accurate predictions and because it is simpler than non-competitive alternatives. But the claim about predictive power is backed up by only cursory empirical evidence (minimum wages and rent control), and sometimes by no evidence at all (the proportionate burden of the sales tax). Further, the predictive power of the perfectly competitive model is not compared against that of alternative models. The key issue should be: which model better applies to any given situation? Answering this would require comparing the full array of predictions and a serious look at the evidence.

With regard to the claim that the competitive model is simpler than non-competitive alternatives, no criteria are proposed to evaluate it. It is a subjective judgement call, but not one shared by all members of the profession (Holt 1992). Alone it is not enough to justify the generic use of the competitive model. This is obvious once one considers coming to an alternative judgement call – that the monopoly model is the simplest market structure. Would that then justify applying the monopoly model generically throughout the whole economy? It certainly would not give the required impression of a well-functioning self-regulated market system. Stiglitz concludes that the competitive paradigm has survived so long 'partly because the belief in that paradigm, and the policy prescriptions that were derived from it, has served certain interests' (2002: 488). In other words, it is an 'enabling myth'. Certainly, the overemphasis given to it in the textbooks can hardly be explained in any other way.

Suggestions for further reading

For a critique of the mainstream textbook treatment of rent controls see Arnott (1995). Krueger (2001) is an excellent source of information about how to teach the effect of minimum wages given the mixed empirical evidence. The whole of Prasch's (2008) little book, *How Markets Work: Supply, demand and the 'real world'* (2008), is worth reading. Particular emphasis could be put on Lectures II to VI, pages 29 to 111.

ADDENDUM: THE INDETERMINATE AND UNSTABLE ECONOMY

This brief addendum considers two questions: Is there likely to be a unique (just one) equilibrium for the economy as a whole? And if the economy is not in equilibrium, is there some price adjustment process that will bring it to equilibrium? While these are questions that are normally considered in upper-level courses, the concepts should be understandable even to introductory students.

General equilibrium and partial equilibrium 'General equilibrium' is when all the markets in an economy are in equilibrium. For example, the 'production possibilities frontier' presented in Chapter 2 is a general equilibrium model of a very simple two-good economy. In this construct, impacts on wheat explicitly have implications for cloth. Both markets are simultaneously in equilibrium. 'Partial equilibrium' looks at just one market at a time, as in the supply and demand model of Chapter 3. For the most part, introductory microeconomics courses use a partial equilibrium approach.

Multiple equilibria and why they matter In Figure 3.7 we illustrated a situation in which an individual market had several possible equilibria, two of which were stable. That meant it was not possible to predict where the market price and quantity might end up. It might, perhaps, require knowing where the market price was originally. In such a situation, it might be possible to take action to achieve the most desirable equilibrium.

The same result can hold for the economy as a whole. That is, there could be many possible equilibria in a general equilibrium model, some of which might be stable and others unstable. Indeed, if the whole economy were to consist of only competitive markets, like the ones in Chapter 3, the Sonnenschein-Mantel-Debreu (or SMD) Theorem implies that the simultaneous equilibrium may not be unique. As a result, it's impossible to say which of the possible equilibria is the one at which the economy would settle (Ackerman 2002: 121). The economy is fundamentally indeterminate. Occasionally the SMD Theorem is referred to as the 'Anything Goes Theorem'.

This may sound like an abstract, technical point of no real relevance, but that's not the case. Economists, when trying to assess the effects of policy changes, sometimes make computer simulation models of the entire economy. Naturally, like any economic model, these general equilibrium computer simulation models are highly simplified descriptions of the real economy. Do these models miss the possibility of multiple equilibria? If so, a researcher could simulate the effect of a policy change (implementing free trade, for example) and reach one conclusion, while perhaps the economy would actually end up in quite a different position. Yet, as Hildenbrand and Kirman observe (1988: 49): 'Almost all of the economic literature, theoretical and applied, turns around models in which the nature of "the equilibrium" is discussed and analysed,' as if that equilibrium were unique.

Does the economy find its way to equilibrium? The question is whether, when the economy is not in equilibrium, some price adjustment process returns the economy to equilibrium. In introductory economics, in the partial equilibrium context, students are told (as in Part One of this chapter) that a market can be brought back into equilibrium by lowering the price when there is excess supply (and raising it if there is excess demand). But Hildenbrand and Kirman (ibid.: 49) note that 'as soon as we leave the two-good case this is no longer true'. To explain, they say: 'Think for a moment of two goods, cars and gasoline. Suppose prices were such that cars were in excess demand and gasoline in excess supply. Normal behaviour ... would be to raise the price of cars and lower that of gasoline' (ibid.: 105). But raising the price of cars also lowers demand for gasoline, increasing the excess supply of gasoline, while lowering gas prices raises the demand for cars, increasing excess demand there. Price adjustments may lead around in circles, with differences between demands and supplies not approaching zero. Ackerman (2002: 122) reviews the issue and the literature.

In the final analysis, the competitive economy is neither determinate nor stable.

4 | People as consumers

'The crucial period for the formation of modern American consumerism was in the 1920s, when manufacturers confronted the
possibility that once basic needs were met mass consumption
might not follow mass production and rising productivity levels.
In response, business helped create the "American Dream", a
materialistic image of success to which everyone might aspire.
But for many families, this dream was a moving target, always
out of reach. Households would aspire to one level of material
affluence, attain it and become habituated to it, and then aspire
to the next level. The role of business in promoting this cycle
of aspiration and habituation is essential to understanding the
cycle of work-and-spend.' Goodwin et al. (1997: 47)[1]

'Will raising the incomes of all increase the happiness of
all? The answer to this question can now be given with somewhat
greater assurance than twenty years ago … It is "no".' Easterlin
(1995: 35)

I THE STANDARD TEXT

This chapter focuses on consumers, buyers in markets for final goods and services. 'Goods' are tangible things, such as economics textbooks or automobiles,
while services are intangible, such as economics lectures or automobile repair
work. For simplicity, we'll just talk about 'goods'. Final goods are consumed by the
buyer rather than used as inputs in making something else. An apple bought by a
bakery to put into an apple pie is an 'intermediate good', not a final good. We're
concerned here only with final goods.

Demand for individual goods results from consumers' attempts to make
themselves as well off as possible, or to maximize 'utility', a word that comes
from the nineteenth-century English philosopher Jeremy Bentham, the originator
of 'utilitarianism'. Utility is the benefit you get from having or doing something.
We use the word interchangeably with 'benefit' or 'welfare' or 'well-being'.

The more of a good that a person consumes in a period of time, the greater
the total benefit (s)he gets from it, but as total consumption increases, the extra
benefit (or 'marginal utility') from having more of it eventually gets less and less.
Consider the utility you get from drinking glasses of water during a day. The

first one feels much needed; the tenth one could be a chore. This is 'diminishing marginal utility'.

To get the highest benefit from a given income, a person must spend appropriately on the goods and services available. Consider a simple example where there are only two goods: pizza and Pepsi. (Students of textbook economics are typically assumed to be junk food addicts, so let's stick to convention.) To get the appropriate balance in your total spending, you must avoid spending 'too much' on any one thing. If the last dollar you spend on pizza gives you less extra benefit than the last dollar you spend on Pepsi, you're spending too much on pizza. Spend less on pizza and more on Pepsi and you'll make better use of your income. The appropriate balance is reached when the last dollar you spend on pizza gives you the same extra benefit as the last dollar you spend on Pepsi.

A consumer's demand for a good summarizes the quantities that would be purchased at various possible prices. In principle, we can ask the consumer (whom we'll call Mary) the maximum amount she would be willing to pay for various amounts of the good (given her income and the characteristics and prices of all other goods) and construct the demand curve from that. Table 4.1 shows her benefit from eating pizzas.

TABLE 4.1 Mary's benefit from eating pizzas

Pizzas (per week)	Total benefit	Marginal benefit	Net benefit of consuming an additional pizza (if price is $12/pizza)	Total consumer surplus
1	$25	$25	$13	$13
2	$45	$20	$8	$21
3	$60	$15	$3	$24
4	$70	$10	-$2	$22

The second column shows that she would be willing to pay at most $25 to get one pizza/week, reflecting her $25 marginal benefit from it. The second pizza gives her only $20 of marginal benefit, reflecting the law of diminishing marginal utility. That's why she'd be willing to pay only a maximum of $45 ($25 + $20) for two pizzas/week.

The table also illustrates the 'net benefit' she gets from her purchases. This is the difference between how much she values the good, as reflected by the maximum amount she's willing to pay for it, and the amount that she actually has to pay. If pizzas happen to cost $12 each, buying the first pizza gives a net benefit valued at $25 – $12, or $13. The second pizza gives a net benefit of $8 ($20 – $12), and so on. A running total of these net benefits (seen in the final column) shows the total net benefit that results from buying different numbers of pizzas.

This total net benefit is called the 'consumer's surplus'. If a consumer is

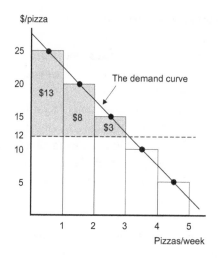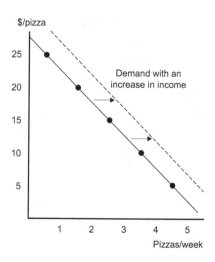

FIGURE 4.1 Marginal benefit and price

spending just the right amount on each good, as described earlier, she is getting the maximum net benefit from her purchases and is maximizing her utility or well-being. If the price happened to be $12/pizza, Mary should buy three pizzas per week to maximize her surplus. Buying the fourth pizza would be an inefficient use of her budget because its marginal benefit is less than the price; the negative net benefit from that would reduce consumer surplus. In general, the consumer should buy more of the good as long as its marginal benefit is greater than or equal to its price.

The left-hand diagram in Figure 4.1 summarizes this. The rectangles show the marginal benefit of each additional pizza; the part of them above the $12 price shows positive additions to consumer surplus from buying that additional pizza. If the price falls to $9/pizza, we can see that it would now be worthwhile to buy the fourth pizza. In general, the marginal benefits tell us the consumer's demand at various possible prices. This example has supposed that pizzas have to be bought in whole units and can't be divided. If we allowed for that, so that people could buy fractions of a pizza (or slices of any size), we could draw marginal benefit as the smooth line in the diagram.

This line is the consumer's demand curve. The consumer's surplus is the area between the demand curve and the price. It's the same as the area of the three shaded rectangles showing the consumer surplus from each individual pizza (with the exception of any surplus from buying a small amount of the fourth pizza, now that pizzas can be bought by the slice).

Other things also influence the amount a consumer wants to buy at each price, such as the income available, and the prices of other goods. They lie in the background here. Changes in any of those other things change demand: an increase in income, for instance, could increase the amount of pizza a person buys at any

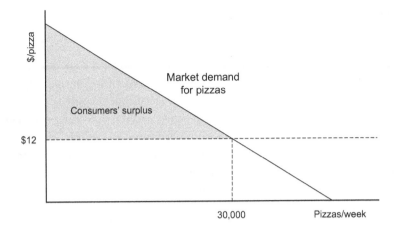

FIGURE 4.2 Market demand

given price, moving demand as shown in the right-hand diagram of Figure 4.1. Or, if income increases a lot, it could reduce demand, as caviar is consumed instead of pizza. In general, more income allows someone to have a different, more preferred, mix of goods giving greater total benefit or utility.

Demand by all consumers is just their total demand at various possible prices. If the price of a pizza is $12, Mary in Figure 4.1 buys three pizzas per week, while weekly demand by all the persons in the market – perhaps a particular geographic region – is 30,000 pizzas, as shown in Figure 4.2. Reflecting individual demands, market demand shows the benefit (measured in dollars) consumers as a whole get from buying various quantities of pizzas. At $12 per pizza, consumers' surplus of all consumers added together is the difference between the maximum prices consumers would be willing to pay (shown by the demand curve) and the market price, the shaded triangle shown in Figure 4.2.[2] If the price falls, consumers buy more and their surplus expands.

The example shows three things: first, the marginal benefit curve is the same as the demand curve; second, the area under the demand curve represents the total benefit from consuming the good; third, the triangle below the demand curve and above the going price is the net benefit (or consumer's surplus) from buying that good.

If the distribution of wealth and income were different then, in general, individual and total demands for goods would change; prices and the amounts produced and sold would also be different. The textbook analysis assumes a particular distribution of income and wealth among people.

For every good, each consumer makes the choices that maximize his or her consumer's surplus, and in aggregate (given everyone's budget constraints) the total surplus of all consumers is maximized too. If something forces consumers to alter their choices compared with this 'free market' outcome, they will be worse off.

2 THE ANTI-TEXT

The previous account of consumer choice offers a reasonable way of thinking about the demand for pizza and how that might change if income changes, the sort of uninteresting question that the textbooks consider at length. But the approach has serious shortcomings that should be a source of concern if we use it as the central or 'default' model to assess the outcomes of consumer decisions in particular markets and in the economy as a whole. In Chapter 1, we described the work of behavioural economists who have examined people's bounded rationality and bounded willpower, concepts that can be applied to understanding consumer behaviour. Here, we will examine further issues that our textbook story quietly swept under the rug.

First, this account says nothing about where our consumer's preferences for pizza, Pepsi or anything else have come from. *Preferences are simply 'given'*. As Milton Friedman put it in his graduate text: 'The economist has little to say about the formation of wants; this is the province of the psychologist. The economist's task is to trace the consequences of any given set of wants' (1976: 13).

This narrow view unduly limits the questions that economics can address. Do some producers and retailers have real influence through advertising and marketing over people's preferences? Why does it matter?

Second, it is assumed that buyers have *perfect information* about what they're buying. When people buy pizzas, if the green peppers on them contain carcinogenic pesticide residues, no worries! The buyers take this into account in their rational calculations when they ask for them on their pizza. In reality, however, *imperfect information* is the rule, not the exception. As well, information is *asymmetric* – in this case the producers of goods have more and better information than their potential customers. Does imperfect and asymmetric information result in important systematic errors when buyers make spending decisions?

Third, the benefit a person gets from consumption in the textbook story has *no social context*. It is entirely unrelated to what other people in the surrounding society have. What happens if social context matters?

We'll consider each of these points in turn. The ideas and their implications are not difficult to understand, so their absence from the textbooks can't be blamed on that. However, they spoil the rosy picture of the operation of the unregulated market economy that an innocent reader can easily take away from the textbook account.

2.1 What if preferences are not 'given'?

The textbook account implicitly assumes that people's wants originate within themselves. For example, a buyer's preferences about pizza and willingness to pay for it reflect how good it tastes compared with other things. If that's true, we don't really have to consider where our taste for pizza comes from; it's just a part of our nature, shaped by evolution to induce us to satisfy our needs for nutrients. This way of thinking clearly does not apply to all goods and services. But the economists who developed the theory of demand were not trying to develop a real theory of people's 'wants'. They sought only a simple account to explain the demand curve, a building block in the supply and demand model that in turn produces a theory of prices, their real goal (Douglas 1987).

Why shouldn't we acknowledge that wants are, in part, determined by people's previous consumption experiences, the social environment in which they live, and attempts by firms to influence individuals' wants?[3] Textbook economics has long been criticized for ignoring this; if preferences are influenced in important ways within the economic system itself, it's hardly convincing for Friedman to claim that it's not economists' business.

Advertising

'Advertising may be described as the science of arresting the human intelligence long enough to get money from it.' Stephen Leacock (1924: 123)

Advertising is the most obvious attempt to influence people's preferences. In textbook economics, people are perfectly informed, so advertising must just provide consumers with accurate information about product characteristics, sellers' locations and prices. This assumes away persuasive advertising that tries to change people's wants and stimulate new wants; and it assumes that advertising never provides biased or misleading information.

The supply and demand model at the heart of textbooks doesn't permit such questions about advertising to arise. Each firm has a very small share of the market and all make identical products, such as a particular variety of apples, for example. We can imagine apple farmers having roadside stands with signs reading 'apples, $4/kg', but no farmer will be so foolish as to try to boost sales by paying for billboards with pictures of celebrities eating apples. (Advertising is acknowledged only later in the textbook when discussing industries dominated by one or a small number of firms, but this has no impact on the theory of consumer behaviour.)

The advertising industry is large. In the United States, probably the world's most advertising-saturated country, it constituted about 2.1 per cent of US gross domestic product in 2008, or about $970 per person.[4] In *The Affluent Society*, John Kenneth Galbraith wrote that advertising expenditures 'must be integrated with the theory of consumer demand. They are too big to be ignored' (1958: 122). Yet textbook economics relegates them to the sidelines.

Some people accuse advertising of contributing to consumerism and an excessively materialistic culture. Clearly, this can't be the goal of any particular advertiser, who, like the apple grower, is only trying to sell a product, but it may be a side effect of the activity of the advertising industry as a whole.

© Andy Singer

For example, in her study of the commercialization of childhood, *Born to Buy*, Juliet Schor (2004: 86) summarizes the results of studies of children's exposure to Channel One. Channel One is a daily news and advertising broadcast shown in a quarter of US middle and secondary schools in exchange for video equipment. They find that the programme affects children's attitudes, making them more likely to agree with statements expressing materialistic views ('designer labels make a difference').

The problem of changing preferences Some economists have given the formation and change of preferences serious thought and reached conclusions that undermine the textbook account. A straightforward example illustrates the central idea.

Suppose that new cell phones receive television signals. You have no interest in watching television and your willingness to pay extra for this feature is zero. The heavily advertised new cell phones are all the rage, however, and your friends look at you with pity and puzzlement. Finally, you trade in your old cell phone for the new model. Evidently, your preferences changed.

How would we evaluate this situation? If we use your initial preferences, when you placed no value on the TV feature, we must conclude that you are worse off: you've paid good money for something you think is worthless. If we use your new preferences, we must conclude that you got some consumer surplus from the deal and are better off after the purchase.

The fundamental problem is that it's not always obvious whether the preferences before or after the change are the ones to use in judging your situation. You have the freedom to change your preferences, after all. On what grounds can we say which preferences are the most valid? Does it depend on why you changed your preferences? The problem is even more complex if people's preferences continually change because of their experience and their changing social environment.

The textbooks implicitly claim that the origin of wants is unimportant by simply ignoring the question. The only thing that apparently counts is the wants of the moment and the extent to which they are being satisfied. But this claim involves a value judgement that reasonable people may – and do – disagree with. How people's preferences are formed is important. While the great economists of the past were often willing to make explicit value judgements about people's wants, now most economists remain silent (McPherson 1987: 403).

Even when a text, such as McConnell and Brue (2005), acknowledges the existence of persuasive advertising that gets consumers to pay high prices for inferior products, it adopts the 'note the problem and then forget it' strategy – not letting the inconvenient observation have any fundamental impact on the analysis.

To open wants up for scrutiny and debate, textbook economics would have to admit that its method for judging individual and social outcomes doesn't always work. Rather than deal with the thorny issues that advertising and marketing raise, the textbooks direct students' attention to socially innocuous questions such as how the demand for pizza might be affected by changes in the price of beer or anchovies.

Controlling advertising in the public interest

'Every time you're exposed to advertising, you realize once again that America's leading industry, America's most profitable business is still the manufacture, packaging, distribution and marketing of bullshit.' George Carlin[5]

In the real world, these issues are too important to ignore and citizens' concern about the harmful effects of advertising and marketing on wants sometimes forces governments to regulate and restrict it in the public interest. Tobacco is a notable example, particularly because much of its advertising and marketing efforts were (and are) directed at children. Children are particularly vulnerable to the army of psychological experts deployed against them. 'Marketing snoops, with cameras, notebooks, and videotapes, can be found in toy stores, clothing shops, and supermarkets, hanging out in the aisles and watching what kids do,' writes Juliet Schor (2004: 86).

Young children can't tell the difference between entertainment programmes and advertising on television, one reason why some western European countries ban the use of children in TV advertising (Nader 2004a: 100). Quebec, Sweden and Norway all ban advertising directed at children under the age of twelve (Goodwin et al. 2005: 241). In the United States, parents' and citizens' groups are campaigning against the growing onslaught of advertising in schools and on school buses.

More than a hundred organizations, including Commercial Alert and the British Medical Association, and dozens of health experts and children's advocates in many countries have called for a ban on junk food advertising to children under thirteen years of age (Commercial Alert 2004). A study suggests that Quebec's ban on all advertising directed at children has indeed reduced junk food spending significantly (Baylis and Dhar 2007).

Example: marketing infant formula One of the most notable examples of an attempt to limit marketing and advertising is the International Code of Marketing Breast-Milk Substitutes (World Health Organization 1981). The Code bans advertising and promotion of infant formula, sets strict labelling requirements, and requires producers to inform potential buyers that breast milk is best for babies. It also requires that formula be used only after consultation with medical professionals. The Code came about after campaigns in the 1970s by nongovernmental organizations against producers, particularly the Nestlé boycott. Infant formula producers simply pursue profits despite the evidence that the use and misuse of their products results in the deaths of enormous numbers of infants.

The World Health Organization and UNICEF agree that for the first six months of life, all babies should be fed only breast milk rather than infant formula. UNICEF's Chief of Nutrition says that 'If we were to breastfeed all children exclusively for the first six months, we could possibly save more than 1 million child lives every year' (Li 2007).[6]

In developing countries, bottle-fed babies are much more likely to die than breast-fed babies, largely because of the use of contaminated water (ibid.). Even in the developed countries, bottle-fed babies have significantly poorer health outcomes than breastfed babies. Yet despite all this, the WHO reports that only about one in three infants worldwide are exclusively breastfed during their first four months. Why?

According to UNICEF, part of the problem is 'aggressive marketing of infant formula'. Individual governments must implement the Code in their own laws and monitor compliance, but many drag their feet. In the United States, the Code's restrictions are not even legally binding.[7] A study by the US Government Accountability Office found that advertising 'is widespread and increasing' and that marketing practices, such as distributing free samples of infant formula to pregnant women or to mothers on discharge from hospital (prohibited under the Code), tend to discourage breastfeeding (US GAO 2006: 34). The editors of the *International Breastfeeding Journal* write that 'the lack of a breastfeeding culture in most industrialized nations is the legacy of decades of commercial marketing of infant formula, often endorsed by medical practices', which leaves parents woefully ignorant (Beasley and Amir 2007).

The bottle-feeding culture has slowly been reversed in some places. This requires a halt to commercial marketing, government support for adequate paid maternity leave, and the implementation of UNICEF's Baby Friendly Hospital Initiative. (This helps mothers begin breastfeeding right after birth.) In Sweden, 72 per cent of babies are exclusively or partially breastfed at six months, while in Norway it's 80 per cent (Sweden 2002: 8; Monbiot 2007a). In contrast, it's 27 per cent in the United States and 21 per cent in the UK (Li et al. 2003; Monbiot 2007a).

A key feature of the problem is the poor information that parents have. For example, in the Philippines, UNICEF reports that 16,000 children under five die annually from 'inappropriate feeding practices, including the use of infant formula'. There, 'poorer families ... are increasingly spending a large part of their income on infant formula, convinced that it is a way to improve their child's intelligence and thus chances for a better life', although breastfeeding is associated with better cognitive development (UNICEF 2007).

Questions for your professor: How do we measure consumer surplus if advertising and marketing change people's preferences? Does it matter if they buy things they would not want with perfect information?

2.2 Incomplete and asymmetric information

The textbook economics story of consumer choice with its assumptions of informative advertising and perfect information leading to optimal choices is particularly misleading in situations where incomplete and asymmetric information is a central feature. This provides an opportunity for manipulative marketing by producers. Let's consider a couple of examples.

Example: marketing prescription drugs No one should have been too surprised when a recent study finally revealed that Prozac, the popular antidepressant taken by 40 million people, and three other drugs in its class are no more effective for most people than a placebo (a sugar pill that the patient believes is a drug). The study 'examined all data available on the drugs, including results from clinical trials that the manufacturers chose not to publish at the time' (Boseley 2008).

While the drug companies raked in tens of billions over the decades these ineffective drugs have been on the market, patients were unknowingly exposed to risks of lethal side effects, such as suicide – a problem the drug companies were aware of, but concealed (Healy 2003).[8]

Unfortunately, the Prozac story is no aberration. Pharmaceutical drugs are complex products that their ultimate users are in no position to understand or assess. Consumers rely on drug companies and supposedly independent researchers, medical journals, healthcare providers and government regulators to make safe products available and to prescribe them properly. This system has been deeply compromised according to recent exposés (e.g. Angell 2004; Moynihan and Cassels 2005).

Drug companies have discovered that they can expand their markets by having drugs prescribed to healthy people: just reclassify them so they become candidates for a prescription drug. Recent decades witnessed highly profitable increases in the number of 'depressed' people, children with 'attention deficit hyperactivity disorder', people with 'high' cholesterol, and on and on. Even shyness has become a major epidemic labelled 'social anxiety disorder' – and a powerful antidepressant (with 'horrendous withdrawal symptoms') found a huge new market (Moynihan and Cassels 2005: ch. 7). The earlier and the longer people can be put on drugs, the more money can be made. In 2008, the American Academy of Pediatrics recommended anti-cholesterol drugs for some children as young as eight (Associated Press 2008; Daniels et al. 2008).[9]

Advertising directed at consumers is effective in inducing prescriptions from doctors, particularly for new drugs that are very expensive and no better than older, less expensive ones or perhaps no better than nothing at all. Citizen groups, such as Commercial Alert, want such ads banned in the United States, but corporate power has blocked it, although such advertising is banned in every other developed country except New Zealand (Angell 2004: 124–5).[10]

Researchers studying drugs and sitting on panels writing guidelines for doctors very often receive money as 'consultants' from the companies whose products they study or recommend. According to a former editor of the *New England Journal of Medicine*, the influence of the industry is such that much published research may be 'seriously flawed', misleading doctors who rely on it to judge the efficacy and safety of new drugs (Angell 2004: xxvi). A significant number of articles published in medical journals have been 'drafted by drug company-sponsored ghostwriters and then passed off as the work of independent academic authors' (Singer and Wilson 2009).

The main targets of drug company marketing are the doctors who write the prescriptions. Sales representatives, who regularly visit doctors' offices to ply their wares, shower them with 'gifts'. Companies spend millions flying doctors on all-expenses-paid trips to conferences where they are presented with one-sided marketing dressed up as 'medical education' (Moynihan and Cassels 2005; Angell 2004: 126–55; Boseley and Evans 2008).

Little wonder, then, that combined with the political power of the companies (which we look at in the next chapter), the drug makers are regularly among the most profitable corporations in the world.

Example: food The food industry is crucial in satisfying one of our most fundamental needs. We can see, smell and taste what we eat and drink, but to find out what it contains at the molecular level is no easy matter. It should not be surprising, then, that much food and drink contains additives to enhance the appearance, texture, flavour or shelf-life of the products – additives that, on closer examination, have serious adverse consequences, such as allergic reactions, behavioural problems in children, such as hyperactivity, and cancers (Hickman 2007).

Books such as Eric Schlosser's *Fast Food Nation* help to reveal what really goes into the products of the fast food industry – everything from shit from slaughtered animals in hamburger meat to the 'natural and artificial flavours' conjured up by the chemists of the flavour industry. Such exposure, however, has had only a minor effect on an industry that maintains an enormous advertising budget to bolster its image, much of it directed at children, whose food preferences form early in life (Schlosser 2001: 4).

Just as obesity is an increasing problem, so too is malnutrition. In 2007, doctors estimated that in Britain there were more than three million malnourished people, including 40 per cent of hospital patients (Woolf 2007; Moreton 2007). The lack of vitamins and vital nutrients is due to excessive reliance on pre-prepared food and not eating enough fresh fruit and vegetables. Yet eating more fresh fruit and vegetables may not be enough. While these are increasingly designed to look good to the buyers, their nutritional content is plummeting. The same is true of industrially produced meat (Pawlick 2006: 15–16, 26–7).

People are also increasingly interested in how their food is produced. Public awareness of the treatment of animals, particularly in factory farming, is rising. For example, in Britain 'free-range' eggs produced by cage-free hens able to walk outside exceed the value of eggs from caged hens. In most cases, however, shoppers are not given the information they would need to make ethical choices about the food they are buying (Singer and Mason 2006: 3–6).

If demand for a product (such as adulterated factory-produced chicken meat) in the presence of imperfect information is greater than it would be in the presence of perfect information, then consumers really do not use their budgets efficiently to maximize their well-being. The misallocation of resources parallels what we saw in the earlier example, where preferences were altered by advertising.

The real default case: incomplete and asymmetric information Despite the pervasiveness of informational problems and the inefficiencies they give rise to, textbook economics focuses on the improbable assumptions of given tastes and perfect information that helps make Adam Smith's good-news story of the invisible hand work for consumers. But incomplete and asymmetric information – that is, buyers and sellers knowing different things – is a better description of reality for almost all goods. As the examples we give suggest, ignorance about what we buy and use is commonplace and in many situations buyers' ignorance has important consequences.

How flammable is your children's clothing? How will your automobile respond to crashes of various kinds? Did you get cheated by the mechanic when you had the car repaired? What hidden defects are there in the house you are considering buying? What are your chances of being a victim of medical malpractice? What chemicals are leaching out of plastics into your food and drink and what are the consequences? Are cell phones really safe? And so on. You can be sure that the producers of these goods or services know much more about the answers than their customers. Even if the customers suspect there is a potential problem, they are unlikely to undertake the time-consuming and perhaps technically demanding research on their own.

What about the news media? Don't investigative reporters uncover problems and inform the public? Don't governments monitor the market and act on the public's behalf, regulating or providing information? We explain the economic basis for corporate power in the next chapter, but for now let's just note that the media corporations that provide most people with their news are primarily interested in profits; systematically upsetting other corporations (which may be major advertisers) is not profitable.

How governments behave depends on the strength of the country's democracy. Where democracy is weak and the power of big business is strong, governments can be expected often to act against the interests of the vast majority of the population.

Everywhere, people and economic institutions try to cope with informational problems. It's not all bad news. Think, for example, of the investments some companies make in a reputation for quality, or those that offer real guarantees and warranties to distinguish their higher-quality products from those of competitors. None of these commonplace features of the business world has a place in the textbook world of perfect information.

In the United States, Ralph Nader has spent a lifetime improving the odds for consumers through organizing citizen and consumer groups and pressing

Questions for your professor: Isn't incomplete and asymmetric information an important problem for consumers? Does the default assumption in the textbook of complete and perfect information divert attention away from these problems? If so, in whose interest?

government to level the playing field through law and regulation. He, and others around the world, have won important victories for consumers, but the cards remain stacked in favour of producers. Business lobbies are always trying to roll back consumer gains.[11]

2.3 Preferences and relative position

Advertising and other actions by producers are not the only way in which people's tastes are shaped within the economic system itself. We are, after all, social animals: we see what others have and that influences our own wants and the utility we get from the things we have.

According to evolutionary psychology, the way we think about our place in society has been shaped, like all the other processes of our minds, by evolutionary forces (Pinker 2002). A concern for status and security is central to the individual's ability to survive, to find mates and to reproduce. We have an innate concern about our relative position in our 'reference group', those people with whom we compare ourselves (Frank 1999; Marmot 2004). As Juliet Schor (1998: 69) reminds us, 'While most critics of consumer society focus on ads and the media, it's important to remember that the more powerful stimulator of desire is what friends and family have.'

The implicit assumption in textbook economics is that the utility people get from things is entirely independent of what others have.[12] But what is the evidence about how other people's consumption affects our utility? The textbook account presents none. How does considering utility in a more realistic way change our judgements about how well the economy is functioning?

John Kenneth Galbraith expressed a central aspect of the problem in *The Affluent Society*:

> If the individual's wants are to be urgent they must originate with himself. They cannot be urgent if they must be contrived for him. And above all they must not be contrived by the process of production by which they are satisfied. For this means that the whole case for the urgency of production, based on the urgency of wants, falls to the ground. One cannot defend production as satisfying wants if that production creates the wants. (1958: 119)

Production creates wants through people's desire to emulate others. 'One man's consumption becomes his neighbour's wish ... The more wants are satisfied the more new ones are born,' as Galbraith wrote (ibid.: 120–21). If this is true, we keep working to produce more and more, yet we remain in the same place in terms of the utility we get from those things. Is there evidence to support this view?

The evidence: surveys of subjective well-being In 1974, Richard Easterlin wrote a path-breaking essay in which he drew economists' attention to work in sociology

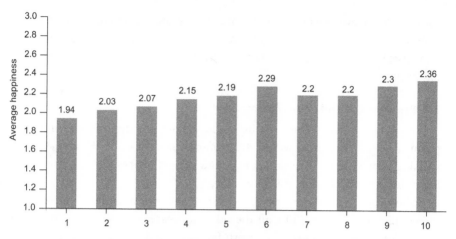

FIGURE 4.3 Happiness in the United States, 1994–96, by income decile
Source: Frey and Stutzer (2002), Table 1

and psychology that tries to measure individuals' feelings of satisfaction and happiness. These are called measures of 'subjective well-being' because they rely on people's own, subjective, assessments rather than objective measures, such as how much income they have.

Happiness within countries across income groups: Easterlin's evidence shows that within countries, people with more income also tended to report themselves as happier, as the textbook model would predict. Figure 4.3 shows the typical picture for the United States, where the population in a national survey is divided into ten equal-sized income groups or deciles. It shows average responses to the question 'Taken all together, how would you say things are these days – would you say that you are very happy, pretty happy, or not too happy?'[13] While no one claims that any one person's happiness can be directly compared with any other person's, the average differences across the groups are meaningful and reflect real differences in well-being.

Average happiness across countries: What happens if we compare average happiness levels across countries with different levels of average income? Figure 4.4 shows data on responses to a question about happiness from seventy countries in the 1999–2004 World Values Survey.[14] For each country, we show the average level of happiness (converted to a ten-point scale) and the best measure available of its real output per person.[15]

Remarkable are the very poor countries (such as Tanzania and Nigeria), whose happiness scores here are even higher than those in the happiest of the wealthy countries.[16] Easterlin observes that such results 'are a testimony to the adaptability of mankind. Income and aspirations ... tend to go together, and people can seemingly make something out of what appears, in some absolute sense, to be a sorry lot' (1974: 119).

There is a problem, however, if, as Angus Deaton puts it, people 'adapt to

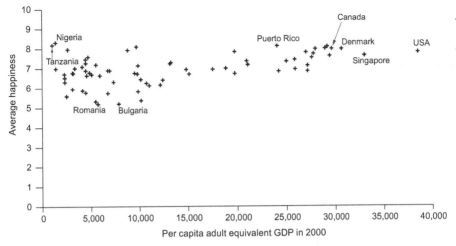

FIGURE 4.4 Happiness and per capita income across countries, 1999–2004

misery and hardship, and cease to see it for what it is. People do not necessarily perceive the constraints caused by their lack of freedom; the child who is potentially a great musician but never had a chance to find out will not express a lack of life satisfaction' (Deaton 2008: 67). To address this concern, Amartya Sen advocates a focus on objective measures such as the actual freedoms and capabilities that people have. In this view, high or growing incomes are not goals in themselves. The goals are things like a long and healthy life, political freedoms, freedom to exchange goods and labour with others, and the ability to participate in social life (Sen 1999).

Nevertheless, the current view of data like those in Figure 4.4 is that countries with higher income per person do tend to have higher average happiness.[17] But the substantial differences between countries with similar income levels suggest that many other things influence happiness in important ways.

Average happiness within countries over time: Easterlin also examined how average happiness changed over time within a country. Figure 4.5 shows that the average level of happiness in the United States has not increased since the first surveys just after the Second World War, yet the average person's material affluence has increased enormously.

The 'Easterlin Paradox' The evidence we have reviewed has paradoxical features. At any time within a country, higher-income persons have a higher level of well-being on average. Yet there seems to be no significant positive relationship between income and average well-being over long periods of time, even when incomes have grown substantially. This puzzle has been dubbed the 'Easterlin Paradox'.

Easterlin's own explanation of the Easterlin Paradox is straightforward: people evaluate their well-being using a standard or norm based on the social conditions

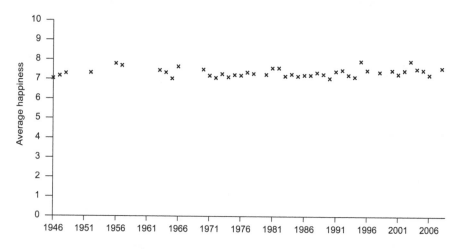

FIGURE 4.5 Happiness in the United States, 1946–2008 *Source*: World Database of Happiness

they experience. If material conditions improve, the social norm changes with it. As a result, on average people feel no improvement in their well-being. Norms and aspirations rise to cancel out the effects of higher real incomes and consumption. This is perfectly consistent with higher-income individuals reporting themselves happier or more satisfied than lower-income individuals at any particular time. That's what makes it sensible for individuals to try to improve their relative position. People don't seem to realize that a gradual rise in norms will take place and they seem to believe that they'll be happier in the future with higher incomes than they really turn out to be (Easterlin 2001).

Easterlin suggests a simple thought experiment: 'Imagine that your income increases substantially while everyone else's stays the same. Would you feel better off?' Of course you would. 'Now, suppose that your income stays the same while everyone else's increases substantially. How would you feel?' He asserts that most people would feel less well off than they did before (Easterlin 1995: 35–6).[18]

In his book *Luxury Fever*, Robert Frank argues that increasing income inequality, particularly in the United States, has moved norms upwards because of the conspicuous consumption among the wealthy. Heavy advertising for status-seeking goods amplifies this. The result, he argues, is a distortion of consumer spending in a futile 'arms race' for status and an explosion of consumer debt.

The Easterlin Paradox can also be explained by the idea that people adapt to changes in income. More income may initially give a feeling of greater well-being, but it wears off because we judge our circumstances relative to our own recent experience. This is a familiar concept in psychology because our senses exhibit this feature. What feels like a warm day in winter would seem like a chilly one in the summer, even if the temperature is the same on both days.

Another way to explain the Easterlin Paradox is to recognize that consuming commodities takes time – a scarce commodity. Yet in the textbooks, 'consumption is regarded as some sort of instantaneous act', imposing a no-time cost (Linder 1970: 7–8).[19] Growing material affluence means greater access to goods, but with no greater time in which to consume them the scarcity of time increases. Linder predicted 'an increasingly hectic tempo of life', less 'time devoted to the cultivation of mind and spirit' and an increase in ultimately unsatisfying materialism (ibid.: 143–4). While textbook economics remains blind to this issue, some people, such as those experimenting with 'simple living' and 'voluntary simplicity', are seeking ways out of the dilemmas that Linder identified.

> Question for your professor: What does the evidence say about whether economic growth and higher average incomes in a country increases feelings of well-being, on average?

Another paradox There is a second, separate puzzle. We've seen that as average incomes grow over time within a country there is no significant increase in average feelings of well-being. You might then predict that average well-being would be the same for countries with different average income levels. Yet we also saw in Figure 4.4 a tendency for countries with higher average incomes to have higher levels of average well-being.

To the extent this is true, it could be due to other systematic differences between high- and low-income countries (Frey and Stutzer 2002: 416–17). For example, higher-income countries tend to have a better quality of democracy and government, as well as greater personal, economic and political freedoms, than low-income countries. These characteristics remain stable over time for many countries and are associated with significant differences in average well-being. As average income within any given country grows, average well-being need not change unless some of these other characteristics also change.

A lively debate has sprung up among economists about what really determines people's well-being.[20] Economists are abandoning the textbook orthodoxy in droves. Whatever conclusions current research will ultimately reach, the standard textbook model is unlikely to survive this confrontation with reality.

2.4 Summing up

The decisions about what and how much to buy are central to the textbook account of how markets work. The textbooks describe consumers who save and spend optimally to maximize their well-being. Yet a careful look reveals just how limited the account's range of applicability really is. It would work nicely for Robinson Crusoe, living in isolation on an island and trying to decide whether to have a banana or a coconut for breakfast. But when applied to the world in which we live, its assumptions about preferences and information and its omission of social context raise serious problems.

It's obvious that the perfect-information model of rational consumer choice is not realistic. The important question is whether the model describes and explains consumer behaviour in a useful way.

Given the systematic ways in which consumers' tastes and information are shaped by producer power and by the social environment around them, the textbook model is a poor guide. It treats people as benefiting from consuming things even if they would not want them if they had accurate information about their characteristics. Businesses can often make it hard for consumers to obtain relevant information. This is only one aspect of the disproportionate power of business organizations in society.

The texts ignore the fact that the utility people get from buying more stuff depends on what other people do, and so they make systematically wrong predictions about their utility. They also give students the impression that economic growth is more important for the well-being of the population than actually seems to be the case. The major theme of standard textbook economics is 'efficiency' – using resources as efficiently as possible to maximize output and consumption. But if additional consumption in wealthy countries provides little or no additional well-being, why is this so important?

Suggestions for further reading

Juliet Schor's books on the cycle of work and spend (1992, 1998) are both perceptive and highly readable. Her latest (2004) explores and exposes the hidden world of marketing to children.

Many recent books have explored the hidden side of the food industry – both what's in our food and how it's made. Eric Schlosser's *Fast Food Nation* (2001) is a classic. Felicity Lawrence's *Not on the Label: What really goes into the food on your plate* (2004) and her subsequent *Eat Your Heart Out: Why the food business is bad for the planet and your health* (2008) are highly recommended. Peter Singer and James Mason point out that what we eat also has ethical consequences in their 2006 book *The Ethics of What We Eat: Why our food choices matter*.

Richard Layard is a prominent economist who has championed the new approach to thinking about well-being. His 2005 book, *Happiness: Lessons from a new science*, is a good account.

We've pointed out the unsatisfactory nature of assuming preferences are 'given' and don't change with our experience. More advanced undergraduate students may want to explore David L. George's *Preference Pollution: How markets create the desires we dislike* (2001).

5 | The firm

'[with] the great concentrations of power in the multinational corporations ... the text books are still illustrated with U shaped curves showing the limitation on the size of the firms in a perfectly competitive market.' Joan Robinson (1972: 4)

'We should expect that individuals and groups will struggle for position; that power will be used to improve one's chances in the economic "game" ... Power should, therefore, be a recurrent theme in economic studies ... Yet if we look at the main run of economic theory over the past hundred years we find that it is characterized by a strange lack of power considerations.' Kurt Rothschild (1971: 7)

I THE STANDARD TEXT

The business firm is an organization within which factors of production – workers, capital (buildings, machinery, equipment and so on) and land – are used with inputs purchased from other firms (raw materials, parts, security services, for example) to produce goods and services for sale. The organization can have different legal forms: a sole proprietorship, a partnership, a cooperative or a corporation.

Although non-profit firms (such as universities) are not uncommon, the firm's goal is assumed to be profit maximization. More precisely, this is the maximization of the present discounted value of the profits it will earn now and into the future.

Production The firm's managers (who may or may not be its owners) make decisions about such things as how much to produce, how they will produce it and what prices to charge. To do this, they have to know the 'technology' of production available to them. 'Technology' just describes how inputs produce outputs. So a peasant weeding a field with a hoe is a possible technology for producing a crop.

Following the textbook tradition, let's consider fictitious data about a firm that produces loaves of bread using 'labour' (workers, all identical in skills and effort) and 'capital' (all the things such as ovens, buildings and so on that workers use to make loaves of bread). Table 5.1 summarizes the technology of production, relating inputs to different rates of bread production.

Production, costs and profits in the short run It's easier and cheaper to change some inputs than others. For example, managers can more easily hire or lay off a worker than build a new building. In our simple two-factor setting, this amounts to saying that capital is effectively fixed for a time, so managers have only choices about varying labour if they want to change production. The period of time during which they face such decisions is 'the short run'. In Table 5.1, the firm is using ten units of capital to produce bread. The first two columns show how bread output (or total product) varies with labour input. The third column, labelled 'Marginal product', shows how output changes as one more worker is hired. (Units of labour are workers per day. Units of output are dozens of loaves of bread.)

TABLE 5.1 Inputs and output in the short run (using 10 units of capital)

Units of labour	Output or total product (dozens of loaves per day)	Marginal product (dozens of additional loaves per day)
0	0	-
1	3	3
2	8	5
3	16	8
4	20	4
5	22	2
6	22	0

The third column illustrates the 'law' of diminishing marginal returns. This shows that increasing the use of any one input, holding all other inputs fixed, eventually reduces the marginal product. This is just a claim about an empirical regularity that economists believe so strongly they label it a 'law'.

The 'law' of diminishing returns does not rule out an initial period of increasing marginal returns. Thus, in column three, the marginal product of the second worker is five dozen loaves of bread, greater than the three dozen of the first worker. Increasing marginal returns occur because, as more workers are used, complicated tasks involved in bread making can be broken up into a series of simple tasks in which workers specialize. This is the idea of the 'division of labour', a concept emphasized by Adam Smith. But once the benefits from the division of labour are exhausted, diminishing marginal returns set in. If they did not, it would be possible to grow the world's food supplies in a flowerpot by adding more and more labour inputs. Marginal productivity of labour must eventually diminish because of the fixed amounts of other inputs it has to work with. While workers can use more flour and yeast (intermediate inputs purchased from other firms) to make more bread, there are only so many dough mixing machines and ovens to use. Figure 5.1 sketches out these general ideas.

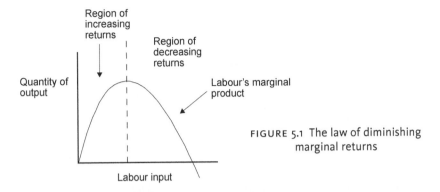

FIGURE 5.1 The law of diminishing marginal returns

The law of diminishing returns determines the shape of all the product curves: marginal, total and average. The marginal product must be an inverted 'U' shape as diminishing returns set in. The total product is derived from the marginal by summing the contribution of each unit of labour. The average product could be derived from the total product by dividing it by the labour input.

We can derive the costs of bread production by using the data in Table 5.1 along with information about the costs of labour and capital. Let's suppose that fixed costs (i.e. costs unrelated to the rate of production) are $250/day, and labour costs $150/day. Table 5.2 shows the results (for which a cup of strong coffee would be a complementary good).

TABLE 5.2 Costs in the short run ($)

(1) Total output	(2) Total fixed cost	(3) Total variable cost	(4) Total cost	(5) Average fixed cost	(6) Average variable cost	(7) Average total cost	(8) Marginal cost
0	250	0	250	∞	∞	∞	
3	250	150	400	83.3	50.0	133.3	50
8	250	300	550	31.3	37.5	68.8	30
16	250	450	700	15.6	28.13	43.8	18.8
20	250	600	850	12.5	30	42.5	37.5
22	250	750	1,000	11.4	34.1	45.4	75
22	250	900	1,150	11.4	40.9	56.8	∞

Note: Calculated using Table 5.1, assuming capital costs $250/day and labour costs $150/day.

Column (1) contains the output data from Table 5.1. Column (2) assumes a fixed cost of $250. Column (3) shows total variable cost, which is just $150 times the number of workers hired. Column (4) is total cost, which is the sum of fixed and variable costs.

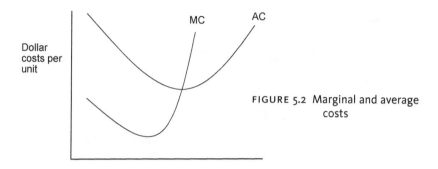

FIGURE 5.2 Marginal and average costs

The next three columns show average costs (average fixed costs, average variable costs and average total costs), obtained by dividing the appropriate 'total' column by output. Note that average fixed cost declines continually as more is produced. Average variable cost falls at first, but later increases as diminishing marginal returns set in. Average total cost falls quite rapidly at first, owing to the rapidly falling average fixed costs and the falling average variable costs. But as the fall in average fixed costs moderates and average variable costs begin to increase, eventually average total costs increase. Like average variable costs, average total costs are U-shaped.

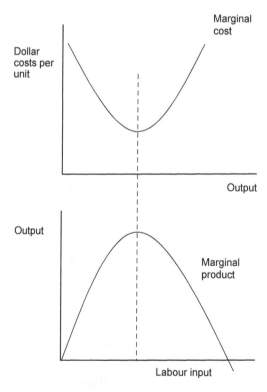

FIGURE 5.3 Marginal product and marginal cost

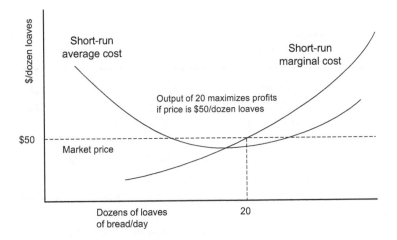

FIGURE 5.4 Marginal benefit and market price

The final column shows the cost of producing additional output, or marginal cost. When the first worker is hired, variable costs rise by $150 and three dozen loaves of bread are made, so their marginal cost is $150/3, or $50 per dozen loaves. We really want the extra cost of producing one more unit of output, but output jumps from zero to three as the firm hires one unit of labour. So, dividing by three units of output gives us the average of the marginal costs as we increase output from zero to three.

When the second worker is hired, costs go up by $150 again, and the bakery makes five dozen more loaves. Their marginal cost is $150/5 or $30 per dozen loaves. The marginal cost of bread falls initially, reflecting increasing marginal returns, but increases later as diminishing marginal returns set in.

Figure 5.2 sketches out these short-run average and marginal costs. (The marginal cost in the numerical example rose in steps as an additional worker was hired for a day; if the firm can hire labour for any length of time it wants, the marginal cost line becomes smooth.)

Note the central importance of the law of diminishing returns; it determines the shape of all the cost curves: marginal, average and total. This follows from the fact that marginal costs go down when marginal productivity goes up. So an inverted U-shaped marginal product curve implies a U-shaped marginal cost curve, as shown in Figure 5.3.

To maximize profits, the firm's managers apply the rational-choice logic of marginal benefit equals marginal cost that we saw in Chapter 1. In this case, consider a perfectly competitive bakery that faces a 'market price' for bread. The marginal benefit of selling a dozen loaves of bread is the market price of (let's say) $50. This is shown in Figure 5.4 as a horizontal line. The firm maximizes profits when the extra revenue from making and selling a dozen loaves of bread just equals the extra costs incurred.

Using the data from Table 5.2, let's suppose that the twentieth unit of output has a marginal cost of just $50 per dozen loaves. (Recall that $37.50 is the average of the rising marginal costs between units sixteen and twenty.) To produce more than that involves a marginal cost greater than $50, which would reduce total profits. The difference between price and average cost, $7.50 (i.e. $50 − $42.50), is profit per dozen loaves of bread; total profits are a princely $150. Using Table 5.1, we can see that in the short run the bakery will hire four workers.

Production, costs and profits in the long run In the short run, the firm could not vary all its inputs. But in the 'long run' it can. This varies the 'scale' of the firm's activities. If, for example, the firm doubled the inputs it used, production must rise, but in what proportion?

Economists classify the possible outcomes into three categories. The first is 'constant returns to scale': output changes in the same proportion as inputs. It's easy to imagine a simple example: one lecture is produced by one professor and one lecture hall. Two professors and two lecture halls produce two lectures.

The second category is 'increasing returns to scale'. As the name suggests, output rises in greater proportion than the change in inputs. Doubling capital and labour inputs more than doubles bread production. There are many reasons for economies of scale. One of the most obvious is that greater scale permits greater division of labour and perhaps more specialized capital equipment.

The third category is 'decreasing returns to scale', in which output rises by a smaller proportion than the increase in inputs. 'Diseconomies of scale can arise because of *coordination* problems that are inherent in any large organization. The more cars Ford produces, the more stretched the management team becomes, and the less effective managers become at keeping costs down' (Mankiw et al. 2006: 289). In effect, the attention of the entrepreneur or management is regarded as a kind of 'fixed factor', bringing back the idea of diminishing marginal returns even in the long run (Kaldor 1934: 67).

The nature of a particular firm's returns to scale is important in describing its long-run costs, and this, in turn, ends up determining how many businesses can survive and coexist in a particular market.

If we assume that the firm can employ inputs at constant prices (so that hiring more labour doesn't raise wages, for example), then with constant returns to scale, costs change in the same proportion as changes in output. Thus, the cost per unit of output (the average cost of production) doesn't change. This constant 'long-run average cost' relationship is shown in Figure 5.5, panel A. This shows the lowest average cost that the firm can attain with current technology and input prices if it has time to adjust its scale of production.

With increasing returns to scale, doubling inputs doubles costs, but more than doubles output. Average costs must be declining as production increases. Conversely, decreasing returns to scale are associated with rising long-run average

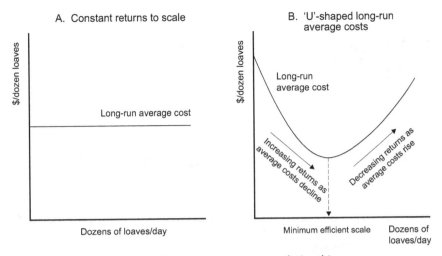

FIGURE 5.5 Long-run average cost relationships

costs. These cases are shown together in Figure 5.5, panel B. The typical textbook story features a long-run average cost relationship that's U shaped, like this one. This reflects increasing returns to scale initially, followed by decreasing returns to scale. The lowest output rate at which the firm can minimize its long-run average costs is the 'minimum efficient scale'.

Two qualifications (usually not in the textbooks) First, the texts discuss a firm's long-run decisions in terms of returns *to scale*, as if the firm scales all inputs up or down, using the same proportions of labour and capital. In reality, these may change. For example, it may make sense in a large-scale manufacturing operation to use more automated production methods and thus more capital relative to labour than would be the case in small-scale operations. Thus, economists typically refer to 'increasing returns', 'constant returns' and 'decreasing returns' to refer to how average costs vary as the firm's output varies in the long run, dropping the restrictive concept of 'returns to scale' (Eatwell 1987).

Second, the texts usually avoid the distinction between increasing or decreasing returns in an individual plant versus increasing or decreasing returns in the firm as a whole. Apparently they are assuming that firms have only one plant, but many firms have several plants. Let's consider our long-run average cost curves to be for the firm as a whole, regardless of the number of plants it has. So, for example, a firm may find it more cost effective to expand production within one plant or to establish another plant to produce a particular total output.

Profit maximization: two cases Figure 5.6 shows the profit-maximizing output in the long run in the case of the perfectly competitive firm, which takes the market price as given. Using the usual profit-maximizing logic, the firm produces output up to the point where its long-run marginal cost equals its marginal revenue, in this case the market price. In the situation illustrated, the firm is just covering all

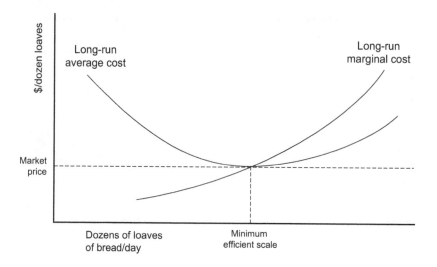

FIGURE 5.6 The long-run equilibrium for the competitive firm

of its costs. (Chapter 6 explains how the assumption of easy entry of firms into the industry ensures this outcome occurs in perfectly competitive industries.)

The alternative case is that of the price-setting firm, rather than the price-taking firm. These are the firms that appear in all other markets other than the perfectly competitive one. (These markets are examined in the next chapter.) Such a non-competitive firm has a choice of prices, as described by the demand curve for its product. In this case, marginal revenue is not the market price. Table 5.3 gives an example.

The first two columns show four points on a downward-sloping demand curve facing the firm. The third column is total revenue (price times quantity sold). The fourth column shows marginal revenue: how the firm's revenue changes as it lowers its price to sell more. Comparing Columns 1 and 4, we see that marginal revenue is consistently less than price. To sell one more unit the firm decreases its price *not just on the last unit, but on all the output that it previously sold at the higher price.*

TABLE 5.3 Downward-sloping demand and marginal revenue

| The demand curve | | Total revenue | Marginal revenue |
Price ($)	Quantity	($)	($)
10	1	10	–
9	2	18	8
8	3	24	6
7	4	28	4

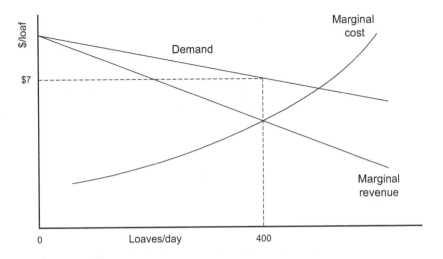

FIGURE 5.7 Relationship between demand and marginal revenue

Figure 5.7 shows the general relationship between demand and marginal revenue. Just like the competitive firm, the non-competitive firm maximizes profits by producing output where marginal revenue equals marginal cost. Once the quantity is determined in this way, the demand curve determines the price, at $7 per loaf in this case.

Implications for market structure Given consumer demand for the good, the number of firms in the industry (the 'market structure') depends on the typical firm's minimum efficient scale (MES) compared with demand. If demand is large relative to MES, there is room for many firms. If economies of scale persist over a wide range of output, there may be room for only a few firms, or perhaps just one.[1]

2 THE ANTI-TEXT

The textbook firm is a strange thing, sketched out with thought experiments and invented data of the sort we used in Part One. Actual empirical evidence about the relationships between inputs and outputs and between outputs and costs in real businesses is virtually non-existent. The next section looks at what the evidence says.

We then briefly re-examine the 'equilibrium' of the firm. It turns out that there are some fundamental problems with the equilibrium concept in the case of the perfectly competitive firm which the textbooks do not acknowledge.

While the textbooks keep students focused on technical details and elaborate diagrams, some important features of the firm are ignored entirely or are so taken for granted that they're invisible. According to the textbooks, firms maximize profits by comparing the extra revenues they get by producing more goods or services with the costs of the inputs needed to produce them. But many firms also find it profitable to incur costs to influence their external environment. These activities are a visible aspect of the political power of business and are the subject of the second section.

Power within the firm is unmentioned too. In the texts, the firm largely remains a 'black box', its internal structure ignored. We'll peek inside the black box in the last section of this chapter.

2.1 What do firms' costs actually look like?

'Ask the teacher to give just one example of a production function describing a real life firm.' Emmanuelle Benicourt (2004: 88)

The theory of production and cost is oriented towards the perfectly competitive firm, as Joan Robinson says in the quote at the beginning of this chapter. The U-shaped long-run average cost curve is supposed to limit the size of the firm's production relative to the size of the market. This keeps each firm small relative to the scale of demand, so we can have 'many' firms in the market and no single firm will have any appreciable power over the price, a central assumption in the perfectly competitive model.

Costs in the short run: is the 'law' of diminishing marginal returns relevant?[2] We saw in Chapter 3 that Piero Sraffa pointed out that the supply and demand curves would not be independent of each other if a change in supply changed input prices, which in turn changed the prices of related products, thus shifting demand. The 'solution' to this problem was simply to assume that *whole industries* are 'price-takers' in input markets; in that case, they cannot affect input prices.

But this Band-Aid fix raises another potential problem. If input prices don't rise as output increases, could a firm's marginal costs remain constant in the short run? An example is shown in panel A of Figure 5.8, where marginal cost is $1 per loaf of bread at all levels of output. Since marginal costs determine the firm's willingness to supply output, the firm's supply curve will be a horizontal line at $1 per loaf. If all firms face the same costs, that means that the industry's supply curve is also a horizontal line at $1 per loaf, and supply must equal demand at that price. But if the price were $1, how much would the individual firm produce? Profit-maximizing output is indeterminate: the marginal revenue from producing an extra loaf of bread is $1 and the marginal cost is also $1 at any level of output. No matter what it does, the firm makes the same profit (or loss in this case, as the firm's fixed costs are not covered). Similarly, we can't say how many firms there would be. One firm could produce all the bread, for example, but then we wouldn't have a competitive market.

Assuming the 'law' of diminishing marginal returns solves the problem,

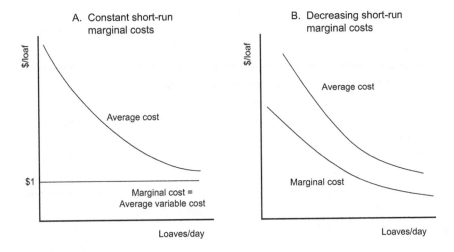

FIGURE 5.8 Short-run marginal costs

however. This ensures that the firm's marginal costs rise in the short run, as we have seen.

But does the claim of rising marginal costs conform to the facts?[3] A widely used intermediate-level text by the late Edwin Mansfield was unusual in offering a review of the evidence. He wrote that

> ... [an] interesting conclusion of the empirical studies is that marginal cost in the short run tends to be constant in the relevant output range. This result seems to be at variance with the theory presented earlier ..., which says that marginal cost curves should be U-shaped ... Although marginal costs may well be relatively constant over a wide range, it is inconceivable that they do not eventually increase with increases in output. (1994: 242)

And so the theory of upward-sloping marginal costs remained, despite the evidence.

More recently, a group of economists at Princeton led by Alan Blinder conducted a representative survey of 200 large American businesses to try to understand better how they set prices.[4] They asked about marginal costs in the short run and report 'overwhelmingly bad news here (for economic theory)': 48 per cent of firms reported constant marginal costs, 41 per cent claimed that marginal costs were decreasing, and only 11 per cent said they had increasing marginal costs (Blinder et al. 1998: 103).

The arithmetic shows that if short-run marginal costs are constant, so are short-run average variable costs; average total costs decline because average fixed costs are falling, as we see in panel A of Figure 5.8. If short-run marginal costs are also declining, then average total costs decline even more rapidly, as shown in panel B of Figure 5.8. They conclude, 'While there are reasons to wonder whether respondents interpreted these questions about costs correctly, their answers paint an image of the cost structure of the typical firm that is very different from the one immortalized in the textbooks' (ibid.: 105).

But is the 'law' of diminishing marginal returns really wrong? After all, it only claims that the additional output produced by variable factors *eventually* diminishes. This can never be proved false. It can be defended, as Mansfield defended it, by saying that in particular cases we simply haven't reached the point where diminishing returns begin.

The point of the evidence we've cited is that the 'law' is apparently *not relevant* in many or most situations: firms have ways of producing available to them that postpone the inevitable. Think about the bakery whose production we described in Part One. It's easy to see how diminishing returns could be postponed. Suppose the bakery had some idle capital in reserve (unused dough mixers and ovens in this case) in the same way that firms typically have unused production capacity. Then as it uses more labour, not only can the work be reorganized to use currently operating capital more effectively, but the unused capital can be brought into use. Rather than leaving capital sitting idle after a shift, the bakery might hire an extra shift of workers, and so on. It can also do this across a variety of different production locations. We might not observe diminishing returns in the actual range of output produced.[5] In practice, rising marginal costs may not limit the firm's production of bread; it is constrained by the demand for bread, as we will see in the next chapter. There, constant or decreasing marginal costs pose no theoretical problems in models of firms in imperfectly competitive markets.

Costs in the long run: are decreasing returns relevant? When we look at the evidence we find that the standard textbook theory about long-run costs fares no better than the short-run theory. Recall that a perfectly competitive market can exist only when each firm experiences decreasing returns at an output level that is small relative to the size of market demand. Then the firm's response to any rise in price would be constrained by rising long-run marginal costs (as shown in Figure 5.6). Increasing managerial costs in coordinating a larger scale of production or obtaining accurate information are the reasons typically given for this.[6]

Piero Sraffa claimed that these convenient U-shaped cost curves didn't resemble the costs of actual businesses. He contended that business people 'would consider absurd' the textbook model's claim that it is rising costs which limit the expansion of a firm's production (1926: 543). Instead, he claimed that average costs would typically be falling as output rose. What ultimately limits firms' production is limited demand for their product: a downward-sloping demand curve, in other words. The assumption in perfect competition that firms face a given market price 'differs radically from the actual state of things'. Sraffa's

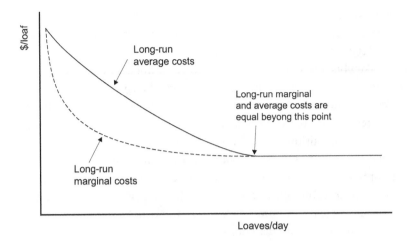

FIGURE 5.9 Long-run average cost with increasing and then
constant returns to scale

essay and the debate it sparked led, by the early 1930s, to work on theories of imperfect competition that we consider in the next chapter.

In his text, Edwin Mansfield also reviewed the evidence about long-run aver-age costs and wrote that 'the long-run average cost function in most industries seems to be L-shaped ... not U-shaped. That is, there is *no evidence* that it turns upward, rather than remaining horizontal, at high output levels (in the range of observed data)' (1994: 242, our emphasis).[7] Figure 5.9 shows this; we see initially increasing returns and then constant returns. The key point here is that if firms don't experience decreasing returns, there's nothing to stop them growing large enough to be able to influence the market price, which is incompatible with a perfectly competitive market. In fact, most introductory textbooks include a diagram like Figure 5.9, but with an upward curve at the right-hand end, insisting upon eventual diseconomies of scale.[8] After this one brief cameo appearance, it is never seen again.

Theories with no empirical support live on The short-run and the long-run U-shaped average costs curves that inhabit the pages of the textbooks and which pose as typical cost curves are bogus constructions that owe their place to the desire to construct and justify a theory of perfect competition. They are not based on empirical evidence about actual costs.

As this is a chapter about firms, we could leave it at that, but this is a good spot to consider why this has happened. It sheds some light on why the main-stream texts, which claim to respect empirical tests of theories, discard the evidence to protect the theory of perfect competition. Avi Cohen explains that the answer lies in what is seen as the even more unattractive nature of the alterna-tive. If nothing limits the growth of the firm, 'the chaotic indeterminateness of oligopoly' (which we examine in the next chapter) replaces 'the elegant determinateness of perfect competition. An indeterminate theory serves little useful purpose' (1983: 218).

As we sketched out in Chapter 2, a paradigm is not abandoned unless there is a more attractive one waiting to replace it. Since the 1930s, initially in response to Sraffa's critique of the competitive model, many economists have been working on potential alternative paradigms. Some of these have centred on models of imperfect competition. Since the 1970s, much work has been done exploring the implications of imperfect and asymmetric information. Joseph Stiglitz argues that 'information economics represents a fundamental change in the prevailing paradigm within economics' (2002: 460). That may well be the case in terms of the cutting edge of economic theory, but it has not yet trickled down to the core of the undergraduate textbooks.

A paradigm's core theoretical framework is surrounded by what Imre Lakatos (1978) termed a 'protective belt' of 'auxiliary assumptions' to prevent it from refutation, as we described in Chapter 2. This is the role of the assumptions of diminishing marginal returns in the short run and decreasing returns to scale in the long run. Avi Cohen explains that 'These auxiliary assumptions provide a basis for questioning and discounting empirical evidence of non-increasing costs and thereby retaining the theory.' Without that, 'normal science – problem-solving activity within the context of an accepted theoretical framework or paradigm' – would not be possible (1983: 218). Cohen asks,

> What happens when you combine the necessary emphasis on unrealistic assumptions in model-building, the clarity of outcomes of simple, unrealistic models, a desire to convince students of the empirical relevance of the *outcomes* of the models, and the tremendous time pressure to cover too much material?
> It is no wonder that introductory instructors often take the shortcut of claiming that real-world outcomes are just like the outcomes of simple, perfectly competitive models. (1996: 86)

As we are stressing throughout this book, real-world outcomes are typically very different. At best, the model of the imaginary perfectly competitive market or of the perfectly competitive economy provides a benchmark of very limited usefulness against which the actual world can be assessed, a theme pursued further in the next chapter.

```
Questions for your professor: Why does the text not refer to
evidence about the costs of actual firms? Is there evidence
that such firms experience diminishing marginal returns?
Is there evidence that actual firms experience decreasing
returns to scale?
```

2.2 The equilibrium of the perfectly competitive firm, re-examined

Figure 5.6 showed the equilibrium of the perfectly competitive firm. As a 'price-taker', its demand is shown as a horizontal line at the market price. The firm simply chooses the profit-maximizing quantity to supply at that market price: the quantity where marginal revenue (just the market price) equals marginal cost.

In an equilibrium, no one, including this firm, should have an incentive to change their actions. So let's ask: will this firm want to continue charging $50 per dozen loaves of bread and producing twenty dozen loaves per day? 'In general, the answer is no,' writes Huw Dixon (1990: 363), who explained very simply why this is not an equilibrium.

> Firms will want to raise price at the competitive equilibrium ... The reason is simple. At the competitive price, firms are on their supply function: price equals marginal cost. This can only be optimal for the firm if the demand curve it faces is actually horizontal. But if the firm raises its price (a little), *it will not lose all its customers* since, although consumers would like to buy from firms still setting the competitive price, *those firms will not be willing to expand output to meet demand* (their competitive output maximizes profits at the competitive price). Those customers turned away [from the other firms] will be available to buy at a higher price. Thus if a firm raises its price above the competitive price, it will not lose all its customers but only some of them. (Ibid.: 363, our emphasis)

In contrast, textbooks feature claims like: 'A competitive firm can sell all its output at the prevailing market price. If it boosts its price above that level, consumers will shop elsewhere' (Schiller 2006: 478).

```
Questions for your professor: In the (textbook) 'equilib-
rium', if the competitive firm increased its price a bit, why
would it lose all its customers? Those customers couldn't
buy from other firms since they already produce their profit-
maximizing output.
```

If the competitive firm does not lose all its customers when it raises its price, then it must face a downward-sloping demand curve and an associated marginal revenue curve, such as we illustrated in Figure 5.7. Now the key question is whether a competitive firm would increase its profits with a small price increase. We can answer this question by referring to Figure 5.10.[9]

In the textbook version, the competitive firm's demand curve is the same thing as its marginal revenue curves. But as soon as the competitive firm's demand curve has a slight slope, *marginal revenue must be below the demand curve.* This means that the firm cannot be maximizing its profits in the textbook version of equilibrium. If demand cuts marginal cost at an output of twenty-two

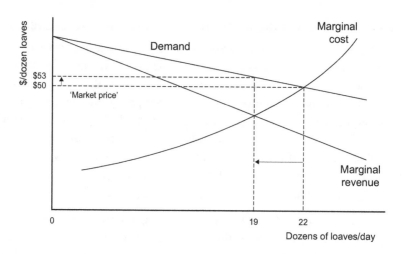

FIGURE 5.10 Why the competitive firm should raise its price above
the market price

dozen loaves, marginal revenue must be less than marginal cost. In the example
shown in Figure 5.10, the firm can cut its output to nineteen dozen loaves and
raise its price to $53 and increase its profits. Of course, the same argument
applies to all the firms in the market; the competitive equilibrium falls apart.

What has gone wrong? It's a reflection of 'Arrow's Paradox', mentioned in
Chapter 3. Again, Huw Dixon explains:

> The basic problem is the contradiction between an equilibrium concept based
> on price taking and the notion of agents (firms or households) setting prices.
> Indeed, it has proven very difficult to provide a coherent account of competitive
> equilibrium which allows for individual agents to do anything other than choose
> demands or supplies at given prices. (1990: 363)

The result is an incoherent account of the market.

2.3 Shaping the external environment: using power for profit

> 'Unlike the political economists who founded the discipline, modern economics
> largely ignores the power element in economic statecraft; and, lacking a theory
> of power, it minimizes the role of power in matters affecting the production and
> distribution of wealth.' Walter Adams and James W. Brock (2004: 14)

Austrian economist Kurt Rothschild made the following insightful observation about economic theory some forty years ago:

> More or less homogeneous units – firms and households – move in more or less
> given technological and market conditions and try to improve their economic
> lot *within the constraints of those conditions* ... [But] people will use power to alter
> the mechanism itself; that uneven power may greatly influence the outcome of

market operations; that people may strive for economic power as much as for economic wealth; these facts have been largely neglected. (1971: 7)

And indeed, textbook economics almost entirely ignores the power that some firms, particularly large ones, have to shape their external environment to enhance profitability. We've already seen examples in the previous chapter in thinking about the use of advertising and marketing to influence potential buyers of the firm's goods and services. But the power of business is most evident in its efforts to shape public policy to its advantage. This touches on virtually every aspect of public affairs, including foreign and military policy, international trade policy, tax policy, environmental regulation, laws about intellectual property (such as patents and copyrights), transportation policy, subsidies to business, unemployment insurance, pensions and other social income supports, and product safety regulation.

More than a century ago, Thorstein Veblen (1965 [1904]: 286) wrote: 'Representative government means, chiefly, representation of business interests. The government commonly works in the interest of the business men with a fairly consistent singleness of purpose.' This retains more than a grain of truth today.

'Think tanks' funded by corporations and foundations established by the very wealthy churn out policy papers guaranteed to reach the desired conclusions; they provide talking heads for television and op-eds for the newspapers.[10] Capital cities swarm with business lobbyists. In Washington, a city Ralph Nader refers to as 'corporate occupied territory', registered lobbyists outnumber members of Congress by sixty-five to one and spend $200 million a month to advance their clients' interests (Moyers 2006).

The recent battle over healthcare reform in the United States saw the industry (largely health insurance and pharmaceutical corporations) employ six lobbyists for every member of Congress, spending hundreds of millions of dollars to block competition from public health insurance and other reforms. 'The largest contribution, totalling close to $1.5m., has gone to the chairman of the senate committee drafting the new law,' writes *Guardian* reporter Chris McGreal (2009). He adds:

> Insurance companies have done even better as the new legislation will prove a business bonanza. It is not only likely to kill off the threat of public health insurance, which threatened to siphon off customers by offering lower premiums and better coverage, but will force millions more people to take out private medical policies or face prosecution.

The result has been 'a total victory for the health insurance industry', according to Harvard medical professor Steffie Woolhander. For their part, the drug companies have ensured that there will be no limits placed on the prices they can charge, and are reportedly ready to spend $120 million on advertising to support the legislation.[11]

Why do the mainstream textbooks ignore this behaviour? After all, investments in influencing public policy are economic decisions about generating higher profits just as much as the building of a new production facility or spending on research and development. Non-mainstream texts recognize this simple fact of life. For example, Lavoie (2006: 36) writes that 'to survive, firms must acquire the means to control their economic environment', including control over government legislation. 'To exercise control, the firm must have power, which is the means by which its survival is guaranteed.'

Perhaps part of the blame for ignoring power can be put on the disciplinary division between 'economics' and 'politics'. But this division has been crumbling for more than fifty years, ever since economists and political theorists began applying the framework of individual rational choice to politics (Bowles et al. 1999; Downs 1957). In fact, that framework, called 'public choice', can help explain an apparent puzzle: how can the few dominate the many? How can a few hundred large corporations and business organizations wield such disproportionate influence in society? If the policies that business owners want are not in the interests of the majority of the population, why don't the citizens simply block them and institute the policies that they prefer? After all, they have democratic institutions at their disposal and corporations have no votes.

Explaining corporate power

'... there is a systematic tendency for "exploitation" of the great by the small.' Mancur Olson (1971: 29)

Before the development of public choice theory, it was often assumed that groups of people with common economic interests would act to further those interests just as a single person would act to further his or her interests, as the late American economist Mancur Olson remarked in introducing his path-breaking book *The Logic of Collective Action* (ibid.: 1). As the title of the book suggests, he was trying to explain when groups of people with a common interest would take collective action to promote their interests. By applying the simple logic of rational choice, the comparison of marginal benefit and marginal cost, Olson showed that some groups would find it much easier to act in their collective interest than others would.

Let's consider a simple example in which apple farmers have an interest in restricting competition from foreign apple growers. Would it pay an apple farmer to retain a lobbyist to persuade the government to limit imports of foreign apples? The answer is clearly 'no' for the same reason we saw in Chapter 4 that it didn't pay the farmer to pay for 'Eat Apples!' billboards. The cost to him would likely exceed the benefits even if he were successful.

© Andy Vine

If an association of apple farmers existed that could hire the lobbyist, the cost to the association might be less than the total benefits all apple farmers would get. But for such collective action to come about, the apple farmers would have to make a contribution to the association. Again, each would have an incentive not to pay and to 'free-ride' on the benefits it might produce (such as government measures to restrict imported apples). Olson predicted that because of this 'free rider problem', such organizations would either not exist or would be small and weak unless they could provide individual farmers with some private benefits they could not otherwise get (cheap crop insurance, for example).

Crucially, the free-rider problem is less severe for small groups. If a few firms account for most of the total production in an industry, they can more easily engage in collective action. The firms will act either together or individually to produce a collective good that benefits them all to some extent. As a result, *'there is a systematic tendency for "exploitation" of the great by the small'*, wrote Olson (ibid.: 29, his emphasis).

Olson explained that 'The high degree of organization of business interests, and the power of these business interests, must be due in large part to the fact that the business community is divided into a series of (generally oligopolistic) "industries", each of which contains only a fairly small number of firms' (ibid.: 43).

The tobacco industry provides a good example. In the United States, the largest four firms account for 99 per cent of total cigarette production (McConnell and Brue 2005: 468). Other countries, such as the United Kingdom, Canada and Australia, also have highly concentrated tobacco industries.

A favourite tactic of corporations and their lobbyists is to create front organizations and phoney 'grassroots' groups that appear to be representing hard-to-organize large groups.[12] The tobacco industry has been particularly active at this. For example, 'Citizens Against Lawsuit Abuse' (CALA) appears to be a citizens' group fighting the supposedly overly litigious culture in the United States whose main victims (its website alleges) are small businesses and consumers themselves.[13] Yet the primary funder of CALA groups has been tobacco giant Philip Morris, which 'both funded and controlled the organizations through the ATRA, the American Tort Reform Association', another front group.[14] Efforts to limit people's ability to sue (marketed in the United States as 'tort reform') can be a profitable investment for insurance companies and for businesses that produce products that harm or kill people (Nader 2000: 275–309, 2004a: 37–48).

The tobacco companies and corporate propaganda (or 'public relations') firms have also been at the forefront in sponsoring front organizations that hang the label 'junk science' on scientific research detrimental to corporate interests. Research into the dangers of second-hand smoke is a prominent example (Michaels 2008: 79–90). Fossil-fuel interests have taken up the 'junk science' crusade in fighting action on climate change. (Chapter 7 gives many other examples of effective collective action by business.)

The flip side of corporate power: public inaction and ignorance Public choice theory also explains why the US health insurance industry and the pharmaceutical industry are able to organize so effectively to shape legislation to protect their profits at the expense of the vast majority of the population. The millions of buyers of overpriced health insurance and pharmaceutical drugs find it difficult to respond to defend their interests with anything like the resources deployed by industry. Despite the supposed power of numbers and of the ballot box, they tend to fall victim to the free-rider problem in two ways. It may pay not to act and it may pay not to have a clue what's going on in the first place.

The free-rider problem and collective inaction As in the earlier example with the apple farmers, if each person compares the costs of political action with the likely benefits, they may not act. Writing to their elected representatives or contributing to a public interest group such as Public Citizen may seem like a waste of time and money.[15] The individual bears all the costs of his or her contribution (which may seem like a drop in the bucket), while the benefits (if any) largely go to others. It's tempting to free-ride and leave the organizing up to someone else.

There are many large groups in society that might have a similar problem organizing to further their collective interests, even where the total benefits to the group would exceed the costs of acting. For example, taxpayers, the unemployed and poor people often fall victim to the free-rider problem and are unable to form groups and to work together in the most effective way. Of course, some such organizations, such as consumer groups, do exist. The theory simply predicts that they will likely be much smaller and less powerful than they would be if people could somehow overcome the free-rider problem.

Rational ignorance It often does not pay the individual member of a large group to know the facts about the issues. In public choice theory, this is called 'rational ignorance'.[16] Information about public policy is not free, and what are the benefits? As a citizen, you can know your interests better and thus decide what causes to support. But if you're not going to act (as we've just discussed), becoming informed would be a waste of time. As a voter, you can cast a more informed vote, but your vote will likely have no effect on the outcome. A more informed vote provides benefits (if any) largely to others, just like any contribution to further the interests of a large group. It pays to 'free-ride', in this case on others' informed votes.

Nor can one expect the mass media to act as 'watchdogs' and hold politicians accountable on the public's behalf. The large corporations that control the media (outside of public broadcasting) have their own goals and taking on corporate power and companies that may be big advertisers is not among them. As Edward Herman and Noam Chomsky contend, one of the functions of the mass media is to 'inculcate and defend the economic, social and political agenda of privileged groups that dominate the domestic society and the state', and 'to fulfil this role requires systematic propaganda' (1988: 298, 1).

Claims about the rational ignorance and inaction of the public should not be taken too far or viewed as a cause for despair. After all, many people enjoy informing themselves about public affairs instead of about the private life of Brad Pitt. They participate in community and national life in many ways, perhaps because they find pleasure in the activities themselves or because they feel it is the right thing to do. We also have our emotions to spur us on.

Rational ignorance does not apply to businesses if there are substantial profits at stake. Tens of thousands of corporate lawyers and lobbyists work full time

> Questions for your professor: If firms can make investments to change public policy to increase their profits, why does the text not discuss this? Where does the text discuss the connection between economic power and political power? If it doesn't, is it sweeping the reality of corporate power under the rug, and in whose interest?

watching laws, regulations and public policy that might affect their clients' interests. Politicians will be under great pressure to look good to the voters, but to be good to big business (Zinn 1990: 255).

American philosopher John Dewey once described politics as 'the shadow cast on society by big business' (Chomsky 2006: 206). But the power of big business doesn't cast any shadows in economics textbooks.

2.4 Power within the firm

'We can learn a great deal about the way the world works by observing what fails to reach the threshold in the ideological institutions.' Noam Chomsky (1993: 109)

In the textbooks, not only does the firm exert no power in the outside world, there is also no power visibly exerted within the firm itself. There are two different power relationships to consider. The first is that between owners and managers; the second is that between managers and all other stakeholders (such as employees, citizens in communities where the firm is located, and its customers and suppliers).

Shareholders versus managers The imbalance of power between owner-shareholders and their elected board of directors on the one hand, and the managers they appoint on the other, has been recognized for a long time. Theory asserts that profit maximization is the firm's sole objective, but managers can have their own objectives. This is an example of the principal-agent problem, studied intensively by economists in recent decades. The principals (shareholders) seek ways to get their agents (the board of directors) to appoint managers (the agents of both shareholders and the board) to maximize profits. They face two important difficulties.

The first is imperfect and asymmetric information; managers have better information about the firm's true performance and the nature of their own efforts. Although outside observers such as auditors, bond-rating agencies and analysts for brokerage firms are supposed to help oversee management, they suffer from asymmetric information too. As well, recent scandals such as the Enron collapse have revealed the potential for conflicts of interest and corruption.

The second difficulty is shareholder-voters' rational ignorance if there are many shareholders and none with a significant block of shares. Top management can gain control of the firm, particularly given the considerable influence managers exert over boards of directors.

The plundering of shareholder assets by managers in recent years has become hard to overlook. In their study *Pay without Performance*, Lucian Bebchuk and Jesse Fried argue that '[t]he pervasive role of managerial power can explain much of the contemporary landscape of executive compensation' (2004: 2). They show that for a large sample of companies, the total compensation of the top five executives rose from 5.2 per cent of the companies' net income in 1993–97 to 8.1 per cent in 1999–2003 (2005: 10). Had compensation remained at 5.2 per cent, shareholders would have saved $69 billion.

When imperfect and asymmetric information is taken into account, the claim that the firm's managers simply maximize the firm's value (i.e. the present discounted value of profits) is not very convincing (Stiglitz 2002: 480–81). A more plausible description of management's goals was sketched out by John Kenneth Galbraith almost forty years ago:

> there must be a relatively high threshold level of profits to keep the stockholders and creditors quiet, ... to avoid takeovers, to minimize recourse to banks, to secure the autonomy of management and the technostructure [his term for the corporate bureaucracy]. In addition, an increase in the profit level from year to year remains an important test of the efficacy of the management and the technostructure ... an important justification for their continued autonomy, power and independence. (Stanfield and Stanfield 2004: 81–2)

In his landmark book *The Visible Hand*, business historian Alfred Chandler agrees, proposing that growth and stability are the main goals of the managers who run firms (1977: 10).[17] Despite the evidence against pure profit maximization, profits are clearly important. In this book, we will generally assume that if a firm's managers can take an action that increases expected profits (although not at their own expense), they will do it. It is hard to see any other way to explain the psychopathic behaviour of many businesses (Bakan 2004: 56–9), the cheating, injuring or killing of customers, workers or members of the general population that adds to the bottom line.

Capitalism and freedom While everyone understands that 'political freedom' requires democratic political institutions, 'economic freedom' apparently doesn't require democratic economic institutions. It means only the freedom to buy and sell with whomever you want, or 'the freedom to shop', in James K. Galbraith's sardonic phrase (2008: 15–24).

The capitalist firm of the textbook is not democratic; it's authoritarian as a matter of principle. The presence or absence of democracy matters for firm behaviour. Managers would pursue different goals if they were elected by the workforce rather than appointed by a board of directors representing only shareholders. For example, as we'll see in Chapter 7, managers in some industries knowingly expose their workers to hazards that lead to illness or death rather than accept reduced profits. The workforce itself would choose differently if given the chance. Similarly, if demand for the firm's product falls, some workers may get laid off in the capitalist firm, but democratic firms seem to prefer to share the work and avoid lay-offs.

The idea of economic democracy is just an extension of the movement for greater democracy that's gone on for centuries. David Colander's introductory text is exceptional in describing its philosophy:

> For one group – the owners of stock – to have all the say as to how the business is run, and for another group – the regular workers – to have no say, is immoral in the same way that not having democracy in deciding on government is immoral. According to this view, work is as large a part of people's lives as is national or local politics, and a country can call itself a democracy only if it has democracy in the workplace. (2004: 369)

Although most textbooks now mention no alternative to the status quo, the idea of workplace democracy has a long history in economic thought. In the mid-nineteenth century, John Stuart Mill wrote of the experiments with worker-managed firms in his *Principles of Political Economy*, the definitive textbook of that time, describing economic democracy as the way of the future.

> The form of association, however, which if mankind continue to improve, must be expected in the end to predominate, is not that which can exist with capitalist as chief, and workpeople without a voice in the management, but the association of the labourers themselves on terms of equality, collectively owning the capital with which they carry on their operations, and working under managers elected and removable by themselves. (Mill 1965: 775)[18]

Democratic firms are not fictional constructs, like the perfectly competitive firm. Both consumer-owned and worker-owned cooperative firms exist and are important in some sectors of the economy. Yet they have virtually vanished from the textbooks (Hill 2000; Kalmi 2007).

For worker cooperatives, there is evidence that worker productivity is higher than in comparable capitalist firms (Bowles et al. 2005: 138). In the Basque region of Spain, the Mondragón Cooperative, comprising more than eighty worker cooperatives and about 30,000 worker members, is a prototype of a cooperative economy in which the primary, manufacturing, financial and service sectors form an interlinked network. It developed from a single small co-op founded fifty years ago (Whyte and Whyte 1991; MacLeod 1997).

But there are real barriers to the growth of democratic firms that leave them greatly outnumbered by capitalist firms. They have trouble raising financial capital from banks and worker-owners face significant risks by having to invest much of their wealth in the same business in which they also have their jobs (Bowles et al. 2005: 340).

It is curious, and revealing, that while the textbooks claim their subject is about choices between alternatives, no alternatives are discussed when it comes to the central institutions of economic life. The capitalist firm is the only game in town.

Questions for your professor: Why does the textbook suppose that democracy must end at the workplace door? In whose interest is it that economic democracy remain off the agenda?

2.5 Summing up: the firm in the textbook and the firm in reality

The mainstream textbook ignores evidence about production and costs of real firms in favour of a fictitious account that does not undermine the apparent relevance of perfect competition. Acknowledging the evidence would underline the irrelevance of the perfectly competitive firm as a description of reality.

The textbook account ignores all questions of power. Apparently, firms sit on the political sidelines, failing to try to shape their environment to their advantage. Power within the firm is deemed a non-issue. Students are apparently supposed to believe that there are no alternatives to the traditional autocratic capitalist firm.

All of this combines to give a bloodless and boring account of production that evades questions of real interest. There is no excuse for this dismal state of affairs.

Suggestions for further reading

Some interesting books have appeared recounting the corporate scandals of recent years. Bethany McLean and Peter Elkind's 2003 book *The Smartest Guys in the Room: The amazing rise and scandalous fall of Enron* is one of them. It inspired the related documentary film, *Enron: The Smartest Guys in the Room*, directed by Alex Gibney.

Law professor Joel Bakan's 2004 book *The Corporation: The pathological pursuit of profit and power* also inspired a thought-provoking documentary film, *The Corporation*, directed by Mark Achbar and Jennifer Abbott. Another insightful study of corporate power is provided by another Canadian law professor, Harry Glasbeek, in his *Wealth by Stealth: Corporate crime, corporate law, and the perversion of democracy* (2002).

A large literature exists on labour-managed firms, producer cooperatives and economic democracy. A readable review of how such firms compare with conventional firms is a 1993 *Journal of Economic Literature* survey article by John Bonin, Derek Jones and Louis Putterman, 'Theoretical and empirical studies of producer cooperatives: will ever the twain meet?'

6 | Market structure and efficiency – or why perfect competition isn't so perfect after all

'Industrial organisation is a field that is in deep intellectual trouble. The source of that trouble is that old textbook theory that we all know so well.' Richard R. Nelson (1976)

I THE STANDARD TEXT

I.I Types of market structure

The point of this section of the standard textbook is to show how firm behaviour and overall efficiency depend on market structure. The exercise supposedly demonstrates that perfect competition represents an ideal market structure, while all other scenarios involve a loss of efficiency. If true, it could provide a compelling reason for the emphasis on the competitive market in the standard textbook. We'll begin with a basic exposition of the four market structures, starting with perfect competition.

I.2 Perfect competition

Large numbers of buyers and sellers, and a homogeneous product, guarantee that market participants are 'price-takers'. Adding easy entry into (and exit from) the industry gives perfect competition long-run optimality properties.

Firms don't need to advertise or worry about their competitors, since they can sell all they wish at the ruling market price. The price – being invariant to an individual firm's output – is both the firm's average *and* marginal revenue.

In Chapter 1 we noted that economics has a very simple framework to explain choice – *all activities are undertaken to the point where marginal cost equals marginal benefit*. This is where total *net* benefit is maximized. For a firm interested only in maximizing profits (the usual textbook assumption) *revenue* is the only *benefit* that matters. So, applying the decision rule to the firm, it should produce up to the point where marginal cost equals marginal *revenue*. At this point total net revenue – or more simply total profit – is maximized.

Derivation of the competitive firm's supply curve Figure 6.1 shows the process in action. The left-hand diagram shows supply and demand in the market as a whole. The right-hand diagram shows a typical firm producing a few thousand litres of milk, which in a market of millions of litres will have no discernible

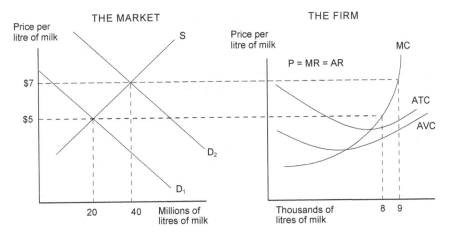

FIGURE 6.1 Derivation of the competitive firm's supply curve

impact on price. The firm equates marginal revenue (or price) to marginal cost. If the market price is $5 per litre, the firm produces 8 thousand litres. If market price increases to $7 a litre (because market demand increases to D_2), the firm produces 9 thousand litres. The key point is that the firm's marginal cost line *is* the firm's supply curve.

There is only one wrinkle: in the short run the price must be above the firm's average variable cost. The difference between variable and total cost is fixed cost. But in the short run, fixed cost is unavoidable. So, as long as the price exceeds average variable costs, the firm's losses are less than its fixed costs, and the firm will stay in production – in the short run at least.

So, more accurately, the section of the firm's marginal cost line that lies above its average variable cost *is* the firm's supply curve. Summing what each firm would supply at any given price determines market supply. This means the market supply curve will shift for two kinds of reasons: first, the position of the typical firm's marginal cost curve could shift; second, the number of firms in the industry could change. Chapter 5 explained the factors that could shift the typical firm's marginal cost curve: changes in prices of factors of production, changes in technology, or changes in the size of the firm (employing more or less capital per unit of labour). What's new is the dependence of the industry supply curve on the number of firms in the industry.

Equilibrium in the long and short runs If firms are earning more than normal profit (called economic profit) other firms will enter the industry. We can be sure of this because in economics cost is always defined as opportunity cost, which includes the cost of the next-best opportunity forgone. When a firm is just breaking even, it is said to be earning *normal* profit – the same as it could have earned in its next-best opportunity elsewhere. When a firm is earning *economic* profit, it is doing better than it could have done elsewhere. If firms are earning an economic profit, there is an incentive for firms in other industries to enter this industry to share in those higher profits. As new entry occurs, the market supply curve shifts right, which reduces the price. This continues until the economic profit disappears, leaving firms earning only normal profit in long-run equilibrium.

For this mechanism to work, all existing firms in the industry, and potential new entrants, must have the same costs. *This is where the assumption of perfect information creeps in again.* If one firm has a particularly efficient chief executive officer (CEO), that firm might enjoy lower costs and hence earn higher profits than its rivals. But with perfect information, the rivals will know about this CEO, and will be prepared to offer more wages to tempt him or her into joining them. At the limit, they will be prepared to offer exactly what the CEO is worth; that is a salary differential that completely offsets his or her greater efficiency.

This same mechanism works for all other factors that could lead to differences in costs. Any differences in efficiency between factors will be completely offset by differences in pay. Thus, all existing firms, and potential new entrants, have the same costs as a result of the assumption of perfect information.

Textbooks contrast short- and long-run equilibrium diagrammatically. In Figure 6.2 the milk industry is initially in long-run equilibrium at a price of $3 a litre. Each firm produces 5,000 litres and just covers its long-run average costs. There is no tendency for firms to enter or leave. Now suppose demand increases to D_2. In the short run, this drives up the price to $7. The firm maximizes profits by equating price (equal to marginal revenue) to its marginal cost. It produces 6 thousand litres at an average cost of $4 per litre. Economic profit per litre is $3 (= $7 – $4). Total economic profit is $3 x 6,000 = $18,000, shown as the shaded rectangle, Z. This encourages new firms to enter the industry.

As new firms enter, so the market supply curve shifts to the right and the price

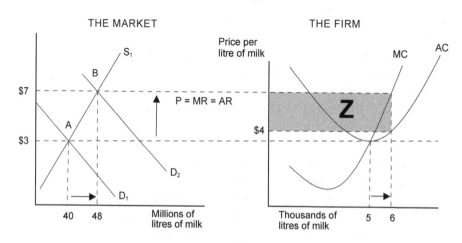

FIGURE 6.2 The short-run response to an increase in demand

is driven back down. How far to the right does the supply curve shift? As shown in Figure 6.3, the supply curve will have to move to S_2, so that the price is bid down to the minimum point on the typical firm's long-run average cost curve. At this point, no firm earns economic profit, and the incentive to enter the industry disappears. The decrease in price from $7 back to $3 causes the original firms to reduce their output from 6,000 litres back to 5,000 litres. But the increase in the number of firms more than offsets this decrease, and ensures that industry output increases from 48 million litres to 70 million litres.

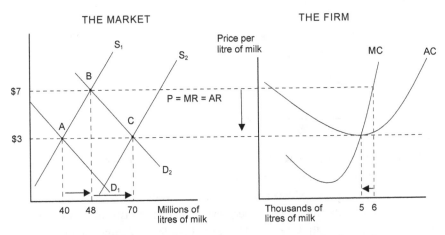

FIGURE 6.3 The long-run response to an increase in demand

The efficiency of perfect competition We showed in Chapter 4 that the demand curve for a commodity is the sum of all individuals' marginal benefit curves. We have just shown that the supply curve is the sum of all firms' marginal cost curves. Hence, the intersection of demand and supply can be reinterpreted as the intersection of the aggregate marginal benefit and marginal cost schedules. Provided there are no 'externalities' (no pollution, for example), this intersection gives us the optimal social quantity, Q*, as shown in Figure 6.4. (Externalities are discussed in Chapter 7.)

At Q_1 (which is less than Q*) the extra benefit of one more unit exceeds the extra cost. Producing this unit increases net benefit. On the other hand, at Q_2 (which exceeds Q*) marginal cost exceeds marginal benefit, and the production of that unit lowers net benefit. In conclusion, the intersection of demand and supply yields the optimal output, which maximizes total net benefit from the production of that good.

The above argument applies to any competitive equilibrium – even the short-run equilibrium at point B in Figure 6.3 where the price exceeds its long-run value. But free entry and exit ensures that the market moves to long-run equilibrium, shown in Figure 6.4, where there is the optimal number of firms, and where

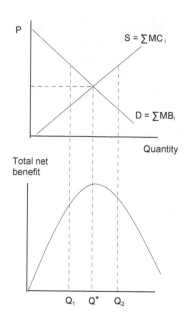

FIGURE 6.4 The optimal quantity

each firm produces at the lowest possible cost per unit. Furthermore, this optimal quantity is distributed to those who value it most.

To see this, suppose we have a fixed quantity of goods – say 1,000 loaves of bread. Now postulate the Ideal Planner, whose job it is to distribute those goods to maximize total benefit. Who should get the bread? The Planner should equate the marginal benefit of a loaf of bread across individuals.

For example, suppose that Muriel's marginal benefit is $4 per loaf, while Virginia's marginal benefit is $9 per loaf. The Planner should take a loaf away from Muriel and give it to Virginia. Muriel's benefit has fallen by $4 but Virginia's has increased by $9. On balance, total benefit increases by $5. As you take bread away from Muriel her marginal benefit of one more loaf increases. As you give bread to Virginia her marginal benefit falls. The Planner can continue to increase total benefit by reallocating bread from Muriel to Virginia until they both have the same marginal benefit. Total benefit is not maximized until everyone has the same marginal benefit of a loaf of bread.

But this is what competitive markets do automatically! We already know that each individual maximizes her own net benefit by buying up to the point where her marginal benefit equals the price. In a competitive market, all consumers face the same price and so all will have the same marginal benefit. So competitive markets work just as an Ideal Planner would only without all the expense we'd need for the Planner's staff.

1.3 Non-competitive markets: there is no supply curve

Turning to non-competitive markets, it is time we demonstrate what we asserted in Chapter 3: there is no supply curve in a non-competitive market. The reason for this key feature is that competitive firms take the market price as given, whereas non-competitive firms do not. Competitive firms equate the given price to marginal cost, giving rise to a unique quantity supplied for any given price; whereas non-competitive firms set their prices, and realize that price decreases lead to quantity increases. Since the best price will depend on the shape and position of the demand curve, there is no unique minimum price necessary to induce the supply of a given quantity – it depends on the nature of demand.

Just like the competitive firm, the non-competitive firm maximizes profits by producing up to the point where marginal revenue equals marginal cost. In the left-hand diagram of Figure 6.5, this occurs at an output of 400 units. Once the quantity is determined in this way, the demand curve determines the price, at $7 per unit.

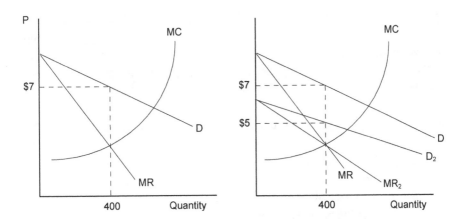

FIGURE 6.5 Non-competitive firms don't have a supply curve

As shown in the right-hand diagram, if demand shifted to D_2 (with associated marginal revenue of MR_2) the new marginal revenue curve would cut the marginal cost curve at the same point as before. Therefore, the firm would produce the same amount, but it would now sell the output at a price of $5. This shows that there is no unique minimum price necessary to induce a given supply, and therefore no supply curve. This is the case for any non-competitive firm.

1.4 Monopoly

Monopoly is the simplest non-competitive market structure since, by definition, there is only one seller. Maintenance of a monopoly position requires barriers to entry associated with: (1) control over at least one crucial input; (2) economies of scale; (3) technological superiority; or (4) a government-created barrier such as patent protection. If the barriers to entry are low, the market may be 'contestable', causing the monopoly to behave more like a competitive industry. To keep things simple, we'll focus on the case where barriers to entry are high.

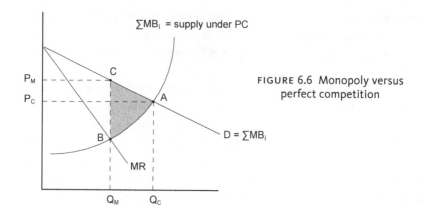

FIGURE 6.6 Monopoly versus perfect competition

Comparing monopoly to perfect competition Suppose all the firms in a perfectly competitive industry were taken over and merged into a single monopolistic supplier. What would be the effect on efficiency and the distribution of income?

The key element in the comparison of the two industry structures is the dual role played by the competitive firms' marginal cost curves. As shown in Figure 6.6, their (horizontal) summation is the supply curve under perfect competition; but under monopoly that same summation is simply the monopolist's aggregate marginal costs.

Under perfect competition, demand and supply intersect at point A. After all the firms are merged, however, the monopoly maximizes its profit by equating marginal cost to marginal revenue at point B. Given output of Q_M, the demand curve determines the price, P_M, at point C.

As shown, monopoly restricts output below the socially optimal level. The monopolist realizes that if it sells less, the price can be raised, whereas each competitive firm cannot raise the price by reducing output, since they are too small to influence it.

We can measure the net loss associated with this output restriction. The value to consumers of the lost output is the area under the demand curve between Q_C and Q_M. The cost of producing this output is the area under the marginal cost curve between Q_C and Q_M. Therefore, the *net* loss (or '*deadweight loss*') due to monopoly is the shaded area ABC.

Two other adverse effects of monopoly stem from the fact that monopolies tend to earn above-normal profits. First, these excess profits probably involve a regressive redistribution of income towards those who are already rich. We can call this the '*equity cost*' of privately created monopolies. Second, individuals will devote time, effort and expertise to secure monopoly profits, perhaps through seeking legal or regulatory protection from potential competitors. This *rent-seeking* behaviour is a further inefficiency – a waste of society's scarce resources over and above that of the deadweight loss.

Deadweight loss and price discrimination There is one interesting exception to the above conclusion: when a monopolist is able to perfectly discriminate among consumers on the basis of their willingness to pay, it produces the efficient amount, and deadweight loss is zero. Perfect price discrimination means that the monopolist is able to sell each unit at a different price, the maximum price given by the demand curve. In effect, the demand curve becomes the marginal revenue schedule, and the monopolist maximizes its profits by producing the competitive quantity at point A. Because the monopolist converts the entire consumer surplus into extra profits, however, perfect price discrimination worsens the equity cost of monopoly.

Perfect price discrimination is extremely rare because the monopolist doesn't know the maximum amount each consumer would be willing to pay. Instead, the monopolist seeks ways to segregate the market into different groups – those willing to pay more versus those who will only pay less. For example, those with less income are willing to cut out coupons in newspaper flyers, or are willing to stay over an extra night to get a cheaper airline ticket. Similarly, we may think student (or senior) discounts are justified on equity grounds, though they too are attempts at price discrimination.

Less than perfect price discrimination means that the monopolist will produce more than Q_M and less than Q_C in Figure 6.6. It lessens the deadweight loss but increases the equity cost of monopoly.

Regulating monopoly Textbooks argue that because monopoly is socially inefficient, government intervention can improve the market outcome. It can put in place anti-trust laws (or competition laws) that prevent monopoly from arising in the first place. If monopoly already exists, it can regulate it.

For example, in certain circumstances price ceilings can eliminate the deadweight loss. The left-hand diagram of Figure 6.7 shows that a price ceiling of P_C causes the demand curve to have a kink. It does not stop the price from falling *below* P_C, so when output is greater than Q_C, the price is given by the original demand schedule. Since the price is constant between P_C and A, however, price equals marginal revenue in this range. Now when the monopolist equates marginal revenue to marginal cost, he finds that they are equal at point A, and produces an output of Q_C. This price ceiling succeeds in getting the monopolist to produce the socially efficient output level. Therefore, we may call this an 'optimal price ceiling'.

This result stands in stark contrast to the effects of price ceilings in competitive markets (analysed in Chapter 3). In the competitive context, price ceilings necessarily cause shortages and black markets. In the monopoly context, those results appear only if the price ceiling is too low – as shown in the right-hand diagram in Figure 6.7. Any price ceiling less than P_C causes a shortage since it is *below* the point of intersection of demand and marginal cost.

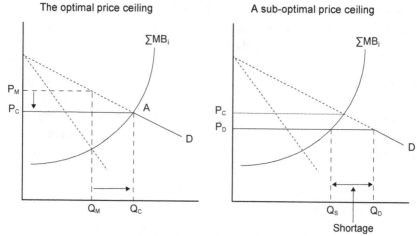

FIGURE 6.7 Price ceilings and monopoly

The government's policy options are more limited in the case of 'natural monopoly'. This occurs when there are large fixed costs of doing business. For example, electricity (and gas) companies incur huge set-up costs to get the grid of wires (or pipes) in place; and they have low and roughly constant marginal costs of adding new users to the network.

Figure 6.8 shows this cost structure. Average costs fall as output increases, because fixed cost is spread over more and more units. Average cost never starts to rise because marginal costs are constant. If several firms were initially in this industry, the biggest firm would have lower costs than its rivals, allowing it to underprice them and capture even more market share – leading to an even greater cost advantage. The logical conclusion is only one firm in the industry.

Trying to establish a competitive industry in the context of a natural monopoly would (a) be doomed to failure, and (b) would result in higher average costs in the unlikely event it succeeded. Anti-trust laws should not be applied to natural

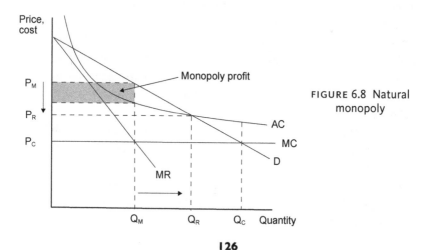

FIGURE 6.8 Natural monopoly

monopolies. Nor can price ceilings induce a natural monopolist to produce the socially efficient output level. A price ceiling cannot be set where marginal cost cuts the demand curve since this would involve setting a price below average cost and the monopolist would be put out of business. Thus, in Figure 6.8 a price ceiling of P_C is not feasible.

Nevertheless, price ceilings can still be beneficial; they lower profits and prices, while increasing output. Without regulation, the monopolist in Figure 6.8 maximizes profits by producing Q_M where MR = MC. The resulting price is P_M and the shaded box shows economic profits. A price ceiling of P_R (where the average cost curve cuts the demand curve) increases output to Q_R and eliminates economic profit. Since output moves towards the competitive level (at Q_C) efficiency is increased.

This all looks terrific: consumers are better off, profits are eliminated, overall welfare increases. Unfortunately, things are rarely that easy in practice. The main problem is that regulators don't have the information required to know where the demand curve crosses the average total cost curve. If they set the price too low, they create shortages; if they succeed in setting price exactly equal to average costs on an ongoing basis, the monopolist loses all incentive to keep costs down.

Even worse, regulators may lose track of the public interest – they may become 'captured' by those they attempt to regulate. This could happen through bribery and corruption or, more innocently, through cross-hiring. Regulators tend to hire ex-industry personnel because of their expertise. Industry tends to hire ex-regulators for their insider connections.

1.5 Other market structures

Perfect competition and monopoly represent two extreme forms of market structure. Both models are relatively simple, and both yield relatively clear-cut predictions. But most markets in modern industrial economies fall between the extremes. There's usually more than one firm in an industry, but rarely are there so many that they are all price-takers. These intermediate market forms – monopolistic competition and oligopoly – rarely lend themselves to definite predictions. But the consensus view is that prices and quantities in those markets fall within the bounds set by the two extremes. The more firms there are, and the more substitutable their products, the more results tend to the perfectly competitive outcome; the fewer the firms, and the less substitutable their products, the more they tend to the monopoly outcome.

Monopolistic competition occurs when there are many firms making slightly different products, with relatively easy entry into (and exit from) the industry. Differentiated products mean that each firm faces a downward-sloping demand curve for its product, giving it some 'market power' or choice over the price it sets.

One of the few predictions we can make concerns long-run equilibrium. Easy

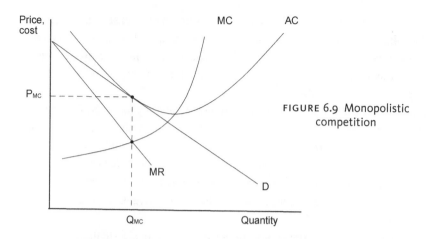

FIGURE 6.9 Monopolistic competition

entry (and exit) ensures that in the long run no firm makes more than normal profit. Therefore, in long-run equilibrium the firm's price equals its average cost. As shown in Figure 6.9 this implies that monopolistically competitive firms produce an inefficiently small output (at Q_{MC}), where marginal benefit (or demand) *exceeds* marginal cost. Nor do these firms minimize their unit costs of production. In effect, they have 'excess capacity'.

Interestingly, while the above represents the typical textbook treatment of monopolistic competition, it represents a serious oversimplification of the original analysis presented by Chamberlin (1933) and Robinson (1933). Both these authors recognize that products can be differentiated by location, by real characteristics, or simply by branding. Branding implies advertising, which simultaneously raises costs and shifts demand. So, while we can confidently predict that in long-run equilibrium there will be zero economic profit, and that output will be on the downward-sloping portion of long-run average cost, we do not know how much of this cost is associated with making the product and how much with advertising it.

There is no strategic interaction between firms in monopolistic competition because they are all too small to pay attention to each other. In contrast, strategic interaction is the core problem in the last industry structure – oligopoly. It occurs when there are relatively few firms in an industry, whether they differentiate their products or not. Strategic interaction makes it the least predictable market structure of all, since no firm knows precisely how its rivals will react to any move it makes.

The mainstream textbook presents some basic game theory to explain the conditions under which firms may collude to achieve the (shared) monopoly outcome. With only two firms the simple 'prisoner's dilemma' is illustrated; neither firm trusts the other and any collusive agreement (or implicit cartel) invariably breaks down. For example, suppose that if Esso and Enron collude by agreeing to charge the monopoly price, each sees profits rise by $2 billion. But if only one of

TABLE 6.1 A pay-off matrix illustrating the prisoner's dilemma

	Enron honours the collusive agreement	Enron offers price discounts
Esso honours the collusive agreement	Enron = +$2 Esso = +$2	Enron = +$6 Esso = – $4
Esso offers price discounts	Enron = –$4 Esso = +$6	Enron = 0 Esso = 0

them honours the agreement while the other cheats (by offering price discounts), the cheater gains $6 billion and the other loses $4 billion. Finally, if both firms cheat (by offering price discounts) they make zero excess profits; each earns only normal profits. This information is displayed in a pay-off matrix in Table 6.1.

Now suppose each firm rationally decides on its best strategy. Esso reasons as follows. They can't trust Enron. Enron will act to maximize its profits whatever Esso does. So, if Esso honours the collusive agreement (the second row of the table), Enron would be better off by offering price discounts. And if Esso offers price discounts (the last row of the table), Enron would still be better off by offering price discounts. So no matter what Esso does, they predict that Enron's best strategy will be to cheat (and offer price discounts). Therefore, given that Enron will cheat (now we look down the last column), Esso's best course of action is also to cheat on the collusive agreement and offer price discounts.

Since the situation is exactly analogous for Enron, neither honours the price-fixing agreement and the firms do not collude. This happens despite the fact that both of them would be better off if they did collude.

This appears to be good news for the consumer – collusion is difficult even when there are only two firms. Repeated plays of the same game, however, allow participants to build reputations. Developing the reputation of always playing 'tit-for-tat' (I'll do to you next period what you do to me this period) brings about a situation where it is in both firms' best interests to abide by the collusive agreement. Table 6.2 illustrates this. Assume Esso plays 'tit-for-tat' and compare three strategies for Enron – honouring the collusive agreement throughout; honouring it only in the first period and cheating thereafter; and honouring it in every period except one (period 2 in this case). The reader can verify the table entries using the profit data from Table 6.1. Clearly, given Esso's 'tit-for-tat' strategy, the best strategy for Enron is to honour the collusive agreement and cooperate (illegally) with Esso.

It is interesting that game theory uses logic and incentives to explain how 'cooperative' (or collusive) behaviour can arise even though neither player is trustworthy. In the repeated game, each trusts that the other will not violate

TABLE 6.2 Repeated plays when Esso plays 'tit-for-tat'

Period	Enron colludes throughout	Enron colludes in period 1 only	Enron cheats in period 2 only
1	+ 2	+ 2	+ 2
2	+ 2	+ 6	+ 6
3	+ 2	0	- 4
4	+ 2	0	+ 2
5	+ 2	0	+ 2
TOTAL	+ 10	+8	+ 8

the agreement, not because either one is an honourable company. Rather it is because they know that the other is a rational calculator who operates only in their own best interests.

2 THE ANTI-TEXT

This chapter has demonstrated what we asserted in Chapter 3: supply curves exist only in perfectly competitive markets. Therefore the demand and supply model is not a different model to perfect competition. Rather, demand and supply is synonymous with, or shorthand for, perfect competition.

Under perfect competition, price ceilings necessarily lead to shortages and black markets. This chapter shows that those predictions do not apply to non-competitive markets. Whenever a firm's demand curve is downward sloping, a price ceiling (which lies above the intersection of demand and marginal cost) leads to an increase in quantity supplied without causing a shortage.

It is strange, therefore, that textbooks seem to regard the competitive model as a generic model with wide applicability to all market structures. One would suppose the reverse to be true: since most markets are non-competitive, wouldn't the predictions of non-competitive models be most applicable? At the very least, textbooks should be highlighting the importance of model selection.

Why is the competitive model given such prominence in the typical textbook? In Chapter 3, we evaluated whether this prominence could be justified by the prevalence of competitive markets in the real world, or by the model's predictive power even in markets that were not strictly competitive. We found neither of these explanations compelling.

This chapter evaluates another possible reason for the emphasis given to perfect competition. Even if no markets were perfectly competitive, and even if the model had no predictive power, perfect competition might still be important as a standard of static economic efficiency against which to compare other market structures. As McConnell and Brue (2005: 193) put it, the competitive model 'provides a standard, or norm, for evaluating the efficiency of the real-world economy'. Colander et al. (2006: 305) note that it provides 'a benchmark for judging policies'. If government policy brings a market closer to the competitive ideal, it is a good policy, at least in terms of the static efficiency criterion.

Unfortunately, the idea that perfect competition is an ideal market structure is seriously flawed. First, perfect competition could lead to an ethically unjust outcome. Can something really be ideal if it is not equitable? Second, perfect competition is an ideal only when we focus exclusively on static efficiency, but this is less important than dynamic efficiency. Third, even in terms of static efficiency, there are many reasons to doubt that perfect competition is an ideal. We'll begin by expanding these arguments before looking at other limitations of the textbook treatment.

2.1 Can something be ideal if it is not equitable?

Perfectly competitive industries produce the efficient quantity, in the most efficient way, and ensure that it is distributed to those who value it most. What could be more ideal than that? Your answer probably depends on your income.

In explaining the efficiency of perfect competition, we compared it to how an Ideal Planner would operate. In order to maximize total benefit the Ideal Planner takes bread away from those with the lowest marginal benefit, and gives it to those with the highest. The final distribution of bread leaves everyone having the same marginal benefit per loaf. That sounds fair, doesn't it?

Actually, it is not necessarily fair at all. Remember, we are measuring benefit in terms of willingness to pay money for one more unit of the good. If people have the same preferences but different incomes, the rich will be more willing to pay more money for one more unit of a normal good than are poor people.[1] We also know that an increase in income shifts the demand curve for a normal good to the right. Since the demand curve *is* the marginal benefit curve, this means that it shifts the marginal benefit curve to the right. The greater is our income, the higher is our marginal benefit curve for most things.

Going back to our earlier example, suppose we know that Muriel's marginal benefit of a loaf of bread is $4, while Virginia's is $9. Efficiency in distribution requires taking bread away from Muriel and giving it to Virginia. But we don't know why Virginia has a high marginal benefit. It could be because she has five children to feed (compared to Muriel's one); or it could be because Virginia is rich, and therefore has a higher willingness to pay. Efficiency in the distribution of goods is not necessarily equitable.

Furthermore, any redistribution of income would change the relative demand for goods. For example, taking money from the very rich and giving it to the very poor would mean fewer luxury yachts and less champagne demanded, and more basic housing. So if all markets exist and they are all perfectly competitive, the economy would produce an efficient quantity of goods *given* the existing distribution of income.[2] But this does not ensure that we produce *the* optimal quantity of goods (or the 'right' goods) in an ethical sense. Only when the actual distribution of income is 'just' will the efficient outcome represent a social optimum.

This is an important point to remember: it's OK to say that perfect competition produces an efficient outcome; it's not OK to say that it produces an 'optimal' outcome (without qualification). We want to avoid implicitly downgrading the equity objective to the point where it is always subservient to the efficiency objective. To rephrase the point using more technical language, perfectly competitive market prices reflect *marginal social valuations* only when the distribution of income is considered socially desirable.[3]

David Colander (2003: 85) points out that 'most authors of principles books ... do not discuss the implications of an existing undesirable income distribution for measures of efficiency'. An efficiently functioning market economy could produce a combination of goods and services that could appear woefully inadequate to meet the needs of society's members, although not their demands. In such situations, singing the praises of the invisible hand seems beside the point.

Question for your professor: If part of the population of a country were starving because they had too little income to buy food (perhaps bad weather destroyed their harvest), would it be inefficient to subsidize their purchases of rice? (The right answer is 'yes': allocative efficiency means rice goes to those who are willing to pay the most for it.)

2.2 Static efficiency is less important than dynamic efficiency

Ask yourself 'what is capitalism really good at?' A good answer is *innovation*. Monopoly power and the associated profits are the reward for innovation. They provide the incentive that drives it. The reward can be bestowed on the firm by a government-granted patent; or it can be extracted from the market via lower costs and a dominant industry position. Far from indicating inefficiency, both patent protection and dominant industry position may reflect dynamic efficiency – the development of new, more efficient techniques of production over time. Moreover, neither of them gives rise to permanent monopoly power.

The law makes patent protection temporary. Most textbooks recognize that such patent protection is necessary to increase incentives to develop new products and technologies, especially products that, once invented, are easily copied. But few consider the optimal length of time such protection should last.[4] The duration of patent protection for drugs is being (or has been) increased in many countries. For example, in 1988 Canada extended drug patent protection from twelve years to twenty years. The pharmaceutical industry argued that it needed this added protection to cover the cost of research and clinical trials. Yet pharmaceutical companies spend twice as much on marketing as they do on research and development (Angell 2004).[5] The extra length of drug patent protection delays the introduction of generic drugs and substantially increases healthcare costs. In 1995, the birth of the World Trade Organization (WTO) also saw a major victory for the pharmaceutical industry lobby: the Agreement on Trade-Related Aspects of Intellectual Property Rights (better known as TRIPs) came into effect. It guaranteed twenty-year patent protection in all WTO member countries.[6]

Monopoly power extracted from technological advantage is similarly temporary – competitors invariably succeed in catching up over time. Joseph Schumpeter believed that dominant firms are constantly subjected to competition as new innovations supplant the old. For example, throughout the 1960s, 1970s and 1980s, IBM had a near-monopoly in the production of computers. This was swept aside by the development of the personal computer and successive waves of technological innovations. Similarly, Intel maintained an advantage in computer-chip manufacture from the 1970s until the 1990s – but recently Advanced Micro Devices has caught up. The moral of these stories is clear: either the dominant firm maintains its monopoly position by reinvesting its profits in technological innovation, or it loses its dominant position and even risks being swept away.

If monopoly power is relatively fleeting, and the companies themselves relatively dynamic, it is hard to see how monopoly power is a problem. In other words, the static inefficiency of non-competitive markets emphasized in textbooks is less important than their dynamic efficiency. As Schumpeter put it, 'Capitalist reality is first and last a process of change. In appraising the performance of competitive enterprise, the question whether it would or would not tend to maximize production in a perfectly equilibrated stationary condition of the economic process is hence almost, although not quite, irrelevant' (1950: 77).

Question for your professor: Could one regard a monopoly as a reward for successful innovation – a carrot that promotes innovation?

While most mainstream textbooks do contain some discussion of innovation and technological change, it is in scattered boxes or in a chapter at the end of the book. This downplays the importance of the topic. Innovation and growth have transformed the industrialized world since the beginning of the Industrial Revolution. Identifying their causes and the market structures that promote them should be central themes.

Indeed, principles textbooks contain precious little historical perspective.

To the extent to which time is mentioned at all, it is usually in reference to 'runs': the 'long run' and the 'short run'. These runs are suggestive of time passing – especially as we move from a short-run equilibrium to a long-run equilibrium. But they are not linked explicitly to calendar time; and once long-run equilibrium is attained, we seem to be frozen into an idyllic dream-state.[7] Viewed as a parable – a story helping us to understand deeper truths about the economy – it contains a germ of truth: that the process of entry and exit from industries is driven by a search for profit. But the parable is inadequate in that the process takes place in an environment of constant technological knowledge, with given resources, given tastes and given products.

The point is that the textbooks barely acknowledge the existence of dynamic efficiency, let alone recognize the possibility of a *trade-off* between static and dynamic efficiency. At best, they acknowledge some ambiguity. For example, Frank et al. (2005: 238) state that in the end we live in an 'imperfect world' and we muddle through as best we can.

The textbook focus on static efficiency may also be linked to the emphasis given to perfect competition. Perfectly competitive firms are the least likely to join in the innovation game. First, they don't have much incentive to innovate since they can already sell all that they like at the market price. Second, they are too small to have the necessary resources to invest in research and development. Baumol (2002: 44–5) states unequivocally: 'the perfectly competitive model has almost nothing to say about the capacity of the market economy to innovate and grow because perfect competition is largely incompatible with innovation'. He agrees with Schumpeter (1950) that oligopoly is where most of the innovation occurs. Oligopolistic firms have the most to gain, and are big enough to be able to afford the outlays.

Question for your professor: Are firms that possess some monopoly power more likely to develop more efficient techniques over time than competitive firms?

In Baumol's opinion, the focus on static efficiency as a guide to government policy interventions has seriously biased modern anti-trust (or competition) policy. He points out (2002: 182) that firms spending substantial amounts on research and development could not price their products at marginal cost (which is often very low) and cover their fixed costs. Yet marginal cost pricing is the centrepiece of the efficient allocation of resources and the focus of competition policy. In his 2006 book, *Regulation Misled by Misread Theory*, Baumol is particularly critical. He notes that while economists generally recognize that perfect competition is an artificial concept, its optimality properties have 'tempted some who are not as careful as they should be' to use it to guide anti-trust rulings. He says:

Never mind that this is a prescription for undermining inter-temporal efficiency. Never mind that marginal-cost pricing would generally preclude recoupment of the research and development (R&D) costs of the innovations at issue, costs that will have to be incurred many times again if innovation is to continue ... Because perfect competition has been shown in certain circumstances to yield efficient results, it is proposed that the regulated firm be constrained to act accordingly. I have witnessed a multiplicity of regulatory proceedings in which this was at least implicit in the positions taken by some parties to the litigation. (Ibid.: 2)

To sum up: innovation and growth are the central features that need explaining. These provide a more compelling case for the market economy than the static efficiency properties of an imagined perfect competition. Since oligopolistic markets must lie at the heart of this story, perfect competition cannot be an ideal market structure.

> Question for your professor: Might regulations that promote competition (and hence static efficiency) harm those companies doing most of the technological innovation (and hence harm dynamic efficiency)?

2.3 Perfect competition is flawed even as a standard of static efficiency

Even if we ignore the issue of dynamic efficiency, there are many reasons why perfect competition is flawed as a standard of static efficiency. Some of these reasons are hardly mentioned in the textbooks despite being well known and routinely taught in upper-level courses. Others are implicitly acknowledged when the texts discuss the many drawbacks with anti-trust policy.

Let's begin with *the theory of second-best*, first set out by Lipsey and Lancaster (1956/57). This states that if one of the standard efficiency conditions cannot be satisfied, then the other efficiency conditions are not desirable. In other words, removing any one distortion, in the presence of others, will not necessarily improve allocative efficiency. In particular, creating a competitive industry out of a non-competitive one, or moving a non-competitive industry closer to the perfectly competitive 'ideal', would not necessarily improve static efficiency.

The intuition for this somewhat surprising result is straightforward. Suppose a non-competitive industry organizes itself into a cartel and restrains output and raises prices. Further suppose this industry produces a good that pollutes the environment. Government intervention that broke up the cartel – increasing industry output and reducing industry price – could worsen overall efficiency by increasing the quantity of pollution. (Pollution is an example of an 'externality', examined in the next chapter.)

© Andy Singer

Of course, the theory of second best is not a criticism of, or flaw in, perfect competition itself. Rather it is a criticism of the false belief that incremental competitive improvements will necessarily improve the allocation of resources in the economy as a whole. It illustrates a serious shortcoming in the usefulness of perfect competition as a benchmark to guide and evaluate actual government policy interventions in the real world where (as we argue in Chapter 7) externalities are pervasive.

Question for your professor: I read that the theory of second best suggests that perfect competition is of little use as an ideal benchmark to guide government regulation. Do you agree?

Next, in showing the deadweight loss associated with monopoly, textbooks assume the monopoly has an *identical cost structure* to the perfectly competitive industry with which it is compared. But there is really no sound basis for such an assumption. The monopolist's cost structure might be lower, or higher, than the sum of the costs of the competitive firms it replaces.

Lower costs are possible if there are synergies or economies of scale or if the monopoly is the result of technological superiority. On the other hand, Leibenstein (1966) has suggested that monopolists may have less incentive to keep costs down. Management may become bloated. Such effects are known in the literature as X-inefficiencies and are particularly likely where barriers to entry are high.

Historically, economists have recognized that the assumption that costs are independent of the market structure is not true. Writing in the 1850s, Cournot was aware that a monopoly's cost structure would differ from that of a perfectly competitive industry. Marshall's elaboration of this in his *Principles* in the 1920s 'actually amounts to denying the existence of a presumption that the price usually set by an industrial monopoly is higher and the quantity produced by it is lower than would be the case if the same commodity were produced under free competition', as Schumpeter pointed out (1954: 977).

Finally, the textbook demonstration of deadweight loss assumes that the perfectly competitive industry has an *identical market demand* to the industry with which it is compared. But whereas monopolists have an incentive to advertise, perfectly competitive firms do not, as we noted in Chapter 4. (Consumers have perfect information and all firms sell the same product, so advertising by any one firm to increase demand for the product in general would not pay.) If the monopolist's advertising increases demand for the product, we cannot assume that both industry structures face identical demand.

Given all of these problems, the texts have shown nothing about the efficiency of perfect competition when compared with monopoly. Their claim that they have shown something is just a bluff.

Furthermore, if perfect competition is ideal, it has to be better than all other non-competitive alternatives. But as soon as we consider market structures where products are differentiated – oligopoly and monopolistic competition – the notion of identical market demand breaks down. As soon as products become differentiated instead of homogeneous, consumers have more choice, a benefit that potentially offsets other costs to society.

Indeed, when discussing the supposed inefficiency of monopolistic competition, all the textbooks recognize this point. Excess capacity in monopolistic competition is the result of product differentiation, which might or might not be wasteful. If product differentiation offers consumers a greater range of real choice – rather than mere branding – there is an advantage that offsets the higher average costs of production. Of course, in practice it is almost impossible to distinguish objectively between what is real choice and what is just branding. Nevertheless, mainstream texts also sweep this problem under the rug when they emphasize the 'ideal' qualities of perfect competition.

Question for your professor: With regard to the deadweight loss supposedly associated with monopoly, is there either evidence or theory to suggest the monopolist would have the same demand and the same costs as the perfectly competitive industry with which it is compared?

2.4 The textbooks concede the point

The texts implicitly concede that perfect competition is of little use as an ideal benchmark. At the very point they begin to discuss government attempts to move markets closer to the competitive 'ideal', they admit that the cure might be worse than the disease. They talk about the possible synergies of mergers; about the benefits of economies of scale; about the problems associated with regulating prices at average costs; about how regulators might become 'captured' by those they attempt to regulate. They quote George Stigler's opinion that the costs of 'market failure' may be smaller than the costs of 'political failure' found in real political systems.

All the above points are genuine concerns. The real world is complicated and these complications mean that perfect competition is of very little use as an ideal market type. This brings us back full circle to our main question: why is the competitive model given such prominence in the typical textbook?

2.5 Evidence, please!

For those who think that perfect competition gives us the 'ideal' output level, the natural question to ask is: how close do we come to it? Harberger (1954) made the first stab at estimating the deadweight loss associated with monopoly power. He concluded that the efficiency cost was less than 0.1 per cent of GDP – so small that economists were wasting their time studying it! Naturally, this stimulated a flurry of methodological criticism and alternative estimates. As a 'make-work project' for economists, this was one of the better ones. Economists worked on refining and critiquing each other's estimates for the better part of thirty years before it finally went out of fashion in the mid-1980s.

Figure 6.10 gives a flavour of the issues involved. Harberger simplified the problem by assuming constant average costs, which determine the competitive price. The monopoly price is somewhat higher, depending on whether the market is contestable or not. We don't need to say how much higher, since that can be determined empirically. The difference between the two prices is the height of the deadweight loss triangle. It can be measured by dividing total profits by total output to get profit per unit, which is the same as price minus average costs, or P_M minus P_C in Figure 6.10. Given the height of the triangle, knowing the elasticity of demand would allow us to calculate its length.[8] Harberger simplified by assuming the elasticity to be 1.

The subsequent debate involved a host of questions. One tricky issue is that data on profit will include all profit – even what economists think of as 'normal' profit. But since economists treat 'normal' profit as a cost, it needs to be subtracted from total profit. Harberger estimated 'normal' profit as the average profit in his data. But depending on the data used, this could end up throwing out the baby with the bathwater. If all firms had equal monopoly power, he would conclude there was no monopoly power at all! A second tricky issue is that

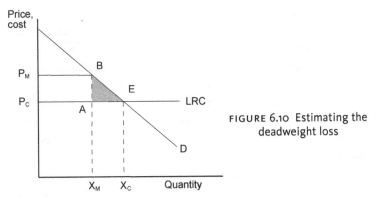

FIGURE 6.10 Estimating the deadweight loss

reported profits will include profits from price discrimination (which increases supply and reduces welfare losses). Such profits also need to be subtracted out but are very difficult to estimate. A third issue is how to measure the actual elasticities of all the demand curves.

If these issues seem complicated enough – and they are – by far the most awkward measurement issues are the very ones that undermine the notion that perfect competition is an ideal. For example, Littlechild (1981) critiqued the whole approach for ignoring dynamic efficiencies. He argued that profits are a short-term phenomenon arising from successful innovation, without which the product *wouldn't be available* to society. If so, both the monopoly *profit* and the consumer surplus at the monopoly output represent a social *gain*.

Many analysts questioned whether costs would be unaffected by market structure. If Leibenstein's X-inefficiencies of monopoly are already embedded in the cost curves of Figure 6.10, Harberger's method will underestimate the deadweight loss. Hay and Morris (1991: 586) comment: 'Sadly, all these arguments must remain at the level of speculation since we have no better evidence on the matter than was available at the time Leibenstein originally wrote.'

Bergson (1973), among others, questioned the extent to which estimates were biased by second-best effects. Scherer and Ross (1990: 666) comment: 'In the strictest sense, we operate with a measuring rod (or triangle) of distressingly elastic rubber. In principle, we cannot even tell the direction of the measurement error imparted by neglecting second-best and other general equilibrium repercussions.' They continue (ibid.: 667): 'Faced with this reality we have two options. We can give up trying to measure the allocative burden of monopoly, or we can cross our fingers and hope the errors from proceeding in a partial equilibrium framework are not too serious.' They admit that they lean towards the second alternative 'more on faith' than logic.

In the first edition of their widely used textbook on industrial organization, Scherer and Ross summarize the literature by guesstimating the deadweight loss of monopoly power at 6 per cent of US gross national product (GNP), with a range of uncertainty running from 3 to 12 per cent of GNP. By the third edition, they eschew any attempt at precision because 'truth was not well served' – the numbers were picked up by journalists or politicians who didn't understand the caveats.[9] Instead, they say (ibid.: 678): 'The most that can be said with reasonable confidence is that the social costs directly ascribable to monopoly power are modest.' Given all the caveats, however, the faith rather than logic, and given the huge range of uncertainty (from 3 to 12 per cent of GNP!), it seems that Scherer and Ross could just as easily have concluded that we really don't know the deadweight loss associated with monopoly. Indeed, we don't really know for many of the same reasons that perfect competition isn't really an ideal benchmark in the first place.

Nevertheless, the conclusion that the deadweight loss is 'modest' somehow became the consensus (or at least the majority) view. It could be taken to mean that the economy is reasonably close to the perfectly competitive ideal (an ideal which assumes perfect information). This interpretation could be used to argue that government 'interference' is not worth the trouble. It could justify blanket deregulation – despite the fact that Scherer and Ross (ibid.: 679) themselves cite the role of anti-trust policy in keeping the costs of monopoly power 'modest'.

Prasch (2008: 3) writes: 'Since the late 1970s American economic policy has been almost exclusively informed by ... market fundamentalism. For a remarkable range of issues ... the "conventional wisdom" has been to aggressively promote deregulation and privatization.' This trend began around the time that economists concluded that the social costs of monopoly power were 'modest'. It was surely a contributing factor to the swing towards market fundamentalism. And this is surely ironic. Instead of concluding that perfect competition isn't really an ideal market type, the result was sold as indicating that the actual economy was pretty close to being ideal! Instead of concluding that existing regulation was working quite well, it justified widespread dismantling of regulation!

> Question for your professor: For thirty years (from the mid-1950s to the mid-1980s) economists attempted to estimate the deadweight loss associated with monopoly power. What did they conclude?

2.6 The omitted legal framework

Unfortunately, the textbooks have a very limited interpretation of the word 'regulation'. Their focus is almost entirely on regulations that control prices or quantities (quotas). But in the broadest sense, market regulations are the legal framework within which markets operate. They are a key factor in determining what markets are allowed to exist and whether those markets function efficiently. We illustrated their importance in Chapter 3 by showing the effects on the rental housing market of poorly designed eviction protection legislation. Yet the legal framework is generally neglected in textbooks.

Moral and ethical judgements are reflected in the law. Where the economics textbooks champion the efficiency of mutually beneficial exchanges, they avoid discussing exchanges that raise sensitive moral questions, as Colander (2003) points out. He asks: 'Where is the market failure in selling babies? You have a willing buyer, a willing seller, and a clear case of comparative advantage' (p. 85). Despite such trades being 'efficient', they are typically prohibited. Apparently, some collective decision has been made that the efficient market outcome would not be socially desirable. Colander writes that the texts shy away from all policy questions that 'must be decided within a broader moral framework', adding that such questions are 'presented as side, not core, issues'. As a result, thoughtful students who are interested in moral questions may drift away from economics to study other subjects, while the 'less thoughtful students ... come out of the course thinking that policy is an easy task if only people listened to economists and understood economic theory' (ibid.: 84).

Just as selling babies is considered immoral, so too is selling body parts, selling sex and selling drugs. To the extent to which such trades occur, these market transactions do not make us better off. Markets fail in these instances to bring about socially desirable outcomes even when the market is working efficiently. These are examples of what David Colander (ibid.: 85) calls 'the failure of markets'. Unfortunately, mainstream neoclassical economics uses an almost identical term – 'market failure' – to refer to situations where markets fail to attain an efficient outcome. By focusing on 'market failure' in this sense, the textbooks exclude discussion of 'failure-of-markets' problems.

Prasch (2008: 8) points out that the legal framework was not always neglected: 'A hundred years ago the teaching of economics, especially in the United States and Germany, began with a discussion of property and contract law ... [which] provides readers with a sense of how the economy is embedded in a set of institutions and norms, rules that may even come to be codified in the laws.' He attributes the modern textbook neglect of the legal framework partly to an oversimplified view of what is exchanged. Textbooks focus on 'an abstract good, by tradition termed a "widget" ... to illustrate the "essence" of the market process' (p. 13). The widget is an example of what Prasch calls an 'inspection-good' – a good whose qualities can be determined by inspection, and is purchased in a 'spot' market. (In a spot market, the transaction is negotiated and settled during a single meeting or interaction – as in a suburban yard sale.)

The opposite of an 'inspection-good' is an 'experience-good' – the quality of which can be ascertained only through long-term experience of it. The opposite of a spot transaction is a 'relational contract', where people (at least implicitly) commit themselves to ongoing business relationships. Such contracts are pervasive in the modern economy. They are involved whenever companies subcontract the production of parts, whenever individuals agree to rent a home or purchase heating oil for delivery over the course of the winter (ibid.: 56). Experience-goods and relational contracts routinely involve asymmetric information, and this may require government regulations to help restrain conflicts of interest and abusive practices.

James Galbraith argues that when people purchase a good they are actually purchasing both the item and some assurance that the product is safe and effective. For him, the necessary and sufficient condition for a market system to work well 'is a *credible* guarantee of product authenticity and quality. The customer must have reason to believe that the product is what it claims to be, and that it will function as it is supposed to do. This is what a strong system of regulation provides' (Galbraith, cited in ibid.: 147).

Labour is a type of 'experience-good'. It takes time for firms to determine the qualities and work habits of workers. But with labour there is an added twist – unlike regular experience-goods, labour not only has needs, it also cares about how fairly it is treated – a typical aspect in relational contracts. We emphasized these points in Chapter 3 when explaining why minimum wage legislation may not cause unemployment because it may elicit more work effort from minimum wage workers, or may prevent a low-level equilibrium in the context of multiple possible equilibria.

Credit markets are a particularly important type of market dealing in 'relational contracts', both because of their central role in a capitalist economy and because asymmetric information is intrinsic to these markets. (We will have more to say about credit markets, and how asymmetric information and limited rationality played major roles in the global financial meltdown of 2008/09, in the Postscript.)

Asymmetric information gives rise to a cluster of well-known problems. First, it allows some people to benefit at the expense of those they are supposed to serve – the so-called 'principal agent' problem. Second, it contributes to 'moral hazard', where incentives are changed by certain kinds of contracts. (For example, individuals may have less incentive to prevent fires after buying fire insurance, and asymmetric information means that we can't easily monitor this changed behaviour.) Third, it contributes to 'adverse selection', where particular contracts disproportionately attract undesirable customers.

Competitive markets cannot function efficiently when these problems are present: government regulation may be required.

Prasch believes the failure to distinguish between inspection-goods and experience-goods, or between spot markets and relational contracts, explains the 'largely fatuous' dichotomy between government regulation and the free market that has become a staple of American political discourse. Another regrettable consequence is that: 'in the making of economic policy, the legal foundations of market systems are either overlooked or, even worse, taken for granted. The debacle remembered as the "Russian transition to capitalism" is only one, terribly tragic, manifestation of this now-conventional error' (ibid.: 14).

Prasch (ibid.: 8–9) notes that the omission of the legal framework contributes to the erroneous belief that the economic realm lies outside of law and politics. He contends that a basic knowledge of the inherent complexity, contingency and importance of contract and property law would illuminate some of the strengths and weaknesses of markets as economic and social institutions.

If government regulations help restrain conflicts of interest and abusive practices, why would anyone favour deregulation? In previous chapters we have emphasized that larger corporations and business associations have the power to change the rules of the game in their favour. Stiglitz (2003: 89–90) explains that the flip side of regulation is that it restrains profits. So deregulation means more profits. Stiglitz argues that those who saw this potential were willing to invest to get it – willing to spend lavishly on campaign contributions and lobbyists. They made the standard argument that deregulation would render markets more competitive, benefiting consumers and society in general. 'But this raised an interesting question: basic laws of economics say that competition is supposed to result in zero profits; if the lobbyists really believed their proposals would result in intense competition, why were they investing so much trying to convince the government to adopt these proposals?' (ibid.: 90).

In the 1990s, deregulation of the electricity market led to Enron's market manipulation, which hurt the California economy. Deregulation of banking opened up new opportunities for conflicts of interest that led eventually to the sub-prime meltdown. Lax regulation of the accounting sector provided opportunities and incentives to provide misleading or wrong information that led to a raft of corporate scandals. Those scandals were not the result of aberrant individuals – a 'few bad apples'. The problem is systemic and relates to incentive structures and to imperfect and asymmetric information. What enabled it was deregulation.

In the big picture, since the financial meltdown that began in March 2008 with the collapse of Bear-Sterns, the world has been on the brink of another depression. We've seen unprecedented fiscal stimulus packages, government bailouts and monetary stimulus packages. But what was the cause of this mess? The banking industry is fairly competitive, especially considering international competition. What went wrong?

Question for your professor: Is it true that the legal and regulatory system within which markets function is important in determining whether markets work efficiently? Do you think we are neglecting this topic?

In seeking answers, some commentators have started to blame economists and their 'competitive markets are efficient' mantra. The point we want to add here is that – in the textbooks at least – the 'efficient markets mantra' was supplemented by a total blindness about the importance of the legislative framework within which markets function.

2.7 Conclusion

This chapter has shown that many of the key predictions of the competitive model do not apply to non-competitive markets. Whenever a firm's demand curve is downward sloping, a price ceiling (which lies above the intersection of demand and marginal costs) can lead to an increase in quantity supplied without causing a shortage. It is strange, therefore, that textbooks regard the competitive model as a generic model whose predictions apparently apply regardless of market structure. One would suppose that since most markets are non-competitive, the non-competitive predictions would be regarded as generic.

A main theme of our *Anti-Textbook* is to try to explain the overwhelming emphasis placed on competitive markets in principles textbooks. Chapter 3 dismissed claims that such emphasis was justified either by the real-world prevalence of competitive markets, or by the generic applicability of the model's predictions. This chapter dismisses the claims that such emphasis is justified by the usefulness of the competitive model as an ideal market type which can be used to guide government policy.

Finally, in emphasizing the importance of the legal framework, we noted the importance of distinguishing between inspection-goods and experience-goods, and between spot markets and relational contracts. Experience-goods routinely involve asymmetric information. In addition, relational contracts involve issues of needs and fairness. In both cases regulations are needed to help restrain conflicts of interest and abusive practices. Ideally, regulation should seek to transform experience-goods into inspection-goods. When it does, it modifies the structure of the market, increasing its size and efficiency.

One way of summarizing this chapter would be to say that even if every good were an inspection-good sold on a spot market, competitive markets would still not guarantee an ideal social outcome because of equity considerations, dynamic considerations, second-best effects, and because market structure affects both demand and costs. The major problems with estimating the social cost of monopoly precisely involve these issues. Ironically, the faith-based conclusion that the social costs were 'modest' supported those who had a vested interest in furthering an agenda of deregulation. The usual arguments were rolled out: deregulation would promote competition and eliminate excess profits. Yet, if the lobbyists really believed that, why were they prepared to invest megabucks to further their proposals?

Suggestions for further reading

Joseph Stiglitz is a prolific author and anything by him is worth reading. On his website (www.josephstiglitz.com) you'll find commentaries on contemporary policy issues, as well as links to his academic articles and a list of his recent books. Of particular interest is his 2003 book, *The Roaring Nineties*, since this shows the pervasiveness of imperfect information, and how deregulation created the wrong incentive structure that led to the scandals and the bubble economy of the 1990s. The lessons still haven't been learnt.

Justin Fox's book, *The Myth of the Rational Market: A history of risk, reward, and delusion on Wall Street* (2009) is an entertaining account of the rise of the efficient market hypothesis and its ultimate failure.

ADDENDUM: WHAT ABOUT THE EFFICIENCY OF ASSET MARKETS?

One way to summarize the content of mainstream textbooks is this: if all markets existed, and were perfectly competitive, the economy would be in a Pareto optimal situation – it wouldn't be possible to make anyone better off without making someone else worse off. The first phrase is necessary because in practice some things aren't traded: we don't (as yet) trade carbon emission permits, or late-night party permits. One consequence of missing markets can be 'externalities', an uncompensated cost (or benefit) imposed on some people by the economic activity of others, something we examine in the next chapter.

The textbooks would have us believe that if all conceivable markets existed, and those markets were competitively structured, the economy would be efficient: resources and goods would be allocated efficiently. Yet, strangely, most microeconomics textbooks do not discuss the efficiency of asset markets (though brief discussions do take place in most macroeconomics textbooks). This is odd given the central role played by asset markets in allocating resources between investment alternatives. If assets markets are competitively structured – yet inefficient – the arguments in favour of laissez-faire are pretty weak.

In the postscript to this book, we present a case study of the 2008/09 global financial meltdown. That postscript contains much more detail on why credit markets are inefficient despite being reasonably competitive. Our focus here is the efficiency of asset markets.

Perhaps unsurprisingly there is a long-held view that asset markets are efficient, because they are competitive markets where information is conveyed very rapidly. This 'efficient market hypothesis' was developed by Eugene Fama (1965), and was the dominant view until the 1990s. It is still very influential today.[10]

i The efficient market hypothesis (EMH)

In theory, the real value of any asset is determined by its discounted stream of future earnings. So if you are trying to determine the real value of IBM stock, you should look at its fundamentals – the underlying determinants of the company's future profits.[11] According to the efficient market hypothesis, if you do this accurately enough using all currently available information, your calculated fundamental value will equal the actual price at which IBM stock is already selling in the market. That is to say, its stock price reflects all publicly available information about IBM's fundamentals. Why? Because any difference between the market price and its fundamental value would indicate a profit opportunity to smart investors, who would sell IBM stock if it looked overpriced, and buy it if it looked underpriced.

Finance theorists produced a great deal of statistical evidence, which seemed strongly supportive. But as Krugman (2009: 3) points out, this evidence was of an oddly limited form.

> Finance economists rarely asked the seemingly obvious (though not easily answered) question of whether asset prices made sense given real-world fundamentals like earnings. Instead, they asked only whether asset prices made sense given other asset prices. Larry Summers, now the top economic adviser in the Obama administration, once mocked finance professors with a parable about 'ketchup economists' who 'have shown that two-quart bottles of ketchup invariably sell for exactly twice as much as one-quart bottles of ketchup,' and conclude from this that the ketchup market is perfectly efficient.

The other form of evidence exploited the fact that asset prices should reflect all publicly available information, and will change only in response to new and unexpected information. But since no one can predict what is by definition unexpected, the markets are inherently unpredictable. As a result, every stock price will follow a random walk – at each moment its next movement is just as likely to be up as down.

The random-walk prediction was extensively tested in the late 1960s and 1970s and it proved very hard to refute. It implies that the 'experts' running mutual funds should do no better at stock picking than they might by throwing darts at a dartboard. As Stiglitz (2003: 61) points out, this conclusion has been supported by numerous studies. The best mutual fund this year will prove to be randomly located in the pack of mutual funds next year.

ii The efficient market hypothesis and the behavioural economists

Markets can be efficient only if market participants are rational calculating machines that do not make systematic mistakes. But as discussed in Chapter 1 (Section 2.6), behavioural economists have shown, at least in laboratory conditions, that we do make systematic mistakes. Of course, you can fool some of the people all of the time. Believers in the efficient market hypothesis would counter that evidence of systematic mistakes by some does not show that the

FIGURE 6.11 Aggregate stock price bubbles

market as a whole is inefficient. As long as there are people around who don't make mistakes – let's call them the *über*-rational – who can capitalize on the mistakes of others, then the market as a whole should be rational.

It is, therefore, extremely interesting that the behavioural economists have recently been able to show systemic deviations from rationality using financial market data. These are known as 'market anomalies'.[12] For example, the same stocks trading in different countries should trade (after adjusting for currency values) for the same amount – but Froot and Dabora (1999) show that large disparities are found. Similarly, closed-end mutual funds should sell on the open market for the same amount as the value of the securities they hold.[13] But Lee et al. (1991) find that they typically trade at substantial discounts relative to their net asset value, and occasionally at substantial premia.

Nor are asset price movements always unpredictable. Building on the psychological finding that individuals tend to overreact to new information (and under-react to prior information), De Bondt and Thaler (1985) hypothesized that stocks that have performed well over a period of years will cause individuals to overreact to the recent good news and drive the prices too high, causing them to underperform in the future. On examining the data, they did indeed find that past 'winners' underperformed – and past 'losers' outperformed – the market.[14] But this detailed evidence of inefficiency is small fry compared to the huge bubbles in aggregate stock prices shown in Figure 6.11.

iii Cycles of boom and bust

Asset markets routinely go through cycles of boom and bust. To date, the biggest stock market collapse on record occurred in October 1929, when, in a few short days following a decade of uninterrupted gains, the US market lost 80 per cent of its value. While cycles of boom and bust are routine, they are not usually of that order of magnitude.

Figure 6.11 plots the S&P 500 – a broad index of the stock prices of the largest 500 companies traded in the USA – from May 1981 to May 2009. As you can see, there have been several setbacks. The two most obvious crashes are the two most recent: the one that began in August 2000 wiped out 44 per cent of equity values by the time the slide finally stopped in October 2002; and the one that began in October 2007 wiped out 56 per cent of equity values by March 2009. Also visible is the October 1987 crash, where the market fell by 23 per cent.

According to Akerlof and Shiller (2009: 131): 'No one has ever made rational sense of the wild gyrations in financial prices, such as stock prices. ... The question is not just how to forecast these events before they occur. ... No one can even explain why these events rationally ought to have happened even *after* they have happened.'

iv Micro near-efficiency and macro inefficiency

Paul Samuelson (1998) often remarked that while the stock market is *mostly* micro efficient, it is macro *inefficient*. The behavioural research (discussed in Section 2 of this addendum) that has shown the existence of market anomalies and predictable price movements undermines the notion that asset markets are *micro* efficient. It doesn't really get to grips with the macro inefficiency associated with bubbles and market crashes. Indeed, one might think macro inefficiency difficult to prove. After all, the fundamental value of an asset is determined by the discounted stream of *expected* future earnings, and not only is the future difficult to predict, but we lack data on people's *expectations* of it.

The way around this problem is to show – once again – that people's expectations are consistently wrong. As Akerlof and Shiller (2009) emphasize with one example after another, when prices are rising we forget about the last bubble. Our 'animal spirits' take over and we get caught up in the current story, the current myth, in the frenzy of making money.[15] We become overconfident and think the current boom will last for ever. And when the bubble bursts, we go to the other extreme – complete pessimism.

This is demonstrated not only by hard empirical evidence – numerous papers have shown that stock prices are much more variable than the discounted streams of profits that they are trying to predict[16] – but also by first-hand experience. Like the 1929 crash, the 1987 crash was swift (occurring in one day), large (wiping out 23 per cent of equity values) and international in scope (it affected stock markets worldwide). But unlike the 1929 crash, there were no obvious fundamental reasons for it. It defies explanation. Completely by chance, Shiller happened to be surveying traders while the stock market was crashing in 1987. They told him they were selling simply because other people were selling. It was mob psychology, not the working of an efficient market.

This illustrates a key point ignored by the efficient market hypothesis – that what something is worth depends not just on its fundamental value, but also on what everyone expects everyone else will be willing to pay for it. The inherent uncertainty over the future of the economy interacts with uncertainty about other people's expectations about the likely actions of other investors! John Maynard Keynes summarized this famously using a beauty contest analogy. He compared the difficulty of predicting asset prices to the difficulty of winning a newspaper competition asking contestants to pick (from a list of 100 female photographs), not the prettiest faces, but the six faces that would be the most chosen by other entrants as the prettiest. Keynes said:

> It is not a case of choosing those [faces] which, to the best of one's judgment, are really the prettiest, nor even those which average opinion genuinely thinks the prettiest. We have reached the third degree where we devote our intelligences to anticipating what average opinion expects the average opinion to be. And there are some, I believe, who practice the fourth, fifth and higher degrees. (Keynes 1936: 156)

Keynes considered it a very bad idea to let such markets, where speculators spend their time chasing one another's tails, dictate important business decisions: 'When the capital development of a country becomes a by-product of the activities of a casino, the job is likely to be ill-done.'

But what about the fabled *über*-rational traders? Assuming that they exist and at least some can recognize a bubble when they see it, why can't they buy when others are selling (and sell when others are buying)? They could not only make a pile of money for themselves, but they would also help to stabilize the market, just as the efficient market theorists believe. The trouble is, as Shleifer and Vishny (1997) recently showed, the market can stay irrational longer than the rational traders can stay solvent. Arbitrageurs, the people who are supposed to buy low and sell high, need capital to do their jobs. A severe plunge in asset prices, even if it makes no sense in terms of fundamentals, would deplete that capital. As a result, the smart money is forced out of the market, and prices may go into a downward spiral.

As a last word on the efficient market hypothesis, perhaps Akerlof and Shiller (2009: 169) say it best with regard to the 2008 financial meltdown: 'The financial-markets egg has broken. If Humpty Dumpty had had the correct view of how the world works, he would not have fallen off the wall in the first place.'

7 | Externalities and the ubiquity of market failure

'The growth fetish, while on balance quite useful in a world with empty land, shoals of undisturbed fish, vast forests, and a robust ozone shield, helped create a more crowded and stressed one. ... Economic thought did not adjust to the changed conditions it helped to create; thereby it continued to legitimate, and indeed indirectly to cause, massive and rapid ecological change.' J. R. McNeil (2000: 336)

'In what industry, in what line of business, are the true social costs of the activity registered in its accounts?' Joan Robinson (1972: 102)

The answer to Joan Robinson's inconvenient question in the quote above is 'none'. Yet the default model of the textbooks assumes that producers of goods and services do pay the full social cost of production. There are no free inputs. Similarly, when someone buys the good or service, she pays the full cost as well. No one else experiences any costs (or benefits).

If producers or consumers impose such costs (or benefits) on others and don't take those into account in their decisions, the result would be an inefficient use of resources. The invisible hand drops the ball, yet again.

I THE STANDARD TEXT

Externalities Suppose that you're making a decision about how much to drive your car in a week. You weigh the benefits to you of doing various things (going to work, shopping and so on) against the costs you have to pay: fuel, and wear and tear on your car, for example.

The result of this rational choice is illustrated in Figure 7.1. You will drive until the marginal benefit to you of an additional kilometre driven just equals the marginal cost to you of driving that kilometre. Beyond that, the extra costs outweigh the extra benefits. If the costs or benefits change, you would respond accordingly. For example, if public transport became cheaper or quicker, the benefits of driving would fall and you would drive less.

Your choices won't lead to the best social outcome, however, because your driving decisions have effects on others which you haven't taken into account.

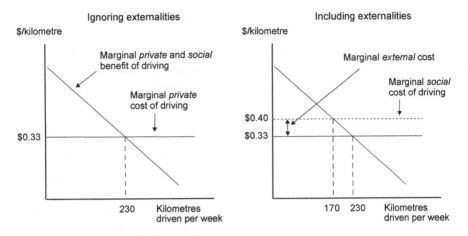

FIGURE 7.1 Markets are inefficient in the presence of externalities

In his original analysis of such situations, Arthur Pigou pointed out that driving led to wear and tear on the road, a cost that others would have to bear either by repairing the road or by having to drive over a poorer surface (1932: 193). There are other costs too: the emission of toxic pollutants, of greenhouse gases into the atmosphere, increased congestion of the roads, which slows the progress of other drivers and increases their chances of having an accident, which, in turn, increases their insurance costs. A recent study has shown that in high-traffic-density regions these added insurance costs are significant. An extra driver in California adds between $2,000 and $3,000 a year to total statewide insurance costs, costs borne by other drivers (Edlin and Karaca-Mandic 2006: 936).

The person driving the car doesn't bear these costs – they are 'external' to her and are borne by others in the society. The marginal social cost is the marginal private cost to the driver herself plus the marginal external costs she imposes on others. Thus, the marginal social cost of driving another kilometre is greater than the marginal private cost.

In an analogous way, an activity could benefit others. If you plant tulips around your house, others can enjoy the flowers in the spring, but the rational-choice model presumes that you plant the tulips only for your own pleasure, ignoring others' external benefits. (The tulips might even impose external costs on the neighbours if they compare their own properties with yours. A wasteful tulip 'arms race' could take place in which gardens become ever more elaborate and expensive! This may sound fanciful, but consumption externalities are a real issue, as we saw in Chapter 4. We'll consider this further in this chapter.)

In the case of the driving example, suppose there are no external benefits, so the marginal social benefit is the same as the marginal private benefit to the driver. Suppose the external cost of driving is 7 cents a kilometre. In Figure 7.1, the dashed line shows the marginal social costs of driving a kilometre as 7 cents greater than the marginal private cost. The socially optimal amount of driving is where the marginal social cost equals the marginal social benefit of driving. Clearly, individual decisions result in 'too much' driving from a social point of view, a 'market failure' because resources are not being efficiently used.

There are two textbook solutions to this externality problem. If persons or producers aren't bearing the full costs of their activities, their costs can be raised through appropriate taxes, called Pigouvian taxes, named after Pigou. In Figure 7.1, a tax of 7 cents per kilometre driven would increase the driver's marginal costs by the amount of the externality. This 'internalizes' the externality; the driver now considers the marginal social cost of driving when deciding how much to drive, reducing kilometres driven to the socially optimal amount.

There is a second, less obvious, solution. Externalities arise because there are no markets for some things and hence no price is paid for them.

In this case, suppose that the government requires producers of fossil fuels to buy permits in an auction market for each kilogram of carbon that the fuel will emit. The number of permits is set to limit total emissions of carbon dioxide. Instead of emissions of CO_2 being a free good, property rights have been established and it now has a price. If total emissions are set appropriately, the driver pays a price for fuel that reflects the social cost of its use, including the costs of climate change in this case, thus internalizing the externality.

Property rights Problems arise in the absence of any property rights. Typically, no one person or group has property rights over common-access resources, such as the air, the water or the fish in the ocean. If open access prevails, so that anyone may use these resources, the potential for inefficient overuse arises. Using the resource does not involve compensating its owner, because there is no owner. One way to address the problem is to require licences for use of the common resource.

Note that an absence of property rights is different from a situation in which individuals share property rights. The classic case is a field on which everyone in a village has the right to graze their animals. The field is common property and offers the potential for overgrazing. If a farmer grazes his cows on the commonly owned field, he may not take into account that he is leaving less grass for other people's cows. If he grazes his cows on his own field, he alone faces the costs of overgrazing. Such common grazing land has existed for millennia, however, and social institutions generally arise to deal with the potential problem.

Public goods The idea of a 'public good' (also called a 'collective good'), introduced in Chapter 5 (pages 112–13), is really just a special case of an externality. As in the example we used there, someone in a group that has a common interest (like the producers of a good) was considering contributing to further the group's goals. Anyone who produces or contributes towards a public good is providing positive external benefits to others. The benefits any one person gets from the public good do not reduce the benefits others can get from it (in the jargon, people are not rivals in consuming it, so it is 'non-rival' in consumption). Nor can any beneficiaries be excluded from enjoying the benefits, even if they have not paid for them (a situation of non-excludability).

In general, goods fall into one of four categories, as depicted in Table 7.1. Some goods have the non-rival characteristic of a public good, but, unlike the public good, it's possible to exclude those who don't pay for it. The computer programs used to write this book are a good example. Excludability means that these goods are artificially scarce; otherwise they would be freely available to anyone. Some computer programs are freely available to everyone and are pure public goods.

TABLE 7.1 Classification of types of goods

	Excludable	Non-excludable
Rival	Private goods, e.g. an apple, fish in a fish farm	Common access resources, e.g. air, water, fish in the ocean
Non-rival	Artificially scarce goods e.g. using a computer program	Pure public goods, e.g. listening to a radio programme; open source software

If you drive a noisy motorcycle down the street, you are instead contributing to a 'public bad', imposing external costs on others. Public bads are also non-rival and non-excludable. Carbon dioxide that contributes to climate change affects everyone to some extent, regardless of whether they contributed to it.

Self-interested behaviour and 'free riding' by individuals results in too few voluntary contributions to public goods, while resulting in over-contribution to public bads, such as smoggy air. Collective action is sometimes needed to deal with the inefficient allocation of resources resulting from these public goods and property rights problems.

2 THE ANTI-TEXT

The late Joan Robinson of Cambridge University was a sharp critic of textbook economics. She commented on 'the notorious problem of pollution': 'The distinction that Pigou made between private costs and social costs was presented by him as an exception to the benevolent rule of laissez-faire. A moment's thought shows that the exception is the rule and the rule is the exception' (1972: 102).

Unfortunately, current textbook economics downplays the importance of externalities by the rhetorical device of 'note and forget' – the texts note the existence of externalities and then largely forget about them.

Mainstream textbook treatment of externalities is remarkably uniform. The topic is always mentioned briefly in an early chapter and is then set aside while the bulk of the book adopts 'no externalities' as its default assumption. Serious consideration of externalities reappears only in a chapter towards the end.[1]

If students get this far, they have spent the bulk of the course admiring the works of the invisible hand. It would be easy to get the impression that externalities are of peripheral, not central, importance. This would be the case if external effects were not significant or if governments address them adequately.

In reality, externalities are pervasive and of great practical importance. Every year, they cost millions of people their lives. They threaten to make the planet uninhabitable for many species, perhaps eventually including our own. They are involved in everyone's consumption decisions every day. They even contribute to the instability of the financial system. The no-externalities default model of the textbooks invites us to forget these simple facts.

Many of the biggest externalities are also remarkably hard to deal with through collective action. It would be easy to get the impression from the textbooks that well-informed economists determine what government policy should be to counteract externalities, and that benevolent politicians then implement it. Is this what happens in practice? The textbooks don't say because, for the most part, they don't deal adequately with how government policy is actually determined. Colander et al. (2006: 130) is a rare exception, remarking 'that government often has difficulty dealing with externalities' because 'government is an institution that reflects, and is often guided by, politics and vested interests'.

As we've argued in Chapter 5, business power combined with the rational ignorance of the public often plays a central role in shaping public policy, and that sensitive topic is off limits. As a result, the textbooks give the misleading impression that externalities are minor blots on the landscape that could be (and perhaps are being) dealt with by a smattering of Pigouvian taxes and subsidies and, where needed, the creation of property rights.

2.1 Externalities in reality

Let's briefly consider some actual externalities to support our contention that they deserve a central place in the analysis of the modern economy. At the same time, we consider whether these externalities can 'easily be put right' in light of the realities of power and information in the societies involved.

Greenhouse gas emissions

'No snowflake in an avalanche ever feels responsible.' Stanislaw Jerzy Lec (1968: 9)

The production of virtually every good or service uses, directly or indirectly, the energy from fossil fuels and results in greenhouse gas (GHG) emissions. These 'emissions are externalities and represent the biggest market failure the world has seen', writes Nicholas Stern (2008: 1), author of *The Economics of Climate Change: The Stern Review* (2007). He explains that

... people around the world are already suffering from past emissions, and current emissions will have potentially catastrophic impacts in the future ... The scientific evidence on the potential risks is now overwhelming, as demonstrated in the recent Intergovernmental Panel on Climate Change (IPCC) Fourth Assessment Report. (2008: 1–2)

The potential consequences of climate change are wide ranging and complex. What is at stake is the habitability of the planet. We have learned that we can change that, perhaps radically.[2]

A source of increasing concern is the understanding that abrupt changes in climate have happened in the past and could happen again, particularly if increasing concentrations of GHGs set up a positive feedback loop in which concentrations spiral upwards, creating a 'runaway greenhouse effect' (Strom 2007: 68–73). This could happen if, for example, substantial amounts of methane, currently trapped in permafrost or in the oceans, were to be released. Rapid climate changes are particularly difficult to adapt to. Even the climate change expected by 2050 seems likely to result in significant extinctions of species (Thomas et al. 2004).

Improved understanding of the rapidity with which large ice sheets can melt has led to growing concern about the potential for a rapid rise in sea levels. Climatologist David Archer thinks that a continuation of 'business-as-usual' could result in an eventual rise in sea levels of about fifty metres (Archer 2009: 141).

Despite this, even by the mid-2000s, almost twenty years after the issue rose to prominence, many textbooks barely mentioned the subject and those that did tucked it away at the back of the book.[3] Is this because the issue has been adequately dealt with? Hardly. The Kyoto Protocol, negotiated in 1997 under the 1992 United Nations Framework Convention on Climate Change, came into effect in 2005. It has achieved neither global emissions reductions nor reductions in expected emissions growth (Tickell 2008: 2).

The climate change externality has a combination of characteristics that make it particularly difficult to address. Its effects come with a long time lag, making procrastination tempting. It's also a global problem, requiring co-ordinated action. Individual countries will be tempted to free-ride on others' actions. Finally, internalizing the externality will require somehow pricing GHG emissions with the aim of greatly reducing the long-term use of fossil fuels. Naturally, corporations with a vested interest in business-as-usual have taken action to protect their shareholders' interests.

Aside from the crude measure of simply renting politicians, the business-as-usual lobby also rents 'climate change sceptics' and funds so-called 'think tanks' to give the policy of inaction some intellectual cover. Their strategy is to create an impression of controversy over the science, the same strategy that was used successfully for so long by the tobacco industry and its public relations advisers, as we saw in Chapter 5.[4] As a consultant to the US Republican Party wrote in 2002, 'Should the public come to believe that the scientific issues are settled, their views about global warming will change accordingly. Therefore you need to continue to make the lack of scientific certainty a primary issue' (Gelbspan 2004: 41).

'There will always be uncertainty in understanding a system as complex as the world's climate,' a joint statement by eleven national academies of science explained, adding that 'the scientific understanding of climate change is now sufficiently clear to justify nations taking prompt action' (Joint Science Academies 2005).[5] But the national academies and the thousands of scientists engaged in research on these questions are perpetrating a 'hoax' and peddling 'junk science', according to the propagandists who find the more subtle strategy of emphasizing uncertainty too tame for their taste.[6]

The campaign can claim some success both with politicians and the public. For example, in Australia, a 'senior figure' in the former government of John Howard said that there was 'an understanding in cabinet that all the science is crap' (McKnight 2008).

Public opinion polls can produce a wide variety of results, depending on the question asked and the context, but as of April 2008 a poll in the United States found that less than half the population believed that there was 'solid evidence' of global warming caused by human activity. One in five did not believe there was solid evidence of global warming at all. The issue ranked at the bottom of the public's policy priorities (Pew Research Center 2008).

In Britain, a 2008 poll found 'the majority of the British public is still not convinced that climate change is caused by humans' (Jowit 2008), although the previous year 62 per cent agreed that 'man-made global warming is threatening the planet', while 25 per cent disagreed (Angus Reid Global Monitor 2008).

Industry's efforts to distort public perceptions have been exposed and are slowly becoming an embarrassment. The Royal Society accused Exxon-Mobil of giving nearly $3 million to thirty-nine climate-denial groups in 2005. In 2008, in the wake of a shareholder revolt(!), Exxon-Mobil 'announced that it would cease funding nine groups that had fuelled a global campaign to deny climate change' (McKnight 2008).

Economists' debate about what action to take on climate change has centred on the comparison of the costs of taking action against the long-term benefits. Largely unnoticed is that the costs in well-being of any ensuing reduction in real consumption are exaggerated by the textbook insistence that well-being depends solely on absolute consumption levels. We saw in Chapter 4 the idea of rapid adaption to new circumstances and of the importance of relative consumption in determining well-being. Canadian economist Pierre Fortin makes a telling point:

... it must be recognized that the *absolute* level of production continues to matter, but in a *negative* sense: by making more and more demands on the local and global environment, demands which have the potential to reduce well-being in the long run. The view that well-being is linked to relative income, whereas the quality of the environment (and hence the long-term sustainability of economic systems) deteriorates with absolute income growth, has stark implications for growth policy. (2005: 4)

Question for your professor: Doesn't the 'biggest market failure the world has seen' (as Professor Stern puts it) deserve more than a passing mention towards the end of the textbook?

Positional externalities in consumption

'I have Traxtar and you don't.' from a Reebok advertisement[7]

As Fortin notes, people's assessment of their own material situation depends in part on what other people have. If few people have their own vehicle, for example, then you won't feel the lack of one nearly as much as if everyone else has one and you don't. The same thing holds for other visible consumption goods: houses, cars, clothing, jewellery, furnishings and appliances, and so on.

What others in society have sets your 'frame of reference', as Robert Frank terms it (1997). That frame of reference is itself a public good: everyone is affected by it and the effect on one person does not detract from the effect that it has on others. Each person's consumption decisions affect the frame of reference in small, subtle but real ways.

For example, suppose that you notice a beautiful pair of $300 Italian shoes in a store window. Carried away, you buy them. Everyone who notices your shoes will now judge their own consumption standards by a slightly altered frame of reference. If their shoes suddenly look second rate beside yours, your purchase devalued them. Your extravagance created a negative externality by lowering their consumption levels relative to yours.

Frank calls these 'positional externalities'; their cumulative effect adds up in the same way that millions of people driving a few more kilometres adds up in terms of air pollution. This results in people systematically engaging in futile 'expenditure arms races' on those goods that most enhance their relative consumption position (Schor 1992, 1998). The other side of the coin is that too few resources are devoted to 'non-positional' goods whose consumption isn't easily observed by others. These include things we produce and consume individually (going for a walk, taking more holidays, socializing with friends) or consume collectively (public libraries, roads, parks). Thus positional

© Andy Singer

externalities distort the entire pattern of consumption, lowering everyone's well-being.

This unhappy result is ruled out by the standard textbook assumption that individual well-being depends only on absolute, not relative, consumption.[8] The problem with this default model is that (as Frank puts it) it 'is inconsistent with our best theoretical understanding of the origins and functions of human motivations; and it is flatly at odds with extensive direct and indirect empirical evidence regarding the nature of utility' (2005a: 141).

Conspicuous consumption can be reined in only by collective action. Frank (1999: 211–26) has argued that progressive taxes on annual consumption spending are the most effective tool to correct this externality. Under such a scheme, people would be able to deduct from taxable income all savings placed in registered accounts.[9] Because income equals consumption plus saving, the tax base is annual consumption spending. The extra tax paid per dollar of spending would rise with an individual's total annual consumption spending; Frank suggests top marginal tax rates of 70 per cent or so. This would make the tax 'progressive' in the sense that total tax paid as a share of a person's income would be higher for higher-income persons.[10] He writes:

> If a progressive consumption tax is to curb the waste that springs from excessive spending on conspicuous consumption, its rates at the highest levels must be sufficiently steep to provide meaningful incentives for people atop the consumption pyramid. For unless their spending changes, the spending of those just below them is unlikely to change either, and so on all the way down. (Ibid.: 216)

Because the tax would collect more from higher-income households and less from lower-income households than the current US tax system, it would reduce total spending on conspicuous consumption goods. Some spending on $14,000 Hermès Kelly alligator handbags would be replaced by increased spending by lower-income families on real necessities. It would also encourage people to engage in untaxed consumption: working less to spend more leisure time with friends and family, going for a walk or reading a library book. All of these activities have been reduced by the wasteful consumption arms race.

Frank asks 'If this tax is such a great idea, why don't we already have one?' (ibid.: 225). He attributes this to the widespread, and false, belief that imposing higher tax rates on the rich will cripple the economy. He's not optimistic about such a policy actually being adopted when political programmes apparently have to be explained in ten-second sound bites.

Other forms of collective action can also help to address these consumption externalities. If spending to keep up with the Joneses leads people to work excessively long hours, increases in legislated minimum holidays could help. Business owners, however, have an interest in promoting the cycle of work-and-spend. As the American abolitionist Frederick Douglass famously put it: 'Power concedes nothing without demand. It never did and it never will.' In the European Union, where social democratic parties have long been strong and unions organize a large part of the labour force, people are entitled to a minimum of four weeks of paid leave per year, although some countries legislate five or six weeks (European Union 1993). In the United States, in contrast, where unions are weak and the very wealthy have disproportionate power, people are entitled to no weeks of paid leave, and about a quarter of the workforce has no paid holidays of any kind (Ray and Schmitt 2007).

> Questions for your professor: Do consumption externalities exist? If so, why doesn't the textbook mention them?

Air pollution

'Unfortunately, the will of our elected officials to curb air pollution and the indifference of corporate polluters to the silent cumulative violence they inflict on our people through air pollution persists.' Ralph Nader (2004b: 168)

The burning of fossil fuels creates carbon monoxide, sulphur dioxide, nitrogen oxides, hydrocarbons and fine particulate matter. Breathing these invisible pollutants and other pollutants that form from them (such as ozone) damages the interior of the lungs and directly influences respiratory and cardiovascular illnesses and lung cancers (Davis 2002: 70). While the thick smog in big Chinese cities gets a lot of attention, even the much lower levels of particulates (achieved through public pressure) in the world's wealthiest countries are still killing substantial numbers of people and causing breathing problems, such as asthma, for many more. About two million people die prematurely every year from the effects of air pollution, according to the World Health Organization (2008b). About 650,000 of these deaths occur in China, more than 500,000 in India and more than 40,000 in the United States (Platt 2007). Recently, the Canadian Medical Association (2008) published a report claiming that 21,000 Canadians will die in 2008 as a result of air pollution.[11]

Major emitters, particularly utilities with coal-fired power plants, adopted the usual strategy of arguing that the links between emissions and death rates are unclear, but the evidence is now conclusive (Pianin 2002). Since the birth of the modern environmental movement in the 1960s, significant progress has been made in reducing these (and other) air pollutants (notably lead), but at the same time, new ones have emerged.

To give just one example, polybrominated diphenyl ethers (PBDEs) are a class of chemicals used as flame retardants in such things as furniture, mattresses, electronics and textiles, and were introduced, ironically, in response to flammability regulations intended to protect consumers. They are structurally similar to the widely banned polychlorinated biphenyls (PCBs) and, like PCBs, are persistent pollutants that accumulate in the body. In rats, PBDEs affect the regulation of calcium in neurons, disrupt thyroid hormonal secretions, and fetal exposure leads to hyperactivity after birth (Coburn et al. 2008).

PBDEs are found in household dust and, in Canadian tests, in everyday foods such as dairy products, beef, pork and fish (Picard 2005). American and Canadian women's breast milk contains concentrations more than forty times higher than those in Sweden, and the levels are rising rapidly, doubling every few years, according to one estimate (Betts 2001). With babies among the most vulnerable, the long-term consequences of this cannot be good.

These are only one group among many industrial chemicals in our bodies which interact in largely unknown ways. There are 85,000 chemicals registered for use in the United States, of which fewer than 2 per cent have been tested for carcinogenicity (Davis and Webster 2002: 25). Aside from the problem of dealing with the complexities of different levels, duration and timing of exposure to a mix of potentially harmful substances, researchers have no 'control group' with whom to compare the affected population because virtually everyone is exposed (Davis 2007).

Workplace health and safety The world's working-age population, currently about 2,700 million, experiences about 1.9–2.3 million deaths per year related to occupation, according to estimates of the International Labour Organization. Of these at least 1.6 million are work-related diseases, including 600,000 cancers, which may take years or decades to develop (Takala 2003: 2).

Textbook economics rules out by assumption any externalities from worker illness and death due to hazardous workplaces. With the assumption of perfect information, it follows that workers demand and get higher wages in exchange for exposure to added risk.[12] These so-called 'compensating differentials' in wages raise firms' costs so that on average firms pay for the costs they inflict on their workers, internalizing these costs and thus ruling out any externality. If this proves too costly, firms may find workers in other countries to accept the risks more cheaply.[13]

In real workplaces, the reality is imperfect information; workers don't know the hazards they face. Employers, however, often know just what they're doing. Friedrich Engels, writing in 1845 on *The Condition of the Working Class in England*, termed such behaviour 'social murder'. He wrote that society 'placed the workers under such conditions in which they can neither retain health nor live long ... and so hurries them to the grave before their time' (Engels 1987 [1845]: 128).

Ignorance of risk and the asbestos holocaust There are many examples from the lead, chemical and plastics industries, but probably the largest single cause of this type of 'social murder' is exposure to asbestos. The fatal dangers of breathing asbestos fibres were observed in the late nineteenth century. Once lodged in the lung, they remain there permanently, causing asbestosis (a fibrous thickening within the lung), larynx cancer and lung cancer, including mesothelioma. The cancers emerge decades after initial exposure (Michaels 2008: 13).

At risk are not just asbestos workers, but

> their families, users of asbestos products, and the public as it is exposed to building materials and asbestos in heating and ventilating systems. In developing countries, where protection of workers and communities is scant to nonexistent, the asbestos cancer epidemic may be even more devastating than it has been in the developed countries. (LaDou 2004: 285)

There are currently about 100,000 cases of asbestos-related cancer a year, according to the World Health Organization. According to one estimate, asbestos will have caused between 5 and 10 million deaths, if exposures to it cease in the near future, which seems unlikely because its use is increasing in some developing countries (Brophy et al. 2007: 237).

While the industry knew of the dangers, it successfully kept the information from workers and the public for decades. The industry also successfully manipulated not only governments but also the International Labour Organization and the World Health Organization, both of which are now, however, finally calling for a worldwide asbestos ban (LaDou 2004; Greenberg 2008).

With the bankruptcy of multinational asbestos companies, due to declining demand and illness-related lawsuits, the single 'most powerful opponent of national and international efforts to ban asbestos around the world' is the Canadian government. Canada has long been one of the world's most important producers and exporters of asbestos, although with about 1,500 workers, the industry is small (LaDou 2004: 289). Chapter 5 sketched out the logic of how narrow interests can dominate public policy and this provides a classic example. The Canadian government has 'used its full influence in international organizations to protect its export market for asbestos, and Canada has aggressively promoted the use of asbestos in developing countries' (ibid.: 289). When France banned the importation of asbestos and asbestos products, the Canadian government challenged it in the World Trade Organization (without success). When the European Union, which has banned asbestos and asbestos products, tried to have chrysotile asbestos added to the UN's Rotterdam Convention (which requires countries importing toxic substances listed under the Convention to give their prior and informed consent), the Canadian government successfully blocked it (Greenberg 2008).

At home, despite the efforts of organizations like Ban Asbestos Canada, the Canadian government remains 'essentially alone among industrialized countries in failing to acknowledge and act upon' the increasing incidence of asbestos-related cancers. It funds an industry lobby group, the Chrysotile Institute (Brophy et al. 2007: 237). It advocates 'controlled use' of chrysotile asbestos while ignoring the fact that almost all Canadian asbestos is exported to developing countries with weak to non-existent regulations. Canada currently exports about 250,000 metric tons of asbestos annually (Greenberg 2008). With about three cancer deaths associated with every 170 tons of asbestos (Tossavainen 2004), these exports should eventually result in about 4,400 deaths a year.

Choosing false beliefs Even if workers know there may be risks to their work, will they evaluate them properly? The textbook model assumes that they will and that appropriate compensation for the extra risk will result.

This won't happen if workers experience what psychologists call 'cognitive dissonance'. People can choose their beliefs about the world, using information selectively to reinforce a belief they would prefer to have (Akerlof and Dickens 1982). In this case, workers have to reconcile their view of themselves as smart people who make the right choices with the actual job they choose. As a result, they can believe their work is safer than it actually is. In this situation, there is no reason to think that wages will, in reality, adequately compensate workers for the risks they face, and thus internalize these costs in the firms' decision-making (Purse 2003). Another idea, leading to the same result, is that workers have differing and incomplete information about job risks. Those who underestimate the risks take the most dangerous jobs.

Question for your professor: Do health and safety risks to workers in the workplace constitute an external cost of production?

The cancer epidemic American men have about a one-in-two chance of developing a cancer during their lifetime, and women a one-in-three chance (Nasca and Pastides 2008: 4). Rates in other industrialized countries such as Canada, Britain and Australia are broadly similar.

TABLE 7.2 Percentage changes in age-standardized cancer incidence rates

	Australia (1973–2002)	Canada (1978–2002)	Scotland (1975–2002)	Sweden (1958–2002)	US, Whites (1972–2002)
All cancers					
Men	38.4	12.2	17.8	48.9	26.1
Women	34.0	11.0	27.6	49.8	15.5
All cancers except lung					
Men	55.4	22.1	42.2	28.0	37.1
Women	31.2	5.5	23.2	22.5	9.7
Lung					
Men	-26.7	-24.1	-32.2	39.3	-16.7
Women	96.6	79.5	66.2	291.9	90.8
Liver					
Men	290.9	90.9	116.7	30.7	119.0
Women	250.0	27.3	112.5	7.7	70.0
Prostate					
Men	176.1	109.7	121.4	208.8	142.2
Breast					
Women	56.2	20.3	31.9	74.6	29.5
Non-Hodgkins lymphoma					
Men	91.8	44.0	74.6	142.5	79.3
Women	78.2	35.1	91.1	126.7	61.4

Note: Data for 'all cancers' exclude 'other skin' cancers.
Source: Authors' calculations from International Agency for Research on Cancer (2005).

Cancer rates for both men and women have been rising steadily for decades throughout the industrialized countries, as can be seen in the sample shown in Figures 7.2 and 7.3. Some data are summarized in Table 7.2 and show increasing rates for the incidence of cancer in general. A decline in smoking and hence reduced lung cancer rates among men in most industrialized countries is one of the few bright spots. More smoking among women is raising their lung cancer rates significantly. Incidentally, as we noted in Chapter 1, in the rational-choice approach of orthodox economics, smoking is a 'rational addiction', an act apparently carried out in full knowledge of the risks. If that were

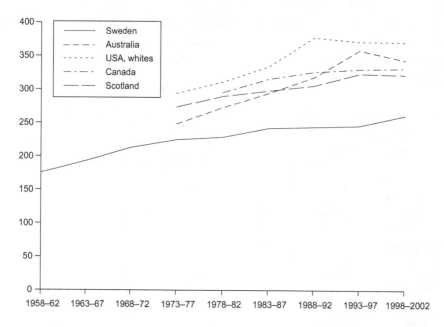

FIGURE 7.2 Cancer incidence per 100,000 males, age-standardized rates

true, none of the 500 million smokers alive today who will die of smoking-related cancers and other disease (Dauvergne 2005: 11) should feel any regret at having smoked.

Excluding lung cancer, male cancer rates are still rising. These increases are not due to the increasing average age of the population. We use cancer statistics where the rates are adjusted to those of a fixed age distribution, allowing comparability across time and across countries.

Such things as increased screening and better diagnosis can account for some of the increase, particularly for breast cancer in women and especially for prostate cancer in men. This can't fully account for breast cancer increases, however, nor does it explain the increasing incidence of cancers such as non-Hodgkin's lymphoma. Other underlying risk factors appear to be at work: workplace and occupational exposures as well as the more familiar culprits, diet and exercise. 'Precautionary policies would urge that exposures to suspected environmental hazards be minimized and that healthful behaviors should be promoted throughout the population with the active involvement of the public and private sectors' (Dinse et al. 1999).

Unfortunately, substantial and influential parts of the private sector have interests in promoting unhealthy products and lifestyles and in covering up workplace and environmental hazards. In the 'cancer industry' itself, attention is naturally directed to the areas where private profit is the greatest (detection and treatment, particularly with expensive drugs) rather than towards prevention (Epstein 1998).

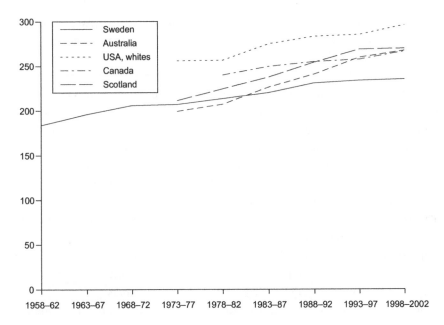

FIGURE 7.3 Cancer incidence per 100,000 females, age-standardized rates

The collapse of the world's fisheries An unregulated fishery is a classic example of an open-access problem. Each fisherman has an incentive to maximize his catch; any fish left behind might be caught by someone else. This sounds like a recipe for disaster, but even in the late nineteenth century, biologists declared the world's fisheries 'inexhaustible' and regulation a waste of time (Gordon 1954: 126).

Advances in fishing technology, however, have proved these optimistic assessments completely wrong. The destruction of the Newfoundland cod fishery (closed, perhaps for ever, in 1992) was not an isolated event. As one group of Canadian biologists explains, '[g]lobally, the rate of fisheries collapses, defined here as catches dropping below 10% of the recorded maximum, has been accelerating over time, with 29% of currently fished species considered collapsed in 2003'. They observe an 'on-going erosion of diversity that appears to be accelerating on a global scale'. This loss of genetic and species biodiversity is the result not only of fishing, but of pollution, habitat destruction and climate change. 'This trend is of serious concern because it projects the global collapse of all taxa [taxonomic units] currently fished by the mid-21st century' if business-as-usual continues. In turn, this implies 'serious threats to global food security, coastal water quality, and ecosystem stability, affecting current and future generations' (Worm et al. 2006: 788, 790).

Governments and international organizations have presided over this growing problem. As one observer comments, 'The world over, bureaucrats and politicians alike assume that commercial fishermen are the constituency they have to satisfy, and not the true owners of the sea, the citizens' (Clover 2006:

316). And what do the fishermen want? They make two demands, according to George Monbiot (2008): 'they must be allowed to destroy their own livelihoods, and the rest of us should pay for it'.

Externalities in the financial industry Given the experience of recent years, no one reading this will need convincing that poorly regulated financial markets don't work well. An important element in their malfunction involves an externality which public regulation and institutions should address.

When a bank makes a loan to a business, it faces some risk of the firm not meeting its obligations. This not only makes the lending bank riskier, it makes other banks with which it is linked in the payments system a little riskier too. This is an externality (Kaufman and Scott 2003). When the bank makes the loan, it thinks only of the additional risk it is assuming, not of the additional risk it imposes on other banks. This has consequences for the stability of the entire financial system if an event (such as a fall in housing prices or a recession) increases the number of defaulting loans faced by all banks.

Public regulation of financial institutions can require individual financial institutions 'to expend the resources necessary to manage risk, to maintain adequate capital, and pay for risk insurance' to internalize these external costs, as John Eatwell and Lance Taylor explain in a study of the Asian financial crisis of 1997. They note that while effective management of these externalities is good for society as a whole, the financial institutions 'tend to resent the costs involved, and argue that, in their case at least, these costs are unnecessary' (1998: 22–3).

The result is an ongoing tension between the regulators and the regulated. In the United States, the last several decades have seen in 'housing and consumer finance ... the consequences of market power, of asymmetric information, and of regulatory capture, leading to rampant predation against both a public system and the public itself, and on a colossal scale', as James K. Galbraith recently put it (2008: 140). We pursue these themes further in the postscript to this book.

Question for your professor: If externalities are really pervasive and important, why doesn't the textbook integrate them throughout the book, rather than leaving them to a chapter towards the end?

2.2 Externalities and the profit motive

'We have always known that heedless self-interest was bad morals; we know now that it is bad economics.' Franklin Delano Roosevelt, second inaugural address, 1937

Many critics of the current economic system deplore the profit motive, seeing it as destructive. From the viewpoint of the textbooks, where the profit motive guides resources to their most valued uses and produces material abundance, it appears that these critics are economic illiterates. Consider this comment by the American historian Howard Zinn:

> [Marx's] perception that the profit motive was ruinous for the human race remains, I think, a great insight. We see that the drive of corporations for profit is done at the expense of human beings all over the world ... the pursuit of money has led chemical companies to pollute the air and water, has led arms manufacturers to create monstrous weapons of destruction without regard to how they will be used or against whom they will be used. (2002: 97–8)

If we take the ubiquity of important externalities seriously, and if we recognize the realities of power and information that hinder effective responses to them, we can see how the profit motive can work in practice. The texts put the externality problem in the background, while assuming away the problems of asymmetric information, corporate power and citizen disorganization that so often tend to give disproportionate power to the kind of narrow interests that Zinn identifies.

Many critics, including Zinn, would argue that only a deep democratization of society can overcome the concentrations of power that inhibit effective collective action to deal with the external costs that the existing economic system generates. In the near term, that could take the form of sufficiently active citizen engagement in civic affairs (Nader 2004a: 1). In the long term, that democratization would have to include the capitalist corporation itself, which operates non-democratically as a matter of principle. In a democratic economy, producing organizations would ultimately have to cover their costs, but the profit motive, in the sense of maximizing profit regardless of the external costs imposed on others, would be discarded.

2.3 Summing up: externalities and the market economy

The ideal of a perfectly competitive market economy that allocates scarce resources efficiently is also one that presumes that there are no externalities. But the conclusion that such a fictitious 'free market' economy is efficient (although, admittedly, not equitable) is no justification for a presumption of laissez-faire. At best, it's an intellectual toy that could be used to stress just how different the actual economy is from this imaginary world.

The modern market economy has indeed produced a high material standard of living for many people in the developed world. But this is not the same thing as 'efficiency'. As we've tried to show, it's perfectly compatible with very serious problems of pollution (of which we have given only a few examples), misuse of resources, and even with long-term catastrophe.

In fact, this does not contradict what is in the texts themselves, if they are read carefully and completely by those willing to draw their own conclusions. But the texts put externalities in the background (and at the back of the book), foregrounding instead the story of markets that work efficiently. A concept that could be woven throughout the book as a repeated theme is instead treated as a secondary matter that could be fixed by appropriate government policy. They fail to provide real information about the actual importance of negative externalities and an analysis of how governments actually respond to them.

Suggestions for further reading

Robert Frank's 1999 book, *Luxury Fever: Why money fails to satisfy in an era of excess*, is a thought-provoking exploration of the effects of consumption externalities. He advocates a consumption tax to address the problem.

Two first-rate accounts of the ruthless behaviour of industrial polluters and the makers of dangerous products are Gerald Markowitz and David Rosner's 2002 study, *Deceit and Denial: The deadly politics of industrial pollution*, and David Michaels's *Doubt is Their Product: How industry's assault on science threatens your health* (2008).

The economics of climate change is an issue of first-rate importance, and Frank Ackerman's brief and accessible 2009 book, *Can We Afford the Future? The economics of a warming world*, is an excellent introduction to the issues.

The disaster facing the world's fisheries is set out by reporter Charles Clover in *The End of the Line: How overfishing is changing the world and what we eat* (2006). It has subsequently been the inspiration for a documentary film, *The End of the Line*, directed by Rupert Murray. See endoftheline.com.

Engels's theme of 'social murder' is taken up by Robert Chernomas and Ian Hudson in their *Social Murder and Other Shortcomings of Conservative Economics* (2007), a critique of corporate power and its absence from mainstream economic theory.

For more advanced undergraduate students, Arild Vatn provides an introduction to institutional economics as applied to environmental economic policy in his 2005 book, *Institutions and the Environment*.

8 | The marginal productivity theory of income distribution – or you're worth what you can get

'Are we so committed to the framework of marginal productivity and its implicit claim … that the distribution of income is legitimated by market forces? Are we prepared to rule the issues of power, monopoly and financial control off the table when we discuss the way incomes are apportioned …?' James K. Galbraith (1998: 37)

'In theory there is no difference between theory and practice. In practice there is.' Yogi Berra

We've emphasized in previous chapters how standard textbooks downplay one of the main economic goals – equity – in favour of the other – efficiency. This emphasis shows up again in the placement of chapters explaining the distribution of income. They are invariably towards the end of the book, and, because of time constraints, the typical introductory economics course may not cover them. The implicit message is that the distribution of income isn't that important.

The textbooks teach the neoclassical model, where the distribution of income is determined primarily by technology, tastes and factor supplies. Mere lip-service is given to conventions or norms, government decisions over public spending, bargaining power, notions of fairness, discrimination, the legal framework, or arbitrary historical accidents.

In its pure form, the neoclassical model assumes perfect competition (including perfect information) and predicts that *all factors earn an amount equal to the value of what they contribute to output.* Though proponents of this view are prepared to admit that almost no markets are perfectly competitive, and there is almost never perfect information, they hypothesize that competitive forces are prevalent enough, and information good enough, to justify using the theory as an approximation.

I THE STANDARD TEXT

I.I Introduction

What are the factors of production? The texts differ on the appropriate classification. The factors of production most often mentioned are: land, labour, capital and entrepreneurship. Baumol and Blinder (2006: 394) also include 'exhaustible natural resources', whereas other authors subsume it under 'land'. Krugman and Wells (2005: 282) include 'human capital' as a separate factor of production, whereas other authors subsume it under 'capital'. (Human capital is the result of past investments in education and skill acquisition.) Finally, not all texts include 'entrepreneurship' as a factor of production. In a survey of the eight leading text-books, however, Naples and Aslanbeigui (1996) found that all but two do include it.

What do these factors of production earn? The usual nomenclature has land earning rent; labour earning wages; capital earning interest; and entrepreneur-ship earning normal profit. In addition, in the short run a residual (economic profit) is earned by the firm's owners, who might be the entrepreneur or the stockholders.

1.2 Demand for factors of production

The demand for any factor of production depends on its productivity, and the revenue generated from selling additional output. Applying the usual marginal reasoning, the profit-maximizing firm will hire an additional unit of a factor as long as it adds more to revenues than to costs.

On the revenue side, an additional unit of a factor produces its marginal prod-uct, MP. Further, each extra unit of output generates some marginal revenue, MR. (For a perfectly competitive firm, marginal revenue is simply the market output price, P.) Hence, the additional revenue from hiring one more unit of a factor is the product of the two, MR x MP, referred to as the marginal revenue product, MRP.

Additional revenue from one more unit of a factor is MRP = MR x MP

If the firm is a price-taker in the factor market, then the cost of one more unit of the factor is simply the factor price, P_F. We'll assume that this price includes all fringe benefits: payroll taxes, paid vacation, paid sick leave and pension contribu-tions.

Additional cost of one more unit of a factor is its market price, P_F

Therefore, the firm should hire each factor up to the point where its price equals its marginal revenue product, P_F = MRP. In other words, the marginal rev-enue product (MRP) is the firm's factor demand schedule. This is downward sloping for two reasons: *the law of diminishing returns* (explained in Chapter 5) guarantees that MP eventually falls as more units of the factor are employed; and second, downward-sloping demand curves guarantee that MR falls as more output is sold.

Applying the decision rule P_F = MRP in the short run (when the only variable factor of production is labour), the firm maximizes its profits by hiring labour up to the point where the wage, W, equals the marginal revenue product of labour, MR x MP_L.

The firm's decision about how much labour to hire also determines how much output it produces. In Chapter 5, however, we saw that to maximize profit, the firm produces up the point where marginal revenue equals marginal cost. Is the new decision rule consistent with the earlier one?

It is easily shown that the two rules are equivalent. The new rule says hire labour until $MR \times MP_L = W$. Divide both sides by MP_L, to get: $MR = W/MP_L$. A moment's reflection confirms that the wage divided by the marginal product of labour is the marginal cost. It costs the firm W (say \$16) to hire one more unit of labour, but the labour produces MP_L units of output (say eight units). Therefore, the cost of producing one of those extra units of output, which is marginal cost, is W divided by MP_L (or \$2 per unit).

In the long run, when all factors of production are variable, they are all hired up to the point where their marginal revenue product equals their factor price, $P_X = MR \times MP_X$. Rearranging this expression gives the optimal combination of factors: $MR = MP_X/P_X = MP_Y/P_Y$, for factors of production X and Y. This is known as the 'least cost rule': the firm will hire every factor up to the point where the productivity of a dollar's worth of every factor is equal.

The least cost rule means that a change in one factor's price will have ripple effects on the demand for all other factors of production. For example, a decrease in the real interest rate, r, makes capital cheaper. This generates two effects: first, firms respond by using more capital and less labour – a substitution effect; second, since costs have fallen, competitive supply curves shift right, leading to increased output – an output effect. The net effect on the position of the labour demand function depends on which effect dominates.

1.3 Determination of wages in a perfectly competitive labour market

To obtain the market demand for a particular type of worker, say welders, we must horizontally sum the *MRP* curves of all the firms across all the industries that employ welders, as shown in Figure 8.1. The supply of a particular type of

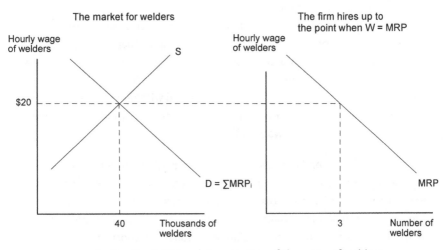

FIGURE 8.1 Competitive determination of the wage of welders

worker is normally depicted as upward sloping, reflecting the assumption that a higher wage is required to induce a greater supply of work time. The overall supply and demand for a particular skill (welding) determines the market wage. The firm then decides how many workers to hire by equating the wage to its *MRP*.

1.4 Wage differentials in competitive labour markets

Why do top professional athletes earn more than surgeons? Why do surgeons earn more than fast-food workers? While each textbook has its own unique categorization of explanatory factors, all of them situate their explanation in the context of forces operating on the demand and supply of different types of labour – in other words, in competitive labour markets. We'll begin with the principle of equal net benefit and proceed through the usual textbook explanations.

The principle of equal net benefit If there were no intrinsic (or innate) differences between workers, and no barriers to entering an occupation, then in equilibrium the *present value of net benefits should be the same* in all jobs. Otherwise people would move from a lower-benefit job to a higher-benefit one.

The principle of compensating differences Because 'net benefits' include non-monetary benefits, dirty, dangerous or dull jobs would receive higher pay than clean, safe and interesting jobs. This could explain why construction workers earn more than sales clerks, since construction involves dirtier and more hazardous conditions, and more irregular employment, than clerical work.

Differences in acquired abilities The principle of equal net benefit implies that wage differentials must be enough to compensate individuals for their investments in acquiring necessary skills. Accountants must earn more than waiters because of the many years of training required. They have acquired human capital, which earns a market return.

On its own, human capital can't explain big wage differentials. If it takes four years and $100,000 to become an accountant rather than a waiter, then (assuming an interest rate of 8 per cent amortized over a twenty-five-year career) accountancy should pay around $9,000 a year more than being a waiter.[1] So, differences in acquired abilities must be supplemented with differences in inherent abilities or barriers to occupational entry (perhaps caused by unions) to come close to explaining real-world wage differentials.[2]

Differences in inherent abilities Large wage differentials require non-competing groups. Textbooks focus on differences in inherited or natural ability. For example, how many of us have the ability (or aptitude) to become a concert violinist, a surgeon or a top athlete? Since the answer is 'very few', and since millions of people are willing to pay billions of dollars on sports entertainment, top professional athletes have very high marginal revenue products.

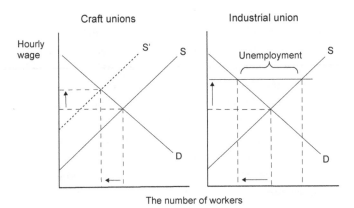

FIGURE 8.2 Two types of unions in otherwise competitive markets

Union-caused wage differentials Unions, by restricting the availability of labour, force up wages. In the left-hand diagram of Figure 8.2, 'craft unions' seek to restrict supply of qualified workers by enforcing long apprenticeships, high initiation fees and limits on the number of new members admitted. Examples are occupational licensing of barbers, physicians, plumbers and cosmeticians. Many progressive social initiatives are seen as having the same effect: for example, laws prohibiting child labour, compulsory retirement or a fixed length of the working week. The benefits of protecting consumers from incompetent practitioners are downplayed because with good enough information such incompetent practitioners would simply go out of business.[3]

In the right-hand diagram of Figure 8.2, the 'industrial' (or economy-wide) union tries to organize all available workers to force wages above equilibrium. As with the craft union, this increases wages at the expense of employment.

Unions are often cited as a cause of unemployment (for example, Mankiw et al. 2006: 432). To try to offset employment reductions, unions could try to increase demand for union workers, for example through efforts to increase productivity or by encouraging consumers to buy goods made by unionized workers (for example, Ragan and Lipsey 2008: 341). Union workers would benefit at the expense of others as demand switches away from the products made by other workers. Another strategy is to support increases in the minimum wage, since this makes non-union workers more costly.

The bottom line is that unions benefit some workers at the expense of other workers. In this view, unions are purely self-serving organizations and any progressive social initiatives they may champion are seen as attempts to attain other goals (Parkin and Bade 2006: 414–15). Clearly, unions get a 'bad press' in mainstream economics textbooks. Parkin and Bade (ibid.: 413) assert that 'labour unions are *the main source* of market power in the labour market' (our emphasis), a claim about the facts that also seems to deny that firms have pervasive market power.

173

Efficiency wages Even without unions, firms may choose to pay more than the equilibrium wage as an incentive for better performance, especially when monitoring work effort is difficult. This makes workers less likely to shirk; being caught and fired now implies a lower wage in an alternative job. If all firms pay wages that are above the market equilibrium, the result will be a pool of workers who want higher-paying jobs but can't find them. The penalty for being caught shirking is now a longer period unemployed.

The theory of efficiency wages is a theory of market failure, which arises because of a lack of information about worker effort. Those who retain their jobs still earn their marginal revenue product since the higher-than-equilibrium wage elicits greater effort. But the market failure manifests itself as unemployment.

Tournament theory Lazear and Rosen (1981: 847) point out: 'On the day that a given individual is promoted from vice-president to president, his salary may triple. It is difficult to argue that his skills have tripled in that one-day period, presenting difficulties for standard theory.' They go on to say: 'It is not a puzzle, however, when interpreted in the context of a prize.' Tournament theory sees CEO pay as like the prizes professional golfers and tennis players receive for winning tournaments. Those prizes increase the productivity of everyone who competes for them. In this view, CEO pay is still based on high productivity, but now it is the productivity of the whole team of executives striving for the top job – not just the CEO alone.

Discrimination All the mainstream textbooks at least mention discrimination; but there is no consensus on how it is treated. The central story is this: over time a competitive market economy will automatically eliminate discrimination (wage differences not based on differences in productivity), provided the forces of competition are not short-circuited by equal pay for equal work legislation. To see this, suppose black and white workers have identical skills and work ethic, but some firms will employ black workers only if the wage is low enough to overcome their dislike of them. If there are not enough non-discriminating firms, some black workers must accept a lower wage at discriminating firms. Since under perfect competition identical workers must earn an identical wage, all black workers must be paid the same wage – a lower one than white workers – and a dual wage structure will emerge.[4]

Unprejudiced firms (which employ more black workers) now experience an economic windfall – their workers are now cheaper – allowing them to expand their market share at the expense of discriminating firms. In the long run, the market share of non-discriminating firms increases, and the wage discount for black workers decreases. Eventually, wages converge.

But what if they don't? Prasch (2008: 120) points out that if we believe that competitive forces are strong enough (perhaps as a matter of faith), but a dual wage structure persists, then logic dictates that the low wage group is not in fact equally capable. Perhaps they lack education, skills or good work habits. Another possibility is that competitive pressures are being frustrated by equal pay for equal work legislation. This prevents non-discriminating employers from paying lower wages, and so prevents them from reaping more profits and expanding their market share. Prejudiced firms will continue to employ white workers whenever possible without being punished by market forces.

The better textbooks point out that competition doesn't automatically eradicate discrimination when customers are themselves prejudiced and willing to pay more to be served by white workers. The worst ones simply emphasize that market forces automatically tend to eliminate discrimination and fail to mention that such a conclusion hinges on the existence of competitive markets and unprejudiced consumers.[5]

1.5 Monopsonistic labour markets

Monopsony means 'single buyer'. The usual context is a single employer of a particular type of labour, which is relatively immobile – either geographically or in terms of skill. The texts universally emphasize that this situation is rare.

Since the monopsonistic employer faces an upward-sloping labour supply curve, to hire an extra worker it must increase the wage for all workers hired. As a result, the marginal cost of an additional worker is not just the wage paid to that worker, but also the additional cost of all the other workers it previously employed at a lower wage.

TABLE 8.1 Marginal cost of labour for a monopsonist

Number of workers (1)	Hourly wage (2)	Total labour cost (3)	Marginal labour cost (4)
1	$6	$6	$6
2	$7	$14	$8
3	$8	$24	$10
4	$9	$36	$12
5	$10	$50	$14

For example, the first two columns in Table 8.1 define an upward-sloping labour supply curve – a higher hourly wage inducing the supply of more workers. The third column shows total labour cost, and is the product of the first two columns. The last column shows marginal labour cost, and is the change in total labour cost as we move from one row to the next of column (3). Note that (except for the first worker) marginal labour cost exceeds the wage.

Figure 8.3 illustrates the problem. To maximize profits, the monopsonist hires labour until its marginal cost equals its marginal revenue product at point

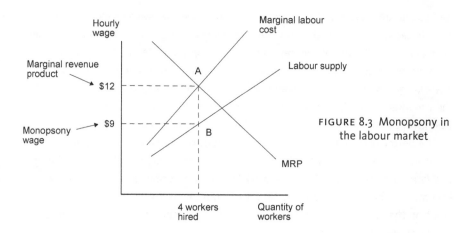

FIGURE 8.3 Monopsony in the labour market

A, where the profit-maximizing number of workers is four. The wage at which they will work is given by the labour supply schedule at point B. According to Figure 8.3, they will be willing to work for $9 an hour even though their marginal revenue product is $12 an hour.

Monopsony and the minimum wage Suppose that the minimum wage is higher than the wage the monopsonist was paying. Since the minimum wage is a legally binding constraint, the marginal cost of labour is just the minimum wage, at least up to the point where the labour supply curve shows that a higher wage is needed to induce a greater supply of labour. Figure 8.4 shows the simple case where the minimum wage is set equal to what the wage would be in a competitive labour market, which we suppose is $10 an hour. The effect is to *increase* employment. In contrast to the competitive model, a binding minimum wage offsets the monopsonist's market power and produces a net social benefit.

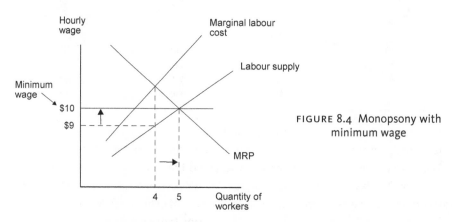

FIGURE 8.4 Monopsony with minimum wage

Monopsony and unions A few texts also explain that a union could offset the market power of the monopsonist. Figure 8.3 shows that the monopsonist could pay up to $12 an hour, the fourth worker's marginal revenue product. Bargaining in a *bilateral monopoly* situation leads to a wage somewhere between $12 and $9 an hour with no adverse effect on employment.

1.6 The returns to capital

The distribution of national income between wages on the one hand and interest, profits and rents on the other is known as the 'functional' distribution of income. It was a major preoccupation of the classical economists. Indeed, David Ricardo called it 'the principal problem in Political Economy' (Glyn 2007). The classical economists explained it using an aggregate production function assuming two homogeneous factors of production – labour and capital. This aggregate model is still a key analytical tool in macroeconomics, and while it is largely absent from microeconomics, it does make an occasional cameo appearance – for example, when deriving the production possibility frontier, when explaining the benefits of trade, and when explaining the return to capital – our current concern.

Assuming perfect competition throughout the economy – in all output and factor markets – we can replace 'marginal revenue' with 'price' in the definition of marginal revenue product. Thus, labour will be hired up to the point where: $W = P \times MP_L$. Dividing through by the aggregate price level, P, allows us to write an expression for the real wage – the nominal wage adjusted for changes in the purchasing power of money (what the money wage can actually buy in terms of goods):

$$\text{The real wage, } W/P = MP_L$$

Similarly, the real return on capital – which is the real rate of interest, r – is determined by the marginal productivity of capital.

$$\text{The real interest rate, } r = MP_K$$

The real returns to each factor are determined by supply and demand. Total labour income (in real terms) is the real wage times the number of workers and is represented in the left-hand diagram of Figure 8.5 by the shaded rectangle. Since the sum of all additional outputs equals total output, the area under the MP_L curve and to the left of labour supply equals total output. Subtracting labour income from total output yields total capital income, shown as the white triangle.

This discussion suggests that the earnings of capital are a residual – what is left over from total output after we subtract labour income. This, however, is just because we arbitrarily chose to plot labour on the horizontal axis and to think in terms of labour's marginal product. We could just as easily have chosen to plot capital on the horizontal axis, and think in terms of capital's marginal product. This is shown in the right-hand diagram of Figure 8.5, which shows the return to capital, *r*, determined by the demand and supply of capital. 'Capital' refers to the structures and stock of equipment used for production. At any moment of time

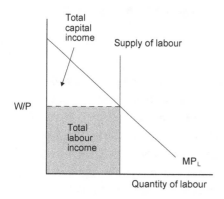

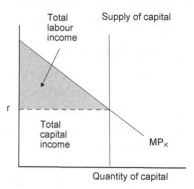

Determination of the wage

Determination of the real interest rate

FIGURE 8.5 The adding-up problem

its supply is given. The demand for capital is the value of its marginal product. The total earnings of capital are equal to the return (*r*) times the quantity of capital, shown as a white rectangle, while this time total labour income is the residual shaded triangle.

Now we face an obvious question. How do we know that the two diagrams are consistent? If both labour and capital are paid the values of their marginal products, how do we know that this just exhausts total output? How do we know that total labour income, shown as the rectangle in the left-hand diagram, is the same as total labour income, shown as the residual triangle in the right-hand diagram?

In general, we cannot be sure that the diagrams 'add up' in this way. Consistency requires a specific technological restriction on production – constant returns to scale. We know, however, that competitive firms in long-run equilibrium operate at the minimum point of their long-run average cost curves – where constant returns to scale occur. If the economy is characterized by competitive firms in long-run equilibrium, then the two diagrams are consistent. Firms hire both labour and capital up to the point where their real reward equals their marginal contribution to output.

2 THE ANTI-TEXT

We'll argue here that the marginal productivity story suffers from logical difficulties – the adding-up problem can be solved only in certain restrictive circumstances. As well, there may be no unique relationship between the supply of capital and real interest rates. Second, the perfectly competitive labour market contains some absurd predictions that are clearly false, but ignored by the textbooks. Third, marginal productivity theory is so amorphous that it's hard to test directly. But fourth, indirect tests refute the prediction of a single market wage for workers of a given quality. To fit the facts, subsidiary theories are needed that deal with fairness and status. These underline the importance of relative position, which undercuts the notion that free markets produce an efficient outcome. We argue that a much better theory, in terms of plausibility and accuracy of predictions, is the dynamic monopsony model. Finally, we turn our attention to executive compensation. We argue that the standard textbook story cannot explain the seismic shift in executive pay relative to average wages. We conclude that instead of 'getting what they are worth', a combination of bad incentives, lax accounting rules and poor oversight led to executives 'getting what they can get away with'.

We'll move on to the theoretical problems after first discussing whether the marginal productivity theory of distribution legitimizes actual market outcomes.

2.1 Does marginal productivity legitimize the actual distribution of income?

There are three ways in which a theory might legitimize a social outcome. The explanation provided by the theory might make the social outcome seem: (1) fair; (2) unavoidable; or (3) beneficial.

In the late nineteenth century, the American economist J. B. Clark explicitly argued that having rewards determined by marginal contribution to output was both fair and unavoidable. It was fair because 'what a social class gets is, under natural law, what it contributes to the general output of industry' (1891: 319). It was unavoidable because competition ensures that if an employer tried to pay a worker less than her marginal product, other employers would offer more, bidding her wages up.

There are two main problems with the fairness argument. First, someone might be unable to make a contribution to output through no fault of their own. This is the rationale for 'the compassionate state' and a social safety net. Second, it confounds the contributions of non-human factors of production (land and capital) with the contributions of those who own them. As Robinson (1973b: 129) points out: 'It says nothing about how the [ownership of] factors are distributed amongst people.' As a result, 'the theory of distribution has nothing to say, one way or the other, about the distribution of income'. Robinson extrapolates the point by saying: 'The theory purports to explain the differences between skilled and unskilled wages, not how the chance to acquire skills is limited. It purports to explain rent per acre, not the size of estates; the rate of interest, not the possession of capital.'

Most modern mainstream textbooks explicitly disavow the fairness argument.[6] But this does not prevent it from continuing to be a pervasive view. Writing in the *New York Times*, Frank Rick (2009) calls it 'the bedrock American dream that virtues like hard work and playing by the rules are rewarded with prosperity'. In other words, rewards are determined by contribution. Furthermore, according to Joan Robinson (1973b: 129), the legitimacy arguments are still made in the textbooks, but are now concealed behind scientific objectivity, allowing them to persuade all the more powerfully. Bok (1993: 15) puts the argument this way:

> The theory of marginal productivity, together with the insights of Adam Smith, seem[s] to have persuaded the general public, as well as economists, that large differences in compensation are indispensable to progress and prosperity. [They] ... are needed both to attract people to the occupations for which they are best suited and to induce them to acquire the skills and exert their best efforts at work for the ultimate benefit of the entire society.

In other words, an unequal distribution of income is legitimate because it is beneficial – meaning that it gives rise to the incentives necessary to give us an efficient and dynamic economy.

To sum up, Clark explicitly made *the fairness argument*, and based it on the maxim: to each according to their contribution. Mainstream textbooks disavow this, but explicitly make *the efficiency argument* and legitimize market outcomes with the maxim: *don't kill the goose that lays the golden eggs.* In doing so, they see themselves as scientific and value free.

Questions for your professor: Does economics support the view that those who receive the greatest rewards are those who have made the greatest contribution? What contribution does the ownership of land or capital make?

2.2 Theoretical problems with the standard textbook story[7]

The adding-up problem At the end of Section 1, we argued that all factors can earn their marginal product only if there are constant returns to scale – otherwise total earnings won't 'add up' to total output. Why is that?

Suppose there are increasing returns to scale. This means that if we increase factor inputs by 1 per cent, output increases by more than 1 per cent. The marginal product of these extra factors is greater than the average output of factors as a whole. So, if we tried to pay all factors their marginal products, there would not be enough available, as a matter of simple arithmetic. (If, on the other hand, the economy experienced decreasing returns, marginal products would be less than average products and there would be output left over.)

Constant returns to scale necessarily prevail in the long-run equilibrium of a perfectly competitive industry, but not in any other industry structure. Therefore, the marginal product theory of distribution requires perfect competition. So, if you don't find perfect competition appealing, must you abandon the marginal product theory of distribution? Not necessarily. You could pin your faith on a combination of increasing returns to scale and imperfect competition. Remember, with increasing returns to scale the sum of the value of the marginal products more than exceeds the value of total output. On the other hand, in imperfect competition factors are paid their marginal revenue products, $MR \times MP$, rather than the value of their marginal products, $P \times MP$. Since marginal revenue, MR, is less than price, P, this might reduce the sum of factor payments enough so that they just exhaust the value of total output. There's no mechanism to guarantee this outcome, however; it could happen only by chance.

```
Questions for your professor: If increasing returns are
pervasive in the modern economy, could every factor earn its
marginal product? Or would income shares more than exhaust
total output?
```

The Cambridge capital controversy This was a debate that raged from the mid-1950s to the mid-1970s over several fundamental concepts, including the meaning of *equilibrium* and the nature of *capital*. The participants in the debate were principally associated either with Cambridge, England, or Cambridge, Massachusetts. While the debate essentially petered out and neoclassical theory survived, Cohen and Harcourt (2003: 200) argue that the issues involved are deep and important and will probably erupt in further controversy until they are resolved.[8]

Consider the textbook story about the determination of the return to capital. This postulates an aggregate production function with capital as one input. From this we determine the marginal product of capital, which in equilibrium equals the real rate of interest. But how do we add up all the different kinds of capital – all the different tools, machines and structures – to get one measure of capital to put into the production function? The answer is that we must add everything up in dollar value terms. But this means that *the value of capital must be known* before it enters the production function, and hence *before the value of capital can be determined*.

This circularity is not, however, the telling point. There are many examples of simultaneous mutual dependence in economics that can be routinely solved. The telling point is that during the 'Cambridge capital controversies' it was shown that there *may be no unique equilibrium solution*. Because of the mutual dependence between the value of capital and the interest rate, it can be shown that one method of production – call it technique A – can be cheaper at both high and low interest rates, while another method – call it technique B – is cheaper at intermediate rates of interest. This is known as the 'reswitching result', and it implies that the demand for capital can have a backward-bending segment, implying the possibility of multiple equilibria, as shown in Figure 8.6.

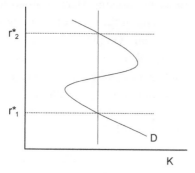

FIGURE 8.6 Reswitching produces the
possibility of multiple equilibria

If the possibility of multiple equilibria means that the impersonal force of marginal productivity isn't enough to determine the interest rate, then what does determine it? Suddenly, the door is open for all kinds of other social forces to matter: social norms, relative power, bargaining, government policies, and so on.

The neoclassical economists responded by arguing that the aggregate model is used only as a simplifying device – they know it isn't intellectually respectable, so showing that it's false isn't damaging their core theory. Rather, the intellectually respectable version is the extremely disaggregated (and complex) general equilibrium theory. In this theory, each disaggregated factor must earn a reward equal to its marginal product and the model economy is Pareto-efficient. Unfortunately, as the critics were quick to point out, these models provide no support for a 'relative scarcity theory of distribution'. For example, one cannot assert that, *ceteris paribus*, an increase in the supply of capital causes real interest rates to fall, as is implied in the right-hand diagram of Figure 8.5. Nor can one assert that, *ceteris paribus*, an increase in the supply of labour causes real wages to fall, as is implied in the left-hand diagram of Figure 8.5. As Cohen and Harcourt (2003: 207) put it:

> [T]he switch to general equilibrium, rather than saving the neoclassical parables, abandoned them for simultaneous equation price systems ... Relinquished, however, were one-way causal claims about unambiguously signed differences in the interest rate associated with differences in the quantity of capital.

Furthermore, general equilibrium theory itself is plagued by difficulties in showing uniqueness and stability (see Ackerman 2002, and the addendum to Chapter 6). It seems that there is something fundamentally wrong with the neoclassical ideal world of perfect competition.

Needless to say, the participants in the debate could not agree about the significance of the results. As we argued in Chapter 2, such disagreements about significance are an endemic problem in economic analysis. Cohen and Harcourt (2003: 207) sum up: 'With neither side able to deliver a knockout punch, issues of faith and ideology entered the ring ... Ideology and methodology, two subjects most economists would rather avoid, were pervasive under-currents fuelling the controversies.'

> Question for your professor: What's your take on the Cambridge
> capital controversy? I hear the English theorists won the
> debate, but lost the war …

2.3 The fuzziness of marginal productivity theory

Can marginal products always be measured? When there are many different outputs produced at the same time, or where output is produced in a complex organization, one person's contribution to overall output might be impossible to decipher. Clearly, information about productivity is crucial, but (as recognized in the efficiency wage theories) information is highly imperfect. Furthermore, someone with low productivity has every incentive to masquerade as someone with high productivity. If marginal productivity cannot be measured, how can it be used by employers to make optimal hiring decisions? And if marginal productivity cannot be measured, how can the theory of distribution be tested?

Indeed, what *does* the marginal product theory of distribution specifically *say*? When MIT economist Lester Thurow set about writing a critique of the textbook marginal productivity analysis, he wrote (1975: viii), 'it is so amorphous that I have been unable to say what it is'.

For example, suppose that we could observe individual workers making widgets. Does the theory say that the workers are paid their actual marginal products every hour or every day? Or will they be paid their average marginal product over some longer period, such as their working life? The textbook theory is ambiguous. Thurow (ibid.: 211–12) points out that 'seniority wage schedules are not evidence contrary to the lifetime marginal-productivity hypothesis, but they are evidence contrary to the instantaneous marginal-productivity hypothesis'.

Similarly, we might observe a group of individual workers of the same seniority all getting the same pay, while some have higher marginal products than others. Thurow (ibid.: 212) asks: 'Are groups or individuals paid their marginal products?' If pay in such cases reflects the average marginal product of the group as a whole, is this consistent with marginal productivity theory? And what defines the group?

Thurow's basic point is that 'subsidiary distribution theories are necessary in every variant except the strict interpretation in which every individual factor is paid his marginal product at every instant of time'. He warns that the theory is in danger of becoming a tautology – something that is true by definition: 'factors in general must be paid in accordance with the productivity of factors in general' (ibid.: 215).

Questions for your professor: Does the marginal productivity
theory say that workers will receive their actual marginal
product at every point in time, or their average marginal product over a longer period? Or will individuals receive the
average marginal product of the group to which they belong?

2.4 Empirical testing of the competitive model

Despite Thurow's misgivings, researchers have attempted to test the marginal
product theory of distribution. As you read this section, ask yourself whether
this research refutes the marginal product theory of distribution, or merely
delineates the subsidiary theories that Thurow suggests are necessary to give
the theory more substance.

Even when marginal products cannot be directly measured there are indirect
ways of testing the competitive labour market model. First, the competitive
model predicts a single market wage for workers of a given quality, doing the
same work, no matter where they do it. A second prediction follows: workers of
different quality should receive different wages even if they work in the same
firm. The evidence refutes both predictions.

Regarding the first prediction, Akerlof and Yellen (1988) cite an impressive
amount of evidence showing that workers of identical characteristics receive
different wages in different industries and occupations.[9] Indeed, industries that
have high wages for one occupation also have high wages for other occupations;
wages are strongly positively correlated with industry profits.

Regarding the second prediction, there is strong evidence that workers' wages
differ by less than their marginal productivities. This phenomenon is known
as *wage compression*. Robert Frank (1984) was one of the first to report it. He
focused on the productivity of real estate and automobile salespeople because
their 'output' was easy to measure, and because of the highly competitive nature
of the industries. He found strong evidence that wage rates vary substantially
less than individual productivity.

The standard version of the efficiency wage model cannot explain these empirical regularities. It suggests that identical workers will receive higher pay in
jobs where monitoring is more difficult as an incentive for work effort. This
cannot explain why identical occupations should receive different pay in different industries. For example, there is no obvious reason why secretaries should
be harder to supervise in the chemical industry, where their pay is high, than
in the apparel industry, where their pay is low (Akerlof and Yellen 1988: 44).

Another variant of the efficiency-wage model, however – the *fairness model* –
provides a natural explanation for both empirical regularities. According to this
model, in industries where it is advantageous to pay some employees highly, it

is considered *fair* to also pay other employees well. And when individuals do not consider themselves to be treated fairly, their motivation and effort suffer.

Lazear (1989) points out a weakness of the fairness model: it is far from obvious that a compressed salary structure is morale-improving for the better workers who receive less than their marginal product. They may feel disenchanted by this scheme. Frank (1984) wonders why those better workers don't split off and form their own firm. He suggests that what's missing from the fairness argument is *relative status* in the firm's hierarchy.

Status is like a non-pecuniary benefit. If the best workers were paid the value of their marginal product, they would receive their high status free of charge. Therefore, they are paid less than their marginal product. Similarly, if the worst workers were paid the value of their marginal product, they would suffer low status without any compensating payment. Therefore, they are paid more than their marginal product.

One very attractive feature of the status explanation for wage compression is that there is abundant evidence that people care about their relative standing in the community, and in the income hierarchies of the groups to which they belong.[10]

Question for your professor: How important are 'fairness' and 'status' in determining a firm's wage structure?

2.5 The importance of fairness and status

Did the previous section refute the marginal product theory of distribution, or merely delineate the subsidiary theories that give the main concept more substance? In these models, wages reflect *both* individual marginal productivities *and* the average productivity of the group as a whole, with the group being the firm. These modifications allow marginal productivity theory to be consistent with broadly observed empirical regularities. So, are these efficiency wage, fairness and status models just the icing on the competitive model's cake?

The monitoring version of the efficiency wage model probably is just icing – though it doesn't sit well with the ethos of reward being determined by contribution. As emphasized by Prasch (2008: 104), the harder-to-monitor tasks need not be more challenging or difficult than the easier-to-monitor tasks. Yet the fact of unequal monitoring costs creates a wage differential between identical workers doing otherwise identical tasks. Nevertheless, the key point is that this outcome is efficient.

On the other hand, hidden within the fairness and status theories is the implication that the competitive market outcome is not efficient. And that means that these models are not just icing on the competitive model's cake. Rather, they are subversive of the key idea that the actual distribution of income is the result of a process that leads to efficient outcomes. Why is that?

Both fairness and status theory emphasize that people care about relative position and this creates an important externality. When reward depends primarily on relative performance, unrestricted choices by rational individuals often yield results that no one favours. To explain why, Frank (2005b) uses the example of hockey players. In an unregulated competitive situation, an individual player would prefer not to wear a helmet since it confers an advantage over those players wearing helmets – the better vision and hearing more than compensate for the increased risk of injury. But if all players go without helmets, it's a race to the bottom – everyone faces more risk and no one benefits. That's why, when they vote in secret ballots, hockey players almost always favour compulsory helmets.

As we document in Chapter 4, abundant evidence has shown that relative income is an important determinant of well-being – for fairness and status reasons among others. Even people who don't care about relative income per se have powerful reasons for caring where they stand in the distribution of income. Frank and Cook (1995: 142) point out that if a parent's goal is to educate her children as well as possible, she can further that goal by having higher relative income, which permits her to purchase a house in a better school district. But when all families spend more, the result is merely to bid up the prices of those houses. Half of all children will still attend bottom-half schools. Thus, a family's quest to provide a better education for its children is similar to the athlete's quest for relative advantage.

People have a variety of possible ways to get ahead of their rivals. They may invest in more or better education. They may accept riskier or less pleasant jobs, which tend to pay more, or they may work longer hours. Any one individual can increase her promotion chances by working longer hours; but when all do it, they are destined to be frustrated.

This helps to explain the attraction of collective measures to reduce the number of hours people work – legislation requiring overtime premiums for national holidays and all hours worked in excess of the standard work week, for example. Free market economists often denounce such laws, arguing that many workers would voluntarily work the longer hours that employers would have offered in the absence of overtime premiums. Yet the incentives confronting workers are similar to those confronting hockey players.

To sum up, *even if labour markets were perfectly competitive*, there is no guarantee that they would produce an efficient outcome since labour supply is influenced by considerations of relative position. The point is that 'if we worked less than we currently do, we would have less income, but then if everyone worked less, we would need less income, because the amount of income we *need* is in part determined by the amount that others have ... private incentives favour excessive work' (ibid.: 144).

> Question for your professor: Is it true that if relative posi-
> tion is important, even perfectly competitive markets lead to
> inefficient outcomes? (Right answer: Yes!)

2.6 The monopsony model of the labour market

As we've seen, the perfectly competitive labour market model (and the marginal product theory of distribution) can be made consistent with well-established empirical regularities by incorporating subsidiary theories such as those concerning fairness and status. The cost of doing so, however, is to overturn the presumption that the unregulated market leads to an efficient situation.

Many economists believe, however, that the competitive labour market model is, in any case, the wrong starting point. Like Alan Manning (2003) of the London School of Economics, they think that a 'dynamic monopsony' model would make a much better starting point, even for markets where there are many small firms. They think that it should be the default model in textbooks.

For Manning, the main problem with the textbook competitive model is that it omits critical features of the labour market, including market power. Did you notice in Figure 8.1 that if a competitive firm reduces its wages by one cent below the equilibrium wage, its entire workforce would quit? Even more implausibly, if the firm's entire workforce did quit, this would be of no great concern to the firm since it could instantly find all the replacement workers it needed by again offering the going market wage. The employer–employee relationship is symmetric, with neither being more powerful than the other. Each has the equivalent power to terminate the relationship and instantly find another job or another worker. Such a depiction is completely implausible as a description of the actual labour market.

In reality, if a firm reduced its wages by one cent below the equilibrium wage, it would not immediately lose all its workers. As Manning says (ibid.: 4), a firm 'may find that workers quit at a faster rate than before or that recruitment is more difficult, but the extreme predictions of the competitive model do not hold'.

Why don't all the workers quit at once? It's because of what are termed 'frictions' in the market. For example, when information is not free it takes time and resources to find a new job, and taking such a job might entail moving home or increased costs of commuting. Other frictions include personal preferences (such as strongly preferring a certain type of work, or attachment to one's co-workers, or a benefit offered by the job), and the firm-specific training and skills that a worker may have. As Manning says (ibid.: 4): 'The existence of frictions gives employers potential market power over their workers. The assumption that firms set wages means that they actually exercise this power.'

Frictions have long been modelled by labour economists in their research. Explicitly incorporating them allows us to see that monopsony is not the rarity that textbooks say it is. Rather, it has general applicability.

> Question for your professor: The competitive labour market model predicts that if a firm reduces its wage by one cent below the equilibrium, its entire workforce will quit. Why don't we test this prediction?

A dynamic reinterpretation of monopsony Consider the effect of frictions on the firm. If it offers a lower wage, it experiences a higher quit rate, which increases the costs of recruiting and training new employees. Job vacancies (unfilled job openings) are a pervasive phenomenon in reality, but are absent from the perfectly competitive labour market where each firm can hire all the workers it wants at the going market wage. In their discussion of the low-wage labour market, Card and Krueger (1995: 373) depict low-wage employers as fighting a constant 'war of attrition' to maintain their workforces.

We illustrate the firm's problem in Figure 8.7. In the left-hand diagram, the upward sloping line $h(W)$ shows that a firm's ability to hire new workers each month increases as its offered wage, W, increases. On the other hand, the monthly quit rate, $q(W)$, decreases as the wage increases. As a result, the absolute number of quits, which is the product of the quit rate and the size of the workforce, L, also decreases as the wage increases. This is shown as the downward-sloping line.

To maintain a workforce of L_0 employees, the firm must set the wage at $5 an hour, such that the number of new hires just balances the number of quits: $h(w) = q(w) \cdot L_0$. As the size of the workforce increases, the schedule showing

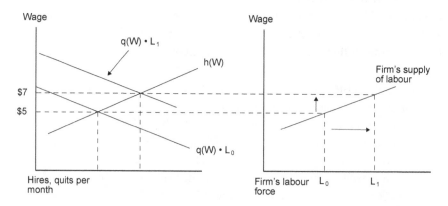

FIGURE 8.7 Derivation of a competitive firm's upward-sloping supply of labour schedule

the absolute number of quits shifts up, necessitating a higher wage. In effect, the firm faces an upward-sloping supply of labour schedule, as shown in the right-hand diagram of Figure 8.7. From that, we can generate a marginal cost of labour schedule as shown in Table 8.1 and generate a gap between marginal productivity and the wage as in the standard monopsony model (shown in Figures 8.3 and 8.4).

Does this model receive empirical support (besides the obvious factors of the coexistence of unemployment and vacancies, and the ability of firms to set wages)? It does.

First, the most direct prediction from Figure 8.7 is that larger firms pay higher wages on average. This is a strong empirical regularity (Oi and Idson 1999).

Second, a slightly more general version of the model presented in Figure 8.7 can explain a widely accepted principle in the personnel field – noted, for example, by Milkovitch and Newman (1987) – that some firms choose a 'low-wage/high-turnover' policy, and others a 'high-wage/low-turnover' policy. In this more general model, the wage offered by other firms is determined within the model itself (Card and Krueger 1995: 379). It turns out that even if workers and firms are identical to begin with, wages will end up differing systematically across firms in equilibrium.

Third, Manning (2003: ch. 7) argues that monopsony is an important cause of the gender pay gap. He cites evidence that women place a higher value than men on the non-wage aspects of a job, such as relationships with co-workers. As a result, the labour market for women is more monopsonistic than that for men, allowing employers to pay them less.

Is the dynamic monopsony model more empirically relevant than the fairness and status models? Campbell and Kamlani (1997) took the unusual step of actually asking firms what considerations were uppermost when setting their wage structure. From their survey of 184 firms, they found that their two main concerns were: (1) to avoid having their better workers quit and (2) to maintain the effort level of their workers by paying them a 'fair' wage. So the survey evidence suggests that concern over quits is at least as important as fairness. This means that firms recognize their power over the wage and the effects their choices have on turnover.

In any event, Machin and Manning (2004) suggest that the dynamic monopsony model can easily coexist with the fairness and status models. Generally speaking, since the structure of wages within the monopsonistic firm is not dictated by workers' marginal productivity, it easily explains why the wage differences between workers that do exist are often unrelated to productivity (ibid.: 383).

Many economists feel that the dynamic monopsony model is a better fit for the way labour markets actually work, and helps to explain many features of the labour market that perfect competition cannot. Moreover, it overturns the laissez-faire mantra concerning the negative impact of labour market regulation.

For example (as we showed in the first part of this chapter), the imposition of a binding minimum wage that is only moderately above the current wage will lead to employment gains in a monopsonistic market, but employment losses would result if the minimum wage is pushed up too far. This can explain why the empirical evidence concerning the effect of minimum wages is so mixed, as we discussed at length in Chapter 2.

Similarly, the formation of a union in the monopsony context creates a bilateral monopoly situation where the wage is determined by bargaining and where wage increases need not be at the expense of employment decreases. In this model, the presence of unions is likely to raise non-union wages – an outcome that is not predicted by standard theory, but is supported by the evidence (Manning 2003: ch. 12).

Question for your professor: If it is costly for workers to move between jobs, could even small firms have some degree of monopsony power?

2.7 CEO and management compensation

Standard marginal productivity arguments suggest that top-level management receive amounts equal to what they add to the net profits of their company. Since their decisions have impacts on the productivity of many workers in the company, it might be possible to justify the huge rewards they earn. Empirically, however, there are no strong or consistent relationships between CEO pay and firm size, profitability or growth, neither across industries nor over time (Finkelstein and Hambrick 1988). This explains why many textbooks emphasize tournament theory. This is the idea that the pay of top-level management, and of CEOs in particular, is like tournament prizes that increase the productivity of everyone who strives for them. This elicits more effort from the whole team of executives competing for the top job and the biggest prize. In short, this arrangement is efficient.

Tournaments might be inefficient The trouble with this argument is that winning a tournament depends on *relative* performance, and we have already established that when reward depends on relative performance, competitive markets lead to inefficient outcomes. For example, corporate management requires teamwork and cooperation, which is likely to suffer. It might even lead to attempts to sabotage rivals. Abegglen and Stalk (1985) document a conscious effort by Japanese corporations to *narrow* the difference between the pay of workers and executives, and between middle management and top-level management, believing it will increase loyalty, cohesion and, ultimately, productivity for Japanese firms.

Evidence concerning executive compensation A key prediction of tournament theory is that the larger the number of contestants (*ceteris paribus*) the larger the prize must be – for two reasons. First, since all the contestants sacrifice some of their income – it goes into the prize pool – the more contestants, the bigger the prize should be. Second, the larger the number of contestants, the lower is the probability of winning and hence the larger must the prize be to have the same incentive effect.

O'Reilly et al. (1988) reject this prediction of tournament theory. Instead, they find a strong association between CEO compensation and the compensation of those members of the board of directors whose job it is to determine the chief executive's pay. This brings up an important conflict of interest: membership of a board usually commands large fees, and while the shareholders nominally elect board members, in practice the shareholders merely ratify the choices of the CEO. So, board members are often more concerned with pleasing the CEO than with providing the fiduciary oversight that their function requires. Finally, since board members are often CEOs of other companies, you have some CEOs determining the pay of another CEO for a nice fat fee, the receipt of which is dependent on pleasing the CEO!

Trends in executive compensation When one looks at the trends in executive compensation in the USA over the last seventy years, it's apparent that there is a puzzle that needs explaining. Figure 8.8 shows that average executive pay hovered around forty times higher than average wages in the USA between 1945 and 1985. But around 1985 there was a seismic shift. Executive pay began a

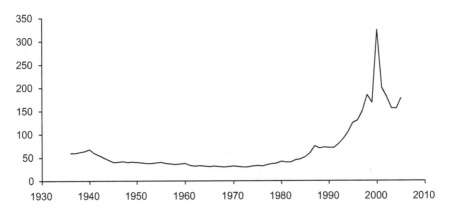

FIGURE 8.8 Average executive pay relative to average wages in the USA (includes salary, bonuses and stock-option grants) *Source*: Frydman and Saks (2008)

steep rise – briefly going stratospheric in 2001 – before 'settling back' to 160 times average wages in 2005.

Marginal productivity theory suggests executive compensation would increase only if there was an increase in the demand for CEOs or a decrease in their supply. But as Stiglitz (2003: 124) observes, 'the number of CEOs on the market didn't suddenly shrink and the productivity or performance of America's CEOs did not rise so much that they suddenly deserved 1,000 percent raises'. Nor does tournament theory do any better. The number of contestants for the top job – normally considered to be the ranks of the vice-presidents – didn't suddenly increase.

Heilbroner and Thurow (1998) suggest that it reflects changing norms of society initiated by explosive growth in the incomes of entertainment icons. CEOs may have said to themselves, 'If Michael Jordan is worth $30 million a year for playing basketball, surely I'm worth $20 million for managing AT&T.' They also suggest that the fall of the Soviet bloc in 1989 eliminated the need to present capitalism in a favourable light.

While Heilbroner and Thurow may have hit on some deep-seated causes, there is a more prosaic proximate cause: the escalation in the use of stock options as part of executive remuneration in the 1980s. Stock options give the holder the right to buy company stock in the future, at prices prevailing when the options are issued.

Ironically, stock options grew out of improvements in economic theory that recognized the importance of imperfect and asymmetric information in causing a potential conflict of interest between owners and management – a conflict referred to as the 'principal agent' problem (which we also discuss in Chapter 5).[11] This helped fuel the 'shareholder value' movement of the 1980s, which aimed to resolve the problem by making management compensation more dependent on

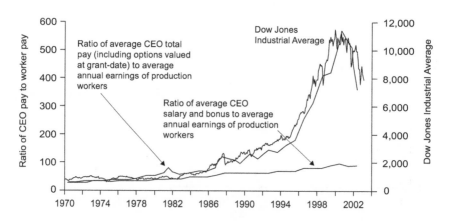

FIGURE 8.9 Dow Jones Industrial Average and CEO pay relative to average pay, 1970–2002 *Source*: Hall and Murphy (2003: 63, Figure 2)

company stock price performance. Stiglitz (2003: 120) quips: 'It was a seductive argument, but as events proved, a deeply flawed one.' The problem is that in a stock market boom, most of the increase in the value of a particular stock has nothing to do with the efforts of management. Figure 8.9 illustrates the extent to which CEO total pay was driven by the overall stock market boom as a result of the use of stock options.[12] A better system would give bonuses only to executives who do better than average (the average of firms in their industry perhaps); it might also penalize those who do worse than average.

The worst aspect of stock options as currently given is that they focus only on *ends* and ignore *means*. For example, profits and stock prices may be driven up by reducing expenditure on R&D; this might enrich management but impoverish the company longer term. Worse, management might deliberately disclose biased information, or massage the financial accounts, to drive share prices up. Stiglitz (ibid.: 116) notes: 'Enron, WorldCom, and Adelphia were only the most flagrant and well publicized of many companies where the vaunted energy and creativity of the nineties would eventually be directed less and less into new products and services, and more and more into new ways of maximizing executives' gains at unwary investors' expense.'

Stiglitz eloquently explains that the succession of corporate scandals from 2000 to 2002 had very little to do with 'a few bad apples' (George W. Bush's explanation) and everything to do with a combination of bad incentives, lax accounting rules and poor oversight. While accounting standards have been tightened up in the United States, the underlying problem of bad incentives remains – as we have seen with the worldwide financial meltdown of 2008/09.[13] (See Chapter 11 for a more detailed discussion.) As we write, the veil of legitimacy for huge bonuses seems to have been torn. Stories of public bailout money being used to pay huge bonuses actually led to armed guards being posted at the offices of AIG in March 2009 to protect employees against death threats.[14] Whether this outrage is permanent or temporary, and whether it leads to new regulations, norms or procedures, is uncertain at this stage.

Is the topic of executive pay of relatively minor importance? Our perspective is that executive pay is the litmus test that reveals important truths about the economic system. The moral of this section on executive compensation is that 'you're worth what you can get' – or perhaps that should be 'what you can get away with'.

> Question for your professor: Executive pay was about forty times average wages in the United States for forty years. But around 1985 it increased, and it is now around one hundred times average wages. Could you explain why?

2.8 Concluding comments

This chapter has covered a lot of ground. We have moved from theoretical critiques of marginal productivity theory to the empirical failings of the competitive model of the labour market. Along the way, we have fired potshots at executive pay, which we argue reveals important imperfections about the current market system.

Yet the perfectly competitive model remains the default model of the textbooks. No one can deny that it has its uses, but it also has serious shortcomings that make it deeply misleading if it is taken literally. It implies that no employer has the slightest power over wages, nor any other kind of power over employees. If the boss threatens to fire you in the morning, you can quit and have another equally good job at the same wage in the afternoon. It implies that questions of 'fairness' and 'status' are irrelevant in determining wages. Wages for different activities simply result from the impersonal market forces of supply and demand.

The predictions of the perfectly competitive model are rejected by the evidence. This is not a trivial matter, because the predictions are about important questions. Furthermore, in every case, the competitive model suggests a laissez-faire approach. It suggests – against the evidence – that minimum wages must decrease employment. It suggests that unions are a force for monopoly, with the usual negative connotations for efficiency. Neither of these predictions survives the change to a monopsony framework, where both minimum wages and unions might improve efficiency. In particular, in such a framework unions are not a market distortion, but an aspect of what John Kenneth Galbraith termed 'countervailing power'. If texts do not discuss this, they offer an anti-union bias because unions then appear to have no role other than to exert monopoly power on employers.

Suggestions for further reading

If you're interested in an up-to-date and non-technical discussion of the Cambridge capital theory controversies, we recommend the article by Cohen and Harcourt (2003). Some argue that since the neoclassical theory has been shown to be logically inconsistent, that fact is reflected in the way the textbooks discuss the determinants of the profit rate. In particular, there is no consistency of treatment. A very good discussion along these lines is found in an article by Naples and Aslanbeigui (1996).

For an excellent and not too technical discussion of the trouble with stock options, see Hall and Murphy (2003).

For a short discussion of the importance of relative position and its implications for the inefficiency of even perfectly competitive markets, see Robert Frank's short column, Frank (2005a). To see the extent to which it applies throughout society, Frank and Cook's 1995 book, *The Winner-Take-All Society*, offers a pleasant and quick read.

On monopsony, one can't do better than read Manning (2003). Non-specialists, however, are advised to stick to the introduction and conclusion of the book.

Finally, Heilbroner and Thurow's *Economics Explained* (1998) is a nice introduction to economics that discusses the distribution of wealth as well as the distribution of income.

9 | Government, taxation and the (re)distribution of income: is a just society just too expensive?

'The people who own the country ought to govern it.' John Jay, first Chief Justice of the US Supreme Court[1]

'The average "owner" among the wealthiest Americans possessed an amount of wealth that was more than sixteen thousand times larger than that of the average household.' Edward Wolff and Ajit Zacharias (2007: 65)

What should governments do? This question is a normative one. It assumes that social goals exist, such as an efficient use of society's resources and an equitable distribution of the goods and services that society produces, and that governments should act to further these goals.

Governments have four main roles. First, governments maintain a legal system within which people can make contracts and have them enforced – a precondition for modern economic life. Second, because the market economy fails to allocate resources efficiently for many reasons, governments have a role in trying to fix these 'market failures'. Dealing with externalities (the subject of Chapter 7) and public goods is a prominent example. Third, because the economy as a whole is potentially unstable, governments can play an important role in stabilizing the overall level of economic activity and keeping unemployment low. This is the domain of macroeconomic policy. Fourth, because there is no reason to expect that the market economy alone will produce an equitable distribution of income among individuals, governments can use taxes, transfers of cash and the direct provision of goods and services to create a more equitable distribution of income and consumption. This chapter examines this last role of government.

I THE STANDARD TEXT

I.I The costs of taxation

Taxation is costly not only because it is costly for government to collect the revenues and for individuals and business to comply with the tax law, but because it influences economic decisions. These include decisions by households about what and how much to buy and how much to save, and decisions by firms about what to produce and how and where to produce those things.

If the decisions of consumers and firms in the absence of taxes would lead to an efficient allocation of resources, then taxes must cause inefficiency if they change those decisions. We saw this in the analysis of an excise tax using the supply and demand framework in Chapter 3. The result was a net loss to society of producing less of the taxed good. This net loss occurs because some mutually beneficial exchanges no longer take place – assuming a perfectly competitive market and no externalities. A similar analysis can be done for any kind of tax. As long as taxes influence choices that would otherwise be optimal, they create 'efficiency losses'.

1.2 Taxes: an international comparison

The best single way to compare taxes across countries is to express total tax revenues collected by all levels of government to the value of the country's total production, or gross domestic product (GDP), as shown in Table 9.1 for the countries of the Organisation for Economic Co-operation and Development (OECD). Clearly, countries differ considerably in their overall levels of taxation. The other side of the coin is that they differ in terms of the goods and services provided by the state.

TABLE 9.1 Taxation as a percentage of GDP, OECD countries, 2005

Country	Taxes (% of GDP)	Country	Taxes (% of GDP)
Sweden	50.7	Germany	34.8
Denmark	50.3	Portugal	34.8
Belgium	45.4	Poland	34.3
France	44.1	Canada	33.4
Finland	44	Turkey	32.3
Norway	43.7	Slovak Republic	31.6
Austria	42.1	Australia	30.9
Iceland	41.4	Ireland	30.6
Italy	41	Switzerland	29.7
Netherlands	39.1	Japan	27.4
Luxembourg	38.6	Greece	27.3
Czech Republic	37.8	United States	27.3
New Zealand	37.8	Korea	25.5
Hungary	37.2	Mexico	19.9
United Kingdom	36.5	EU average	39.7
Spain	35.8	OECD average	36.2

Source: Organisation for Economic Co-operation and Development (2008a: 58–9)
Note: Averages for the EU and the OECD are unweighted averages.

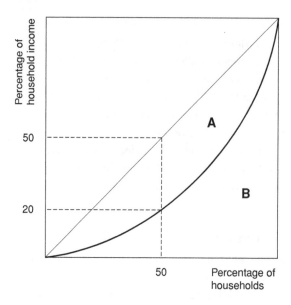

FIGURE 9.1 The Lorenz curve

1.3 The distribution of income and wealth

Countries are usually compared using per-person average income. Because of inequality, however, we need to know something about the distribution of income and of wealth to judge how a society is doing in terms of equity.

The distribution of income Household income is the focus of attention because it is the basic consumer unit. Income can be measured in different ways. 'Before-tax market income' includes wages and salaries and income from savings (dividends, interest, capital gains). Alternatively, 'disposable income' is market income plus cash transfers from government minus income taxes and other direct taxes on wages and salaries (e.g. premiums to national pension plans or for unemployment insurance). Comparing the two allows us to see some of the effects of government on the distribution of income.

Suppose, as in Figure 9.1, households are lined up on the horizontal axis from the lowest income on the left to the highest income on the right. The vertical axis shows the percentage shares of total household income that various groupings of households have. In this example, the poorest 50 per cent of households have 20 per cent of total income. If household incomes were equally distributed, those households would have 50 per cent of total income, the amount shown on the 45-degree line. The gap between the points showing actual household incomes (called the Lorenz curve) and this reference line indicates the nature and extent of income inequality.

Income inequality is usually summarized in a single number to aid in comparing inequality over time and across countries. One simple way is to calculate the ratio of the shares of total income held by the top 10 or 20 per cent of

TABLE 9.2 Measures of income inequality

Country	Top 10% to bottom 10%	Top 20% to bottom 20%	Gini coefficient
Some OECD countries			
Denmark	8.1	4.3	0.247
Japan	4.5	3.4	0.249
Sweden	6.2	4	0.250
Norway	6.1	3.9	0.258
Finland	5.6	3.8	0.269
Hungary	5.5	3.8	0.269
Germany	6.9	4.3	0.283
Austria	6.9	4.4	0.291
Netherlands	9.2	5.1	0.309
Korea, South	7.8	4.7	0.316
Canada	9.4	5.5	0.326
France	9.1	5.6	0.327
Belgium	8.2	4.9	0.330
Ireland	9.4	5.6	0.343
Poland	8.8	5.6	0.345
Spain	10.3	6	0.347
Australia	12.5	7	0.352
Italy	11.6	6.5	0.360
United Kingdom	13.8	7.2	0.360
New Zealand	12.5	6.8	0.362
Portugal	15	8	0.385
United States	15.9	8.4	0.408
Mexico	24.6	12.8	0.461
Some non-OECD countries			
India	8.6	5.6	0.368
Russia	12.7	7.6	0.399
Nigeria	17.8	9.7	0.437
China (excluding Hong Kong)	21.6	12.2	0.469
Venezuela	48.3	16	0.482
Chile	33	15.7	0.549
Brazil	51.3	21.8	0.570
South Africa	33.1	17.9	0.578
Colombia	63.8	25.3	0.586

Note: Values are for income or expenditure shares. Dates of underlying survey data vary from 1990s, to early 2000s.

Source: UNDP (2007): 281–4, Table 15

households with the bottom 10 or 20 per cent, as shown in Table 9.2. This, however, omits information about the households between them. The most commonly used measure that summarizes the entire income distribution is the Gini coefficient. This is the ratio of the area between the Lorenz curve and the

45-degree line (marked 'A' in Figure 9.1) and the entire area under the 45-degree line (A + B in the figure). So the Gini coefficient = A/(A + B). It's zero if income is equally distributed; it's 1 if one household has everything. Table 9.2 also shows estimates of the Gini coefficient for a selection of countries. With the exception of India, the developing countries shown have much higher income inequality than the developed countries. Among the OECD countries, there is considerable variation in inequality, with the United States being the most unequal.

The distribution of wealth This is typically ignored in the texts, but note the differences between wealth and income. A household's wealth is the value of its assets, net of its debt. Wealth is important because it offers economic security, status and power (including borrowing power), things not adequately captured by measures of income alone. Similarly, debt adds to economic insecurity (Wolff and Zacharias 2007: 66–7).

TABLE 9.3 Distribution of household net worth

Country	Share of total wealth held by			Percent of house-holds with zero or negative wealth	Gini co-efficient
	Top 10%	Top 5%	Top 1%		
Italy, 2002	42	29	11	10	0.61
United Kingdom, 2000	45	30	10	17	0.66
Finland, 1998	45	31	13	17	0.68
Canada, 1999	53	37	15	23	0.75
Germany, 2002	55	38	16	38	0.80
United States, PSID 2001	64	49	25	24	0.81
United States, SCF 2001	71	58	33	25	0.84
Sweden, 2002	58	41	18	32	0.89

Note: The definition of net worth excludes business equity. Including it reduces the Gini coefficient, sometimes significantly. (See Organisation for Economic Co-operation and Development 2008b, Table 10.6.) For the United States, PSID is Panel Survey of Income Dynamics; SCF is the Survey of Consumer Finances.

Source: Organisation for Economic Co-operation and Development (2008b): 263, Table 10.3

Wealth is typically distributed even more unequally than income, as Tables 9.2 and 9.3 show. Many households have zero or negative wealth (i.e. their debts exceed their assets).[2] The United States stands out among these countries as having a particularly large share of wealth held by the top groups within the population.

The Gini coefficient for the United States (equal to 0.81) is explained by Wolff and Zacharias (ibid.: 66) with this analogy: imagine dividing an 'aggregate economic "pie" worth $100 among a hypothetical group of ten families … suppose that one family got $91, while the remaining families received only $1 each. The Gini coefficient of this distribution is 0.81.'

1.4 Poverty

Poverty can be defined in absolute or relative terms. In the United States, the official poverty line uses an absolute measure of poverty that is not adjusted for changes in average living standards.[3] Some textbooks accept this approach. Others reject this and argue for relative approaches such as a definition of poverty as income that is less than half that of the median household.[4] (The median household is the middle one in a ranking from richest to poorest.) The justification for using a relative measure of poverty is that 'necessities' are culturally determined. Lack of indoor plumbing or hot water may not be out of the ordinary in a poor country, but it would be in a rich one. Hence, as community standards increase, those left behind experience a feeling of relative deprivation, or poverty, even if they experience no absolute change in their condition. The growing gap between themselves and others causes them to experience 'social exclusion' as opposed to 'social inclusion'.

Question for your professor: If poverty is defined with respect to the income that others have, this indicates that well-being is determined by relative income, not just a person's own income in isolation. Shouldn't this idea and its implications [e.g. as explored in Chapter 7 of this book] be mentioned elsewhere in the text?

Poverty among families with children is sometimes viewed with particular concern because it violates the generally accepted principle of equality of opportunity. Table 9.4 shows the enormous range of variation across the rich countries; the child poverty rate is nine times higher in the United States than in Denmark.

There are useful absolute measures of poverty and deprivation, however, which have become more widely used as a result of arguments such as those of Amartya Sen (1999), which stress the importance of also measuring people's capabilities to lead a decent life. Fundamental to this are people's abilities to avoid premature death and to receive adequate nutrition. These are reflected in the development indicators reported by the World Bank (2008: 354) in its annual World Development Report. These include the prevalence of malnutrition of children under age five and the under-five mortality rate. One of the United Nation's Millennium Development Goals is to reduce under-five mortality by two-thirds between 1990 and 2015.[5] Other goals for 1990–2015 include other absolute measures of poverty: halving the proportion of people whose income is less than US$1/day and halving the proportion who suffer from hunger.

TABLE 9.4 Percentage of children in households with less than half of median household income, circa 2000

Country	%	Country	%
Denmark	2.4	Hungary	13.1
Finland	3.4	Austria	13.3
Norway	3.6	Canada	13.6
Sweden	3.6	Japan	14.3
Belgium	6.7	New Zealand	14.6
Switzerland	6.8	Poland	15.6
Czech Republic	7.2	Spain	15.6
France	7.3	Ireland	15.7
Netherlands	9.0	Italy	15.7
Germany	10.9	United Kingdom	16.2
Australia	11.6	United States	21.7
Greece	12.4	AVERAGE	11.2

Note: Country data range from 1999–2001. Household income is adjusted for household composition. The overall average is not weighted by population.

Source: Bradshaw et al. (2006, Appendix Table 1)

The idea can also be applied to developed countries. The Human Poverty Index in the United Nations Development Programme's Human Development Reports (e.g. UNDP 2007) includes the probability of survival to age sixty, a measure of functional literacy and a measure of long-term unemployment (attempting to capture an aspect of social exclusion).

1.5 Income redistribution

'Should economic policy makers always strive to achieve economic efficiency? Well, not quite, because efficiency is not the only criterion by which to evaluate an economy. People also care about issues of fairness or equity. And there is typically a trade-off between equity and efficiency: policies that promote equity often come at a cost of decreased efficiency in the economy, and vice versa.' Krugman and Wells (2005: 15)

How much redistribution of income should take place is a normative question about which economists have no more ethical expertise than other citizens. What they hope to contribute is a framework for thinking clearly about the question. The benefits of income redistribution are greater 'equity', or social justice. The costs are presumably less efficiency. This trade-off is illustrated by Arthur Okun's famous 'leaky bucket' metaphor which we referred to in Chapter 1: redistributing income is like carrying water from the rich to the poor using a leaky bucket – the result may be more equitable, but comes at a cost of water spilled on the ground, normally assumed to be wasted.

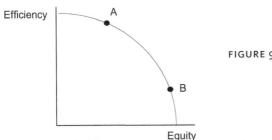

FIGURE 9.2 The equity–efficiency trade-off

The set-up is an application of the familiar logic of comparing marginal benefits and marginal costs. The general idea of the trade-off is sketched out in Figure 9.2. So that we have something measurable on the horizontal axis, let greater 'equity' mean less income inequality. Thus to get more equity, one has to accept less efficiency. Lower average incomes are the price of reducing income inequality.

As drawn, the line shows diminishing returns: when equity is low (and inequality is high), as at A, equity improvements have relatively little cost in terms of economic efficiency. The leaks in Okun's 'leaky bucket' are small. Further reductions in inequality and poverty require sacrificing increasing amounts of efficiency, and hence income. The bucket gets leakier and leakier.

The leaks are chiefly the adverse effects on incentives as redistribution takes place. Redistribution is not just cutting up the 'economic pie' in different slices; it affects the size of the pie itself. For example, it may affect the work effort of those who pay taxes and those who get transfers. A certain amount of inequality is necessary to maintain individual incentives to produce income.

According to the official version, the job of the economist is not to say where on this trade-off society should be. Rather the job of the economist is just to do positive economics: to inform public debate, and if possible to think of ways of improving the trade-off. Where a society ends up depends on individual preferences about social justice and how society's political institutions translate these into a collective choice about taxes and transfers and other measures affecting the distribution of income.[6]

2 THE ANTI-TEXT

Our goal for the remainder of the chapter will be to make a case for the following claims:

1 The texts contain a subtle bias against government action in general and against redistribution in particular. Economic inequality and issues of equity get relatively little treatment compared with the problems of seeing that resources are used efficiently.

2 Both economic theory and the empirical evidence support the view that there

is no significant equity–efficiency trade-off, if policies are well designed. Poverty and inequality in many countries can be greatly reduced without any cost in terms of economic growth.

3 A great deal of evidence (entirely ignored by the textbooks) shows that social and economic inequalities within societies are responsible for large inequalities in health and life expectancies that cost millions of people many years of life.

2.1 The subtle bias against government and against redistribution

In a perceptive study of the rhetoric of the textbooks, David George points out that given the order of topics in the texts, government 'tends to be treated as an entity emerging only after the private sector has established itself' (1990: 863). The government then 'interferes' with markets for private goods.

With taxes, the texts focus attention on how the 'burden' will be shared and on technical explanations of the efficiency cost of taxes. (Ironically, the goods usually chosen to illustrate the 'efficiency loss' of excise taxes are goods that have externalities. Hence, there may not be any efficiency loss at all, as discussed in Chapter 7.)[7] The benefits from increased government spending that taxes make possible are made much less clear. In a book already weighted towards the attainment of efficiency in the use of scarce resources, what choice is the reader invited to make when it comes to the equity–efficiency trade-off?

The emphasis on the inefficiency of taxes reinforces the examples given in the texts in the supply and demand applications (reviewed in Chapter 3). They are typically ones in which the government appears to mess things up: minimum wages increase unemployment, rent controls create apartment shortages, subsidies create inefficiencies and taxes create efficiency losses. This might have been what former US president Ronald Reagan was referring to when he said: 'The nine most terrifying words in the English language are "I'm from the government and I'm here to help"' (Vitullo-Martin and Moskin 1994: 130).

The order of topics in the texts almost invariably buries the discussion of government, taxation and redistribution deep in the book. (In fact it's in the same relative location as we have placed this chapter given that we decided to parallel the structure of the typical text.) We suspect that many economics courses never quite manage to get to the topic.

This placement of topics in textbooks reflects authors' judgements about the relative importance of topics, or, given the profit-oriented nature of textbooks, it reflects their judgement about what other economics professors consider important. The main part of the microeconomics textbooks is spent developing an imaginary world of perfect competition in which resources are used efficiently, and then comparing that with other market structures. This can only reflect a value judgement that income distribution and the government's role in redistribution are not very important.

A different value judgement is possible. In the first words written in the *Journal of Radical Political Economics*, John Weeks wrote:

> The overriding reality of the American economy is inequality – inequality of income, inequality of power, inequality with regard to the ability to determine one's life. Inequality is what economics should be all about. But, in fact, economics as it is taught and practiced by economists deals very little with inequality. (1969: 1)

This remains true today, with the exception that in economics research there has been a greatly increased interest in inequality, perhaps because inequality is growing so rapidly in some countries, particularly the United States.

We made the case (in Chapter 4) that a person's situation relative to others strongly influences well-being. Growing income and wealth inequalities fuel the wasteful 'conspicuous consumption' arms race that we examined in Chapter 7. We'll see more evidence shortly of the damage that inequality causes. So why is this chapter buried towards the end of the book? Why is redistribution viewed as relatively unimportant? John Weeks believed that it was just self-interest: 'our profession gains disproportionately from the existing social and economic order. This is why economics provides no guide to an alternative social and economic system in which inequality, acquisitiveness, and exploitation would be eliminated' (ibid.: 1).

He might be right, but our concern here is simply to illuminate the value judgements, not to explain them. Gunnar Myrdal (1969) dismissed any pretence that social scientists might make about their 'objectivity' and pointed out that value judgements must permeate their work. Instead, he advocated making one's value judgements explicit so the reader would be aware of them and could decide whether to accept them. Sadly, his advice has gone largely unheeded and readers must be alert to detect hidden value judgements on their own.

Questions for your professor: Why does the text give so little attention to economic inequality? Does that reflect a value judgement that it's not very important?

The Pareto principle: when is 'society' better off? Let's consider a specific example of a hidden value judgement. Introductory textbooks rarely give a careful and explicit discussion about how we can think about the welfare of society as a whole. 'When professional economists think about economic policies, they generally start with the principle that a change is good if it makes someone better off without making anyone else worse off. That idea ... is referred to as the Pareto principle,' explains Harvard professor Martin Feldstein (1999: 34).

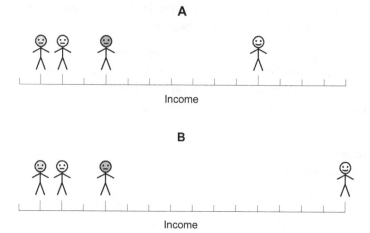

FIGURE 9.3 Income distribution and equality

When it's not possible to make anyone better off without making someone else worse off, we have a 'Pareto optimal' outcome. If 'better off' and 'worse off' refer to individuals' utilities, determined as they see fit, at first glance this seems innocuous. As Colander et al. (2006: 356) put it, 'It's hard to object to the notion of Pareto optimal policies because, by definition, they improve life for some people while hurting no one.'

But, as Marglin (2008: 180) notes, 'this appears to offer a way of talking about societal well-being without invoking value judgements', yet 'value judgements continue to be present, hidden in the foundational assumptions that social well-being consists of satisfying the rational, calculating individual's self-interested pursuit of consumption'.

If we accept that value judgement, and if we also accept the claim that individuals' utilities can't be compared directly, how do we implement the Pareto principle to think about whether an economic policy is desirable? As discussed in Chapter 4, the texts assume that utility goes up if income goes up (with prices unchanged) and, despite the evidence, slip in an unstated assumption that no one cares about what others have.[8] Then the Pareto principle becomes: *'If some people's incomes go up and other people's incomes are unchanged, society is better off.'*

It's easy to overlook the assumption that the income distribution doesn't matter, that it's irrelevant whether a policy increases inequality or not. Consider situations A and B in Figure 9.3. The only difference between them is that one person's income has gone up in B compared with A. If people care about how their incomes compare to those of others, the people whose absolute incomes remain the same will judge themselves worse off in B than in A. If so, the Pareto principle can't be used to say that B is better than A because some people's utilities have decreased.

Rather than sweeping the question of rising inequality under the rug, Martin Feldstein confronts it in an interesting way. He writes,

> I am interested only in evaluating changes that increase the incomes of high-income individuals without decreasing the incomes of others. Such a change clearly satisfies the common-sense Pareto principle: It is good because it makes some people better off without making anyone else worse off. I think such a change should be regarded as good even though it increases inequality. (1999: 34)

Feldstein has neatly substituted the original 'common-sense Pareto principle' that refers to utilities for the version that refers to incomes. He does this while going on to acknowledge that some people 'regard increasing the income of the wealthy as a "bad thing", even if that increased income does not come at any-one else's expense'. How does Feldstein conclude that even when some people feel worse off there has been a Pareto improvement? He does it by labelling such malcontents 'spiteful egalitarians' whose views should be rejected. They simply don't count as members of society! Given that concern about one's relative position seems to be a part of human nature and not some moral defect, Feldstein's position is peculiar. It is also a politically expedient position at a time when incomes at the top soared while the incomes for the rest of the US population largely stagnated.

When the texts offer the Pareto principle (or words to that effect) and define whether people are 'better off' and 'worse off' in terms of changes in individual incomes, they are agreeing with Feldstein. They just don't state the consequences as openly and candidly as he did.

There is evidence of how people actually think about this Feldstein/textbook version of the Pareto principle. Yoram Amiel and Frank Cowell investigate this through a series of carefully constructed surveys, asking people to evaluate situations like that illustrated in Figure 9.3. They noted that it 'is perfectly reasonable to suppose that ... well-being may be affected by other people's incomes' (1999: 54). They found that in situations like Figure 9.3, the greater the addition to the income of the 'rich' person, the smaller the proportion of respondents who considered that the society as a whole was made better off (ibid.: 64).[9]

The 'Pareto optimal' outcomes available to society depend on the initial distribution of wealth and income. Each possible distribution leads to demands and supplies that result in a particular 'Pareto efficient' allocation of society's re-sources. A highly unequal society might see a lot of resources devoted to security systems to protect the mansions of the rich; a society where wealth was initially distributed equally might devote resources to universal childcare and healthcare. Both outcomes could be 'Pareto efficient', but not equally desirable.[10]

In any case, given the distribution of income and wealth, the scope for Pareto gains is virtually non-existent. Economic policy typically results in some people being made better off and some worse off. We'll discuss in the next chapter how economists judge society as a whole to be better off or worse off in such situations.

> Questions for your professor: If a policy increases the incomes of the rich without decreasing any other people's incomes, would that be a desirable policy? What does the text say about such policies?

The rhetoric of reaction Claims of an equity–efficiency trade-off fit neatly into a pattern identified by Albert Hirschman in *The Rhetoric of Reaction*, his study of the arguments used over the last 200 years against the development of civil, political, social and economic rights. What we're interested in here are arguments against the 'welfare state', which

> ... in the twentieth century extended the concept of citizenship to the *social and economic* sphere by recognizing that minimal conditions of education, health, economic well-being, and security are basic to the life of a civilized being as well as to the meaningful exercise of the civil and political attributes of citizenship. (Hirschman 1991: 2)

The welfare state programmes typically include: a guaranteed minimum income of some kind (insurance against destitution); cash transfers to provide greater security in the event of illness, unemployment and old age; and equality of access to certain social services as a right of citizenship, regardless of ability to pay. These include public education and public health services, but also possibly housing and personal social services (Gough 1987).

Hirschman identifies several claims made in opposition to welfare state programmes. One is that 'the proposed change, though perhaps desirable in itself, involves unacceptable costs or consequences of one sort or another' (1991: 81). Arthur Okun's influential book on the equity–efficiency trade-off appeared just after the economic turmoil of the early 1970s. At this time, the argument against the welfare state became 'that it was at odds with economic growth' and 'would jeopardize the conspicuous economic successes of the postwar period' (ibid.: 115). Okun himself was no reactionary, and was optimistic that if his leaky bucket 'is filled in reasonable ways' then 'it can still hold plenty when it reaches the deprived' (1975: 101). This makes the question an empirical one: how leaky is Okun's bucket if 'filled in reasonable ways'?

2.2 The equity–efficiency trade-off, reconsidered

Does it make sense to talk about an 'equity–efficiency' trade-off? Julian LeGrand points out that 'efficiency' by itself is not a primary social objective like

"YOU GET WHAT YOU PAY FOR"

© Andy Singer

'equity'; it's just a means to an end, namely attaining primary social objectives, whatever those might be. We have efficiency if it's not possible to get closer to achieving one social objective without getting farther away from attaining another.

In the context of an 'equity–efficiency' trade-off, 'efficiency' seems to mean something else, such as maximizing the value of total production or its rate of growth. But LeGrand raises a fundamental point: increasing production or its growth rate is also not a primary social objective. It is only useful if it contributes to some primary objective, like a measure of what he calls 'aggregate want-satisfaction' (LeGrand 1991: 30). If there is a trade-off, it is between primary objectives like aggregate well-being and equity. But that is not the trade-off that appears in the texts or in the economics literature.

LeGrand is surely right in suggesting that production and its growth have been elevated 'to the status of a primary objective' because it's assumed that 'increases in production lead to increases in individuals' utilities' (ibid.: 31). We saw the dubious evidence for this assumption in Chapter 4 when considering subjective well-being in wealthy countries. But LeGrand points out another problem: 'the utility *costs* of increased production should also be taken into account. Yet these are frequently neglected' (ibid.: 31).

He illustrates with an example of a simple policy change that induces a person to work more and so to earn more income, while taking less leisure time (ibid.: 35–6).[11] The person ends up with more money income, but less utility. It looks as if 'efficiency' has been increased, but well-being has gone down because of the reduction in leisure. LeGrand argues that it would be better to separate 'the idea of efficiency from that of economic growth and to discuss the issue of any trade-offs between growth and equity explicitly, rather than obscuring the issue by reference to efficiency' (ibid.: 32).

The demise of the equity–efficiency trade-off in theory

'Equity is complementary to the pursuit of long-term prosperity. Greater equity is doubly good for poverty reduction. It tends to favour sustained overall development, and it delivers increased opportunities to the poorest groups in a society.' François Bourguignon, chief economist, World Bank (World Bank 2005)

The economists who participated in the development of the advanced welfare states of northern Europe in the middle of the twentieth century learned from experience its growth-enhancing effects. Gunnar Myrdal explained that welfare state policies were created despite the belief that they would result in lower growth. But then 'the idea emerged that welfare reforms, instead of being costly for a society, were actually laying the basis for a more steady and rapid economic growth'. Investing in housing, nutrition, health and education and redistributing income to families with children, especially to underprivileged families, pays off by avoiding future costs and increasing future productivity (Myrdal 1973: 40–41).

By the late 1980s, this view was reflected in the 'new growth theory'. Many of these ideas about 'endogenous growth' stress the importance of human capital (as reflected in education and skills), and the importance for growth of the 'intergenerational transmission of human capital' – a fancy way of saying that children's prospects are importantly influenced by their parents' socio-economic situation.[12] Those models that examine explicitly the effects of inequality on growth predict that lower inequality should be associated with higher long-term growth (Osberg 1995).

This touches on an important distinction between 'static efficiency' and 'dynamic efficiency' that we mentioned in Chapter 6 in the context of Schumpeter and Baumol's ideas about the dynamic efficiency of oligopolistic industries. The textbook story of the efficiency loss due to taxation is about 'static' inefficiency; reducing taxes and the inefficiencies associated with them would give a one time gain in income. An economy that is 'dynamically efficient' is one that optimizes its growth rate. If the statically inefficient taxes are used to reduce inequality and that, in turn, increases the rate of economic growth even slightly over time, then the result can be dynamically efficient. The higher growth rates eventually lead to much higher levels of income (Osberg 1995).

The evidence about an equity–efficiency trade-off Table 9.1 shows that taxes amount to half of Denmark's total production; Table 9.2 shows its comparatively low levels of economic inequality, while Table 9.4 shows that Denmark has almost eliminated child poverty. In Figure 4.4 we saw that Denmark is among the world's most prosperous countries and its people among the happiest. How can a place like Denmark exist if there is a serious trade-off between efficiency and equity?

While a lot can be learned from the experience of places like Denmark or Gunnar Myrdal's Sweden, economists also like to consider the combined experience of many countries. The endogenous growth theories were developed at the same time as enough data had accumulated to make statistical examination of a large sample of countries possible (Lindert 2004a). Studies examined the growth–inequality relationship looking at groups of countries, while taking into account the many other factors that economic theory suggests will also influence growth (Persson and Tabellini 1994; Alesina and Rodrik 1994; Barro 2000).

In reviewing such studies, Sarah Voitchovsky (2005: 274) writes: 'The debate continues ... as to whether the ultimate effect of overall income inequality on growth is positive, negative, or not significant. Nevertheless, it seems that studies' conclusions depend notably on the econometric method employed, and the data considered.' This is not surprising in light of our discussion in Chapter 2 of the difficulties of conclusive empirical testing. She points out that ideas about the growth-retarding effects of inequality centre around inequality at the bottom of the income distribution, while inequality at the top end of the distribution is sometimes seen as facilitating growth. Testing the effects of income inequality using a single measure of inequality such as the Gini coefficient misses these differences and looks only at some average of the effects (ibid.: 273–4).

Instead, she examines a group of relatively high-income countries using data on their income distributions. She finds 'that growth is facilitated by an income distribution that is compressed in the lower part of the distribution, but not so at the top end. In this view, redistributive policies – such as progressive taxation and social welfare – are likely to facilitate growth through their impact on the bottom of the distribution, and to inhibit growth through their impact on the top of the distribution' (ibid.: 290). The net effect remains unclear.

Andrew Sharpe concludes that,

> it is probably imprudent to make the case for a more equitable society on the basis of the efficiency effects of increased equality. The empirical evidence of the positive impact of greater equality on efficiency is still inconclusive. In any case, for many a more equitable society is a goal in itself and any positive efficiency effect is an added bonus. Equally, there is little conclusive evidence of major negative effects on efficiency from equality. (2003: S13)

In an important study, Peter Lindert examines the relationship between the social transfers (unemployment insurance, income support, pensions, public healthcare spending, housing subsidies) that are a central part of the welfare state and economic growth. Looking at the experience of about twenty OECD countries between the early 1960s and the mid-1990s, he found no significant effect of social transfers on economic growth (Lindert 2004b: vol. 2, ch. 18).

'It is well-known that higher taxes and transfers reduce productivity. Well known
– but unsupported by statistics or history.' Peter Lindert (ibid.: vol. 1, p. 227)

Why is the equity–efficiency trade-off lingering on in the textbooks if, in fact,
there is so little evidence for it, at least within the range of income inequality
that we actually observe? Peter Lindert explains that '[t]he source is ideology
and a valid theory that if governments were run badly, they would drag down
economic growth'. It is true that 'if governments did nothing but tax people on
the basis of their productivity and give it to other people who were unproductive – encouraging them to be unproductive with those grants – it would make
everybody work less, take less risk, and innovate less' (2004a: 7).

The evidence seems to show that, on average, governments haven't been run
badly. More social spending to attain more egalitarian outcomes does not seem
to have come at any significant cost in terms of either the level of per-person
incomes or their rate of growth. It provides a nice counter-example to what is
supposed to be a central truth of economics: 'There's no such thing as a free
lunch' because there are *always* trade-offs. If society collectively wants more of
one good (greater income equality) it must give up some other good (the size
of the 'economic pie').[13]

The research we've described suggests that the real equity–efficiency trade-off
may look something like Figure 9.4. Over a wide range of income inequality,
there is essentially no relationship between equity and efficiency, as reflected
by the growth rate. Beyond that range, for degrees of equality or inequality not
actually observed, the empirical evidence doesn't say anything directly.

So is the trade-off featured in the textbooks really a myth? Perhaps it's about

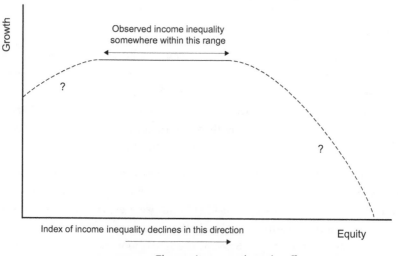

FIGURE 9.4 The equity–growth trade-off

as much a myth as the 'law' of diminishing marginal returns. As we saw in Chapter 5, there are theoretical ideas to support the possible existence of diminishing marginal returns, but in actual practice good management of production seems to be able to make it irrelevant in practice in the great majority of firms. The same can be said for the equity–efficiency trade-off: there are some theoretical ideas that would suggest its existence at some (perhaps very low) level of income inequality (as sketched out in the downward-sloping part of the curve in Figure 9.4), but it is irrelevant in practice.

Questions for your professor: What is the evidence for a significant equity-efficiency trade-off? If there is a significant trade-off, why haven't the high-tax welfare states in Europe experienced low growth and low average living standards compared with lower-tax countries?

2.3 The pervasive costs of inequality

'Social injustice is killing people on a grand scale.' Commission on the Social Determinants of Health, World Health Organization (CSDH 2008: 26)

We've seen earlier, particularly in Chapter 4, evidence of the importance of relative position for individuals' feelings of well-being. But the focus of textbook economics is on the individual removed from social context. As a result, it largely ignores the question of individuals' relative position in society except for admitting its existence briefly by defining poverty as a relative phenomenon. Yet a fundamental feature of human (and most other primate) societies is their social hierarchy and the acute awareness everyone has of their place in it.[14]

The social gradient of health Those at the top of the hierarchy experience not only feelings of greater well-being (as we saw in Chapter 4), but also significantly better health than those at the bottom. Epidemiologist Sir Michael Marmot, one of the foremost researchers in this area, explains that 'these social inequalities in health … are not a footnote to the "real" causes of ill-health in countries that are no longer poor; they are the heart of the matter'. He points out that in places of great inequality, such as the area around Washington, DC, there is a twenty-year difference in life expectancies between the poor and the rich – a gap as big as that between men in Japan and in Kazakhstan (2004: 2). Men in an affluent area in Glasgow live to an average of eighty-two; men in a poor area of the city average fifty-four years (CSDH 2008: 32). In Canada, there is a five-year gap in men's life expectancies between the top fifth and the bottom fifth of the income distribution and a two-year gap for women (Health Disparities

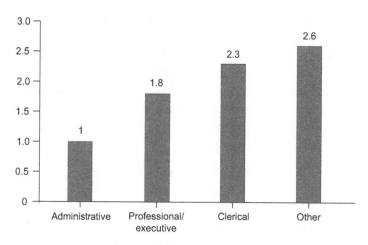

FIGURE 9.5 Relative risk of CHD death excluding other risk factors
Source: Adapted from Marmot et al. (1978: Fig. 3)

Task Group 2004: 1).[15] Such gaps in life expectancies within affluent countries are not unusual, but they are largely preventable.

While the health of those at the top and those at the bottom of the social hierarchy can differ greatly, the health of everyone in between is also affected by their socio-economic position. Figure 9.5 illustrates one example, the results of a major study of coronary heart disease (CHD) among British civil servants. Those in the professional/executive grade had a 1.8 times greater chance of having CHD than those just one rung above them in the hierarchy, the policy-makers in the top administrative grade. The lower the grade in the civil service, the higher the risk of CHD.

The idea of socio-economic inequality as a primary determinant of ill-health may seem surprising. Most public debate about health policy centres on how well the healthcare system works, and issues of public health regulations (e.g. food and water quality) and individual behaviour (such as anti-smoking campaigns). Yet there is ample evidence to show that the effects of socio-economic inequality are deadly. If African-Americans had the same death rates as whites, there would have been 886,000 fewer deaths between 1991 and 2000 in the United States (CSDH 2008: 30).

While average life expectancies don't differ much between wealthy countries, within those countries life expectancies differ systematically and significantly between different groups of people. People's income, their occupation and the social status attached to it, the degree of economic security and control over work and home life, and their social connectedness (all of which are inter-related) are all important determinants of individual health. Deficiencies in these things result in increased chances of poor mental and physical health and premature death. This is the so-called *social gradient of health* – the idea

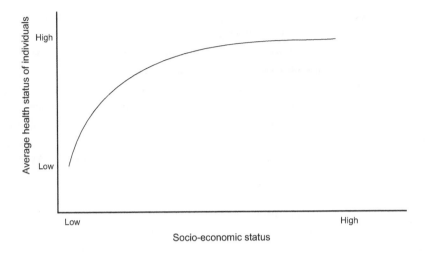

FIGURE 9.6 The social gradient of health

that average health and life expectancy decline systematically the lower people are in the social hierarchy.

In general, the relationship is not linear, but resembles a field hockey stick, as shown in Figure 9.6 (Health Disparities Task Group 2004: 4). Average health status is systematically lower the lower one's socio-economic status, but falls more rapidly at lower levels.

In their book for the World Health Organization, *The Social Determinants of Health: The solid facts*, Richard Wilkinson and Michael Marmot review both the evidence of the social gradient of health and its policy implications. They ask:

> Why do these psychosocial factors affect physical health? In emergencies, our hormones and nervous system prepare us to deal with an immediate physical threat by triggering the fight or flight response: raising the heart rate, mobilizing stored energy, diverting blood to muscles and increasing alertness ... [T]urning on the stress response diverts energy and resources away from many physiological processes important to long-term health maintenance. Both the cardiovascular and immune systems are affected. For brief periods, this does not matter; but if people feel tense too often or the tension goes on too long, they become vulnerable to a wide range of conditions including infections, diabetes, high blood pressure, heart attack, stroke, depression and aggression. (2003: 12–13)

The effects of socio-economic inequality begin before birth and have life-long consequences. Wilkinson and Marmot state that 'the foundations of adult health are laid in early childhood and before birth' (ibid.: 14). For example, maternal stress and anxiety reduce blood flow to the uterus, while the fetus also experiences the stress hormones directly.[16] Weight at birth is related to the mother's circumstances and shows a remarkably strong correlation with health throughout life. For example, birth weight is negatively associated with the likelihood of heart disease and strokes (Wilkinson 2005: 81ff.) and with diabetes in middle and old age (Wilkinson and Marmot 2003: 15).

The conditions of early childhood have similarly important effects on long-term physical health. UNICEF issues periodic report cards on OECD countries' performance. Its recent study of early childhood education and care showed large differences between countries. UNICEF has set out ten benchmark measures as 'a set of minimum standards for protecting the rights of children in their most vulnerable and formative years' (UNICEF 2008: 2). Sweden scored 10/10; Canada and Ireland were dead last at 1/10, even worse than the United States (3/10) and Australia (2/10). Perhaps it's no surprise that Sweden may have been the first country to have eliminated the relationship between children's height and weight and the social class and income of their parents (Lindgren 1976).

The gradient, internationally To this point, the discussion of health inequalities has been only about inequalities within countries. But international inequalities in health and life expectancies are huge and are entirely due to the circumstances in which people find themselves. For instance, if infant mortality in the world were the same as that in Iceland (2 per 1,000 live births), there would be 6.6 million fewer infant deaths every year.[17] The lifetime risk of death in childbirth is 1 in 8 in Afghanistan; in Ireland it's 1 in 47,600 (CSDH 2008: 29, 154).

If domestic inequalities are unjust, these international ones must be even more so. Philosophers make a strong case for extensive redistribution (Pogge 2008; Nagel 2005), governments acknowledge it with their foreign aid, while in many countries international redistribution has widespread public support through charitable contributions to non-governmental organizations such as Oxfam.

Yet the way the equity–efficiency trade-off is discussed in the texts, only people within the national borders count. Redistribution outside the borders is virtually off the agenda.

Flattening the social gradient

'There will always be inequalities in society but the magnitude of their effects on health is within our control. Why not make things better? It is in all our interests.' Michael Marmot (2004: 266)

The World Health Organization's Commission on the Social Determinants of Health has recently set out a detailed plan to close the health gap between people within countries and between countries within a generation (CSDH 2008). It writes:

The poor health of the poor, the social gradient in health within countries, and the marked health inequities between countries are caused by the unequal distribution of power, income, goods, and services, globally and nationally, the consequent unfairness in the immediate, visible circumstances of people's lives – their access to health care, schools, and education, their conditions of work and leisure, their homes, communities, towns, or cities – and their chances of leading a flourishing life. This unequal distribution of health-damaging experiences is not in any sense a 'natural' phenomenon but is the result of a toxic combination of poor social policies and programmes, unfair economic arrangements, and bad politics. (Ibid.: 1)

The Commission's recommendations include measures to provide affordable housing, improve working conditions, and to enhance economic security through adequate social insurance so that people have assistance in the event of illness, disability, unemployment or lack of adequate income. Most people live in countries with little or no social insurance, but there are serious health inequities even in most industrialized countries.

Health equity is a matter of life and death for millions of people and the knowledge and resources exist to address it. The evidence we've reviewed in this chapter suggests that the growth costs of such measures are (at worst) about zero.

Wealth, externalities and political power We have focused our discussion only on the health and mortality effects of inequality, which we suspect are not very widely known. In our examples of externalities in Chapter 7, we explained the idea that visible consumption leads to external costs for others because of its influence on consumption norms. Because these externalities flow from the top down the social hierarchy, societies with greater income and wealth inequalities should experience more of these external costs.

More commonly understood is that great inequalities in income and wealth are associated with inequalities in political power and influence that are incompatible with a healthy democracy. As Edward Wolff says about the United States, 'We're becoming an oligarchic society, with an extreme concentration of wealth. This concentration of wealth is protected through a political process that's making it difficult for anyone but the monied class to have a voice' (quoted in Mattern 2002).

Question for your professor: If 'social injustice is killing people on a grand scale', as the World Health Organization's Commission on the Social Determinants of Health claims, why is doing something about this not a major theme in an introductory economics course?

2.4 Summing up

What have we seen? While giving lip-service to equity as a social objective, in practice the texts relegate questions of income distribution and redistribution to the back of the book, as if these are of secondary importance to the pursuit of 'efficiency'.[18] It doesn't have to be this way. For example, Goodwin et al. (2005) place it in a core chapter in the centre of their book. This reflects a different value judgement on their part, one that we obviously endorse.

For the students who get to this topic in the conventional text, the authors suggest, despite the absence of convincing evidence, that there is a real trade-off between efficiency and equity. They then ignore the evidence about the pervasive effects of economic inequality on health and mortality, documented in detail and beyond dispute, that result in millions of premature deaths every year just in the wealthy countries alone. A simple presentation of the facts would lead inevitably to the question of what to do about them.

But the world-view in the mainstream textbooks is sympathetic to the basic features of the status quo. It appears that textbook authors reflexively shy away from raising questions that would challenge the existing distribution of power and wealth, both within countries and between them. Perhaps they fear that doing so would open them up to accusations of being 'ideological'. But it is equally ideological to avoid raising uncomfortable and inconvenient questions.

Suggestions for further reading

Peter Lindert (2004a) provides a clear and compelling case for his views in the July/August 2004 issue of *Challenge*, an excellent journal with clearly written articles and interviews accessible to undergraduate economics students.

Marmot's 2004 book, *The Status Syndrome: How social standing affects our health and longevity*, is a book that may change the way you understand human nature and our social world. He played a leading role in the World Health Organization's Commission on the Social Determinants of Health whose 2008 report sets out how a better world is possible.

Wilkinson and Pickett's *The Spirit Level: Why more equal societies almost always do better* (2009) provides a wealth of information on the pervasive effects of inequality on societies.

10 | Trade and globalization without the rose-tinted glasses

'There is no branch of economics in which there is a wider gap between orthodox doctrine and actual problems than in the theory of international trade.' Joan Robinson (1973a: 14)

We saw the idea of comparative advantage and the gains from specialization and trade in the production possibilities frontier model in Chapter 2. We considered there the 'gains from international trade', a theme we examine further here. The case for free trade, presented to students as unassailable wisdom, rests on shallow arguments and the shaky ground of value judgements shared by economists, but not, it seems, by the general public.

1 THE STANDARD TEXT

1.1 The extent and growth of international trade

The importance of trade is typically expressed relative to the size of a country's economy as measured by its gross domestic product (GDP). Trade takes place not only in goods, but also in services such as shipping, tourism and education. Table 10.1 shows the relative size of exports and imports for a variety of countries and their shares of total world trade.

Clearly, the trade/GDP ratios of the countries vary greatly and require careful interpretation. Belgium, for example, does not really export more than its entire GDP; the large value of exports relative to GDP must reflect goods made elsewhere that are both imported and then re-exported through its ports. As well, there are very large differences between exports and imports in some cases. Saudi Arabia's exports are more than 30 per cent of GDP larger than its imports. This trade surplus reflects an accumulation of assets as it sells more than it buys from the rest of the world. Similarly, the substantial US trade deficit reflects an ongoing accumulation of debt.

1.2 The economics of tariffs and import protection

Let's consider the effects of a tariff (i.e. tax on imports) on nails. For simplicity, we consider the 'small country' case, where the importing country takes the world price of nails (here, $10/kilo of nails) as given: its imports are too small to influence the price in any appreciable way. Figure 10.1 illustrates this situation. At the world price, demand exceeds domestic supply; the difference is imports.

TABLE 10.1 International trade, 2007 (%)

Country	Exports/ GDP	Imports/ GDP	Share of world exports	Share of world imports
Some OECD countries				
Belgium	112.9	107.9	3.1	2.9
Netherlands	84.7	76.7	4	3.5
Sweden	52.4	44.8	1.2	1.1
Germany	46.5	39.7	9.5	7.4
Korea, South	44.7	45.3	2.7	2.5
Canada	36.2	35.4	3	2.7
Mexico	32.4	35.8	2	2.1
France	26.9	28.9	4	4.3
United Kingdom	26.1	29.8	3.1	4.4
Australia	22.0	24.8	1	1.2
Japan	19.2	17.6	5.1	4.4
United States	11.7	17.1	8.3	14.2
Some non-OECD countries				
Saudi Arabia	63.4	31.6	1.7	0.6
Nigeria	43.0	26.2	0.5	0.2
China (excluding Hong Kong)	40.8	33.1	8.7	6.7
Russia	30.5	21.8	2.6	1.6
South Africa	29.9	38.6	0.5	0.6
India	20.1	25.1	1	1.5
Brazil	13.9	12.3	1.2	0.9

Note: GDP is not adjusted for purchasing power parity. This increases the ratios of exports and imports to GDP significantly for developing countries.

Source: World Trade Organization Statistics, Country Profiles, October 2008

If the government imposes a tariff of $1/kilo on nails, the domestic price rises by the same amount. Foreign suppliers of imported nails must get $11/kilo of nails so that after paying the tariff they still get the world price of $10/kilo. Otherwise, they would sell their nails elsewhere. The rise in price reduces the quantity demanded and increases the quantity produced domestically. As a result, imports decline.

The effect of the tariff is to make consumers of nails worse off and domestic producers of nails better off, while giving the government some revenue from that tariff. What is the net effect?

First, note that the price increase reduces consumers' surplus (the area under the demand curve and above the price) by the areas a + b + c + d in Figure 10.1. Area c is the government's tariff revenue, which involves no loss to society. (Imagine that it is returned to the population as a cash transfer.) The domestic nail producers get areas a + b as they produce more and at a higher price. Part of

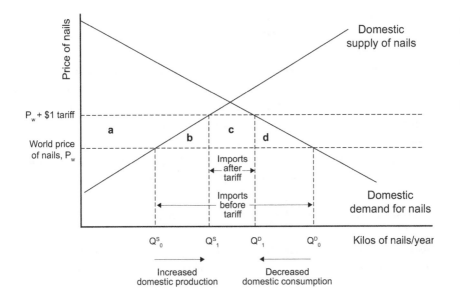

FIGURE 10.1 The effects of a tariff

that (area 'b'), however, represents additional marginal costs of production above the world price, P_W, so really only area 'a' adds to their profits. If those who get these added profits are domestic residents, that results in no loss to society. The net result is that consumers have lost a + b + c + d, producers get 'a', governments get 'c'; thus 'b + d' is the *net loss to society as a whole* from the tariff. The loss comes from two sources: reduced consumption lowers consumer surplus ('d') and the society has accepted higher domestic costs of production of nails than it could have paid to get the nails from abroad ('b').

The analysis of a policy that limits imports to a certain maximum level (called an import quota or a quantitative restriction) is the same with the exception that in that case the government gets no tariff revenue. Either domestic importers or foreign producers get the benefits of the higher price, depending on who gets the valuable rights to import the limited amount of foreign nails.

1.3 The argument for free trade

The net costs of a tariff or a quota are the same as the net gains from removing them. Consumers gain consumer surplus from the lower price and greater consumption; on the production side, society's resources are directed more towards the goods in which it has a comparative advantage. Total income in the country is higher and, as we saw in Chapter 2, every consumer can potentially have more of all goods. The textbooks then make claims like this: 'the gains are larger than the losses. Thus, free trade raises the total welfare' (Mankiw et al. 2006: 189) or 'By engaging in free trade, … we can make ourselves better off

and the citizens of other countries better off' (Parkin and Bade 2006: 768–9) or
'[I]nternational trade produces mutual benefits to the countries that engage in it'
(Krugman and Wells 2005: 423).

If all countries carry out such policies, 'the world economy can achieve a more
efficient allocation of resources and a higher level of material well-being than it
can without trade' (McConnell and Brue 2005: 696). Exposure to foreign competition also keeps domestic producers on their toes, adopting the best technologies
to keep costs low and productivity high. The linking of economies around the
world through trade (part of the broader process of 'globalization') also promotes
peace between trading partners by making war more costly.

1.4 Arguments for protecting domestic production against foreign imports

As part of their World Trade Organization obligations, many countries have
agreed to increase tariffs only in special circumstances (described below). In
international trade negotiations, countries' negotiators label tariff reductions as
a 'concession', as if these were costly, rather than beneficial as economic analysis
suggests. There are, however, some theoretically defensible arguments for some
protection against imports, at least in some circumstances.

National defence Depending on its location and history, a country may view the
higher costs of domestic production as a worthwhile price to pay to be able to
feed and defend itself in the event of war. How far such a policy should go isn't
easy to say, however.

Infant industries and strategic trade policy Comparative advantage is not static; a
country's relative costs of production can change over time. If a domestic industry were protected from foreign competition, a sufficiently large domestic market
might enable it to expand to take advantage of increasing returns to lower average costs. Average costs could also fall with the experience of producing output
('learning by doing') and with research and product development that, without
protection, would not be viable. Eventually, when the fledgling industry finally
grows up, it survives without protection and could possibly start exporting its
product. In the case of an oligopolistic industry where there might be economic
profits to be had, this policy secures some of those profits for countries with
firms in that industry.

Unfortunately, it may not be clear which industries are good candidates for
such treatment, while there will be no shortage of applicants for protection.
Other countries could retaliate with tariffs if their exports are affected. Economists also argue that production subsidies would be a more efficient policy.
These would support producers without raising consumer prices. (This assumes
that taxes needed to pay for the subsidy have no efficiency costs.)

Diversification of production Relying on one or two export industries (usually agricultural commodities or natural resources) exposes the country to risks of large economic fluctuations if world prices are volatile. This is most relevant for developing countries that produce raw materials and for some oil-producing countries. But are tariffs that create a high-cost domestic industry the answer? Perhaps a country could promote other kinds of exports (e.g. tourism, education and other services) through investments in education and infrastructure.

Retaliation against unfair trade practices: subsidies and dumping Under international trade agreements, countries may prevent damage to domestic industries if foreign competitors get subsidies from their governments. Similarly, if foreign firms 'dump' goods in the domestic market at below their cost of production, tariffs can legally be applied to prevent injury to domestic firms. This makes sense if foreign firms are using 'predatory pricing' to destroy domestic firms and establish a monopoly, but not if foreign firms are simply selling in the domestic market at a lower price than they are charging in other markets ('price discrimination'). Yet anti-dumping tariffs may be applied in this way.

Changing the terms of trade The 'terms of trade' reflects the relative value of a country's exports in terms of the imports they can purchase. A country's total consumption can rise if its terms of trade improve: it can export the same amount and get more imported goods. If a country is large enough, it can influence world prices. A tariff on imports, by reducing demand for those products, can drive down their prices in world markets; at the same time, as resources are drawn into the production of import-competing goods, the supply of the country's exports falls, thus raising their price. The country's terms of trade improve. This 'optimal tariff' policy makes the country better off at the expense of people in other countries whose terms of trade worsen. If other countries respond by raising their own tariffs, however, they can cancel out the effects on the terms of trade, leaving everyone worse off.

1.5 Illegitimate arguments for protection

The texts state that some arguments for protection are wrong. Here are two examples.

Tariffs increase employment Will the purchase of imports instead of domestic goods cost jobs at home? The texts say no. If the country is on its production possibilities frontier, so all resources are employed, tariff protection can only move workers from the export industry to the import-competing industry, with the losses that we saw earlier in Figure 10.1. If there is unemployment, the claim is true for one country, but it can't be true for all countries. If all countries try this, as in the 1930s, everyone's exports fall and so does employment.[1]

Since we can't compete against low-wage foreign labour, tariffs prevent a 'race to the bottom' Textbooks argue that this is also false. High-wage countries sell goods to low-wage countries (and vice versa), so clearly it's possible to 'compete' against low-wage labour. Comparative advantage shows that it is relative, not absolute, costs which matter for the ability to trade. Wage differences reflect productivity differences, as we saw in the 'textbook' part of Chapter 8.[2]

1.6 The global trading system

Countries make agreements among themselves about trade policy. These can be bilateral agreements, such as the Canada–US free trade agreement, or multilateral, as in the treaties that have been negotiated under the General Agreement on Tariffs and Trade (GATT) and its successor, the World Trade Organization (WTO).

The WTO replaced the General Agreement on Tariffs and Trade (GATT) in 1995. It is an international organization whose primary tasks are: overseeing trade-related agreements between countries which provide predictability and stability for importers and exporters, resolving disputes between member states, and providing a forum to negotiate new agreements.

Alongside the WTO and allowed within its rules are preferential trade agreements between pairs or groups of countries. These agreements allow trade (and perhaps investment and labour) to move freely between the countries that are members of the preferential agreement, while they maintain separate rules for countries outside it. The European Union is an example of a 'customs union', where all countries within it maintain a common trade policy. The North American Free Trade Agreement (NAFTA) is an example of a 'free trade area', where the countries within it maintain independent trade policies with countries outside the NAFTA.

2 THE ANTI-TEXT

We will first set out some important points that the textbook analysis slides over. How do the textbooks, and economists more generally, add together the gains and the losses of different people to proclaim that 'the country' as a whole is better off or worse off as a result of some economic policy change? All too often, economists claim to have an answer to this question when they really don't.

What happens if we change the simple assumptions of the Ricardian model? What happens if technologies can change, perhaps moving with foreign investment between countries? What happens if firms face increasing returns instead of constant returns? The simple conclusions of the textbook Ricardian model no longer hold.

Finally, we will see that the problems of externalities, imperfect information and power are just as serious in the international sphere as they are in the domestic sphere. Globalization is a much more complex and double-edged process than the textbooks let on.

2.1 Problems with the textbook model

The analysis of the tariff The analysis of tariff removal compares two equilibrium positions. The implicit assumption is that the economy moves instantly and costlessly from one equilibrium to the other. This is not just a simplification for the convenience of students; it is common in empirical studies of changes in trade policy. These typically simulate what the economy would look like after a change in trade policy, but only consider the new equilibrium when all adjustments have taken place.

Perfectly competitive models of factor markets could be used to describe just such instantaneous and costless reallocations of resources. But in reality, the economy does not hop from one position on the production possibilities frontier to another; it follows a path inside the frontier as factors of production leave the import-competing sectors, and spend time unemployed before perhaps becoming re-employed in other sectors. The income lost during unemployment and the costs of becoming re-employed should be counted. 'Economists have sometimes dismissed such adjustment costs with the comment that the displaced factors become re-employed "in the long run". But this is bad economics, since in discounting streams of costs and benefits ... the near-present counts more heavily than "the long run",' as Baldwin et al. (1980: 407) rightly observe.

As well, the argument is commonly made (as we saw in Figure 10.1) that consumers benefit from lower prices for imported goods, resulting in an expansion of consumer surplus. But did you notice in our earlier 'textbook' exposition that this is only half the story? Driskill writes (2007: 12–13) that in their enthusiasm for free trade, exponents of its benefits sometimes neglect to note that when tariffs are removed, the relative price of exportable goods must rise. People buying those goods will see their consumer surplus shrink. Whether any particular consumer is better off or worse off depends on the balance between the importable and exportable goods they buy.

Questions for your professor: Why do we just compare the equilibrium with the tariff with the equilibrium without it? Are we forgetting the costs of getting from one to the other?

When is 'society' better off? The compensation principle The Pareto principle, which we examined in Chapter 9, does not apply to changes in trade policy. Lowering protection against imports makes some people in society worse off, while others become better off. As in so many practical situations, the Pareto principle offers no guidance.

Recognizing this, British economists John Hicks (1939) and Nicholas Kaldor (1939) proposed the *compensation principle*. Compare free trade with import protection. If with free trade it is *hypothetically* possible to redistribute income between individuals so that some people have more income and no one has less income than with protection, then free trade is better than protection.[3] So, as Mankiw et al. (2006: 184) write, with free trade 'the gains of the winners exceed the losses of the losers, so the winners could compensate the losers and still be better off'. They conclude: 'Thus, free trade raises the total welfare' (ibid.: 189).

That is the essence of the texts' argument for free trade. By asserting the Hicks–Kaldor compensation principle (implicitly, if not explicitly), it gives primacy to the supposed social objective of efficiency while ignoring questions of equity or income distribution.

We saw in the previous chapter the dubious nature of the Pareto principle as a general criterion for judging whether society is better off or not. The Hicks–Kaldor compensation principle, with its *hypothetical*, not actual, compensation, is far less convincing. Yet despite that texts assert: 'Free trade makes the country as a whole better off, even though it may not make every individual in the country better off' (Ragan and Lipsey 2008: 824). Similarly, Schiller writes that 'the country as a whole stands to benefit from trade' despite the lost jobs of some (2006: 746).

In a refreshing commentary (aptly entitled 'Why do economists make such dismal arguments about trade?'), Vanderbilt University's Robert Driskill (2008: 2) asks: 'Why should people think economists can be, in effect, high priests who tally up benefits and losses to different individuals and pronounce the outcome good or bad for the group as a whole? In fact, people shouldn't.' Judging the outcome is 'a matter of moral philosophy, not number-crunching', and economists are no better moral philosophers than anyone else. 'It's really that simple.' It is hard to overstate the importance of this basic point, which applies to the textbook analysis of economic policy in general.

It's not obvious that everyone would share the value judgement of the textbooks concerning trade policy. What if many people each gain a little bit while a few suffer losses that are 'often large, painful, and traumatic, requiring dramatic life changes' (ibid.)? Jacobson et al. (1993: 685) report annual long-term losses of 25 per cent of pre-unemployment earnings for 'high tenure' workers who lose their jobs in failing firms, with losses remaining 'large even for those who find new jobs in similar firms'. They have only a small fraction of their monetary losses compensated through unemployment insurance, while considering only these monetary losses greatly understates their loss in well-being (Winkelmann and Winkelmann 1998).

Is 'society as a whole' *necessarily* better off if the sum of the gains and losses is positive? A reasonable person could easily say 'no'. Note that the example here also assumes that a rise in everyone's real income makes everyone better off, but, as we've seen in Chapter 4, this is open to question. A relatively small increase in real income experienced by most people could have little effect on well-being as they quickly adapt to it, while the few who suffer large losses would indeed be worse off as their relative position worsens.

Trade and growing wage inequality While issues of income distribution are important in assessing policy changes, they are also important in judging whether changes in patterns of comparative advantage and trade are making countries as a whole better off or worse off. Trade economists have been debating for years the extent to which globalization and the increasing trade of the industrialized countries with developing countries has put downward pressure on wages of less-skilled workers in the developed countries, contributing to growing income inequality there (Krugman 2008b).

A basic model found in every trade textbook explains trade as the result of differences in the relative amounts of factors of production in countries.[4] Some countries have a relative abundance of skilled labour and capital, some have a relative abundance of unskilled labour, for example. The model predicts that countries will specialize in and export goods that use a lot of the relatively abundant factors relative to the less abundant ones.

If a country with an abundance of skilled labour increases imports of goods that use a lot of unskilled labour, the wages of less skilled labour fall. At the same time, an increase in exports of goods that use a lot of capital and highly skilled labour raises the incomes of capital owners and of high-skilled workers. Earnings and income inequality grow. But there are also other explanations for increasing wage inequality. So far, it seems, the debate about the extent to which trade is responsible remains unresolved, if only because of the enormous difficulty in disentangling the causes of changes in wages.[5] As we will see shortly, though, there are further reasons for thinking that trade and globalization will be putting downward pressure on wages more generally in the industrialized countries.

> Questions for your professor: When some people gain and some lose following some policy change, how do economists say whether society as a whole is better off or worse off? Is it sufficient to have net gains so that total incomes go up?

2.2 Relaxing the textbook's assumptions

The simple Ricardian model that illustrates comparative advantage and the gains from trade makes some critical assumptions. Technologies can differ permanently between countries; neither the technology nor factors of production can move between them. Only consumption goods can move internationally. It also assumes perfect competition and constant returns in production.

We will briefly consider what happens when each of these assumptions is relaxed. We then get a glimpse of the real world where corporations offshore production, taking their technology with them. Workers lose their jobs, putting downward pressure on wages in rich countries. Increasing returns lead to arbitrary patterns of specialization both within and between countries.

Technological change Paul Samuelson (2004) describes what happens to countries' national incomes if technology changes as a result of local developments. To adapt his analysis to our simple Ricardian wheat and cloth example from Chapter 2: suppose England experiences a technological improvement in wheat production, the good in which Canada has a comparative advantage. This lowers the world price of wheat and reduces Canada's gains from trade. Canada's national income falls as its terms of trade fall (i.e. it must export more to get a given amount of imports). In the worst case, it eliminates Canada's gains from trade and trade stops.

Samuelson (ibid.: 142–3) thinks that this kind of technological catch-up on the part of less developed, lower-wage regions has been common through history, both within countries and between countries. While total incomes rise in the areas 'catching up', income falls in the previously more advanced regions.

Workers, owners, internationally mobile technology and capital The Ricardian model treats everyone like worker-owners, such as farmers who grow wheat and who keep sheep. They consume some of their own produce and trade the rest. In this simple setting, there are no winners and losers; everyone can gain from trade. Yet, as Marglin remarks (2008: 278), 'the distinction between worker and owner is basic to capitalism, as is the distinction between producer and consumer', adding: 'it is not just a simplification to ignore these realities but a distortion'.

Marglin offers a more realistic model in a simple numerical example to illustrate what happens when workers and owners are considered separately (ibid.: 274–81). In the case he considers, a multinational corporation located in an industrialized country offshores some of its nail production to a developing country.[6] Technology, and the physical capital in which it is embodied, both move. This is an example of a way in which technological differences between countries can change that is different in an important way from Samuelson's analysis, where the technology change took place abroad, but without a flow of capital.

As a result of their foreign investment, owners of multinational corporations, or MNCs, enjoy larger profits. Nail production falls in the industrialized country as it imports some nails from abroad. Some workers lose their jobs, obtaining instead involuntary 'leisure'. They are worse off, not only from lost income during unemployment, but also from lower future earnings and, if they have to move, the costly disruption in their lives as they become uprooted from friends, family and community.

In the case Samuelson examined, foreign investment did not bring about the technological change in the foreign country so there was no flow of foreign investment income back to the developed country. This income to capital owners can offset the income losses of workers who lose their jobs as a result of production cuts, so that national income in both places may rise, unlike in Samuelson's example. But as we have seen, even if the total income in the industrialized country increases, there is no reason to conclude that the nation collectively is better off.

In the developing country, there is greater material prosperity. This benefits people there, particularly if basic needs have not yet been met, and possibly even people in other countries if they care about the international distribution of income. It also involves, however, 'the disruption of community and the substitution of forced-march Westernization for a more gradual evolution' of the indigenous culture (Marglin 2008: 280), a cost that has no place in textbook thinking. Whether that society is better off or not, or at what pace its transformation should take place, also requires value judgements.

> Question for your professor: The Ricardian model in the text does not allow capital or labour to move internationally. What if capital moves to 'offshore' some production. Does this make workers at home worse off?

Increasing returns and globalization Gomory and Baumol (2000, 2004) have examined broadly similar scenarios, but ones in which firms have increasing returns instead of the constant returns of the Ricardian model. In their model, which country ends up specializing in which good is completely arbitrary. The country that first starts producing a particular industrial good has lower average costs than its potential rivals would if they entered the market at initially low levels of output. They will find it more profitable to produce something else instead.

Here, the outcome depends on accidents of history. Except in the unlikely event that average costs are the same in each country, this arbitrary pattern of production will not maximize total world income. Figure 10.2 gives an example.[7] Portugal can produce nails more cheaply than England, but if England gets a head start, its declining average costs may lock Portugal out of the market.

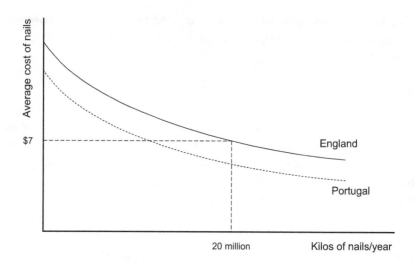

FIGURE 10.2 Average costs of producing nails in two countries

England produces 20 million kilos of nails at an average cost of $7/kilo. If Portugal tried to enter to take a portion of the world market, its producers would face much higher average costs. When there are increasing returns, 'the invisible hand can blunder' (Gomory and Baumol 2000: 94) and can lead to highly inefficient patterns of production.

If increasing returns are an important feature in the production of many goods, the textbook default model of perfect competition is misleading. In that model, free trade produces a globally efficient allocation of resources. In the world of increasing returns, it does not.

Question for your professor: According to the textbook, specialization with free trade results in the most efficient use of the world's resources. Are other, inefficient, outcomes possible?

As in the Samuelson and Marglin accounts, the transfer of technology from high-income to low-income countries and the 'resulting growth in the effectiveness of competition ... drives wages toward the middle. They end up above the initially low levels in the less-developed economy, but below [their] former level in the wealthier countries' (Gomory and Baumol 2004: 438).

None of this means that industrialized countries should sabotage technological progress in developing countries or restrict imports from them. All of these examples serve to stress that comparative advantage evolves and that the distribution of the gains from trade changes with it. The process of 'globalization' produces complex and ever-changing outcomes. No simple conclusions are possible.

Instead of the traditional trade policies – tariffs, quotas and so on – examined in the textbooks in the context of an infant industry, these ideas highlight the importance of broad, economy-wide policies to influence productivity and technological change, and thereby the dynamic pattern of comparative advantage. These could include tax policy and support for research and development, and for education.

2.3 What's missing from the textbooks

Once again, the usual suspects are missing in the textbook account: externalities, asymmetric information and power. In the international context, they raise new problems.

The problem of externalities The textbook analysis of trade assumes the usual default case of no externalities. As we stressed in Chapter 7, externalities are everywhere. When they are not taken into account in decision-making, international trade will be inefficiently large.

The most obvious externalities are global: the greenhouse gas (GHG) emissions that are involved in the transportation of all kinds of traded goods and services, whether it is fresh flowers flown from Kenya to England, container ships sailing from China to Rotterdam, or millions of tourists flying to exotic locations. With current technology, serious action to reduce GHG emissions would surely increase transportation costs significantly and reduce the volume of world trade.

Partha Dasgupta (2007: 121) of Cambridge University gives a nice example of more local externalities. Suppose that the government of a developing country offers timber concessions to private companies which cut down the forest and export the wood. This damages watersheds and the livelihoods of farmers and fishers downstream. They have too little political power to get compensation for the damage they suffer. This effectively subsidizes the country's timber exports and transfers wealth from the poorest people in a poor country to the owners of the forestry companies and to importers in rich countries.

How big are such subsidies and how much is trade influenced by them? Dasgupta (ibid.: 121) writes: 'Unfortunately, I can give you no idea ... because they haven't been estimated. International organizations have the resources to undertake such studies; but, to the best of my knowledge, they haven't done so.' He rightly adds that examples like this do not make a case against free trade, as such, but they do show that the case for free trade must include a consideration of its environmental impacts.

Defenders of globalization, such as economist Martin Wolf of the *Financial Times*, dismiss such concerns about exports being, in effect, subsidized by externalized costs.

Differences in incomes, preferences and geography could quite reasonably give different localities, or countries, entirely different environmental standards for local environmental spillovers. If polluting industries were then to migrate from high-standard regions or countries to low-standard regions or countries, the world would be unambiguously better off. The high-standard regions or countries would be able to consume the products of polluting activities without having to host them, and the low-standard regions or countries would have more economic activity, in return for pollution to which they are, relatively speaking, indifferent. (Wolf 2004: 191)

That government policy in authoritarian regimes and dictatorships may not accurately reflect the public's preferences does not seem to occur to him. Setting that aside, there is also the problem of the powerlessness of parts of the population (as Dasgupta noted) and the problem of information. People have to know that the pollution is taking place and to understand fully its consequences.

In recognition of these realities, there are actually legal restrictions on international trade in toxic materials and toxic waste, although they are failing spectacularly to stop the flow of waste from rich to poor countries. Electronic equipment that contains lead, mercury, cadmium, chromium and polyvinyl chlorides is causing growing problems, particularly as manufacturers are not required to bear the costs of their proper disposal and thus have no incentive to try to produce them in other ways. Richard Wray (2008) reports that 'Thousands of discarded computers from western Europe and the U.S. arrive in the ports of west Africa every day, ending up in massive toxic dumps where children burn and pull them apart to extract metals for cash.' A CBS *60 Minutes* (CBS News 2008) investigation found a flow of illegal e-waste from the United States to a place in southern China run by 'gangsters' with 'the highest levels of cancer-causing dioxins in the world' and where 'seven out of ten kids have too much lead in their blood'.

Martin Wolf's view, quoted earlier, is the economist's standard response to this situation: all the exchanges here are voluntary, so everyone must be better off than they would otherwise be. The Chinese workers, for example, felt sick and knew that their work was damaging their health, but their pay of $8 a day looked good given their destitution. An end to toxic exports from the rich countries would leave them worse off.

If we set aside the children who have no say in the matter and the fact that the workers still have far from complete information, this could actually be true. What the standard response ignores, because of its narrow focus on efficiency, is the bigger framework of injustice into which all this fits.[8] It is an example of a 'failure of markets' (as opposed to a market failure), David Colander's distinction, which we explained in Chapter 6. The market may be working efficiently, but it is producing an ethically unacceptable outcome.[9] The CBS *60 Minutes* report quotes James Puckett, founder of the non-governmental organization Basel Action Network: 'desperate people will do desperate things ... it's a hell of a choice between poverty and poison. We should never make people make that choice.'[10]

> Questions for your professor: Is trade in toxic waste efficient? Why does it seem to be an unpopular idea?

Information, fair trade and product certification Consumers may care about how the products they buy were produced. Everyone is aware of controversies over child labour and clothing made in 'sweatshops' and other goods produced in poor labour conditions. By not raising these issues, textbook theory seems to suggest that all that matters to the utility-maximizing consumer is the price and information about the physical characteristics of the final good.

Suppose that you are going to buy a $2 cup of coffee. As playwright Wallace Shawn (1991: 20–21) writes, its 'price comes from its history, the history of all the people who were involved in making it and selling it and all the particular relationships they had'. By buying the cup of coffee, you also 'form relationships with all of those people ... The cup of coffee contains the history of the peasants who picked the beans, how some of them fainted in the heat of the sun, some were beaten, some were kicked.' If instead the coffee beans were grown by independent farmers, perhaps buyers with monopsonistic power forced down the price, leaving them in poverty. Perhaps the farming practices were environmentally destructive.

© Andy Singer

If coffee buyers recognize their place in this web of relationships with people and with nature instead of behaving like textbook consumers, they will want to know how the coffee was produced. But how can they find out? Buyers will have no practical way of distinguishing among sellers' claims unless some trusted, independent third party can provide a widely recognized certification.

The development of 'fair trade' certification for coffee and other products is just one example of this. It offers buyers credible assurance that the products were produced by democratically run small farmer cooperatives that are offered above-market prices as a way of reducing poverty and promoting grassroots economic development (Fridell et al. 2008: 11–12).

Other examples of certification are those for organic products or certification about how animals were treated in the production of a variety of food products. The development of these certification systems and the rapid growth of sales of 'fair trade' products show that many buyers do indeed care about more than just the price and the physical characteristics of the goods they buy.

When textbook economics ignores these issues, it is only being consistent with its default assumptions, which we have repeatedly highlighted. With perfect information, no externalities, no market power, and the unimportance of economic democracy (in this case, producer cooperatives) because of the absence of power more generally, then the fair trade movement makes no sense.

Question for your professor: Does the textbook provide any explanation about why 'fair trade' products exist?

The problem of power

'The strong do as they can, while the weak suffer as they must.' Thucydides (quoted in Chomsky 2007: 175)

Countries differ greatly in terms of population, total production and income per person. In turn, these features influence their bargaining power when dealing with each other. The texts' general neglect of power is particularly apparent when we consider their treatment of the international economy and international economic institutions.

As philosopher Thomas Pogge (2007: 139) explains,

Economic systems, both global and national, are characterized not only by a (generally wholesome) competition under standing rules of the game, but also by a fierce struggle over the design of these rules themselves. The outcomes of this continuous struggle reflect not the well-informed insights of an impartial planner, but the interests, bargaining power and expertise of the various groups of participants.

In the international arena, the 'rules of the game' are formally set out both in international organizations, such as the World Trade Organization (WTO), the World Bank and the International Monetary Fund (IMF), and in separate bilateral agreements between countries. Over the last two decades, the activities of these organizations and the establishment of such bilateral agreements have drawn increasing criticism and opposition. Based on the contents of their textbooks, however, economics students would be hard pressed to understand what all the excitement is about.

The World Trade Organization Unless the problem of power is recognized clearly, a good deal of the criticism of the WTO can be baffling. Its decisions are made by consensus; most of its members are at least nominally democratic. What's the problem?

Even sympathetic mainstream economists agree that 'a few rich countries dominate the WTO' negotiations and that 'it is dominated by large corporations', something that is 'probably inevitable, since it is large corporations that do most trade. Corporations have both the incentive and the resources to influence policies, and they do, both within countries and internationally' (Deardorff and Stern 2002: 418). (Such views do not appear in the texts.)[11]

One of the worst examples of the exertion of corporate power has been the creation of the Trade-Related Aspects of Intellectual Property Rights (TRIPs). It was a top priority of US-based multinationals, and thus of the US government, in the negotiations leading up to the formation of the WTO in 1995. The agreement, to which all WTO members must ultimately adhere, created worldwide protection for 'intellectual property' such as copyrighted materials, including computer programs, protected for fifty years, and patents, protected for twenty years.

It was clear from the beginning that the result would be a substantial increase in transfers to the developed-country monopolists who were getting additional protection for their intellectual property. Significant net losers are developing-country residents; patents in those countries are almost entirely controlled by foreign MNCs. The MNCs may enjoy a further benefit of preventing the emergence of potential competitors in developing countries given the increased protection given to patenting processes, as in the production of pharmaceuticals (Dunkley 2000: 189–90).

Bilateral trade agreements between large and small countries Recent years have seen a growing number of bilateral trade agreements between countries. These are sometimes called 'preferential' trade agreements because they give the exports of the partner country preferential tariff-free treatment. As of the time of writing, the United States has negotiated such free trade agreements with Australia, Bahrain, Chile, Colombia, Mexico, Israel, Jordan, South Korea,

Malaysia, Morocco, Oman, Panama, Peru and Singapore.[12] Under the North American Free Trade Agreement (NAFTA), the United States also has free trade with both Canada and Mexico. Under the Central America–Dominican Republic Free Trade Agreement, it has free trade with El Salvador, Guatemala, Honduras, Nicaragua, Costa Rica and the Dominican Republic. It has also signed 'bilateral investment treaties' with forty countries. Aside from NAFTA, Canada has bilateral trade agreements with Chile, Colombia, Costa Rica, Israel, Peru and the countries of the European Free Trade Association (Iceland, Norway, Liechtenstein and Switzerland).[13]

Standard trade theory suggests that the gains from such agreements go disproportionately to the small country. The argument is straightforward. We saw from Figure 2.2 (on page 30) that a country's consumption possibilities expand more the greater the difference between its prices before trade and its prices after trade begins.

Imagine a simple situation where the world consists of a 'large' and a 'small' country. World supply and demand determine world prices. World prices must be close to those that would prevail in the large country alone before trade because adding the small country's supply and demand to that of the large country does not change supply or demand very much. As a result, the large country's consumption possibilities do not increase much with trade, while those of the small country increase a lot. The small country gets the lion's share of the total gains from trade, although it also gets the lion's share of the unemployment costs of readjusting its pattern of production – something downplayed by the conventional analysis, as we noted.

Acknowledging the existence of oligopoly and increasing returns reinforces this conclusion. The large country, because of the size of its internal markets, will have already realized the lower average costs associated with increasing returns. In contrast, by obtaining easier and more secure access to the large country's markets, producers in the small country can lower their average costs considerably.

Canadian economists advanced these ideas when considering the consequences of a free trade agreement with the United States in the 1980s. If the large country signs a preferential trade agreement with a smaller one, the large country is being a good neighbour to the small one. Given that history is replete with examples of large countries kicking sand in the faces of small countries, this claim of disinterested benevolence may be too good to be true.

Gerald Helleiner of the University of Toronto seems to think so (Helleiner 1996). He suggests that the large country will seek 'side payments' – perhaps unrelated to trade – as a price for preferential access to its markets. He warns that 'It is therefore quite misleading to address the benefits and costs of integration agreements exclusively, or even primarily, on the basis of trade effects', as economists invariably do.[14]

The point is crucial. By focusing attention on the simple arguments from trade theory, economists can make a persuasive-sounding case for freer trade. But by ignoring the actual or potential 'side payments', whose costs may also be hard to quantify, they are ignoring a critical part of the story.

Helleiner suggests that these 'side payments' could include things like: extending monopoly protection of 'intellectual property' (namely patents and copyrights), special protection of foreign investors, privatization of parts of public sector production, 'harmonizing' some laws and regulations to those of the large country, and acceptance by the small country of restrictions on some of its economic policies (e.g. screening of foreign takeovers of domestic firms). The 'side payments' will benefit certain powerful interests in the large country, while at the same time restricting the policy autonomy of the small country in ways that could end up being much more important than just lowering tariffs. Furthermore, as time passes and the economies become more integrated, it could become prohibitively costly to cancel the agreement, effectively locking in these policy constraints.

A notorious example of a potential for ongoing side payments is Chapter 11 of NAFTA, which effectively permits companies to sue governments for lost profits as a result of policy changes. For example, as a result of growing public concern, the government of Quebec banned many pesticides in 2006. Dow AgroSciences, the maker of the herbicide 2,4-D, is challenging this in court and demanding $2 million in compensation for 'expropriated' profits (Mittelstaedt 2009).

The large country's demands for 'side payments' may well not end once the agreement has been signed. The small country remains vulnerable to selective non-compliance or to threats of cancellation or 'renegotiation' of the agreement. This reflects the imbalance in bargaining power that comes from the asymmetry in size between the two countries. It does not just influence the outcome of the initial negotiations, but persists and raises real risks for the smaller country. Helleiner asks an important question: 'will powerful actors actually submit to disagreeable developments, whatever they may previously have said, if they do not suffer greatly in consequence of the failure to do so?' (1996: 762)

The large country could stretch or flout the rules and make the small country bear the disproportionate costs of trying to make it comply through whatever time-consuming dispute resolution institutions are set up under their agreement. The US–Canada softwood lumber disputes that began in the early 1980s are an example of such behaviour.

The US government's allegations that Canadian softwood lumber is subsidized and American softwood producers thereby damaged has been defeated at every stage in NAFTA and WTO dispute settlement panels and before American courts. Instead of the dispute settlement process having resolved the problem, however, the end result has not been free trade, but a victory for power politics and managed trade. The most recent dispute (2002–06) ended with capitulation by the Canadian government to a negotiated settlement in which the American government and industry (after losing in every legal forum available) got to split $1 billion in tariffs collected from Canadian producers, funds which the industry lobby will find handy in future litigation (Feldman 2007). The reason given by defenders of the deal was that Canada had to 'accept the need to pay off the U.S. industry to obtain peace', as a legal victory would only be followed by renewed harassment. Given the power imbalance, 'paying extortion to the protectionist lobby' was the only practical solution (Ritchie 2006).

As one observer comments, 'the rules of the game have been periodically rearranged on an ad hoc basis to suit the short-term interests of the most powerful country, namely the United States' (Gagné 2002: 27). He adds (p. 26) that 'Canadian industries should thus be aware that continued access to the American market depends critically on not exceeding some explicit or implicit market share'.

In the end, it's unclear whether the gains, such as they are, from such agreements are worth the risks for the small country. The main alternative is greater reliance on multilateral institutions when small countries can band together and have allies (perhaps even other large countries), rather than facing the large country one on one.

Questions for your professor: 'Free trade' agreements seem to be about a lot more than tariff reduction. They have about as much in common with free trade as pre-nuptial agreements have with free love. Do you agree?

Foreign direct investment: the problem of power ... again The topic of foreign direct investment (i.e. foreign ownership or effective control of firms located in a country) is almost entirely absent from the introductory texts, despite its prominence in many countries. Indeed, multinational corporations (MNCs) receive barely a mention, let alone any serious treatment, despite their central role in the international economy. By leaving MNCs out of the picture, the texts are implicitly taking the position that they are a non-issue. Yet surely the debate about their role deserves serious attention.

It's important to note that if the textbooks don't bother to distinguish between whether a firm is domestically owned or foreign owned, they're implying that ownership doesn't matter. All firms in the textbooks maximize profits, so they behave in the same way, regardless of who owns them. But as a general proposition, hardly anyone seems to believe this. Countries routinely prohibit, restrict or review foreign ownership, particularly in sectors associated with cultural and political sovereignty, such as the military industries and the media and publishing industries.

TABLE 10.2 Estimates of the stock of foreign direct investment (FDI), by sector, 2006 (trillions of dollars)

	Developed countries	Developing countries
Inward FDI Stock	9.4	2.8
Primary (%)	8	8
Manufacturing (%)	29	26
Services (%)	62	64
Outward FDI Stock	11.4	1.4
Primary (%)	8	3
Manufacturing (%)	28	9
Services (%)	62	84

Note: (1) Countries of south-east Europe and the Commonwealth of Independent States are not included. (2) Some assets are not classified by sector.

Source: UNCTAD (2008), Annex Tables A.1.5 and A.1.6, pp. 207–8

Most foreign investment, like most trade, takes place between the developed economies. Table 10.2 summarizes the broad picture. More than three times as much inward FDI takes place in the developed countries than in the developing countries. In both cases, the bulk of it is in service sectors. Ownership of these assets rests overwhelmingly with residents of developed countries.

Our particular concern here is with the activities in developing countries of MNCs owned in developed countries. This is where disparities in power may be most significant. These activities also draw the most criticism of MNCs' activities. For instance, if the government of a developing country gets into a dispute with an American corporation, the relevant power disparity is that between the United States and the developing country.

In Chapter 4, we mentioned the deaths of 16,000 children a year in the Philippines that result from inappropriate feeding practices, including the use of infant formula in unsafe conditions. In 2006, the Philippines Department of Health imposed new rules that would enforce the World Health Organization's International Code of Marketing of Breastmilk Substitutes. The Supreme Court of the Philippines rejected the producers' appeal to suspend the new rules. US government representatives then began lobbying the Philippines government and the head of the US Chamber of Commerce wrote to the Philippines president warning that the measure would damage 'investors' confidence'. 'Four days later', reports George Monbiot (2007b), 'the Supreme Court reversed its decision.' In the end, though, the Philippine government did not cave in and with the assistance of domestic and international activists, the new rules were largely reinstated (Baby Milk Action 2007).

State sponsorship and protection of domestic businesses carrying out foreign direct investment have a long, if unattractive, history. In their study of the economics of British imperialism, Lance Davis and Robert Huttenback (1988: 279) conclude that British 'imperialism can best be viewed as a mechanism for transferring income from the middle to the upper classes'. The British middle class paid most of the taxes to support the military and administrative structure of the empire, while the upper classes enjoyed higher rates of return on investments abroad than would otherwise have been available to them: 'socialism for the rich, capitalism for the poor'.

American business owners have long enjoyed a similar subsidy. Even before the United States became the dominant world power, it routinely invaded countries in Central America and the Caribbean in support of US business interests. General Smedley Butler of the US Marine Corps (quoted in Chomsky 1987: 94–5) described his own exploits this way:

> I spent 33 years ... being a high-class muscle man for Big Business, for Wall Street and the bankers ... I helped purify Nicaragua for the international banking house of Brown Brothers in 1909–1912. I helped make Mexico ... safe for American oil interests in 1914. I brought light to the Dominican Republic for American sugar interests in 1916. I helped make Haiti and Cuba a decent place for the National City [Bank] boys ... I helped in the rape of half a dozen Central American republics for the benefit of Wall Street.

After the Second World War, when American power was unrivalled, the pattern continued but on a larger scale. Particularly notable were the 1953 coup that overthrew the Iranian parliamentary government on behalf of Anglo-American oil companies (installing the Shah as dictator), the 1954 military coup in Guatemala on behalf of the United Fruit Company, and the 1973 military coup in Chile ousting a democratic government opposed by the International Telephone and Telegraph Corporation.[15]

Currently, the Colombian military is the major recipient of US military aid in the Americas. In 2007, Amnesty International issued a report entitled *Colombia. Killings, arbitrary detentions, and death threats – the reality of trade unionism in Colombia.* It detailed how more than two thousand trade unionists had been killed in the preceding twenty years. In the mining, oil, gas and energy sectors, an area of particular interest to MNCs and foreign governments, Amnesty states:

> Trade unionists in these sectors have faced repeated human rights violations, often because of their opposition to privatization. Trade unionists representing mine workers in artisanal mines whose livelihoods are potentially threatened by large-scale investment by international mining interests have also faced repeated human rights violations. Trade unionists representing workers in multinational firms have also faced human rights violations often in the course of labour disputes. (Amnesty International 2007: 23)

Both the United States and Canada have concluded free trade agreements with Colombia.[16]

It's important to acknowledge that, in many places, MNCs have brought real benefits, bringing useful capital investment while assisting in the transfer of technologies and know-how between countries, and offering no threat to local political autonomy. But in other places, destruction and repression follow in their wake. By not offering any serious discussion of the role of MNCs in the international economy, the texts decline to address an issue of worldwide relevance.

> Questions for your professor: Does foreign ownership of firms matter? What does our textbook have to say about this?

2.4 Summing up

We have not attempted to make a case either for free trade or for some form of restricted trade. One of our central points is that things are much less clear cut than the texts let on. In the end, economic theory can prove nothing about whether free trade or some form of restricted trade is best from the point of view of the people living in a particular country. It can provide a framework to help to understand the consequences of alternative policies and to identify who is likely to experience gains and losses. Other 'non-economic' considerations may come into play as well, such as national autonomy. Ultimately, value judgements are inescapable.

The second major theme here is that textbook economics slides over a number of important issues concerning globalization. Pervasive externality and informational problems are compounded by inequalities in power, particularly at the national level.

Why do so many economists support free trade and offer advocacy to students rather than an accurate presentation of the benefits and costs? Driskill (2008: 2) speculates that in economists' culture, the arguments for free trade are a kind of institution: '200 years of tradition that has short-circuited their critical thinking'. Perhaps, but something deeper may be at work. William Poole (a free trade advocate) stresses that 'the case for free international trade is really part of a more general case for free markets' (2004: 4). If so, what is at stake is much bigger than just whether tariffs are good or bad; it's the ideology of laissez-faire itself.

Suggestions for further reading

Driskill's brief 2008 article, 'Why do economists make such dismal arguments about trade?' is essential reading.

Students of international trade will find much of interest in Dunkley (2000) and in his follow-up book on free trade doctrine and trade and development (2004).

The fair trade movement has taken off. Hudson and Hudson (2003) links fair trade to Marx's concept of commodity fetishism, an idea we sketched out in Section 2.3 using the words of Wallace Shawn. We also recommend their later article with Mara Fridell (Fridell et al. 2008), which examines how the major coffee companies have responded to the fair trade movement by attempting to undermine it while at the same time branding themselves as ethical.

11 | Conclusion

'Tim Harford: "I was not surprised to read your lop- sided and
unconvincing caricature of orthodox economics ('textbooks' are
such a convenient straw man)."

'Pete Lunn: "Textbooks are a straw man? To me they are like a
vice on the mind of economists, who get tetchy when you present
results that reveal the behaviour of real people to be not as
those textbooks assume."' *Prospect* magazine, issue 150

In this short chapter, we want to gather together the main points we've raised about what's unsatisfactory with the standard microeconomic textbook – and why it matters.

The distinction between positive and normative economics

The idea that positive and normative economics are clearly distinct is misleading. Implicit value judgements are embedded throughout so-called 'positive' economics. The very definition of economics as the attempt to satisfy *unlimited wants* with limited resources is rooted in judgements about what makes human beings happy. It's an individualistic view that ignores our social links, while shifting our attention towards efficiency (and away from questions of equity).

Indeed, one could argue that the main thrust of textbook economics is not positive. The texts are not describing the world as it is. Instead, the texts explicitly or implicitly make the claim that competitive markets are a reasonable approximation to the real world and that they produce a reasonably efficient outcome. Thus, Krugman and Wells (2005: 15) write, 'Markets usually lead to efficiency.' The reader is invited to adopt the normative view that, broadly speaking, there should be laissez-faire: a free market system, with a minimum of government interference.

As Marglin (2008: 3) puts it: 'The problem with the idea that economics is purely, or even primarily, a descriptive undertaking is that the apparatus of economics has been shaped by an agenda focused on showing that markets are good for people rather than on discovering how markets actually work. And from this normative agenda has come the constructive agenda.'

What evidence is there for this claim? We've seen in Chapters 3 and 6 how demand and supply were applied to all areas of the economy, regardless of the actual market structure prevailing there. We've seen how demand and supply are applied to explain income distribution and the gains from trade. We've seen how the predictions of the perfectly competitive model – that price ceilings lead to shortages, for example – are presented as universally valid even though a non-competitive market setting results in different conclusions. Finally, we've seen how the textbooks often claim there is a clear body of evidence confirming the inefficiencies resulting from minimum wages and rent control.

In making the argument for markets and for limited government, textbook economics relies on value judgements implicit in its fundamental assumptions about self-interested individuals, their full rationality and their unlimited wants, and the nation-state being the only valid measure of community, as Marglin (ibid.) argues. Normative value judgements pervade microeconomics.

The rational individual

Modern research challenges the notion of rational individuals constantly and instantly calculating the best action to maximize their individual well-being. Bounded willpower, bounded selfishness and bounded rationality are now well established in the behavioural economics literature, although they have made little impact on textbook economics. We know that 'animal spirits' – individuals' impulses to action in the face of uncertainty – play a dominant role in many of our most important decisions. We also know that individuals make systematic mistakes. Collective euphoria can result, fuelled by whatever myth about the economy prevails at the time.[1] These irrationally exuberant booms end in busts that are hugely expensive for the economy, as we have seen in recent years.

TABLE 11.1 Conventional economics and the blank cells of Akerlof and Shiller

	Rational responses	Irrational responses
Economic motives	Mainstream textbook economics	
Non-economic motives		

Akerlof and Shiller argue that the current mainstream macroeconomic model focuses on how the economy would behave if people had only the economic motives identified in the textbooks and were fully rational. But the same point can be made about the focus of the microeconomics principles textbooks. In Table 11.1 textbooks and mainstream models inhabit only the upper left-hand cell. These address only the question: How does the economy behave if people have only economic motives and rational responses? It's time that the mainstream textbooks took the blank cells seriously.

Akerlof and Shiller say (2009: 173):

Indeed if we thought that people were totally rational, and that they acted almost entirely out of economic motives, we too would believe that government should play little role in the regulation of financial markets ... But on the contrary all those animal spirits tend to drive the economy sometimes one way and some-times another. Without intervention by the government the economy will suffer massive swings in employment. And financial markets will, from time to time, fall into chaos.

While endorsing the importance of animal spirits and limited rationality, we do not agree with Akerlof and Shiller that if individuals were rational and had only economic motives then there would be little role for the government in regulating financial markets. Problems of imperfect and asymmetric informa-tion are pervasive and are particularly important in financial markets. They give rise to principal-agent problems, moral hazard problems and adverse selection. This suggests a key role for the government in regulating many markets, in-cluding financial markets.

The goals of equity and efficiency

Textbooks emphasize the importance of efficiency and downplay the impor-tance of equity. In textbook treatments, the equity goal is always subservient to the efficiency goal. For example, textbooks implicitly use the compensation principle in cost–benefit analysis to justify efficiency-enhancing policies; as long as winners *could* compensate losers and still be better off, society as a whole is supposedly better off, although no one can explain why in any convincing way.

Furthermore, textbooks claim that there is a trade-off between equity and effi-ciency: transferring income between people is like transferring water in a leaky bucket. They emphasize that taxation causes inefficiencies, while conveniently forgetting that taxing things we want less of (such as pollution) can improve efficiency. Similarly, the transfers that make up the social safety net are allegedly costly because they reduce incentives to work. Yet at the same time, the texts ignore the arguments and evidence that equity is good for growth. In reality, it seems that, within limits, people in many countries have opportunities to attain both more equity *and* more efficiency.

Recent research has emphasized that equity promotes social cohesion and trust, whereas inequality weakens people's sense of reciprocity, and increases the sense of 'us' versus 'them' (Wilkinson and Pickett 2009). By ignoring this subject, textbooks seem to imply that there is no role for virtues like loyalty and trust. Joseph Stiglitz argues that Adam Smith didn't make this mistake: he was aware of the limitations of markets, and knew this was not so. Indeed, modern economics explains why economic systems in which such virtues are prevalent actually work better than those in which they are absent. Stiglitz writes (2003: 274):

Older theories had simply assumed that it was costless to write and enforce contracts, so that every time anybody did anything for anybody else, there was a contract that was rigorously adhered to. But in the real world, contracts are ambiguous, contract disputes abound, litigation is extremely expensive, and most economic dealings go on without contracts. In the real world there are often implicit contracts, understandings, norms, which enable society to function well. What makes economic systems work, by and large, is trust.

And, as we have said, trust is enhanced by equity.

The assumption that more is better

When textbooks emphasize the importance of efficiency, they explicitly assume that 'more is better'. At the individual level, well-being and happiness depend only on a person's real income and consumption. This story stumbles into a fallacy of composition by assuming that if one person is better off with more stuff, everyone is better off if everyone has more stuff.[2] This fallacious assumption invites readers to adopt a pro-growth consumerist outlook.

The evidence, ignored entirely in the textbooks, shows that in rich countries measures of average happiness have not increased as average incomes have risen substantially. People simply seem to get used to their new circumstances, which quickly become the norm. Good evidence suggests, however, that relative position and status within groups matter a great deal to individuals' happiness.

Methodological problems

Textbooks teach that we judge the usefulness of a model by the accuracy of its predictions, not by the realism of its assumptions. Textbooks gloss over the difficulty of actually refuting a theory. It is very difficult to reject core hypotheses because they are protected by auxiliary assumptions. If the theory does not seem to fit the facts, this can be blamed on the failure of at least one of these auxiliary assumptions to hold, leaving the core hypothesis untouched. Hence, Deepak Lal's (2000: 18) memorable comment: 'ideas – good or bad – never die in economics'.

Economics is better represented as the art of persuasion or, as McCloskey prefers, 'the art of rhetoric'. In this context 'rhetoric' means 'debate', and in this debate all and every kind of reasoned argument is admissible: analogies (or metaphors), thought experiments, natural experiments, historical precedents and appeals to authority. Even the 'official methodology' – predictive power and hypothesis testing – is used rhetorically according to McCloskey; it's just one more way of trying to persuade.

It is interesting, and perhaps ironic, that the textbooks do not apply the methodology they espouse to the material they present. They do not develop a series of models, generate a variety of predictions, confront these predictions with the facts, and in this way evaluate which model is best. Instead, evidence is presented sporadically and selectively. Evidence is nearly always presented to support the textbook claim that the competitive model is good enough to use as a generic model to answer any question – but contrary evidence is too often ignored.

Ironically, when the textbooks present non-competitive market structures, they choose real-world applications by how closely the market in question conforms to the model's assumptions. They never attempt to apply these models generically to markets that don't conform to the model's assumptions to see how accurate the predictions are. For example, monopsony is said to be of little relevance because the case of a single employer is rarely seen, but a corresponding analysis of the realism of the assumptions of the perfectly competitive labour market is omitted. Adding to the irony is the fact that modern labour economists recognize that monopsony power may derive from imperfect information and imperfect mobility of workers. Since information and mobility are always imperfect, it is entirely reasonable – on a priori grounds – to think that the monopsony model might be a useful generic model.

Overemphasis on perfectly competitive markets

Students learn that the realism of a theory's assumptions is irrelevant just before they learn the highly unrealistic perfectly competitive model (in its shorthand 'demand and supply' version). They are then invited to apply it to markets in virtually all sectors of the economy.

Could it be that this model is simpler than others, and this is why it is presented as a generic tool? We don't think so. The perfectly competitive model is rather complex – even if its shorthand version makes it appear simpler than it really is. In any event, one would be hard pressed to show that the competitive model is simpler than (say) the monopoly model. So, why is the competitive model so emphasized?

A main theme of our *Anti-Textbook* is to argue that the overwhelming emphasis placed on the competitive model in principles textbooks reflects – and may produce in readers' minds – a particular ideological outlook. For example, Chapter 3 dismisses claims that the emphasis on competitive markets is justified by either their real-world prevalence, or by the generic applicability of the model's predictions. Chapter 6 dismisses claims that such emphasis is justified by the usefulness of the competitive model as an ideal market type that can be used to guide government policy.

Nor is the competitive model a useful parable – a story that helps us to understand deeper truths about the economy. Certainly, perfect competition contains a germ of truth: the process of entry and exit from industries is driven by a search for profit. But the parable is inadequate in that the process takes place in an environment of constant technological knowledge, with given resources, given tastes and given products. Therefore, it says nothing about some of the most important facts that need explaining – innovation and growth. If there is one thing that capitalism is remarkably good at, it is *innovation*. Monopoly power and the associated profits are the reward for innovation. They provide the incentive that drives it. Focusing on a world filled with perfectly competitive markets omits this vitally important feature of the economic landscape.

We believe the overemphasis placed on perfectly competitive markets arises because it is possible to tell a story about their purported ideal characteristics. Textbooks spin a yarn about how competitive markets produce Pareto-efficient outcomes, how they allocate resources to their highest-valued uses and distribute goods to those who value them most. In this market structure, government intervention to change prices or quantities inevitably produces adverse side effects and reduces efficiency. So, the emphasis on competitive markets imparts a market fundamentalist bias to the standard textbook – it is biased against government intervention and government regulation.

Textbooks ignore their own ideological leanings

Textbooks do not acknowledge the possibility that they have adopted a particular ideological position. The authors seem to be unaware that it is impossible for any social science, or any individual researcher, to avoid adopting some world-view. After all, there is necessarily a fine line between explaining why something is the way it is, and justifying the way it is. Since the start of the scientific revolution in the seventeenth century, there have been inevitable interrelationships between science and society.

Social science in particular has largely tended to play a legitimizing role, and economics is no exception. Economics can legitimize aspects of society either through what its dominant theories focus attention on and attempt to explain, or through what they ignore. As Dowd (2000: 14) says: 'it is often alarming to note what mainstream economists do and do *not* examine, what questions they do and do *not* ask, what aspects of the economy (and important connections with the rest of the social process) they do and do *not* take into account'.

As we have seen, textbook economics asks few uncomfortable questions about consumerism. Consumer theory has the notion of 'consumer sovereignty' – that consumers ultimately rule the economy by deciding what to buy and what not to buy. This downplays the role of business in forming consumers' preferences and in determining the products on offer to consumers. All buying decisions are portrayed as the free exercise of individual preferences formed by some unexamined process that apparently falls outside the realm of economics.

Similarly, if corporations pollute the air and water when producing the goods consumers want, this must just reflect voters' rational choices about the trade-offs involved, not a lethal mixture of individual ignorance and corporate influence over the political system. When questions of power are routinely ignored, as they are in the textbooks, this is a subtle way of legitimizing the existing distribution and exercise of power. Similarly, the lack of attention paid to the distribution of income among households and to its equity serves to legitimize existing inequalities. If these issues merit only a few pages towards the end of a large textbook, how can they be that important?

The same ideological position is not present in all economic paradigms. Different paradigms contain different world-views. But textbooks don't bother teaching students about how the paradigms reflect world-views, nor do they bother teaching students anything other than one world-view that comes out of the dominant neoclassical paradigm.

Indeed, 'economics' has come to be synonymous with the economics of a particular view of capitalism. It wasn't always this way. At one time, economic textbooks routinely contained chapters on alternative economic systems, on the evolution of economic doctrines, and the advantages and disadvantages of the corporate form.[3] In dropping these subjects, perhaps mainstream textbooks have been 'dumbed down'. Certainly, the range of thinking has been narrowed.

The central idea that smaller government is better

This follows if – as textbook economics maintains – markets can be generically analysed as if they were perfectly competitive, and if externalities can be analysed as if they are exceptions rather than ubiquitous. Therefore, *in general*, government intervention is neither necessary nor beneficial.

The popular presumption that governments are inefficient compared to the private sector and compared to markets rests more on ideological belief rather than on evidence. Herbert Simon, who received his Nobel Prize for important contributions to understanding how organizations behave, put the matter this way:

> Most producers are employees of firms, not owners. Viewed from the vantage point of classical theory, they have no reason to maximize the profits of firms, except to the extent that they can be controlled by owners. Moreover, profit-making firms, non-profit organizations, and bureaucratic organizations all have exactly the same problem of inducing their employees to work toward the organizational goals. There is no reason, *a priori*, why it should be easier (or harder) to produce this motivation in organizations aimed at maximizing profits than in organizations with different goals. If it is true ... that organizations motivated by profits will be more efficient than other organizations, additional postulates will have to be introduced to account for it. (Simon 1991: 28)

Downplaying the importance of the legal framework within which markets operate

As noted earlier, trust is important because contracts are necessarily incomplete, potential disputes abound, and litigation is expensive. As Prasch (2008: 8) observes: '[A] rudimentary knowledge of the principles of property and contract law opens our minds to their inherent complexity, contingency, and importance. This knowledge, in turn, illuminates some of the strengths and weaknesses of markets as economic and social institutions.'

The recent global financial meltdown (discussed in the postscript to this book) illustrates – among other things – the importance of the legal and regulatory framework within which markets operate. Imperfect and asymmetric information creates possible conflicts of interest that allow some people to profit at the expense of others. The invisible hand isn't supposed to work like that; it is supposed to transform everyone's selfishness into the greater good.

Prasch (ibid.) explains that the invisible hand only works to produce an efficient allocation of resources if the economy consists of certain special kinds of markets. There must be no externalities, but additionally the quality of the product must be known, and exchanges must be instantaneously completed in 'spot' markets. This describes the proverbial 'widget' of the microeconomic textbooks and occupies the upper left-hand cell in Table 11.2. On the other hand, if quality cannot be determined without owning the product for a while (experience-goods as opposed to inspection-goods), or if exchanges are ongoing and involve issues of fairness and needs ('relational contracts' as opposed to spot markets), the invisible hand mechanism breaks down and resources will not be efficiently allocated.

TABLE 11.2 Conventional textbook economics and the blank cells of Robert Prasch

	Spot markets	Relational contracts
Inspection goods	The mythical 'widget'	
Experience goods		

Whenever information about quality is imperfect, markets can break down – as in the market for good used cars (the 'lemons' problem) or the market for asset-backed commercial paper. Even though most consumer durables and capital goods would fit in the lower left cell of Table 11.2, and most labour market contracts and credit market transactions would fit in the lower right-hand cell, textbooks treat all of these as if they were widgets – hence we draw the table with blank cells. Textbooks pretend these cases don't exist. In so doing, they underestimate the importance of the laws and regulations needed to make these markets function more efficiently. In all the blank cells of Table 11.2, regulations are needed to help restrain conflicts of interest and abusive practices.

Prasch (ibid.: 13–14) explains: 'The lack of concern for specifics is aggravated when an abstract good, by tradition termed a "widget," is used to illustrate the "essence" of the market process. In this pedagogy, the student's attention is then directed to the theory of exchange and price. It concludes once the student has been successfully drilled in "the theory of the market".'

The omission of power

Textbooks assume all economic relationships are voluntarily entered into. But the choices people make are constrained by the circumstances in which they find themselves. In turn, those circumstances may be shaped by the power of others in the society around them. Should we say that a person 'voluntarily' allows her children to work in a sweatshop or that circumstances forced her into this unwelcome decision? As we explained in Chapter 3, Prasch (ibid.) shows that where needs are a consideration, such markets may differ from the conventional demand and supply found in the textbooks.

The only power that appears in the textbooks is 'market power' – the power of some sellers to influence the prices of their products. Yet in the actual economy, power appears in many forms.

Most people spend much of their lives at work, as employees of companies governed by authoritarian chains of command. Their employers' monopsonistic power influences the pay they receive, which, in turn, rests on the difficulties employees would have in finding another comparable job. As consumers, people's preferences are influenced by a continuous barrage of propaganda crafted by the marketing industry. Perhaps the most glaring example of the omission of power in the standard textbooks is their silence about the influence of business on government policy, and on the legal and regulatory framework within which markets operate.

The presumption in favour of free trade

While mainstream texts may appear to take a balanced view on the costs and benefits of free trade, in fact they bias the discussion to favour free trade. How is this done? First, the texts downplay adjustment costs and effects on the distribution of income. As usual, the focus is on efficiency and increasing national income, with the presumption that this, in turn, will increase the well-being of society as a whole.

Second, state power is ignored, yet power relations between countries affect the 'rules of the game' that govern trade and international economic relations. 'Free trade agreements' can include rules governing patents and copyright, foreign investment and access to energy resources, for example. Finally, they ignore the environmental costs of trade – in particular, the production of greenhouse gases in transporting goods and raw materials from one side of the world to the other.

The omission of community

According to the standard account, expanding the realm of the market expands the possibilities for specialization and trade, expands freedom of choice,

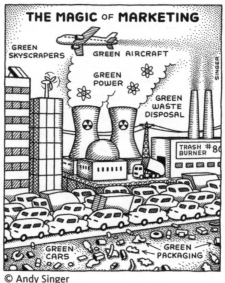

© Andy Singer

and necessarily makes people better off. We have noted repeatedly that it doesn't necessarily make *everyone* better off, creating distributional problems that may be compounded when people care about relative position. But there is another issue. Even if everyone were absolutely better off, and even if no one cared about their relative position, there is still a potential problem: markets often undermine community. Marglin (2008) asks what limits should be placed on markets for the sake of community.

The greater the role for markets, the more life is commercialized; personal relationships are replaced by anonymous market transactions. Sometimes this not only damages the community, it can even backfire on the economy. For example, the US sub-prime meltdown arose because, instead of bankers knowing their customer's profile individually and being able to assess it, the market became more and more anonymous. The community was taken out of the marketplace.

Marglin gives the example of two ways in which a farmer can protect himself against the risk of his barn burning. The old-fashioned way, still practised by the Amish, is to have a commitment to economic reciprocity in the form of community barn-raising. The modern way is to buy insurance. Insurance is much more efficient in terms of time and cost. But it is only more efficient if we focus exclusively on the users of the barn as individuals. If we're interested in the community, then the Amish are on to something by rejecting insurance and sticking to barn-raisings. Economic reciprocity is part of the glue that keeps the community together.

The concept of community doesn't easily fit within the mainstream neoclassical framework, which views society as merely a collection of individuals. Leonard (2009: 490) argues in his critique of Marglin that if communities are

252

beneficial to individuals, then people will form them, join them or leave them as they see fit. But the problem here is that community ties are deeper than merely chosen associations. Marglin claims that since the benefits of community ties are hard to measure, economists have chosen to ignore them altogether. With wry humour he notes (2008: 9): 'The nineteenth century physicist Lord Kelvin insisted that we know only what we can measure. Economics takes the dictum a step further … what we can't measure – entities like community – doesn't exist.'

Incidentally, the fixation on quantitative measurement has broader implications than the omission of community. It also plays its part in our neglect of the environment. Stiglitz (2009: 2) notes:

[W]hat we measure affects what we do. If we have poor measures, what we strive to do (say, increase GDP) may actually contribute to a worsening of living standards. We may also be confronted with false choices, seeing trade-offs between output and environmental protection that don't exist. By contrast, a better measure of economic performance might show that steps taken to improve the environment are good for the economy.

Downplaying the ecological crisis facing the planet today

Perhaps it is absurd that this point appears at the end of our list, given the severe risks human societies face from climate change. The textbooks could help students understand that there is a problem and why it exists.

In part, the origins of our environmental problems can be laid at the door of economics itself. As historian J. R. McNeil writes,

Anglo-American economists (after about 1880) took nature out of economics. The growth fetish, while on balance quite useful in a world of empty land, shoals of undisturbed fish, vast forests, and a robust ozone shield, helped create a more crowded and unstressed one … Economic thought did not adjust to the changed conditions it helped to create; thereby, it continued to legitimate, and indeed indirectly to cause, massive and rapid ecological change. (McNeil 2000: 336)

Economists such as Kenneth Boulding and Herman Daly have written about this distinction between this 'empty-world economics' and the 'full-world economics' that is needed now (Boulding 1966; Daly and Cobb 1989). But the textbooks are still teaching empty-world economics.

Marglin explains the importance of the distinction:

But now that we live and work at close quarters to one another, our non-market interactions are much more part of the fabric of our lives, and externalities are of central concern. Pollution, once again, is a case in point. When people lived in small communities with a lot of space between settlements and produced and consumed at relatively modest levels, air and water pollution were relatively minor problems. They become major problems only with the advent of cities and the accompanying growth in population density. (Marglin 2008: 284).

The economic system not only produces these increasingly important problems, but some of its features make these problems difficult to address. Firms have an interest in preventing externalized costs from being internalized. They may seek to lessen public pressure for regulation to reduce pollution by 'going green' to improve their image among consumers. But, given imperfect and asymmetric information, appearance rather than reality counts. Too often the result is 'green-washing' rather than really going green. Alternatively, public ignorance and apathy may allow firms simply to use their political influence to alter or block environmental regulations.

The textbook accounts of externalities ignore these problems and put forward the central story that markets are generally efficient and that market failures, such as pollution, can be remedied. Then the net effect of the market system is, or can be, roughly efficient.

Marglin (ibid.: 283–4) asks:

Are externalities an occasional nuisance or anomaly ...? Or are externalities everywhere, something we rarely escape? It obviously makes a huge difference. In the first case, externalities can be treated as relatively minor, second order effects ... In the second case externalities are central to the discussion and are ignored at the peril of making the discussion irrelevant to the world we actually inhabit.

Critical thinking about economics

Our fundamental aim in writing this *Anti-Textbook* has been to provide economics students with the basic ideas with which they can begin to think critically about what they read in their textbooks. As Noam Chomsky (1988: 623) once remarked: 'If the schools were doing their job, which of course they aren't, ... they would be providing people with means of intellectual self-defense' – in this case, the means to defend themselves against the unconscious acceptance of the ideology presented in the textbooks. As a result, students have to think for themselves, not an easy matter to do alone and without some guidance.

Our intention in writing this book has not been to discourage anyone from studying economics. After all, economics deals with matters that are central to individual well-being and to the functioning of human societies. But simply to study a conventional textbook (and to solve the multiple-choice questions that supposedly test understanding of the subject) is not enough. One needs to read with a critical eye, and to note what is omitted and what is unsupported. Such critical thinking will be rewarded with a very different and far more interesting perspective on the world.

Suggestions for further reading

Aldred (2009) *The Skeptical Economist* focuses on the hidden ethical values of economics, and is highly recommended. Fullbrook's (2008) *Pluralist Economics* presents alternative approaches to economics.

Moshe Adler's book, *Economics for the Rest of Us*, has not yet been published as we write this. But what appear to be its main themes – examining the misuse of 'efficiency' to justify opposition to policies that promote greater equity, and a critical examination of the marginal productivity theory of wage determination – reflect themes we have examined in this book.

Postscript: a case study on the global financial meltdown

In this postscript we want to connect our main themes with the global financial meltdown that exploded into headline news in March 2008 with the collapse of Bear-Sterns, one of the world's largest investment banks.

This financial debacle illustrates the importance of many of the issues highlighted throughout this *Anti-Textbook* – issues that are downplayed and underemphasized by the mainstream texts. It illustrates the importance of imperfect and asymmetric information, externalities, limited rationality and inappropriate incentives. In particular, it illustrates the necessity of appropriate government regulation, and the ability of powerful business interests to change the rules of the game through lobbying – especially in the USA (which was the epicentre of the global collapse).

Let's begin with some general points about credit markets and ask whether the supposed generic applicability of the demand and supply model holds in this case.

The importance of imperfect and asymmetric information

Textbooks claim that the demand and supply model can be applied as a generic model to all markets throughout the economy. Then why not apply it to credit markets? Credit markets in the USA seem reasonably competitive. There are thousands of banks and finance companies within easy reach by phone producing a reasonably homogeneous product – loans. But in Chapter 6 we noted that asymmetric information is routinely involved in relational contracts, of which loan contracts are a prime example. Banks cannot know everything relevant to a customer's creditworthiness – people have an incentive not to divulge damaging information about their past; and their future ability to repay loans depends on a host of uncertain elements better understood (perhaps) by the individuals themselves. Nor can depositors and shareholders know everything about the solvency and risk profile of any given bank; nor (it turns out) can borrowers know everything about how honestly the terms, conditions and fees associated with loans may be presented.

We noted in Chapter 6 that asymmetric information gives rise to a cluster of well-known problems: the principal-agent problem, the moral hazard problem and the adverse selection problem. Competitive markets cannot function efficiently when these problems are present: government regulation is required. So, how do these problems manifest themselves in credit markets?

Let's begin with the principal-agent problem (where some people benefit at the expense of those they are supposed to serve). This played its part in the global financial meltdown when the management of banks focused on maximizing their own short-term reward by, for example, inflating short-term profits to maximize the value of their stock options. Managers ignored the long-run interest of the entities that employed them and their shareholders. It was involved when financial institutions gave predatory loans to individuals who had little chance of paying them back – the infamous NINJA (no income, no job, no assets) mortgages. It was involved when those same financial institutions repackaged these loans into an alphabet soup of investment vehicles and sold them on to unsuspecting investors.[1]

Moral hazard (where incentives are changed by certain kinds of contracts, which leads to a change in behaviour that is hard to monitor) played its part in the meltdown for at least four reasons. First, because the banks didn't hold the mortgages they extended but sold them on to other investors, they had little interest in the real creditworthiness of the borrowers. So, the normal incentive of banks to vet the creditworthiness of its customers was short-circuited (or distorted) by the creation of the new investment vehicles. Second, the agencies that assigned credit ratings to the investment vehicles were compromised by the fact that their fees depended on the quantity of ratings they gave. (The better the ratings they gave, the more business they would be given.) Third, the investors who purchased the 'alphabet soup' of investment vehicles didn't sufficiently care about their ultimate riskiness because they insured against the possibility of default (or at least they thought they did) by buying CDSs (credit default swaps) from huge insurance companies like AIG. Fourth, depositors at the banks didn't have to worry about the risk of bank collapse since their deposits were insured by the government-owned Federal Deposit Insurance Corporation.

Finally, adverse selection (where particular contracts disproportionately attract undesirable customers) is always involved in credit markets, since experience suggests that those who are dishonest, desperate or overly optimistic are much less likely than others to drop out of the loan market as interest rates rise. This makes the business of extending loans more risky as interest rates rise.

The role of externalities

The temptation of high returns might lull a bank into ignoring the increasing riskiness of loans as interest rates rise. Such a bank not only jeopardizes its own future, but might also weaken the banking system as a whole.

As long ago as 1776, Adam Smith worried that banks would be tempted by the possibility of high returns to ignore increasing risk. As noted by Prasch (2008: 59): 'His concern was less for the irresponsible bank, but rather for the tendency for one bank failure to cast doubt on the reputation of nearby banks, thereby contributing to a potential crisis within the broader financial system.'

If my failure jeopardizes your possibilities for success, there is a negative externality. Clearly, there is an externality in banking since failure by any one bank negatively affects the reputation of all banks – and not just banks' reputations with households; it even affects their reputations with each other. For example, in the 2008/09 crisis banks became so suspicious of each other that they refused to lend to each other – exacerbating the credit crunch. This is often referred to as a 'systemic externality' since problems at one bank have implications for the *banking system* as a whole.

Limited rationality

Real estate and stock market bubbles are driven by investor overconfidence. Akerlof and Shiller (2009) argue that this overconfidence is fed by 'stories' that gain such widespread acceptance that they seem undeniably true. For example, in the 1990s it was commonly believed that real estate was the single best investment anyone could make, because land is limited while the population (and hence the demand for land) is constantly growing. Akerlof and Shiller (ibid.: ch. 12) point out that after the bubble bursts, the story conveniently disappears.

Just as overconfidence characterizes the upswing, irrational pessimism characterizes the downswing. When prices begin to fall, people focus on trying to preserve their capital. This necessitates selling more quickly than others. In the mad scramble to sell, prices fall precipitously. Fundamental values suddenly don't matter. Individuals and companies that borrowed heavily to participate in the real estate boom find themselves with negative net asset values. When the loans are called in, bankruptcy looms.

Interest rates aren't always at their market clearing level

Bankruptcies highlight an important point: the destruction of wealth in the downturn isn't limited to decreases in asset prices – real wealth is also destroyed. Machines are mothballed, factories are closed. Some may never reopen.

Financial institutions find themselves not only short of liquidity, but also short of capital. Many of them in the 2008/09 crisis had liabilities far exceeding the (now reduced) value of their assets and were effectively insolvent – hence the call for massive government bailouts. In such circumstances even sound businesses are unable to find the funding they require and may be forced into bankruptcy.

This is what is meant by a 'credit crunch'. Interest rates may be low (even approaching zero) but loans are difficult to obtain – especially if you need the money! *This is a classic case of how the demand and supply model is inadequate to explain the credit market.*

The importance of the regulatory framework and the impact of deregulation

Stiglitz (2003) argues that the main problems were caused by deregulation. In the early 1930s the Roosevelt administration enacted three key pieces of legislation in an effort to avoid a repeat of the Great Depression. The system worked well for about fifty years.

Roosevelt's first piece of legislation was the Glass-Steagall Act (1933), which prevented commercial banks (which take deposits and grant loans to both households and business) from acting as investment banks (which issue stocks and shares, and organize huge business deals such as mergers). Investment banking is inherently more risky than commercial banking, and the Glass-Steagall Act kept the two separate.

The second key piece of legislation was the Federal Housing Administration Act (1934), which regulated the terms of mortgages and insured them against default. For example, it established interest rate ceilings on mortgages (making them more affordable) and minimum down-payment requirements (making them less risky since borrowers were less leveraged). The idea was to prevent a repeat of the Great Depression scenario, where millions of Americans defaulted on their mortgages, precipitating the collapse of thousands of banks. To further safeguard the banking system, the Federal Housing Administration Act insured long-term mortgages.

The final piece of legislation was the creation in 1938 of the Federal National Mortgage Association (known as Fannie Mae), which purchased the now federally insured mortgages from banks and other financial lenders. Fannie Mae would then resell these mortgages to investors needing safe assets. The process funnelled cash into the banks, allowing them to make more mortgages.

Beginning in the early 1980s, Roosevelt's reforms began to be dismantled.

Deregulation in the 1980s Unfortunately, in the late 1970s (and early 1980s) the US central bank (the Federal Reserve) raised interest rates to record high levels in an effort to fight inflation. As market interest rates approached and then exceeded the ceiling on mortgage rates, it became unprofitable to issue mortgage loans and their supply dried up. This inspired two policy responses.

First, interest rates were deregulated in 1980 for any company that lent more than $1 million a year – regardless of whether it accepted deposits.[2] According to C. L. Mansfield (2000: 492): 'This ... is the statute that ultimately set the stage for the subprime home equity lending industry of today.' No one predicted the kind of predatory lending tactics that would take hold when mortgage rate ceilings were eliminated.

Second, the terms and conditions of mortgages were deregulated in 1982, allowing lenders to promote a hodgepodge of 'alternative' mortgage features.[3] These included: adjustable-rate mortgages, 'negative amortization' loans (whereby borrowers don't pay off the principal) and 'balloon' mortgages (which oblige borrowers to make a large payment at the end of the loan's maturity in exchange for lower monthly charges). These 'alternative' mortgages figure prominently in the sub-prime crisis, either through predatory lending, poor risk controls or hidden punitive charges that tipped people into foreclosure. Taken together, these two legislative overhauls opened the door for small consumer finance companies to move into the mortgage business and begin peddling exotic, high-interest loans.

There was one last legislative change made in the 1980s, which enticed people to use their homes as piggy banks. Prior to 1986, interest payments on most types of consumer loans – credit cards, car loans and house loans – were tax deductible. After 1986 interest deductibility was allowed only for first- or second-home mortgages. This change focused people's attention on house mortgages as the only way to get a tax break. Combined with the two earlier reforms that deregulated the terms, conditions and interest rate on mortgages, the interest-deductibility rule turned homes into automated teller machines. A host of finance companies were only too happy to step up with the money for refinancing – at rates of their choice.

Calculations by Mansfield (ibid.: 522) show that by 1988, a scant two years after the tax code was changed, 68 per cent of home equity loans were used to fund things other than home improvements, compared with just 35 per cent in 1984. Running parallel to this growth was the growth in small consumer finance companies. In 1977, these little consumer finance companies owned a mere 0.5 per cent of the home equity loan market. But by the end of the 1980s, they had 32 per cent.

The repeal of Glass-Steagall in 1999 The Glass-Steagall Act prohibited commercial banks from owning other financial companies such as investment banks or insurance companies.[4] It was this feature which was abolished in 1999 by the Gramm-Leach-Bliley Bank Deregulation Bill.

The consolidation of commercial and investment banks was supposed to allow the resulting 'full-service' banks to better compete and to enjoy economies of scale.[5] Instead, it enhanced the scope for conflicts of interest and perverse incentives. Because full-service banks make most of their money selling equities and bonds and arranging 'deals', *the creditworthiness of the companies to which they extended loans became secondary.* For example, we now know that major full-service banks continued to give loans to Enron even as it approached bankruptcy because of the lure of mega-profits from new deals, if it avoided bankruptcy.[6]

Stiglitz (2003: 143–4) says: 'The bubble – and the bad behaviour – were re-inforcing: the stronger the bubble, the stronger the incentives to take the actions to keep it going. The banks must surely have known that when the bubble burst, many of the loans they had made would fail. Thus, the banks' loan portfolios depended on keeping the stock market bubble going.' The bubble Stiglitz is referring to is the stock market bubble of the late 1990s – the one that burst in August 2000. But the same set of incentives was at work in generating the real estate and stock market bubble that burst seven years later.

Deregulation or evolution?

Akerlof and Shiller's (2009) book, *Animal Spirits*, explains that the main problem was not deregulation, but the natural tendency of corporations to develop their business in a way that avoids existing regulation. In particular, they cite the evolution of the privately issued mortgage-backed security.

Securitization was not new: banks had been able to sell their mortgages (as assets) to Fannie Mae since its establishment in 1938. But Fannie would buy only federally insured mortgages, which were backstopped by the US government. The securities it sold were relatively safe.[7]

What was new was the securitization of assets that were not federally insured. These new investment vehicles were more risky and more profitable. Because of the higher risk, big investors sought reassurance. This was met in part by credit rating agencies assigning grades to securitized bundles – a lucrative job which had its own perverse incentives to give overly generous ratings. But it was also met by the development of credit default swaps – ways of insuring against default by the ultimate borrowers upon whom the value of the securities depended. The value of these credit default swaps was estimated in 2008 to be around $62 trillion and involved complex interrelationships between financial institutions.[8]

It might be helpful to think of credit default swaps as like a fire insurance policy on a house. The householder pays a small sum – say $300 a year – to insure a home worth, say, $300,000. The insurer makes money by gearing rates to the likelihood of a home fire. If for some bizarre and unforeseen reason a large proportion of the insured houses suddenly burnt down, the insurance company would certainly go bankrupt. And if it did, the homeowners who now have dud insurance claims would probably also be forced into bankruptcy. But this scenario isn't very likely. Usually the risk of any one home burning down is independent of any other burning. So, by insuring lots of houses, the insurance company diversifies its risk.

Similarly, the financial institutions that insured the mortgage-backed securities against default thought that the risk of any one householder defaulting on his or her mortgage was independent of any other householder defaulting. So, by issuing lots of credit default swaps, they were 'diversifying'. But this reasoning ignores the possibility of a systemic event – such as a real estate bubble bursting – creating huge swathes of mortgage defaults.

The financial institutions that issued the credit default swaps faced a catastrophic liability. It was this which led to Lehman Brothers going bankrupt on

3 September 2008. The fact that they couldn't pay up jeopardized every financial institution that had insured against credit default with them. The resulting panic convinced the US authorities not to allow AIG – another huge player in these markets – to similarly collapse. As a result, on 16 September 2008 AIG was bailed out and given (what grew to be) a $182 billion loan, and was effectively 'nationalized' by the government, which received in return 79.9 per cent of its equity.[9]

Now, one could say that the growth of the credit default swap market was one way in which financial institutions evolved to avoid regulation. But the *unsupervised* growth in this market was due to the last – and perhaps most important – piece of deregulation (also introduced by Phil Gramm) – the Commodity Futures Modernization Act (CFMA) of 2000. This legislation guaranteed that the credit default swaps would not be regulated like other 'futures contracts'.[10] It also whacked the Securities and Exchange Commission's budget when they asked for more funding to oversee all these new types of deals.[11] This illustrates a crucial point: it is not sufficient to have regulations in place. The agency whose job it is to enforce the regulations needs a budget sufficient to do the job.

So, while it is true that institutions did evolve ways to avoid legislation – as Akerlof and Shiller argue – deregulation played a huge role in causing the subprime collapse and the global financial meltdown.[12]

Why did this happen?

Why did successive US administrations opt for deregulation? Akerlof and Shiller attribute it to public antipathy towards regulation. The United States was deep into a new view of capitalism – the no-holds-barred interpretation of the game. They argue (2009: 173): 'We had forgotten the hard-earned lesson of the 1930s: that capitalism can give us the best of all possible worlds, but it does so only on a playing field where the government sets the rules and acts as a referee.' The US administration was trapped into the mantra of deregulation.

Some commentators, such as Rodrik (2009), specifically blame economists. He says:

> [E]conomists (and those who listen to them) became over-confident in their preferred models of the moment: markets are efficient, financial innovation transfers risk to those best able to bear it, self-regulation works best, and government intervention is ineffective and harmful. They forgot that there were many other models that led in radically different directions. Hubris creates blind spots. If anything needs fixing, it is the sociology of the profession. The textbooks – at least those used in advanced courses – are fine.

Finally, we mustn't forget Stiglitz's point that deregulation made a lot of people very rich. Those who saw this potential were willing to invest to get it – spending large amounts on campaign contributions and lobbyists to secure the necessary legislative changes and financing 'think-tank' propaganda to influence public opinion.

Suggestions for further reading

Akerlof and Shiller's (2009) book explains how human psychology is prone to waves of irrational optimism and pessimism, and how these generate bubbles and slumps. A different view is presented in Baker's (2009) book *Plunder and Blunder*. As the title suggests, his thesis is how a combination of policy blunders and powerful vested interest have caused market bubbles and meltdowns.

Notes

Introduction

1 Ironically, the difficulty of defining neoclassical economics is the lasting impression one gets from reading the brave attempt by Arnsperger and Varoufakis (2008) to identify its three identifying features.

2 Stiglitz sees his work as changing the neoclassical paradigm. For example, the title of his Nobel lecture (Stiglitz 2002) was 'Information and *the change in the paradigm* in economics' (emphasis added).

3 Market fundamentalism is essentially a laissez-faire view. The core belief is that markets are efficient and that governmental attempts to 'interfere' with markets necessarily create inefficiencies. The term was popularized by George Soros in his book *The Crisis of Global Capitalism* (1998), but has been used by many others – for example, Stiglitz (2002) and Prasch (2008).

4 The 'Nobel Prize in economics' is a commonly used term for 'The Sveriges Riksbank Prize in Economic Sciences in Memory of Alfred Nobel'. Established in 1968 by the Bank of Sweden, which also funds it, it is not one of the original prizes established by Alfred Nobel.

I What is economics?

1 Quoted in John K. Galbraith's 1973 book, *Economics and the Public Purpose*.

2 The stand-up economist, Yoram Bauman, quips that a microeconomist is someone who is wrong about specific things, whereas a macroeconomist is someone who is wrong about things in general (see his website: www.standupeconomist.com/).

3 For example, Lavoie (2006: 10) says: '... since full employment of resources is not assumed, the discussion of their

efficient allocation is not a major issue. Rather, what is emphasized among post-Keynesian economists is the degree to which these resources are utilized.'

4 While it is true that economists recognize problems with markets, the solution to these problems is always more and better markets.

5 In the next chapter we discuss the difficulties of coming to a definitive conclusion through empirical testing. While the conclusions of Persson and Tabellini (1994) and Alesina and Rodrik (1994) have been challenged, it is still correct to say that there is no firm evidence that greater inequality lowers growth. This is discussed more fully in Chapter 9.

6 We noted earlier that mainstream economics does not restrict preferences to the purely selfish, so that altruism is allowed. Still, the typical model does assume pure self-interest.

2 Introducing economic models

1 Objecting to the placing of observables at the heart of the new quantum mechanics, during Heisenberg's 1926 lecture at Berlin; related by Heisenberg, quoted by Salam (1990: 99).

2 John Maynard Keynes in a letter to Roy Harrod, 1938, cited by Vickers (1999: 210).

3 See McCloskey (1983, 1985), Klamer et al. (1988) and Klamer et al. (2010).

4 Card (1992a, 1992b), Katz and Krueger (1992), Card et al. (1994), Card and Krueger (1994, 1995, 2000). Neumark and Wascher (2004) point out that conflicting empirical evidence can be found for nearly every country in the world.

5 So, David Levine was being diplomatic because he was suggesting that

minimum wage researchers were trying to avoid all such non-robustness; but in the attempt to do so, they were guiding their results in a desired direction, possibly unconsciously.

6 Perhaps because it really wasn't credible that it was 'unconscious' author biases at work; and 'conscious' author biases go by a different name – though we still have the option to use a polite one. The polite one is 'data mining' and, according to an article by Denton (1985), it's a pretty prolific industry.

7 William Broad and Nicholas Wade, in *Betrayers of the Truth* (1983), present examples where the inability of other researchers to replicate published scientific findings revealed both inadvertent errors and outright fraud. On the other hand, Dewald et al. found that the errors did not significantly affect the conclusions in the majority of cases.

8 Another example would be whether asset markets are efficient. There has been a long-running battle between Eugene Fama and his associates in support of the efficient market hypothesis, and Andrei Shleifer, Richard Thaler and others in support of the inefficient market hypothesis.

9 Donald McCloskey and Deirdre McCloskey are the same person, the transition occurring (from Donald to Deirdre) in 1995.

10 A good Internet source is the History of Economic Thought website developed through the New School of Economic Research. Check out the website at cepa. newschool.edu/het/.

11 www.census.gov/foreign-trade/balance/c0004.html#2008.

3 How markets work

1 The S&D model is also identified as the competitive model in McConnell and Brue (2005: 48); Mankiw et al. (2006: 66); Parkin and Bade (2006: 60); and Stiglitz and Boadway (1997: 23).

2 Krugman and Wells (2005: 209) also argue that easy entry into and exit from the industry are not required for price-taking behaviour.

3 The four texts that explicitly note the requirement of perfect information are Baumol and Blinder (2006), Case and Fair (2004), Ruffin and Gregory (2001) and Stiglitz and Walsh (2002). The remaining seven texts are Ayers and Collinge (2005), Gwartney et al. (2006), Hall and Lieberman (2005), Krugman and Wells (2005), Mankiw (2004), O'Sullivan and Sheffrin (2003) and Parkin (2005).

4 For a brief description of how DeBeers' Central Selling Organization controlled 70 per cent of the world's diamond supply, see Hazen (1999: 132–3). With regard to aluminium, Alcoa's near-monopoly position has decreased over the years, but the heavy entry costs and the key element of control over bauxite deposits have led to a long-lived oligopolistic structure. (See www.wa.gov/esd/lmea/sprepts/indprof/pmetal.htm.) With oil, we are referring to OPEC.

5 For example, for inputs, a small number of firms dominate markets for nitrogen fertilizer and farm machinery. On the output side, the same is true for the meat-packing sector and for the milling of grain.

6 Statistics Canada, CANSIM Table 379-0017, 'Gross domestic product by industry'.

7 But even if prices and output in these oligopolistic markets generally move in the directions predicted by a competitive analysis, these markets won't reach an efficient equilibrium, nor would government interference automatically create inefficiencies.

8 There are exceptions. For example, the discussion in Ragan and Lipsey (2008: 101–3) is carefully nuanced and makes the distinction between first- and second-generation controls. O'Sullivan and Sheffrin (2003: 148–50) provide a surprisingly conventional view of rent controls, despite the fact that the first author is a leading urban economist.

9 This is mere anecdotal evidence collected by Myatt (2004) while living in Paris from 2001 to 2002. He claims that the plural of 'anecdote' is 'data'.

4 People as consumers

1 This is from a summary of Schor (1992: 107–37).

2 There are technical problems with this measure of consumers' surplus (e.g. the requirement that the marginal utility of income be constant and that consumers' utilities can be added up) that we will not discuss (Takayama 1987).

3 Bowles et al. (2005: ch. 3) has an excellent discussion.

4 Advertising Age (adage.com) data centre reported an estimate by Robert Coen of $294 billion for all forms of advertising in 2008. US GDP in mid-2008 was estimated by the Bureau of Economic Statistics to be $14.3 trillion and, based on Bureau of the Census estimates for 2007, its population in 2008 would be about 304.7 million.

5 From George Carlin's 'Advertising lullaby', currently posted on YouTube.

6 For further information, see who.int/nutrition/topics/infantfeeding/en/index.html, accessed 23 November 2008, and World Health Organization (2008a).

7 The United States was the only UN member to vote against the Code (*Time*, 1 June 1981, p. 26). It finally endorsed it in 1994.

8 See also www.healyprozac.com/default.htm.

9 No conflicts of interest are stated in the journal article, although the press report notes that the lead author had worked as a consultant to Abbott Laboratories and to Merck.

10 See commercialalert.org for more details.

11 Nader (2000) is a great collection of essays detailing problems facing consumers.

12 The textbook assumption is defensible only if it focuses on one person's demand, taking the incomes and consumption of everyone else as given. Whether the person's preferences are independent of what others have or are interdependent doesn't matter in this case (Pollak 1978).

13 The average is calculated using '3' for 'very happy', '2' for 'pretty happy' and '1' for 'not too happy'. Source: Frey and Stutzer (2002: Table 1)

14 The question in its English version was 'Taking all things together, would you say you are very happy, quite happy, not very happy or not at all happy?' We calculated aggregate values using weights 9.3, 7.2, 3.9 and 1.0 for each response respectively. (Weights are those current in the World Database of Happiness.) There are seventy-three surveys for sixty-nine countries; three were sampled twice and the former East Germany and West Germany were surveyed separately.

15 The values are from the variable *rgdpeqa* in the Penn World Tables, Version 6.2. Gross domestic product is expressed in US dollars of the year 2000, with exchange rates adjusted for purchasing power parity, to give a more appropriate comparison between countries than market exchange rates permit. Rather than divide GDP by population, an adjustment is made to give less weight to children, whose consumption needs are less.

16 Satisfaction with life is significantly lower in these countries, however (Deaton 2008). Questions about happiness elicit information about experienced emotional states, while questions about satisfaction with one's life ask for an overall evaluation of one's situation. The factors that influence each of these are not necessarily the same.

17 The relationship looks like a curved line that gets flatter as income gets higher, but which continues to rise as income rises. This implies that a given dollar increase in incomes will have a bigger impact on happiness in poor countries. A similar relationship holds for satisfaction with life (Deaton 2008). In the recent past, many have held the view that beyond a certain level of average income, increases in happiness were negligible (e.g. Layard 2005).

18 Solnick and Hemenway (1998) report survey evidence supportive of this.

19 Schwartz (2004) gives a psychologist's view about why the expansion of

choice that comes with increasing incomes has significant costs. In textbook economics, more choice is always better.

20 Other recent studies include Di Tella and MacCulloch (2006, 2008), Clark et al. (2008) and Stevenson and Wolfers (2008).

5 The firm

1 In reality firms often produce more than one product. Here, 'the size of the firm' refers only to how much of the relevant product the firm produces because the concern is about its share of this one market.

2 The following sections draw heavily on two valuable articles by Avi Cohen (1983, 1996).

3 Keen (2009: 134–6 and 2001: ch. 3) asks a similar question.

4 The firms were representative of the economy as a whole outside of government, non-profit firms, agriculture and firms with regulated prices (Blinder et al. 1998: 60).

5 This description of costs is standard fare in the post-Keynesian approach to the firm (Lavoie 2006: 40–41).

6 Putterman and Kroszner (1996: 13–16) survey recent theoretical ideas.

7 A recent text, Shepherd and Shepherd (2004: 162–6), also cites no evidence.

8 We surveyed nine widely used texts, of which the first six had such a diagram or a discussion of it: Colander et al. (2006: 202), Frank et al. (2005: 203), Mankiw et al. (2006: 287), McConnell et al. (2007: 164), Krugman and Wells (2005: 200), Ragan and Lipsey (2008: 174); Baumol and Blinder (2006), Parkin and Bade (2006), Schiller (2006).

9 Dixon (1990: 364) has a similar diagram, as does Keen (2009: 126). Keen's account of why the competitive equilibrium is really a disequilibrium is different: 'Once a single firm has changed its output, then all firms will receive the new market price, and *there is no seller charging a lower price to whom the consumers can turn*.' This presumes that once one firm reduces its output, all firms raise their price. In Dixon's account, one firm can raise its price, while other firms maintain theirs at the initial level.

10 The Center for Public Integrity (www.publicintegrity.org) is an excellent source of reports about lobbying activities in the United States.

11 The healthcare legislation has not yet been finalized as this book goes to press.

12 For examples, see www.source-watch.org/index.php?title=Portal:Front_groups, accessed 24 November 2008.

13 See www.cala.org/cause.html, accessed 24 November 2008.

14 www.sourcewatch.org/index.php?title=Citizens_Against_Lawsuit_Abuse, accessed 24 November 2008.

15 The situation is a prisoner's dilemma, a concept described in Chapter 6, Part One.

16 Caplan (2008: ch. 4) explains the concept and critiques it.

17 Surveys of firms reviewed by Blinder et al. (1998: 40–44) provide mixed evidence: profit maximization, target rate of return, and maintaining market share figured among managers' goals. In his post-Keynesian text, Lavoie (2006: 37) concludes that firms seek growth, and the pursuit of power and profits is a means to that end.

18 For other editions, see his *Principles of Political Economy*, Book IV, ch. vii, §6.

6 Market structure and efficiency

1 This is the same as saying that high-income persons will, on average, have a lower marginal utility of income than a low-income person. The marginal dollar is simply worth less to them so they'll be willing to pay more of them for an extra loaf of bread, for example.

2 See Section 1.7 of Chapter 1 for an explanation of the condition concerning the necessity for all markets to exist.

3 In more advanced economics courses, the problem is ignored in a more sophisticated way. Preferences are assumed to be such that the distribution of income does not affect total market

demand for any product. In this special case, prices must equal marginal social valuations. This means, however, that a transfer of $1 from a rich person to a poor person does not affect the demand for anything, which is clearly untrue.

4 We surveyed nine widely used texts and found a discussion of the trade-offs of patent length in only the first two: Frank et al. (2005), Krugman and Wells (2005); Baumol and Blinder (2006), Colander et al. (2006), Mankiw et al. (2006), McConnell et al. (2007), Ragan and Lipsey (2008), Parkin and Bade (2006), Schiller (2006).

5 Marcia Angell (2004: 12) documents that between 1990 and 2000 'marketing and administration' were two and a half times the size of R&D expenditures. She says: 'These figures are drawn from the industry's own annual reports to the Securities and Exchange Commission (SEC) and to stockholders, but what actually goes into these categories is not at all clear, because drug companies hold that information very close to their chests. It is likely, for instance, that R&D includes many activities most people would consider marketing, but no one can know for sure. For its part, "marketing and administration" is a gigantic black box that probably includes what the industry calls "education," as well as advertising and promotion, legal costs, and executive salaries – which are whopping.'

6 This is being phased in, with the least-developed countries allowed to delay granting pharmaceutical patents until 2016. Many economists have been critical of extending patent protection across the world in this way (e.g. Scherer 2004).

7 As Wheat (2009: 70) puts it, it is ironic that the long run depends 'on the passage of time to dismiss the significance of time'.

8 The elasticity is the percentage change in quantity divided by the percentage change in the price. Knowing this and how much price has changed allows the change in quantity (the base of the triangle) to be estimated.

9 This change in treatment from the earlier edition to the third edition is explained in a footnote on p. 678.

10 Nowadays it is seriously challenged by behavioural economics. One indication that behavioural economics has become mainstream is the 9 December 2002 article by Justin Fox in *Fortune* entitled 'Is the market rational? No, say the experts. But neither are you – so don't go thinking you can outsmart it'.

11 The amount it pays out as dividends is immaterial. Either the firm disperses its profits as dividends or it ploughs them back to grow its assets – either way, the shareholder benefits.

12 The next several paragraphs draw heavily on Mullainathan and Thaler (2004).

13 Closed-end funds are like typical (open-end) mutual funds except that to cash out of the fund, investors must sell their shares on the open market. This means that closed-end funds have market prices that are determined by supply and demand, rather than set equal to the value of their assets by the fund managers as in an open-end fund.

14 More recent studies found under-reaction rather than overreaction over shorter periods of time. Over periods of six months to one year, stocks display momentum – the stocks that go up the fastest for the first six months of the year tend to keep going up. So, markets sometimes overreact and sometimes under-react (Mullainathan and Thaler 2004).

15 The stories vary, but always seem convincing at the time. In the dot-com bubble the story was all about the new technology breaking the mould. Everything was going to be different. In real estate booms the story is usually about a fixed amount of land confronting a growing population and a growing economy that has always (and will always) propel prices higher. It's a myth, but people believe it during the boom.

16 See, for example, Shiller (1981), Campbell and Shiller (1987) and Jung and Shiller (2005).

7 Externalities

1 We surveyed nine widely used texts, eight of which had this structure: Baumol and Blinder (2006), Colander et al. (2006), Frank et al. (2005), McConnell et al. (2007), Krugman and Wells (2005), Parkin and Bade (2006), Ragan and Lipsey (2008) and Schiller (2006). The only exception was Mankiw et al. (2006), where externalities get a chapter in the middle of the book.

2 Archer (2009) is a good introduction to the physical science. See also the most recent report of the Intergovernmental Panel on Climate Change (2007).

3 Of the sample of nine texts in endnote 1, only three – Baumol and Blinder (2006), McConnell et al. (2007) and Schiller (2006) – offer any factual evidence about climate change.

4 For details see Monbiot (2006: ch. 2) and Gelbspan (2004: ch. 3).

5 The academies were those of Brazil, Canada, China, France, Germany, India, Italy, Japan, Russia, the United Kingdom and the United States. See also American Association for the Advancement of Science (2006).

6 See www.junkscience.com for a sample. The site www.sourcewatch.org is a valuable guide to the background and sources of funding of industry-funded organizations and 'experts'.

7 Cited in Schor (2004: 48).

8 Of the texts listed in endnote 1, only Frank et al. (2005: 298, 427) mention consumption externalities. It plays no role in the central chapter on consumption, however.

9 Some countries, such as Canada and the United States, already have such schemes, but they limit the amounts that can be put in these accounts each year.

10 This contrasts with existing 'regressive' sales taxes and value-added taxes where higher-income persons tend to pay a lower percentage of their income in tax than lower-income persons.

11 This claim seems inconsistent with the figures for the United States in the previous sentence.

12 From the texts in endnote 1, only Colander et al. (2006: 463) explicitly acknowledge the importance of laws governing workplace health and safety. No other texts mention the issue.

13 The 2004 documentary film *Shipbreakers* provides a case study of the dirty and dangerous work of breaking up ships carried out in Alang, India. For details, see the National Film Board of Canada, www3.nfb.ca/collection/films/fiche/?id=51361.

8 Marginal productivity theory

1 It's the same as a simple mortgage calculation. You can find many mortgage calculators online. Set the amortization period to twenty-five years, and choose the interest rate and principal amount.

2 The fact that estimated returns to schooling are much greater than that required from a mortgage amortization point of view suggests that there are barriers to entering occupations – including differences in inherited ability – which raises the return above levels implied by the principle of equal net benefits. McConnell et al. (2007: 305) inform us that: 'Rates of return are estimated to 10 to 13 percent for investments in secondary education and 8 to 12 percent for investments in college and university education. One generally accepted estimate is that *each year* of schooling raises a worker's wage by about 8 percent' (emphasis added).

3 For example, McConnell et al. (2007: 300) say: 'The purpose of licensing is supposedly to protect consumers from incompetent practitioners – surely a worthy goal. But such licensing also results in above-competitive wages and earnings for those in the licensed occupation.'

4 Employers are rational – so that even non-prejudiced employers seek to maximize profits. If they can employ black workers at a discount, they'll seize the opportunity. Prasch (2008: ch. VII) contains an excellent discussion.

5 Perhaps the worst treatment of discrimination is contained in Parkin and Bade (2006), who seem to confuse shifts in demand with changes in quantity

demanded. They correctly say that lower prices act 'as an incentive to encourage people who are prejudiced to buy from the people against whom they are prejudiced'. But then they strangely suggest: 'This force could be strong enough to eliminate the effects of discrimination altogether' (p. 429). In brief, only four of nine texts in our sample of mainstream textbooks mention that discrimination can persist in competitive markets if customers themselves are prejudiced.

6 For example, Krugman and Wells (2005: 307) say: 'many wrongly believe that marginal productivity theory gives a moral justification for the existing distribution, implying it is fair and appropriate'.

7 This section contains more advanced material and may be omitted without loss of continuity.

8 They point out that the same issues erupted in huge controversies on two previous occasions – once at the turn of that century and again in the 1930s.

9 Large differences exist even after controlling for union status and observed worker and job characteristics.

10 Much of this evidence is summarized in Chapter 4.

11 The owner is the principal, and the management team the agent. In modern corporations, shareholders are the principals.

12 An indication of its phenomenal growth is that in 1992 firms in the 'Standard & Poor's 500' index granted their employees options worth a total of $11 billion at the time of grant; by 2000, option grants in S&P 500 firms increased to $119 billion (Hall and Murphy 2003: 49).

13 The Sarbanes-Oxley Act of 2002 tightened up accounting standards in the US. Among the major provisions of the act are: criminal and civil penalties for securities violations, auditor independence and increased disclosure regarding executive compensation.

14 See *The Times*, 18 March 2009, business.timesonline.co.uk/tol/business/industry_sectors/banking_and_finance/article5927610.ece.

9 Government, taxation

1 Quoted in Chomsky (1987: 3).

2 Negative wealth is possible because 'human capital', a person's ability to earn income in the future, is not measured in surveys, although it is an important asset. For example, most students graduating from university have negative wealth if they have substantial student loans.

3 The official US poverty line is based on 1964 estimates of a minimum adequate diet, then multiplied by three (the purchase of other necessities taking up two-thirds of the budget). It has since been adjusted only for changes in the cost of living. See www.census.gov/hhes/www/poverty/poverty.html.

4 We surveyed nine widely used texts. The absolute measure of poverty was the choice of: Krugman and Wells (2005), Mankiw et al. (2006) and Schiller (2006). Of these, only Mankiw mentioned the idea of relative poverty. The relative measure of poverty was supported by: Baumol and Blinder (2006), Colander et al. (2006) and Parkin and Bade (2006). The remaining three texts took no clear position: Frank et al. (2005), McConnell et al. (2007) and Ragan and Lipsey (2008).

5 For details see www.un.org/millenniumgoals/.

6 The income distribution is a 'public good' (a concept discussed in Chapter 5): people may value it differently, but everyone 'consumes' the same amount.

7 In fairness, the examples are probably chosen for simplicity: an excise tax changes the relative price of a single good.

8 This follows from the unstated assumption that individual utility is independent of others' incomes and consumption.

9 Amiel and Cowell (1999: 120) report stark differences between Israeli economics and sociology students who answered these questions. Economics students were almost twice as likely to agree that society was better off in moving from situations like A to B in Figure 9.3.

10 Colander et al. (2006: 305) is exceptional in making this point clearly, point-

ing out that one Pareto optimal position would be for one person to have all the world's income and everyone else nothing.

11 The policy change is a reduction in a guaranteed minimum annual income and a reduction in the tax rate on labour income.

12 Endogenous growth means that the growth rate is generated within the theoretical model itself rather than being determined outside it, i.e. exogenously. For example, the neoclassical theory of economic growth fashionable in the 1960s and 1970s featured exogenous technological change, driven by some scientific progress that lay outside the model.

13 The 'no free lunch' idea also does not survive a course in macroeconomics: in situations of mass unemployment of resources, when the economy is far below its production possibility frontier, appropriate macroeconomic policy can expand the production of all goods by putting unemployed resources to work. There is only a trade-off if the economy is moving from one point to another on the production possibilities frontier itself.

14 Robert Sapolsky's (2001) account of hierarchy in a baboon troop is both entertaining and instructive.

15 Wolfson et al. (1993) examines the relationship between death rates after retirement and earnings before retirement in Canada and finds a similarly significant social gradient.

16 Experiments with rats have determined causation between maternal stress before birth and subsequent health. Otherwise there would be an open question as to whether poorer health was instead due to post-natal conditions (Wilkinson 2005).

17 This probably does not take into account that if family size is a matter of choice, the number of births would be lower if infant mortality were lower too.

18 We surveyed nine texts. The discussion of income inequality and poverty was located in the following chapter numbers: 21st of 22 chapters (or 21/22, for short) in Baumol and Blinder (2006); 19/20 in Colander et al. (2006); 15/15 in Frank et al. (2005); 21/22 in Krugman and Wells (2005); 16 and 18/18 in Ragan and Lipsey (2008); 20/22 in Mankiw et al. (2006); 14/17 in McConnell et al. (2007); 18/19 in Parkin and Bade (2006); and 17/20 in Schiller (2006).

10 Trade and globalization

1 For example, McConnell et al. (2007: 419); Ragan and Lipsey (2008: 829).

2 For example, McConnell et al. (2007: 419–20); Ragan and Lipsey (2008: 828).

3 The original compensation principle was stated in terms of unobservable utilities, but it is typically implemented using incomes, as we saw in the last chapter. Hicks and Kaldor made the simplifying assumption that the redistribution of income would not cost anything: total income would remain unchanged.

4 The model is called the Heckscher–Ohlin model after its Swedish originators. In it, all industries are perfectly competitive and all factors are assumed to be unable to move between countries. At first glance, this model appears to be most applicable to trade between developed and developing countries, which are thought to differ the most in terms of relative quantities of factors of production.

5 For example, technological change could change wages, but also be a response to import competition.

6 Production is 'outsourced' if it is contracted out to another company. If it is 'offshored' it takes place in another country, whether in the same company or not.

7 The figure is adapted from Figure 1 in Palley (2006: 11).

8 It also does not consider that people may view differently their responsibility for acts of commission (e.g. sending their toxic waste to places where it won't be disposed of properly) and acts of omission (e.g. failing to act to address global economic injustice).

9 The outcome would be acceptable only if the initial distribution of income and wealth in the world were acceptable.

10 The Basel Action Network works to promote adherence to the Basel

Convention, which governs trade in hazardous materials.

11 We surveyed nine texts. None raised the question of corporate influence over the WTO's agenda, nor of the power of large countries to dominate the WTO: Baumol and Blinder (2006), Colander et al. (2006), Frank et al. (2005), McConnell et al. (2007), Krugman and Wells (2005), Mankiw et al. (2006), Parkin and Bade (2006), Ragan and Lipsey (2008) and Schiller (2006). Only Schiller (p. 744) remarked that 'many Third World nations are concerned about playing by trade rules that always seem to benefit rich nations (e.g. copyright protection, import protection, farm subsidies)'. Why the rules are like this is apparently a mystery.

12 For texts of the agreements and their status, and an up-to-date list, see the website of the Office of the United States Trade Representative: www.ustr.gov/ Trade_Agreements/Section_Index.html.

13 The Department of Foreign Affairs and International Trade has details at www.international.gc.ca/trade-agreements-accords-commerciaux/agr-acc/ index.aspx.

14 Of the texts listed in endnote 11, only Frank et al. (2005: 52) acknowledges Helleiner's point, warning that a trade agreement with a superpower that 'can use trade as an instrument of foreign policy' reduces 'the sovereignty of the smaller partner'.

15 On Iran, see Curtis (2003: 303–15). On Guatemala, see Schlesinger and Kinzer (1983). On Chile, see Hersh (1983: 258–96) and Klein (2007).

16 As of the time of writing, the US Congress has not ratified the agreement with Colombia. A bill implementing the agreement is currently before the Canadian parliament.

11 Conclusion

1 In the 1990s, the prevailing myth was that the boom in information technology made all other cycles obsolete; from 2000 to 2005 it was that property prices could only go up because land is in limited supply while population continues to grow.

2 The compensation principle really amounts to the claim that everyone is better off if everyone, on average, has more stuff. As we've noted, this is unconvincing for other reasons.

3 The ninth edition of Samuelson's principles textbook, published in 1973, contains all of these topics.

Postscript

1 Three of the better-known acronyms are SIVs (structured investment vehicles), CDOs (collateralized debt obligations) and ABCPs (asset-backed commercial paper).

2 This was the Depository Institutions Deregulation and Monetary Control Act of 1980.

3 This was the Alternative Mortgage Transaction Parity Act of 1982.

4 It also established the Federal Deposit Insurance Corporation (FDIC), which provided government insurance on bank deposits to prevent bank runs. This aspect of Glass-Steagall is still in place.

5 In this case the economies were called 'economies of scope' (the benefits that come from producing a variety of goods and services).

6 These consequences came to light only as the corporate and banking scandals emerged with the bankruptcy of Enron in 2001 and Worldcom in 2002.

7 Fannie Mae (and its 'younger brother' Freddie Mac) did themselves need bailouts. But this was because when the real estate bubble burst even regular borrowers – who did have down payments and assets – found themselves underwater. The value of their mortgages now exceeded the value of their properties. This led to foreclosures and the downfall of Freddie and Fannie. See Krugman (2008a).

8 This estimate was made by the International Swaps and Derivatives Association (ISDA), www.isda.org/.

9 Source: www.bloomberg.com/apps/ news?pid=20601103&sid=aaog3i4yUopo& refer=us.

10 It also exempted commodity futures trading from federal oversight. In stepped

Enron, to take advantage of that loophole (and we know how that turned out).

11 For his favours to Enron and the banks, Gramm was rewarded with a cushy job at UBS Warburg. And Gramm's wife, Wendy, was rewarded with a job at Enron.

12 We've argued (at least in previous endnotes) that neither Fannie Mae nor Freddie Mac was responsible for the sub-prime mess. But there is a case against them bound up with their peculiar status: although they're private companies with stockholders and profits, they're 'government-sponsored enterprises' and receive special privileges. The most im-portant of these is implicit: investor belief that if Fannie and Freddie are threatened with failure, the federal government will come to their rescue. This implicit guar-antee means that profits are privatized but losses are socialized. If they do well, their stockholders reap the benefits; but if things go badly, Washington picks up the tab. Heads they win, tails you lose. Such one-way bets can encourage the taking of bad risks, because the downside is someone else's problem. See Krugman (2008a).

Bibliography

Abegglen, J. and G. Stalk (1985) *Kaisha: The Japanese Corporation*, New York: Basic Books.

Ackerman, F. (2002) 'Still dead after all these years: interpreting the failure of General Equilibrium Theory', *Journal of Economic Methodology*, 9(2): 119–39.

— (2009) *Can We Afford the Future? The economics of a warming world*, London: Zed Books.

Adams, W. and J. W. Brock (2004) *The Bigness Complex: Industry, labour and government in the American economy*, 2nd edn, Stanford Economics and Finance, Stanford, CA: Stanford University Press.

Adler, M. (2010) *Economics for the Rest of Us: Debunking the science that makes life dismal*, New York: New Press.

Akerlof, G. A. and W. T. Dickens (1982) 'The economic consequences of cognitive dissonance', *American Economic Review*, 72(3): 307–19.

Akerlof, G. A. and R. J. Shiller (2009) *Animal Spirits: How human psychology drives the economy and why it matters for global capitalism*, Princeton, NJ, and Oxford: Princeton University Press.

Akerlof, G. A. and J. L. Yellen (1988) 'Fairness and unemployment', *American Economic Review: Papers and Proceedings*, 78(2): 44–9.

Aldred, J. (2009) *The Skeptical Economist: Revealing the ethics inside economics*, London and Sterling, VT: Earthscan.

Alesina, A. and D. Rodrik (1994) 'Distributive policies and economic growth', *Quarterly Journal of Economics*, 109(2): 450–90.

Alston, R. M., J. R. Kearl and M. B. Vaughan (1992) 'Is there a consensus among economists in the 1990s?', *American Economic Review, Papers and Proceedings*, 82: 203–9.

American Association for the Advancement of Science (2006) 'AAAS board statement on climate change', 9 December, available at www.aaas.org/news/releases/2007/0218am_statement.shtml.

Amiel, Y. and F. A. Cowell (1999) *Thinking about Inequality: Personal judgement and income distributions*, Cambridge: Cambridge University Press.

Amnesty International (2007) *Colombia: Killings, arbitrary detentions, and death threats – the reality of trade unionism in Colombia*, AMR 23/001/2007, July.

Angell, M. (2004) *The Truth about the Drug Companies: How they deceive us and what to do about it*, New York: Random House.

Angus Reid Global Monitor (2008) 'Global warming a real threat for Britons', 10 January, available at www.angus-reid.com/polls/view/global_warming_a_real_threat_for_britons/.

Archer, D. (2009) *The Long Thaw: How humans are changing the next 100,000 years of Earth's climate*, Princeton, NJ: Princeton University Press.

Arnott, R. (1995) 'Time for revisionism on rent control', *Journal of Economic Perspectives*, 9: 99–120.

Arnsperger, C. and Y. Varoufakis (2008) 'Neoclassical economics: three identifying features', in E. Fullbrook (ed.), *Pluralist Economics*, London: Zed Books.

Arrow, K. (1959) 'Towards a theory of price adjustment', in M. Abramovitz (ed.), *The Allocation of Economic Resources*, Stanford, CA: Stanford University Press, Stanford.

Associated Press (2008) 'Cholesterol drugs recommended for kids as young as 8: pediatricians', 7 July, available at www.cbc.ca/health/story/2008/07/07/kids-cholesterol-report.html.

Ayers, R. and R. Collinge (2005) *Micro-economics: Explore and apply*, Upper Saddle River, NJ: Pearson Prentice Hall.

Baby Milk Action (2007) 'Significant protection for infant health in the Philippines achieved as court rejects "restraint of trade" argument – but more needed', Press release, 10 October, available at www.babymilkaction.org/press/press10oct07.html.

Badger, G. J., W. K. Bickel, L. A. Giordano, E. A. Jacobs, G. Loewenstein and L. Marsch (2007) 'Altered states: the impact of immediate craving on the valuation of current and future opioids', *Journal of Health Economics*, 26: 865–76.

Bakan, J. (2004) *The Corporation: The pathological pursuit of profit and power*, Toronto: Viking Canada.

Baker, D. (2009) *Plunder and Blunder: The rise and fall of the bubble economy*, Sausalito, CA: PoliPoint Press.

Baldwin, R. E., J. Mutti and J. D. Richardson (1980) 'Welfare effects on the United States of a significant multilateral tariff reduction', *Journal of International Economics*, 10(3): 405–23.

Barro, R. (2000) 'Inequality and growth in a panel of countries', *Journal of Economic Growth*, 5(1): 5–32.

Baumol, W. J. (2002) *The Free-market Innovation Machine: Analyzing the growth miracle of capitalism*, Princeton, NJ: Princeton University Press.

— (2006) *Regulation Misled by Misread Theory: Perfect competition and competition-imposed price discrimination*, Washington, DC: AEI-Brookings Joint Centre for Regulatory Research.

Baumol, W. J. and A. Blinder (2006) *Microeconomics: Principles and policy*, 10th edn, Mason, OH: Thomson South-Western.

Baumol, W. J. and R. E. Gomory (2001) *Global Trade and Conflicting National Interests*, Cambridge, MA: MIT Press.

Baylis, K. and T. Dhar (2007) 'Effect of the Quebec ad ban on junk food ex-penditure', Working paper, University of British Columbia, 2 November, available at www.works.bepress/kathy_baylis/15.

Beasley, A. and L. H. Amir (2007) 'Editorial. Policy on infant formula industry funding, support or sponsorship of articles submitted for publication', *International Breastfeeding Journal*, 2(5): 1–3.

Beaulier, S. A. and S. Mounts (2008) 'Asymmetric information about perfect competition: the treatment of perfect information in introductory economics textbooks', in F. Mixon, Jr, and R. Cebula (eds), *Expanding Teaching and Learning Horizons in Higher Education: Essays on economic education*, New York: Nova Science Publishers.

Bebchuk, L. A. and J. M. Fried (2004) *Pay without Performance: The unfulfilled promised of executive compensation*, Cambridge, MA, and London: Harvard University Press.

— (2005) 'Pay without performance: an overview of the issues', *Journal of Applied Corporate Finance*, 17(4): 8–23.

Benicourt, E. (2004) 'Five pieces of advice for students studying microeconomics', in E. Fullbrook (ed.), *A Guide to What's Wrong with Economics*, London: Anthem Press.

Bergson, A. (1973) 'On monopoly welfare losses', *American Economic Review*, 63: 853–70.

Betts, K. S. (2001) 'Rapidly rising PBDE levels in North America', *Environmental Science and Technology Online News*, 7 December, available at pubs.acs.org/subscribe/journals/esthag-w/2001/dec/science/kb_pbde.html.

Blinder, A. S., E. Canetti, D. Lebow and J. B. Rudd (1998) *Asking about Prices: A new approach to understanding price stickiness*, New York: Russell Sage Foundation.

Bok, D. (1993) *The Cost of Talent*, New York: Free Press.

Bonin, J. P., D. C. Jones and L. Putterman (1993) 'Theoretical and empirical studies of producer cooperatives: will ever the twain meet?', *Journal of Economic Literature*, 31(4): 1290–320.

Boseley, S. (2008) 'Prozac, used by 40 m people does not work, say scientists', *Guardian*, 26 February.

Boseley, S. and R. Evans (2008) 'Drug giants accused over doctors' perks', *Guardian*, 23 August.

Boulding, K. E. (1966) 'The economics of the coming Spaceship Earth', in H. Jarret (ed.), *Environmental Quality in a Growing Economy*, Baltimore, MD: Johns Hopkins Press, pp. 1–3.

Bowles, S., R. Edwards and F. Roosevelt (2005) *Understanding Capitalism: Competition, command, and change*, Oxford: Oxford University Press.

Bowles, S., M. Franzini and U. Pagano (eds) (1999) *The Politics and Economics of Power*, London: Routledge.

Bradshaw, J. P., P. Hoelscher and C. Richardson (2006) 'Comparing child well-being in OECD countries: concepts and methods', UNICEF Innocenti Centre Working Paper IWP-2006-03, December.

Broad, W. and N. Wade (1983) *Betrayers of the Truth: Fraud and deceit in the halls of science*, New York: Simon and Schuster.

Brophy, J. T., M. M. Keith and J. Schieman (2007) 'Canada's asbestos legacy at home and abroad', *International Journal of Occupational and Environmental Health*, 13(2): 236–43.

Campbell, C. M. and K. S. Kamlani (1997) 'The reasons for wage rigidity: evidence from a survey of firms', *Quarterly Journal of Economics*, 112(3): 759–89.

Campbell, J. Y. and R. J. Shiller (1987) 'Cointegration and tests of present value models', *Journal of Political Economy*, 97(5): 1062–88.

Canadian Medical Association (2008) *No Breathing Room: National illness costs of air pollution*, August, available at www.cma.ca.

Caplan, B. (2008) *The Myth of the Rational Voter: Why democracies choose bad policies*, Princeton, NJ: Princeton University Press.

Card, D. (1992a) 'Using the regional variation in wages to measure the effects of the federal minimum wage', *Industrial and Labor Relations Review*, 46: 22–37.

— (1992b) 'Do minimum wages reduce employment? A case study of California 1987–89', *Industrial and Labor Relations Review*, 46: 38–54.

Card, D. and A. Krueger (1994) 'Minimum wages and employment: a case study of the fast food industry in New Jersey and Pennsylvania', *American Economic Review*, 84(4): 772–93.

— (1995) *Myth and Measurement: The new economics of the minimum wage*, Princeton, NJ: Princeton University Press.

— (2000) 'Minimum wages and employment: a case study of the fast-food industry in New Jersey and Pennsylvania: a reply', *American Economic Review*, 90: 1396–420.

Card, D., L. Katz and A. Krueger (1994) 'Comment on David Neumark and William Wascher: employment effects of minimum wages and subminimum wages', *Industrial and Labor Relations Review*, 47: 487–96.

Case, K. and R. C. Fair (2004) *Principles of Microeconomics*, 7th edn, Upper Saddle River, NJ: Pearson Prentice Hall.

CBS News (2008) 'Following the trail of toxic e-waste', *60 Minutes*, 9 November, available at www.cbsnews.com/stories/2008/11/06/60minutes/printable4579229.shtml, accessed 14 February 2009.

Chamberlin, E. (1933) *The Theory of Monopolistic Competition: A re-orientation of the theory of value*, Cambridge, MA: Harvard University Press.

Chandler, A. D., Jr (1977) *The Visible Hand: The managerial revolution in American business*, Cambridge, MA: Harvard University Press.

Chernomas, R. and I. Hudson (2007) *Social Murder and Other Shortcomings of Conservative Economics*, Winnipeg: Arbeiter Ring Publishing.

Chomsky, N. (1987) *Turning the Tide: The US and Latin America*, 2nd revised edn, Montreal: Black Rose Books.

— (1988) *Language and Politics* (ed. C. P. Otero), Montreal: Black Rose Books.

— (1993) *Letters from Lexington: Reflections on propaganda*, Monroe, ME: Common Courage Press.

— (2006) *Failed States: The abuse of power and the assault on democracy*, New York: Metropolitan Books.

— (2007) *Interventions*, San Francisco, CA: City Lights Books.

Clark, A. E., P. Frijters and M. A. Shields (2008) 'Relative income, happiness and utility: an explanation for the Easterlin Paradox and other puzzles', *Journal of Economic Literature*, 46(1): 95–144.

Clark, J. B. (1891) 'Distribution as determined by a law of rent', *Quarterly Journal of Economics*, 5: 289–318.

Clover, C. (2006) *The End of the Line: How overfishing is changing the world and what we eat*, Berkeley and Los Angeles: University of California Press.

Coburn, G. C., M. C. Currás-Collazo and P. R. S. Kodavanti (2008) 'In vitro effects of environmentally relevant polybrominated diphenyl ether (PBDE) congeners on calcium buffering mechanisms in rat brain', *Neurochemical Research*, 33: 355–64.

Cohen, A. J. (1983) '"The laws of returns under competitive conditions": progress in microeconomics since Sraffa (1926)?', *Eastern Economic Journal*, 9(3): 213–20.

— (1996) 'Why haven't introductory textbooks resolved Sraffa's 1926 complaints? The realism of U-shaped cost curves and the dominance of perfect competition', in N. Aslanbengui and M. I. Naples (eds), *Rethinking Economic Principles: Critical essays on introductory textbooks*, Chicago, IL: Irwin, pp. 81–91.

Cohen, A. J. and G. Harcourt (2003) 'Whatever happened to the Cambridge capital theory controversies', *Journal of Economic Perspectives*, 17(1): 199–214.

Colander, D. C. (2003) 'Integrating sex and drugs into the principles course: market-failures versus failures-of-markets outcomes', *Journal of Economic Education*, 34: 82–91.

— (2004) *Economics*, 5th edn, Boston, MA: Mc-Graw-Hill Irwin.

Colander, D., R. P. F. Holt and J. B. Rosser, Jr (2004) *The Changing Face of Economics: conversations with cutting edge economists*, Ann Arbor: University of Michigan Press.

Colander, D. C., C. Richter and D. W. Rockerbie (2006) *Microeconomics*, 3rd Canadian edn, Toronto: McGraw-Hill Ryerson.

Commercial Alert (2004) 'Experts call for worldwide ban on marketing of junk food for kids', Press release, 27 February, available at www.commercial alert.com.

CSDH (Commission on the Social Determinants of Health) (2008) *Closing the Gap in a Generation: Health equity through action on the social determinants of health*, Geneva: World Health Organization.

Curtis, M. (2003) *Web of Deceit: Britain's real role in the world*, London: Vintage.

Daly, H. E. and J. B. Cobb, Jr (1989) *For the Common Good*, Boston, MA: Beacon Press.

Daly, H. E. and J. Farley (2004) *Ecological Economics: Principles and applications*, Washington, DC: Island Press.

Daniels, S. R., F. R. Greer and the Committee on Nutrition (2008) 'Lipid screening and cardiovascular health in childhood', *Pediatrics*, 122(1): 198–208.

Darley, J. and D. Latane (1968) 'Bystander intervention in emergencies: diffusion of responsibility', *Journal of Personality and Social Psychology*, 8: 377–83.

Dasgupta, P. (2007) *Economics: A very short introduction*, Oxford: Oxford University Press.

Dauvergne, P. (2005) 'Cancer and global environmental politics', *Global Environmental Politics*, 5(3): 6–13.

Davis, D. L. (2002) *When Smoke Ran Like Water: Tales of environmental deception and the battle against pollution*, New York: Basic Books.

— (2007) *The Secret History of the War on Cancer*, New York: Basic Books.

Davis, D. L. and P. S. Webster (2002)

'The social context of science: cancer and the environment', *Annals of the American Academy of Political and Social Science*, Vol. 584, *Health and the Environment*, November, pp. 13–34.

Davis, L. E. and R. A. Huttenback (1988) *Mammon and the Pursuit of Empire: The economics of British imperialism*, abridged edn, Cambridge: Cambridge University Press.

Dawnay, E. and H. Shah (2005) *Behavioural Economics: Seven principles for policy makers*, London: New Economics Foundation.

Dayton-Johnson, J. (2001) *Social Cohesion and Economic Prosperity*, Toronto: James Lorimer and Co.

De Bondt, W. and R. Thaler (1985) 'Does the stock market overreact?', *Journal of Finance*, 40(3): 793–805.

Deardorff, A. V. and R. M. Stern (2002) 'What you should know about globalization and the World Trade Organization', *Review of International Economics*, 10(3): 404–23.

Deaton, A. (2008) 'Income, health and well-being around the world: evidence from the Gallup World Poll', *Journal of Economic Perspectives*, 22(2): 53–72, also available at media.gallup.com/dataviz/ www/Angus_Deaton_Gallup_Poll_ Article.pdf.

Denton, F. (1985) 'Econometric data mining as an industry', *Review of Economics and Statistics*, 67(1): 124–7.

Dewald, W. G., J. G. Thursby and R. G. Anderson (1986) 'Replication in empirical economics: the Journal of Money, Credit, and Banking Project', *American Economic Review*, 76(4): 587–603.

Di Tella, R. and R. MacCulloch (2006) 'Some uses of happiness data in economics', *Journal of Economic Perspectives*, 20(1): 25–46.

— (2008) 'Gross national happiness as an answer to the Easterlin Paradox?', *Journal of Development Economics*, 86(1): 22–42.

Dinse, G. E., D. M. Umbach, A. J. Sasco, D. G. Hoel and D. L. Davis (1999) 'Unexplained increases in cancer incidence in the United States from 1975 to 1994: possible sentinel health incidators?', *Annual Review of Public Health*, 20(1): 173–209.

Dixon, H. (1990) 'Equilibrium and explanation', in J. Creedy (ed.), *Foundations of Economic Thought*, Oxford: Blackwell, pp. 356–93.

Douglas, M. (1987) 'Wants', in J. Eatwell, M. Milgate and P. Newman (eds), *Palgrave Dictionary of Economics*, vol. 4, New York: Palgrave Macmillan, pp. 874–6.

Dowd, D. (2000) *Capitalism and Its Economics: A critical history*, London: Pluto Press.

Downs, A. (1957) *An Economic Theory of Democracy*, New York: Harper.

Driskill, R. (2007) 'Deconstructing the arguments for free trade', Unpublished manuscript, Vanderbilt University.

— (2008) 'Why do economists make such dismal arguments about trade?', *Foreign Policy*, May/June, available at www.foreignpolicy.com/story/cms. php?story_id=4320.

Dunkley, G. (2000) *The Free Trade Adventure: The WTO, the Uruguay Round and globalism*, London and New York: Zed Books.

— (2004) *Free Trade: Myth, reality and alternatives*, London and New York: Zed Books.

Easterlin, R. A. (1974) 'Does economic growth improve the human lot? Some empirical evidence', in P. A. David and M. W. Reder (eds), *Nations and Households in Economic Growth: Essays in honor of Moses Abramovitz*, New York: Academic Press.

— (1995) 'Will raising the incomes of all increase the happiness of all?', *Journal of Economic Behavior and Organization*, 27(1): 35–47.

— (2001) 'Income and happiness: towards a unified theory', *Economic Journal*, 111(473): 465–84.

Eatwell, J. (1987) 'Returns to scale', in J. Eatwell, M. Milgate and P. Newman (eds), *Palgrave Dictionary of Economics*, vol. 4, New York: Palgrave Macmillan, pp. 165–6.

Eatwell, J. and L. Taylor (1998) 'The performance of liberalized capital markets', Center for Economic Policy Analysis Working Paper Series III, Working Paper no. 8, New School for Social Research, New York, September.

Edlin, A. S. and P. Karaca-Mandic (2006) 'The accident externality from driving', *Journal of Political Economy*, 114(5): 931–55.

Einstein, A. (1926) 'Remarks on new quantum mechanics', quoted in A. Salam, *Unification of Fundamental Forces: The first of the 1988 Dirac memorial sectures* (1990), Cambridge: Cambridge University Press, p. 99.

Engels, F. (1987 [1845]) *The Condition of the Working Class in England*, London: Penguin.

Epstein, S. (1998) *The Politics of Cancer Revisited*, Hankins, NY: East Ridge Press.

European Union (1993) Council Directive 93/104/EC of 23 November 1993 concerning certain aspects of the organization of working time, *Official Journal*, L 307, 13/12/1993, 18-24, available at eur-lex.europa.eu/LexUriServ/LexSriServ.do?uri=CELEX:31993L0104: EN:HTML.

Fama, E. (1965) 'The behavior of stock market prices', *Journal of Business*, 38(1): 34–105.

Farmer, R. (1993) *The Macroeconomics of Self-Fulfilling Prophecies*, Cambridge, MA: MIT Press.

Feldman, E. J. (2007) 'Deal or no deal. Snatching defeat from the jaws of victory', *International Trade Law and Regulation*, 13(5): 91–7.

Feldstein, M. (1999) 'Reducing poverty, not inequality', *The Public Interest*, 137: 33–41.

Finkelstein, S. and D. Hambrick (1988) 'Chief executive compensation: a synthesis and reconciliation', *Strategic Management Journal*, 9(6): 543–58.

Fortin, P. (2005) 'From productivity to well-being: keep the focus on basic skills', *International Productivity Monitor*, 11: 3–13.

Fox, J. (2009) *The Myth of the Rational Market: A history of risk, reward and delusion on Wall Street*, New York: HarperCollins.

Frank, R. H. (1984) 'Are workers paid their marginal products?', *American Economic Review*, 74(4): 549–71.

— (1997) 'The frame of reference as a public good', *Economic Journal*, 107: 1832–47.

— (1999) *Luxury Fever: Why money fails to satisfy in an era of excess*, New York: Free Press.

— (2005a) 'Positional externalities cause large and preventable welfare losses', *American Economic Review*, 95(2): 137–41.

— (2005b) 'Of hockey players and housing prices', *New York Times*, 27 October, also available at www.robert-h-frank. com/timescolumn.html.

Frank, R. H. and P. J. Cook (1995) *The Winner-Take-All Society*, New York: Penguin.

Frank, R. H., T. Gilovich and D. Regan (1993) 'Does studying economics inhibit cooperation?', *Journal of Economic Perspectives*, 7(2): 159–71.

Frank, R. H., B. S. Bernanke, L. Osberg, M. Cross and B. MacLean (2005) *Principles of Microeconomics*, 2nd Canadian edn, Toronto: McGraw-Hill Ryerson.

Frey, B. S. and A. Stutzer (2002) 'What can economists learn from happiness research?', *Journal of Economic Literature*, 40(2): 402–35.

Fridell, M., I. Hudson and M. Hudson (2008) 'With friends like these: the corporate response to fair trade coffee', *Review of Radical Political Economics*, 40(1): 8–34.

Friedman, M. (1953) *Essays in Positive Economics*, Chicago, IL: University of Chicago Press.

— (1976) *Price Theory*, Chicago, IL: Aldine Publishing.

Froot, K. A. and E. M. Dabora (1999) 'How are stock prices affected by the location of trade?', *Journal of Financial Economics*, 53(2): 189–216.

Frydman, C. and R. E. Saks (2008) 'Executive compensation: a new view from a long-term perspective, 1936–2005', NBER Working Paper no. 14145.

Fullbrook, E. (ed.) (2008) *Pluralist Economics*, London and New York: Zed Books.

Fuller, D. and D. Geide-Stevenson (2003) 'Consensus among economists: revisited', *Journal of Economic Education*, 34(4): 369–87.

Gagné, G. (2002) 'The NAFTA and the softwood lumber dispute: what kind of Canada–US partnership?', Research Paper 12–02, Groupe de recherche sur l'integration continentale, University of Quebec at Montreal.

Galbraith, James K. (1998) *Created Unequal: The crisis in American pay*, New York: Free Press.

— (2008) *The Predator State: How conservatives abandoned the free market and why liberals should too*, New York: Free Press.

Galbraith, John K. (1958) *The Affluent Society*, London: Hamish Hamilton.

— (1973a) 'Power and the useful economist', *American Economic Review*, 63(1): 1–11.

— (1973b) *Economics and the Public Purpose*, Boston, MA: Houghton Mifflin.

— (1985) *The New Industrial State*, 4th edn, Boston, MA: Houghton Mifflin.

— (2004) *The Economics of Innocent Fraud: Truth for our time*, New York: Houghton Mifflin.

Gelbspan, R. (2004) *Boiling Point*, New York: Basic Books.

George, D. L. (1990) 'The rhetoric of economics texts', *Journal of Economic Issues*, 24(3): 861–78.

— (1996) 'The rhetoric of economics texts revisited', in N. Aslanbeigui and M. I. Naples (eds), *Rethinking Economic Principles: Critical essays on introductory textbooks*, Chicago, IL: Richard D. Irwin, Inc., pp. 28–43.

— (2001) *Preference Pollution: How markets create the desires we dislike*, Ann Arbor: University of Michigan Press.

Glasbeek, H. (2002) *Wealth by Stealth: Corporate crime, corporate law, and the perversion of democracy*, Toronto: Between the Lines.

Glyn, A. (2007) 'Explaining labor's declining share of national income', Policy Brief no. 4, Intergovernmental Group of Twenty-four (G-24).

Gneezy, U. and A. Rustichini (2000) 'A fine is a price', *Journal of Legal Studies*, XXIX(1), pt 1: 1–18.

Gomory, R. E. and W. J. Baumol (2000) *Global Trade and Conflicting National Interests*, Cambridge, MA: MIT Press.

— (2004) 'Globalization: prospects, promise and problems', *Journal of Policy Modeling*, 26: 425–38.

Goodwin, N. R., F. Ackerman and D. Kiron (eds) (1997) *The Consumer Society*, Washington, DC, and Covelo, CA: Island Press.

Goodwin, N., J. A. Nelson, F. Ackerman and T. Weisskopf (2005) *Microeconomics in Context*, Boston, MA: Houghton Mifflin.

— (2008) *Microeconomics in Context*, 2nd edn, New York: M. E. Sharpe.

Gordon, H. S. (1954) 'The economic theory of a common-property resource: the fishery', *Journal of Political Economy*, 62(2): 124–42.

Gough, I. (1987) 'Welfare state', in J. Eatwell, M. Milgate and P. Newman (eds), *Palgrave Dictionary of Economics*, vol. 4, New York: Palgrave Macmillan, pp. 895–7.

Greenberg, M. (2008) 'The defence of Chrysotile, 1912–2007', *International Journal of Occupational and Environmental Health*, 14(1): 57–66.

Gwartney, J., R. Stroup, R. Sobel and D. Macpherson (2006) *Microeconomics: private and public choice*, 11th edn, Mason, OH: Thomson South-Western.

Hahn, F. H. (1987) 'Review of The Rhetoric of Economics', *Journal of Economic Literature*, XXV(1): 110–11.

Hall, B. and K. J. Murphy (2003) 'The trouble with stock options', *Journal of Economic Perspectives*, 17(3): 49–70.

Hall, R. and M. Lieberman (2005). *Microeconomics: Principles and applications*, 3rd edn, Mason, OH: Thomson South-Western.

Harberger, A. C. (1954) 'Monopoly and

resource allocation', *American Economic Review*, 44: 77–87.

Hay, D. A. and D. J. Morris (1991) *Industrial Economics and Organisation: Theory and evidence*, Oxford: Oxford University Press.

Hazen, R. M (1999) *The Diamond Makers*, Cambridge: Cambridge University Press.

Health Disparities Task Group (2004) 'Reducing health disparities – role of the health sector', Discussion paper, Public Health Agency of Canada, Ottawa, December.

Healy, D. (2003) *Let Them Eat Prozac*, Toronto: James Lorimer and Co.

Heilbroner, R. L. (1998) 'Rhetoric and ideology', in A. Klamer, D. McCloskey and R. Solow (eds), *The Consequences of Economic Rhetoric*, Cambridge: Cambridge University Press, pp. 38–44.

Heilbroner, R. L. and L. Thurow (1998) *Economics Explained: Everything you need to know about how the economy works and where it's going*, New York: Touchstone Books.

Helleiner, G. K. (1996) 'Why small countries worry. Some neglected issues in current analyses of the benefits and costs for small countries of integrating with large ones', *World Economy*, 19(6): 759–63.

Helliwell, J. (2003) 'How's life? Combining individual and national variables to explain subjective well-being', *Economic Modelling*, 20: 331–60.

Herman, E. S. and N. Chomsky (1988) *Manufacturing Consent: The political economy of the mass media*, New York: Pantheon.

Hersh, S. M. (1983) *The Price of Power: Kissinger in the Nixon White House*, New York: Summit Books.

Hickman, M. (2007) 'E211 revealed: evidence highlights new fear over drinks additive', and 'Caution: some soft drinks may seriously harm your health', *Independent*, 27 May.

Hicks, J. R. (1939) *Value and Capital*, 1st edn, Oxford: Oxford University Press.

Hildenbrand, W. and A. P. Kirman (1988)

Equilibrium Analysis: Variations on themes by Edgeworth and Walras, Amsterdam: North-Holland.

Hill, R. (2000) 'The case of the missing firms', *Journal of Economic Education*, 31(3): 281–95.

Hirschman, A. O. (1991) *The Rhetoric of Reaction: Perversity, futility, jeopardy*, Cambridge, MA: Belknap Press of Harvard University Press.

Holt, S. (1992) 'The sequence of market structures: teaching perfect competition last', Unpublished paper.

Hudson, I. and M. Hudson (2003) 'Removing the veil? Commodity fetishism, fair trade, and the environment', *Organization and Environment*, 16(4): 413–30.

Hunt, E. K. and H. J. Sherman (2008) *Economics: An introduction to traditional and radical views*, 7th edn, New York: M. E. Sharpe.

Intergovernmental Panel on Climate Change (2007) *Climate Change 2007: The physical science basis*, Cambridge: Cambridge University Press, available at www.ipcc.ch/ipccreports/ar4-wg1.htm.

International Agency for Research on Cancer (2005) *Cancer Incidence in Five Continents*, vols 1–8 (updated) and vol. 9, Lyons: International Agency for Research on Cancer, available at www-dep.iarc.fr/.

Jacobson, L. S., R. L. La Londe and D. G. Sullivan (1993) 'Earnings losses of displaced workers', *American Economic Review*, 83(2): 23–6.

Joint Science Academies (2005) 'Joint science academies' statement: global response to climate change', available at royalsociety.org/document.asp?id=3222.

Jowit, J. (2008) 'Poll: most Britons doubt cause of climate change', *Observer*, 22 July.

Jung, J. and R. J. Shiller (2005) 'Samuelson's Dictum and the stock market', *Economic Inquiry*, 43(2): 221–8.

Kahneman, D. (2002) 'Maps of bounded rationality: a perspective on intuitive judgement and choice', Nobel Prize Lecture, December.

Kaldor, N. (1934) 'The equilibrium of the firm', *Economic Journal*, 44(173): 60–76.

— (1939) 'Welfare propositions and interpersonal comparisons of utility', *Economic Journal*, 49: 549–52.

Kalmi, P. (2007) 'The disappearance of co-operatives from economics textbooks', *Cambridge Journal of Economics*, 31(4): 625–47.

Katz, L. and A. Krueger (1992) 'The effect of the minimum wage in the fast food industry', *Industrial and Labor Relations Review*, 46: 6–21.

Kaufman, G. G. and K. E. Scott (2003) 'What is systemic risk? And do bank regulators retard or contribute to it?', *Independent Review*, 7(3): 371–91.

Kearl, J. R., C. L. Pope, G. C. Whiting and L. T. Whimmer (1979) 'A confusion of economists', *American Economic Review, Papers and Proceedings*, 69: 28–37.

Keen, S. (2001) *Debunking Economics: The naked emperor of the social sciences*, London: Zed Books.

— (2009) 'A pluralist approach to micro-economics', in J. Reardon (ed.), *The Handbook of Pluralist Economics Education*, London: Routledge, pp. 120–49.

Keynes, J. M. (1936) *The General Theory of Employment, Interest and Money*, London: Macmillan.

— (1963 [1931]) 'Economic possibilities for our grandchildren', in *Essays in Persuasion*, New York: W. W. Norton.

Klamer, A., D. McCloskey and R. M. Solow (1988) *The Consequences of Economic Rhetoric*, Cambridge: Cambridge University Press.

Klamer, A., D. McCloskey and S. Ziliak (2010) *The Economic Conversation*, London: Palgrave Macmillan.

Klein, N. (2007) *The Shock Doctrine: The rise of disaster capitalism*, Toronto: Knopf Canada.

Knack, S. and P. Keefer (1997) 'Does social capital have an economic payoff? A cross-country investigation', *Quarterly Journal of Economics*, 112: 1251–88.

Krueger, A. (2001) 'Teaching the minimum wage in econ 101 in light of the new economics of the minimum wage', *Journal of Economic Education*, 32: 243–58.

Krugman, P. (2008a) 'Fannie, Freddie and you', *New York Times*, Op-Ed column, 14 July.

— (2008b) 'Trade and wages, reconsidered', *Brookings Papers on Economic Activity*, 1: 103–37.

— (2008c) *The Return of Depression Economics and the Crisis of 2008*, New York: W. W. Norton.

— (2009) 'How did economists get it so wrong?' *New York Times Magazine*, 2 September, available at www.nytimes.com/2009/09/06/magazine/06Economic-t.html.

Krugman, P. and R. Wells (2005) *Microeconomics*, New York: Worth Publishers.

Kuhn, T. S. (1962) *The Structure of Scientific Revolutions*, Chicago, IL, and London: University of Chicago Press.

LaDou, J. (2004) 'The asbestos cancer epidemic', *Environmental Health Perspectives*, 112(3): 285–90.

Lakatos, I. (1978) *The Methodology of Scientific Research Programmes: Philosophical papers vol. 1*, ed. J. Worrall and G. Currie, Cambridge: Cambridge University Press.

Lal, D. (2000) *The Poverty of 'Development Economics'*, 2nd revised and expanded US edn, Cambridge, MA: MIT Press.

Lavoie, M. (2006) *Introduction to Post-Keynesian Economics*, Houndsmill, UK and New York: Palgrave Macmillan.

Lawrence, F. (2004) *Not on the Label: What really goes into the food on your plate*, London: Penguin.

— (2008) *Eat Your Heart Out: Why the food business is bad for the planet and your health*, London: Penguin.

Layard, R. (2005) *Happiness: Lessons from a new science*, London: Penguin/Allen Lane.

Lazear, E. P. (1989) 'Pay equality and industrial politics', *Journal of Political Economy*, 97(3): 561–80.

Lazear, E. P. and S. Rosen (1981) 'Rank-order tournaments as optimum labor contracts', *Journal of Political Economy*, 89(5): 841–61.

Leacock, S. (1924) *The Garden of Folly*, New York: Dodd, Mead and Co.

Lec, S. J. (1968) *More Unkept Thoughts*, New York: Funk & Wagnalls.

Lee, C., A. Shleifer and R. H. Thaler (1991) 'Investor sentiment and the closed-end fund puzzle', *Journal of Finance*, 46(1): 75–109.

LeGrand, J. (1991) *Equity and Choice: An essay in economics and applied philosophy*, London and New York: HarperCollins.

Leibenstein, H. (1966) 'Allocative efficiency v. X-efficiency', *American Economic Review*, 56: 392–415.

Leonard, T. C. (2009) 'Review of S. A. Marglin's *The Dismal Science*', *Journal of Economic Literature*, 47(2): 489–91.

Leontief, W. (1983) 'Foreword', in A. Eichner (ed.), *Why Economics is Not Yet a Science*, New York: M. E. Sharpe.

Levine, D. (2001) 'Editor's introduction to "The employment effects of minimum wages: evidence from a prespecified research design"', *Industrial Relations*, 40: 161–2.

Li, K. (2007) 'World Breastfeeding Week 2007: an early start on breast milk saves infants' lives', 1 August, available at www.unicef.org/nutrition/index_40463.html.

Li, R., Z. Zhao, A. Mokdad, L. Barker and L. Grummer-Strawn (2003) 'Prevalence of breastfeeding in the United States: evidence from the 2001 Immunization Survey', *Pediatrics*, 111(5), pt 2: 1198–201.

Linder, S. B. (1970) *The Harried Leisure Class*, New York: Columbia University Press.

Lindert, P. (2004a) 'Social spending and economic growth. Interview with Peter Lindert', *Challenge*, 47(4): 6–16.

— (2004b) *Growing Public: Social spending and economic growth since the eighteenth century*, 2 vols, Cambridge: Cambridge University Press.

Lindgren, G. (1976) 'Height, weight and menarche in Swedish urban school children in relation to socio-economic and regional factors', *Annals of Human Biology*, 3(6): 501–28.

Lipsey, R. G. and K. Lancaster (1956/57)

'The general theory of the second best', *Review of Economic Studies*, 24(1): 11–32.

Littlechild, S. (1981) 'Misleading calculations of the social costs of monopoly power', *Economic Journal*, 91: 348–63.

Lombardini-Riipinen, C. and M. Autio (2007) 'Coverage of behavioral and experimental economics in undergraduate microeconomics textbooks', SSRN, December, available at ssrn.com/abstract=1088076.

Lunn, P. and T. Harford (2008) 'Behavioural economics: is it such a big deal?', *Prospect Magazine*, 150, September.

Machin, S. and A. Manning (2004) 'A test of competitive labor market theory: the wage structure among care assistants in the south of England', *Industrial and Labor Relations Review*, 57(3): 371–85.

MacLeod, G. (1997) *From Mondragón to America: Experiments in community economic development*, Sydney, Nova Scotia: University College of Cape Breton Press.

Mankiw, N. G. (2004) *Principles of Microeconomics*, 3rd edn, Mason, OH: Thomson.

Mankiw, N. G., R. D. Kneebone, K. J. McKenzie and N. Rowe (2002) *Principles of Microeconomics*, 2nd Canadian edn, Toronto: Thomson Nelson.

— (2006) *Principles of Microeconomics*, 3rd Canadian edn, Toronto: Thomson Nelson.

Manning, A. (2003) *Monopsony in Motion: Imperfect competition in labor markets*, Princeton, NJ: Princeton University Press.

Mansfield, C. L. (2000) 'The road to subprime "hell" was paved with good congressional intentions: usury deregulation and the subprime home equity market', *South Carolina Law Review*, 51: 473–589.

Mansfield, E. (1994) *Microeconomics*, 8th edn, New York: W. W. Norton.

Marglin, S. (2008) *The Dismal Science: How thinking like an economist undermines community*, Cambridge, MA: Harvard University Press.

Markowitz, G. and D. Rosner (2002) *Deceit*

and Denial: The deadly politics of industrial pollution, Berkeley: University of California Press.

Marmot, M. (2004) The Status Syndrome: How social standing affects our health and longevity, New York: Times Books.

Marmot, M. G., G. Rose, M. Shipley and P. J. S. Hamilton (1978) 'Employment grade and coronary heart disease in British civil servants', Journal of Epidemiology and Community Health, 32(5): 244–9.

Marwell, G. and R. Ames (1981) 'Economists free ride, does anyone else?: experiments on the provision of public goods, IV', Journal of Public Economics, 15: 295–310.

Mattern, D. (2002) 'Millennium: status and vision', The Humanist, November/December.

McCloskey, D. (1983) 'The rhetoric of economics', Journal of Economic Literature, XXI(2): 481–517.

— (1985) The Rhetoric of Economics, Madison: University of Wisconsin Press.

McConnell, C. R. and S. L. Brue (2005) Economics: Principles, problems and policies, 16th edn, Boston, MA: McGraw-Hill Irwin.

McConnell, C. R., S. L. Brue and T. P. Barbiero (2007) Microeconomics, 11th Canadian edn, Toronto: McGraw-Hill Ryerson.

McCullough, B. D. and H. D. Vinod (2003) 'Verifying the solutions from a non-linear solver', American Economic Review, 93(3): 873–92.

McCullough, B. D., K. A. McGeary and T. D. Harrison (2006) 'Lessons from the JMCB archive', Journal of Money Credit and Banking, 38(4): 1093–107.

McGreal, C. (2009) 'Revealed: millions spent by lobby firms fighting Obama health reforms', Guardian, 1 October.

McKnight, D. (2008) 'Who is behind the climate change deniers?', The Age (Melbourne), 2 August.

McLean, B. and P. Elkind (2003) The Smartest Guys in the Room: The amazing rise and scandalous fall of Enron, New York: Portfolio.

McNeil, J. R. (2000) Something New Under the Sun: An environmental history of the twentieth century, New York: W. W. Norton.

McPherson, M. S. (1987) 'Changes in tastes', in J. Eatwell, M. Milgate and P. Newman (eds), Palgrave Dictionary of Economics, vol. 1, New York: Palgrave Macmillan, pp. 401–3.

Michaels, D. (2008) Doubt is Their Product: How industry's assault on science threatens your health, Oxford: Oxford University Press.

Milkovitch, G. T. and J. M. Newman (1987) Compensation, 2nd edn, Plano, TX: Business Publications Inc.

Mill, J. S. (1965) Collected Works, vol. 3: Principles of Political Economy, bks III, IV and V, Toronto: University of Toronto Press.

Miller, R. L. (2004) Economics Today, 12th edn, Boston, MA: Pearson/Addison Wesley.

Mittelstaedt, M. (2009) 'Dow to sue over Quebec pesticide ban', Globe & Mail, 9 April.

Monbiot, G. (2006) Heat: How to stop the planet from burning, London: Allen Lane.

— (2007a) 'Not what it says on the tin', Guardian, 19 June, also available at www.monbiot.com.

— (2007b) 'G8: watch what they do, not what they say', Guardian, 5 June, also available at www.monbiot.com.

— (2008) 'Fishermen cling on as ecosystem suffers', Guardian Weekly, 18 July.

Moreton, C. (2007) 'We are eating ourselves ill: treating malnutrition costs NHS more than obesity', Independent, 6 May.

Moyers, B. (2006) 'A culture of corruption', Washington Spectator, 1 April, available at www.washingtonspectator.com/archive.cfm.

Moynihan, R. and A. Cassels (2005) Selling Sickness: How the world's largest pharmaceutical companies are turning us all into patients, Vancouver and Toronto: Greystone Books.

Mullainathan, S. and R. Thaler (2004)

'Behavioural economics', *International Encyclopaedia of the Social and Behavioural Sciences*, Science Direct, Elsevier, pp. 1094–100.

Musgrave, A. (1981) '"Unrealistic assumptions" in economic theory: the F-twist untwisted', *Kyklos*, 34: 377–87.

Myatt, A. (2004) 'Getting the most from a principles discussion of rent control', *Economic Research Network, ERN Educator: Courses, Cases and Teaching*, Abstract no. 485422, 1–17 January.

Myrdal, G. (1969) *Objectivity in Social Research*, New York: Pantheon Books.

— (1973) *Against the Stream: Critical essays on economics*, New York: Pantheon.

Nader, R. (2000) *The Ralph Nader Reader*, New York: Seven Stories Press.

— (2004a) *The Good Fight: Declare your independence and close the democracy gap*, New York: Regan Books.

— (2004b) *In Pursuit of Justice: Collected writings 2000–2003*, New York: Seven Stories Press.

Nagel, T. (2005) 'The problem of global justice', *Philosophy and Public Affairs*, 33(2): 113–42.

Naples, M. I. and N. Aslanbeigui (1996) 'What does determine the profit rate? The neoclassical theories presented in introductory textbooks', *Cambridge Journal of Economics*, 20: 53–71.

Nasca, P. C. and H. Pastides (2008) *Fundamentals of Cancer Epidemiology*, 2nd edn, Sudbury, MA: Jones and Bartlett Publishers.

Nelson, R. (1976) 'Review: Goldschmid, Mann, and Weston's industrial concentration: the new learning', *Bell Journal of Economics*, 7(2): 729–32.

Neumark, D. and W. Wascher (2004) 'Minimum wages, labor market institutions, and youth employment: a cross-national analysis', *Industrial and Labor Relations Review*, 57: 223–48.

Northrop, E. (2000) 'Normative foundations of introductory economics', *American Economist*, 44(1): 53–61.

Oi, W. Y. and T. L. Idson (1999), 'Firm-size and wages', in O. Ashenfelter and D. Card (eds), *Handbook of Labor Economics*, vol. 3, Amsterdam: North Holland, pp. 166–214.

Okun, A. (1975) *Equality and Efficiency: The Big Tradeoff*, Washington, DC: Brookings Institution Press.

Olson, M. (1971) *The Logic of Collective Action: Public goods and the theory of groups*, Cambridge, MA: Harvard University Press.

O'Reilly, C. A., B. G. Main and G. S. Crystal (1988) 'CEO compensation as tournament and social comparison: a tale of two theories', *Administrative Science Quarterly*, 33(2): 257–74.

Organisation for Economic Co-operation and Development (2008a) *OECD in Figures 2008*, Paris: OECD, available at www.oecd.org.

— (2008b) *Growing Unequal? Income distribution and poverty in OECD countries*, Paris: OECD, available at www.oecd.org.

Osberg, L. (1995) 'The equity–efficiency trade-off in retrospect', *Canadian Business Economics*, 3(3): 5–20, available at www.myweb.dal.ca/osberg/.

O'Sullivan, A. and S. Sheffrin (2003) *Microeconomics: Principles and tools*, Upper Saddle River, NJ: Prentice Hall.

Palley, T. I. (2006) *Rethinking Trade and Trade Policy: Gomory, Baumol and Samuelson on comparative advantage*, Public Policy Brief 86, Levy Economics Institute of Bard College.

Parkin, M. (2005) *Microeconomics*, 7th edn, Toronto: Pearson Addison Wesley.

Parkin, M. and R. Bade (2006) *Microeconomics: Canada in the global economy*, 6th edn, Toronto: Pearson Addison Wesley.

Patinkin, D. (1965) *Money, Interest and Prices: An integration of monetary and value theory*, 2nd edn, New York: Harper & Row.

Pawlick, T. F. (2006) *The End of Food: How the food industry is destroying our food supply – and what you can do about it*, Fort Lee, NJ: Barricade Books.

Persson, T. and G. Tabellini (1994) 'Is inequality harmful for growth?', *American Economic Review*, 84(3): 600–21.

Pew Research Center (2008) 'An increase in GOP doubt about global warming deepens partisan divide', 8 May, available at pewresearch.org/pubs/828/global-warming.

Phillips, P. (2003) *Inside Capitalism: An introduction to political economy*, Halifax: Fernwood Publishing.

Pianin, E. (2002) 'Study ties air pollution to risk of lung cancer', *Guardian Weekly*, 14 March, p. 36.

Picard, A. (2005) 'Common foods laced with chemical', *Globe & Mail*, 14 February.

Pigou, A. C. (1932) *The Economics of Welfare*, 4th edn, London: Macmillan.

Pinker, S. (2002) *The Blank Slate: The modern denial of human nature*, New York: Viking.

Platt, K. H. (2007) 'Chinese air pollution deadliest in world, report says', *National Geographic News*, 9 July, available at news.nationalgeographic.com/news/2007/07/070709-china-pollution.html.

Pogge, T. W. (2007) 'Why inequality matters', in D. Held and A. Kaya (eds), *Global Inequality: Patterns and explanations*, London: Polity Press.

— (2008) *World Poverty and Human Rights*, 2nd edn, London: Polity Press.

Pollak, R. A. (1978) 'Endogenous tastes in demand and welfare analysis', *American Economic Review*, 68(2): 374–9.

Poole, W. (2004) 'Free trade: why are economists and noneconomists so far apart?', Federal Reserve Bank of St Louis *Review*, 86(5): 1–6.

Prasch, R. E. (2008) *How Markets Work: Supply, demand and the 'real world'*, Cheltenham: Edward Elgar.

Pugel, T. A. (2007) *International Economics*, New York: McGraw-Hill Irwin.

Purse, K. (2003) 'Work-related fatality risk and neo-classical compensating wage differentials', *Cambridge Journal of Economics*, 28(4): 597–617.

Putnam, R. (1993) *Making Democracy Work: Civic traditions in modern Italy*, Princeton, NJ: Princeton University Press.

Putterman, L. and R. S. Kroszner (1996) 'The economic nature of the firm: a new introduction', in L. Putterman and R. S. Kroszner (eds), *The Economic Nature of the Firm: A reader*, 2nd edn, Cambridge: Cambridge University Press.

Ragan, C. T. S. and R. G. Lipsey (2005) *Microeconomics*, 11th Canadian edn, Toronto: Pearson Addison Wesley.

— (2008) *Economics*, 12th Canadian edn, Toronto: Toronto: Pearson Addison Wesley.

Ray, R. and J. Schmitt (2007) 'No-vacation nation', Washington, DC: Center for Economic and Policy Research, available at www.cepr.net.

Redelmeier, D., P. Rozin and D. Kahneman (1993) 'Understanding patients' decisions: cognitive and emotional perspectives', *Journal of the American Medical Association*, 72: 73.

Ricardo, D. (2005 [1817]) *The Principles of Political Economy and Taxation*, Indianapolis: Liberty Press.

Rick, F. (2009) 'Bernie Madoff is no John Dillinger', *New York Times*, 4 July.

Ritchie, G. (2006) 'Peace in our time', *Ottawa Citizen*, 29 April.

Robinson, J. (1933) *Economics of Imperfect Competition*, London and New York: Macmillan.

— (1965) 'Teaching economics', *Collected Economic Papers*, vol. 3, ch. 1, Oxford: Basil Blackwell.

— (1972) 'The second crisis of economic theory', *American Economic Review*, 62(2); reprinted in *Collected Economic Papers*, vol. 4, ch. 10, Oxford: Basil Blackwell.

— (1973a) 'The new mercantilism', *Collected Economic Papers*, vol. 4, ch. 1, Oxford: Basil Blackwell.

— (1973b) 'Marginal productivity', *Collected Economic Papers*, vol. 4, ch. 14, Oxford: Basil Blackwell.

Rodrik, D. (2009) 'Blame the economists, not economics', *Guatemala Times*, 11 March, available at www.hks.harvard.edu/news-events/news/commentary/blame-the-economists.

Rothschild, K. (1971) 'Introduction', in

K. Rothschild (ed.), *Power in Economics: Selected readings*, London: Penguin, pp. 7–17.

Ruffin, R. and P. Gregory (2001) *Principles of Microeconomics*, 7th edn, Toronto: Addison Wesley.

Russell, T. and R. Thaler (1985) 'The relevance of quasi rationality in competitive markets', *American Economic Review*, 75(5): 1071–82.

Salam, A. (1990) *Unification of Fundamental Forces: The first of the 1988 Dirac memorial lectures*, Cambridge: Cambridge University Press.

Samuelson, P. A. (1973) *Economics*, 9th edn, New York: McGraw-Hill.

— (1998) 'Summing up on business cycles: opening address', in J. Fuhrer and S. Schuh (eds), *Beyond Shocks: What causes business cycles*, Boston, MA: Federal Reserve Bank of Boston, pp. 33–6.

— (2004) 'Where Ricardo and Mill rebut and confirm arguments of mainstream economists supporting globalization', *Journal of Economic Perspectives*, 18(3): 135–46.

Samuelson, P. A. and W. D. Nordhaus (1992) *Economics*, 14th edn, New York: McGraw-Hill.

Sapolsky, R. M. (2001) *A Primate's Memoir*, New York: Scribner.

Scherer, F. M. (2004) 'A note on global welfare in pharmaceutical patenting', *World Economy*, 27: 1127–42.

Scherer, F. M. and D. Ross (1990) *Industrial Market Structure and Economic Performance*, 3rd edn, Boston, MA: Houghton Mifflin.

Schiller, B. R. (2006) *The Economy Today*, 10th edn, New York: McGraw-Hill Irwin.

Schlesinger, S. and S. Kinzer (1983) *Bitter Fruit: The untold story of the American coup in Guatemala*, Garden City, NY: Anchor Books.

Schlosser, E. (2001) *Fast Food Nation: The dark side of the American meal*, Boston, MA, and New York: Houghton Mifflin.

Schor, J. B. (1992) *The Overworked American: The unexpected decline of leisure*, New York: Basic Books.

— (1998) *The Overspent American: Upscaling, downshifting, and the new consumer*, New York: Harper Perennial.

— (2004) *Born to Buy*, New York: Scribner.

Schumpeter, J. (1950) *Capitalism, Socialism and Democracy*, New York: Harper and Row.

— (1954) *History of Economic Analysis*, New York: Oxford University Press.

Schwartz, B. (2004) *The Paradox of Choice: Why more is less*, New York: HarperCollins.

Sen, A. K. (1999) *Development as Freedom*, New York: Knopf.

Sharpe, A. (2003) 'Linkages between economic growth and inequality: introduction and overview', *Canadian Public Policy*, 29, Supplement, pp. S1–S14.

Shawn, W. (1991) *The Fever*, New York: Grove Press.

Shell, E. R. (2002) *The Hungry Gene: The inside story of the obesity industry*, New York: Grove Press.

Shepherd, W. G. and J. M. Shepherd (2004) *The Economics of Industrial Organization*, 5th edn, Long Grove, IL: Waveland Press.

Shiller, R. J. (1981) 'Do stock prices move too much to be justified by subsequent changes in dividends?', *American Economic Review*, 7(3): 421–36.

Shleifer, A. (2000) *Inefficient Markets: An introduction to behavioral finance*, Clarendon Lectures, Oxford: Oxford University Press.

Shleifer, A. and R. Vishny (1997) 'The limits of arbitrage', *Journal of Finance*, 52(1): 35–55.

Simon, H. (1991) 'Organisations and markets', *Journal of Economic Perspectives*, 5(2): 25–44.

Singer, N. and D. Wilson (2009) 'Medical editors push for ghostwriting crackdown', *New York Times*, 17 September.

Singer, P. and J. Mason (2006) *The Ethics of What We Eat: Why our food choices matter*, Emmaus, PA: Rodale.

Smith, A. (1979 [1776]) *The Nature and Causes of the Wealth of Nations*, Indianapolis: Liberty Press.

Solnick, S. J. and D. Hemenway (1998) 'Is

more always better? A survey on positional concerns', *Journal of Economic Behavior and Organization*, 37: 373–83.

Soros, G. (1998) *The Crisis of Global Capitalism: Open society endangered*, PublicAffairs, New York: Perseus Books Group.

Sraffa, P. (1926) 'The laws of returns under competitive conditions', *Economic Journal*, 36(4): 535–50.

Stanfield, J. R. and J. B. Stanfield (eds) (2004) *Interviews with John Kenneth Galbraith*, Jackson: University of Mississippi Press.

Stern, N. (2007) *The Economics of Climate Change: The Stern Review*, Cambridge: Cambridge University Press.

— (2008) 'The economics of climate change', *American Economic Review*, 98(2): 1–37.

Stevenson, B. and J. Wolfers (2008) 'Economic growth and subjective well-being: reassessing the Easterlin Paradox', *Brookings Papers on Economic Activity*, 1: 1–87.

Stiglitz, J. E. (1985) 'Information and economic analysis: a perspective', *Economic Journal*, 95, Supplement: Conference Papers, pp. 21–41.

— (2002) 'Information and the change in the paradigm in economics', *American Economic Review*, 92(3): 460–501.

— (2003) *The Roaring Nineties: A new history of the world's most prosperous decade*, New York: W. W. Norton.

— (2009) 'GDP fetishism', *Economists' Voice*, 6(8), Article 5.

Stiglitz, J. E. and R. Boadway (1997) *Principles of Microeconomics and the Canadian Economy*, 2nd Canadian edn, New York: W. W. Norton.

Stiglitz, J. E. and C. Walsh (2002). *Principles of Microeconomics*, 3rd edn, New York: W. W. Norton.

Strom, R. (2007) *Hot House: Global climate change and the human condition*, New York: Copernicus Books.

Sweden (2002) *Amning av barn födda 2000* [Breastfeeding of children born in 2000], Stockholm: National Board of Health and Welfare and Official Statistics of Sweden, available at www.soe.se/ epc/amning/amning.htm.

Takala, J. (2003) 'ILO's role in the global fight against asbestos', *Asbestos: European Conference 2003*, Conference report, www.hvbg.de/e/asbest/konfrep/ konfrep/index.html.

Takayama, A. (1987) 'Consumer surplus', in J. Eatwell, M. Milgate and P. Newman (eds), *Palgrave Dictionary of Economics*, vol. 1, New York: Palgrave Macmillan, pp. 607–13.

Taylor, J. B. (2004) *Economics*, Boston, MA: Houghton Mifflin Co.

Thaler, R. H. and S. Bernartzi (2004) 'Save more tomorrow: using behavioural economics to increase employee savings', *Journal of Political Economy*, 112(1): S164–S187.

Thomas, C. D. et al. (2004) 'Extinction risk from climate change', *Nature*, 427(6970): 145–8.

Thurow, L. (1975) *Generating Inequality: Mechanisms of distribution in the US economy*, New York: Basic Books.

Tickell, O. (2008) *Kyoto2: How to manage the global greenhouse*, London: Zed Books.

Titmuss, R. M. (1970) *The Gift Relationship*, London: Allen and Unwin.

Tucker, I. B. (2005) *Economics for Today*, 4th edn, Mason, OH: Thompson/South-Western.

Tossavainen, A. (2004) 'A global use of asbestos and the incidence of mesothelioma', *International Journal of Occupational and Environmental Health*, 10(1): 22–5.

UNCTAD (United Nations Conference on Trade and Development) (2008) *World Investment Report 2008: Transnational corporations and the infrastructure challenge*, New York and Geneva: United Nations.

UNDP (United Nations Development Programme) (2007) *Human Development Report 2007/2008*, New York: Palgrave Macmillan, available at hdr. undp.org/en/.

UNICEF (2007) 'WHO and UNICEF call for renewed commitment to breastfeed-

ing', Press release, 20 June, www.
unicef.org/media/media-40135.html.
— (2008) *The Child Care Transition*, Innocenti Report Card 8, Florence: UNICEF
Innocenti Research Centre.

US GAO (United States Government
Accountability Office) (2006) *Breastfeeding: Some strategies to market
infant formula may discourage breastfeeding; state contracts should better
protect against misuse of WIC name*,
GAO-06-282, February.

Valentine, T. (1996) 'The minimum wage
debate: politically correct economics?',
Economic and Labour Relations Review,
7: 188–97.

Vatn, A. (2005) *Institutions and the Environment*, Cheltenham: Edward Elgar.

Veblen, T. (1965 [1904]) *The Theory of Business Enterprise*, Reprints of Economic
Classics, New York: Augustus M. Kelley.

Vickers, J. (1999) 'Economic models and
monetary policy', *Bank of England Quarterly Bulletin*, May, pp. 210–17.

Vitullo-Martin, J. and J. R. Moskin (1994)
The Executive's Book of Quotations, New
York and Oxford: Oxford University
Press.

Voitchovsky, S. (2005) 'Does the profile of
income inequality matter for economic
growth?', *Journal of Economic Growth*,
10(3): 273–96.

Weeks, J. (1969) 'Political economy and
the politics of economists', *Journal of
Radical Political Economics*, 1(1): 1–10.

Wheat, I. D. (2009) 'Teaching economics
as if time mattered', in J. Reardon (ed.),
*The Handbook of Pluralist Economics
Education*, London: Routledge.

Whyte, W. F. and K. K. Whyte (1991) *Making Mondragón: The growth and dynamics of the worker cooperative complex*,
2nd revised edn, Ithaca, NY: Industrial
and Labor Relations Press.

Wilkinson, R. (2005) *The Impact of Inequality: How to make sick societies healthier*,
New York and London: New Press.

Wilkinson, R. and M. Marmot (eds) (2003)
*Social Determinants of Health: The solid
facts*, 2nd edn, Geneva: World Health
Organization.

Wilkinson, R. and K. Pickett (2009) *The
Spirit Level: Why more equal societies
almost always do better*, London: Allen
Lane.

Winkelmann, L. and R. Winkelmann
(1998) 'Why are the unemployed so
unhappy? Evidence from panel data',
Economica, 65(1): 1–15.

Wolf, M. (2004) *Why Globalization Works*,
New Haven, CT: Yale University Press.

Wolff, E. and A. Zacharias (2007) 'The impact of wealth inequality on economic
well-being', *Challenge*, 50(4): 65–87.

Wolfson, M., G. Rowe, J. F. Gentleman and
M. Tomiak (1993) 'Career earnings and
death: a longitudinal analysis of older
Canadian men', *Journal of Gerontology*,
48(4): S167–S179.

Woolf, M. (2007) 'Junk food nation.
3.6 million people in Britain suffer
from malnutrition', *Independent*, 6 May.

World Bank (2005) *Equity and Develop-
ment: World Development Report 2006*,
Washington, DC: World Bank and
Oxford University Press.

— (2008) *World Development Report 2009*,
Washington, DC: World Bank and
Oxford University Press.

World Health Organization (1981)
*International Code of Marketing of
Breast-Milk Substitutes*, Geneva: World
Health Organization, available at
www.who.int/nutrition/publications/
infantfeeding/en/index.html, accessed
23 November 2008.

— (2008a) 'International Code of
Marketing of Breast-Milk Substitutes, frequently asked questions,
updated version 2008', Geneva:
World Health Organization, available
at whqlibdoc.who.int/publications
/2008/9789241594295_en.pdf, accessed
23 November 2008.

— (2008b) 'Air quality and health', August,
available at www.who.int/topics/
air_pollution/en/.

Worm, B. et al. (2006) 'Impacts of biodiversity loss on Ocean Ecosystem Services',
Science, 314: 787–90.

Wray, R. (2008) 'Breeding toxins
from dead PCs', *Guardian*, 6 May,

available at www.guardian.co.uk/
environment/2008/may/06/waste.
pollution/print, accessed 14 February
2009.

Zinn, H. (1990) *Declarations of Independ-* *ence: Cross-examining American ideol-* *ogy*, New York: HarperCollins.

— (2002) *The Future of History: Interviews* *with David Barsamian*, Monroe, ME: Common Courage Press.

Glossary

Adding-up problem: if labour is paid its marginal product, will the residual amount be just enough to pay capital its marginal product? Answer: only if there are constant returns to scale!

Arrow's Paradox: if everyone is a price-taker in a perfectly competitive demand and supply model, how do prices change? Who or what adjusts them in response to surpluses or shortages?

Behavioural economics: the attempt to study how human beings actually behave instead of focusing on how rational beings should behave. Notions of limited selfishness, limited self-control and limited rationality have emerged from this discipline.

Bubbles: ongoing increases in prices (often asset prices such as stock market price or real estate prices) that in retrospect turn out not to have been justified.

Cambridge Capital Controversy: a debate that raged from the mid-1950s to the mid-1970s that eventually showed inconsistencies in the neoclassical aggregate model that purports to explain income distribution.

Comparative advantage: a lower opportunity cost of production. Used to 'demonstrate' that trade is mutually advantageous. Some texts acknowledge that other theories are needed to explain some aspects of trade, such as trade in similar goods between similar countries.

Competitive market: requires large numbers of buyers and sellers who are all small relative to the market such that no one can individually influence the market price. (See *Arrow's Paradox*.) Also requires free entry and exit, and perfect information.

Deadweight loss of monopoly: the supposed cost of monopoly compared to a competitive market. It includes the loss of net benefit from a smaller quantity produced, the loss from 'rent-seeking' behaviour (the diversion of time, effort and expertise away from productive activities towards efforts to secure monopoly profits), and an equity cost of a less equitable distribution of income.

Demand: the maximum price consumers are willing to pay for any given quantity demanded.

Dynamic efficiency: an optimal rate of technological progress resulting from optimal investments in research and development. Relevant to the debate about whether monopolists and oligopolists are more likely to develop better techniques over time than competitive firms. In contrast, static efficiency assumes given technology and products.

Dynamic monopsony: when a firm has market power to set its wage owing to 'frictions' and imperfect information. Since the conditions are pervasive, so is dynamic monopsony. See *Frictions.*

Easterlin Paradox: empirical evidence showing: (1) a positive relationship of income to well-being among people at any point in time, and (2) no relationship between average income and average well-being in a society over long periods of time. It is explained by the ongoing importance of relative position and gradual adaption or adjustment in people's aspirations over time to higher living standards.

Efficiency: a situation of no waste. See *Pareto optimal.*

Equilibrium: a situation where there is no tendency to change. Plans of all relevant economic decision-makers are consistent with each other. An equilibrium may be stable (the system returns to the equilibrium following a small disturbance) or unstable (a small disturbance drives the system away from equilibrium).

Equity: a synonym for fairness. What is equitable or fair requires an ethical or normative judgement. For example, equity may involve the idea of a 'fair go' where everyone has equal opportunity. It may instead involve judgements about the equitability of outcomes, as in utilitarianism. The ultimatum game (described in Chapter 1) shows that people are prepared to make themselves absolutely worse off in order to punish others who have not treated them 'fairly'.

Externalities: cost or benefits imposed on others that do not influence the decisions by the original actor and which are not reflected in market prices. These are of second order of importance according to their treatment in mainstream texts. In reality they are all-pervasive and many are of first-order importance.

Failure of markets: a situation in which the market may produce an efficient outcome, but it is one which is socially or ethically unacceptable. Term suggested by Colander (2003). Compare with *Market failure.*

Free rider problem: exists whenever an individual can receive a benefit from others' contribution to the cost of a good that benefits them all. Using the principles of rational choice, the individual may decide not to contribute but to 'free ride' on the contributions of others. See *Public good.*

Frictions: often refers to things that prevent either job or geographic mobility of the labour force. For example, changing jobs might necessitate retraining.

Includes the time and resources it takes to find information, or switch jobs, or move home.

General equilibrium: occurs when all markets in the economy are in equilibrium simultaneously.

Heterodox economics: an umbrella term used to cover approaches that are outside of mainstream, orthodox economics. It includes institutional, post-Keynesian, socialist, Marxian, feminist, Austrian, ecological and social economics among others.

Ideology: a theoretical perspective or world-view; a view of human nature and the possibilities for change; usually embodies value judgements about what is good and bad. Different political ideologies give rise to different schools of thought in the social sciences.

Inefficiency: exists when there is the potential to use resources more efficiently, to make at least one person better off without making anyone worse off, i.e. to move to a Pareto optimal situation. In practice, eliminating an inefficiency may make some better off and some worse off, but those made better off would be able, in principle, to compensate those made worse off.

Laissez-faire: the doctrine that society is better off if the government refrains from intervening in the market economy.

Macroeconomics: the study of the economy as a whole. Topics include the determination of GDP, the growth of GDP, unemployment, inflation, interest rates, and the balance of payments.

Marginal benefit: the extra benefit from doing a bit more of something. For a firm: selling another unit of a good or service. For a person: getting some utility from a bit more of some activity, like consuming a good or earning some extra income.

Marginal cost: the extra cost of doing a bit more of something. For a firm: producing another unit of a good or service. For a person: doing a bit more of some activity. Marginal cost, like all costs, reflects opportunity costs.

Marginal thinking: the attempt to maximize monetary or psychological satisfaction by pursuing any activity up to the point where marginal cost equals marginal benefit.

Market failure: a situation in which markets fail to allocate resources efficiently owing to an inherent characteristic of the market, such as monopoly, externalities or imperfect information.

Market fundamentalism: the belief that the model of a perfectly competitive market approximates how actual markets operate in the real world. See *Laissez-faire.*

Microeconomics: the study of individual markets. Topics include the determination of prices, quantities, and relative efficiency of different market structures.

Monopsony: a firm that has market power to choose the wages it offers. Traditionally it was thought to require a single buyer of labour, and therefore to be extremely rare. But see *Dynamic monopsony.*

Multiple equilibria: an economic model may have more than one equilibrium. For example, neither demand nor supply curves have to be linear and they could intersect more than once, resulting in multiple equilibria. See *Equilibrium.*

Neoclassical economics: often used to describe the orthodox or mainstream approach that dominates the undergraduate textbooks. It emphasizes individual rational choice, marginal analysis, and the efficiency of resource allocation at a point in time (static efficiency). It focuses attention on equilibrium outcomes in individual competitive markets and the general equilibrium of the economy as a whole.

Normative: that which embodies a norm, value or moral precept. Normative statements often (though not always) contain the word *should.* For example: there should be no child poverty in a country as rich as Canada. See its opposite, *Positive.*

Opportunity cost: what must be given up to get something; the value of the next best alternative forgone.

Pareto optimal: has the property that it is not possible to make anyone better off without making at least one person worse off – in other words, there would be no waste anywhere in the economy. See *Inefficiency.*

Partial equilibrium analysis: the analysis of the equilibrium of a single market in isolation. Other markets may or may not be assumed to be in equilibrium, but they are not analysed explicitly.

Positive: dealing only with facts, descriptions of the world. In principle, positive statements can be shown to be right or wrong, although it may not be easy to do so in practice. See its opposite, *Normative.*

Price ceiling: a government-determined maximum price. It will not be 'binding' unless it is below the equilibrium price. Example: rent controls.

Price floor: a government-determined minimum price. It will not be binding unless it is above the equilibrium price. Example: minimum wages.

Principle of compensating differences: because 'net benefits' include non-monetary benefits, dirty, dangerous or dull jobs would receive higher pay than clean, safe and interesting jobs, all else equal.

Principle of equal net benefit: if there were no intrinsic (or innate) differences between workers, and no barriers to entering an occupation, then in equilibrium the present value of net benefits should be the same in all jobs – otherwise people would move from a lower-benefit job to a higher-benefit one.

Prisoner's dilemma: a situation Robert Frank calls 'smart for one, dumb for all'. People make rational choices to do the best they can for themselves, but collectively the result is worse than other outcomes that are possible. The standard example is that of two firms who fail to collude to charge the monopoly price and set a lower price instead. The dilemma also exists whenever people would be collectively better off if everyone contributed to a public good (or reduced their contributions to a public bad, such as pollution) but rational choice leads them to 'free ride' on others' contributions. It is a pervasive social problem.

Private good: a good that provides benefits only to the person who consumes it, also termed a 'rival good'. It's assumed that a system of property rights exists to exclude anyone who has not paid for the good from consuming it ('excludable'). See its opposite, a *Public good*.

Public bad: like a public good, only a public bad reduces utility instead of adding to it. Examples: an unjust distribution of income, incompetent and corrupt government, pollution.

Public good: a good is something that provides benefits. A pure public good is not only non-excludable, it is also non-rival. The opportunity cost of another person consuming it is zero. Static efficiency requires a socially optimal price of zero. See its opposite, a *Private good*.

Rational choice theory: this assumes that individuals are rational, self-interested, have a stable set of internally consistent preferences, and wish to maximize their own happiness (or 'utility'), given their constraints.

Scarcity: the starting point for neoclassical economics. It arises out of unlimited wants confronting limited resources.

Self-fulfilling prophecies: an expectation that (say) the price will increase by 10 per cent leads to changes in behaviour such that the actual price does increase by 10 per cent.

Speculation: attempting to buy low and sell high to make a profit. Textbooks tell us that speculation must be stabilizing. Modern research is showing how speculation can be destabilizing through buying high and selling even higher.

Sraffa, Piero: The Italian-born economist at Cambridge University who in 1926 argued that several requirements for the competitive demand and supply model were mutually incompatible.

Supply: the maximum quantity sellers are willing to sell for any given price. It must be independent of demand. The supply curve exists only for price-taking firms – not for firms that set their price with an eye on how that will affect demand for their product.

Utility: a measure of happiness or benefit.

Wage compression: when wage differences between workers are much smaller than their productivity differences. It refutes a prediction of marginal productivity theory, and suggests the importance of fairness and status considerations.

Index

Channel One, 80
chemicals, registration of, 160
child labour, prohibition of, 173
child mortality, 83, 216; in Philippines, 239
child poverty, 210
children, vulnerable to advertising, 81–2
choice: freedom of, 42; individual, 38; public, 110, 112; rational, 9 17, 22, 110, 150, 163
Chomsky, Noam, 113, 114, 254
Chrysotile Institute, 162
cigarettes *see* tobacco industry
Citizens Against Lawsuit Abuse (CALA), 112
Clark, J. B., 179–80
climate change, 112, 152–3, 154–7, 165, 253; denial of, 156
closed-end mutual funds, 147
coffee, price of, 233–4
cognitive dissonance, 162
Cohen, Avi, 105, 106, 181, 182–3
Colander, David, 116, 132, 141, 154, 206, 232
collective good, 111, 152 *see also* public goods
Colombia, US military aid to, 240
Commercial Alert, 82, 84
Commodity Futures Modernization Act (CFMA) (2000), 262
common resources, use of, 152
communities, destruction of, 16, 18
community: notion of, 25–6; omitted from analysis, 251–3; relation to individual, 17–18
comparative advantage, 28–30, 222, 224, 227, 230–1; evaluation of, 43–5; technological change and, 228
comparative static analysis, 48–9, 64
compensation principle, 225–6, 245
competition, 13; imperfect, model of, 66, 106; perfect, 46, 53, 54–7, 60, 65, 93, 102, 104, 107–8, 130, 131, 132, 138, 169, 194, 204, 230 (analysis of, 118–22; efficiency of, 121–2; flawed nature of, 135–8; in labour markets, 63; incompatible requirements of, 65–6; limits of, 118–49; overemphasis on, 247–8)
competitive market, definition of, 46
competitive model, 106; as useful

approximation, 57–62; empirical testing of, 184–5; inconsistency of, 64–5
computer waste, disposal of, 232
conspicuous consumption, 90, 158, 205
consumer loans, 260
consumer's surplus, 75–6, 221
consumerism, 79, 248; formation of, 74 *see also* conspicuous consumption
consumers, people as, 74–92
contracts, 60; perceived costlessness of, 245–6; relational, 141–2, 250, 256
conventions, 169
Cook, P. J., 186
cooperation, importance of, 21
cooperative (or collusive) behaviour, 129–30
cooperative firms, 116
coronary heart disease, in civil service, 214
corporations, power of, 84, 110–14; relation to individual, 18–20 *see also* multinational corporations
costs, private versus social, 150–3
costs of production, theories of, 94–100, 102–6; empirical support lacking, 105–6
Cowell, Frank, 207
credit crunch, 258
credit default swaps (CDS), 257, 261–2
credit markets, in USA, 256
crime rates, 20
Crusoe, Robinson, 27–8, 91
cycles, 15, 147–8

Daly, Herman, 253
Dasgupta, Partha, 231, 232
Davis, Lance, 240
Dayton-Johnson, J., 26
deadweight loss, 125, 136, 137, 138, 139–40
Deaton, Angus, 88–9
demand: relation with marginal revenue, 101; theory of, 74–81
demand and supply model, 53
demand curve, 46–7, 76, 77, 104, 107, 131
democracy, 21, 86, 91, 115–16, 167, 217; economic, 116, 234
Denmark, taxation in, 210–11
deregulation, 143, 144, 261–2; impact of, 259–61
Dewald, W. G., 34
Dewey, John, 114
differences, principle of compensating, 172

malnutrition, of children, 201
management compensation *see* executive compensation
Mankiw, N. G., 54, 226
Manning, Alan, 187, 189
Mansfield, Edwin, 103, 104, 105, 259, 260
marginal benefits, 10–11, 13, 118, 122, 131, 150
marginal costs, 10–11, 38, 97, 118, 119, 175, 176, 203; social, 151–2
marginal productivity of labour, 94–7
marginal productivity theory of income distribution, 169–95; empirical testing of, 184–5; fuzziness of, 183
marginal revenue product (MRP), 170
marginal utility, 75–6
Marglin, Stephen, 9, 16–18, 25, 26, 44, 206, 228, 243, 252–4
market: anomalies of, 147, 148; as means of organizing activity, 12–13; efficiency of, 18; equilibrium, 48; failures, ubiquity of, 150–68; frictions in, 187–9; idolization of, 4; non-competitive, 122–3; structure of, 118–49; types of, 54, 118; workings of, 53 (imagined, 46–73) *see also* failure of markets
market fundamentalism, 4–5, 140, 248
Marmot, Michael, 213, 216
Marx, Karl, 167
McCloskey, D., 32, 36–40, 246
McConnell, C. R., 81
McGreal, Chris, 109
McNeil, J. R., 150, 253
metaphors, use of, 38
methodology, 14, 25; fudging of, 31–2; implicit and unofficial, 36, 37–40; inability to refute core propositions, 35–6, 106, 246; problems of, 246–7
micro near-efficiency, 148–9
military-industrial complex, 19
Mill, John Stuart, *Principles of Political Economy*, 116
minimum efficient scale, 101
minimum wage, 5, 50–1, 63, 173, 190, 244; effect of, on unemployment, 3, 31, 32–5, 58–9, 204; laws regarding, 67; monopsony and, 176; predictions concerning, 58–9
models, building of, 27; selection of most appropriate, 5, 130
Monbiot, George, 166, 239

Mondragón Cooperative, 116
monopolistic competition, 54, 127
monopoly, 54, 123–7, 132, 248; bilateral, 177; compared to perfect competition, 124; cost structures of, 136; fleeting nature of, 133; model of, 62, 71; natural, 126–7; regulation of, 125–7
monopsonistic labour markets, 175–7, 187–90
monopsony, 58, 233, 247, 251; and minimum wage, 176; and unions, 176–7; dynamic, 58; reinterpretation of, 188–90
moral and ethical judgements, 141
moral hazard, 142, 245, 256, 257
more is better, assumption of, 246
Morris, D. J., 139
mortgages, 257; alternative, 259–60; NINJA mortgages, 257; regulation of, 259 *see also* sub-prime mortgage crisis
Mullainathan, S., 69
multinational corporations, 228, 235, 238, 241
Musgrave, Alan, 38–9
Myrdal, Gunnar, 205, 210, 211

Nader, Ralph, 86–7, 109, 159
National City Bank, 240
natural experiments, 39
needs, absolute, 16
Nelson, R., 118
neoclassical economics, 1, 169, 181, 252; ideology of, 42
non-competitive markets, 122–3
non-rivalry, 153
normative economics, 31, 37, 243–4
North American Free Trade Agreement (NAFTA), 224, 236, 237; Chapter 11, 237
Northrop, Emily, 16
'note and forget' device, 153

objectivity, myth of, 3
offshoring, 44; example of, 228
Okun, Arthur, 14, 202–3, 208
oligopoly, 54, 58, 127, 128, 135, 236; model of, 62
Olson, Mancur, *The Logic of Collective Action*, 110–11
opportunity cost, 10, 27–30
O'Reilly, C. A., 191
organic products, 234

rent controls, 49, 244; predictions concerning, 59–61
rent freeze: in New York, 70; in Paris, 70–1
rent-seeking behaviour, 124
rents: ceilings on, 31, 59; freezing of, 60
replication of results, problem of, 34
research and development (R&D), 135, 193
reswitching result, 181
retirement, compulsory, 173
returns to capital, 177–8
returns to scale, 98–9, 180–1
rhetoric of reaction, 208
Ricardo, David, 44, 177, 224, 227, 228
Rick, Frank, 179
risk, ignorance of, 161–2
Robinson, Joan, 1, 9, 93, 128, 150, 153, 179, 180, 219
robust equation, search for, 33–4
Rodrik, Dani, 5, 262
Roosevelt, F. D., 166, 259
Rosen, S., 174
Ross, D., 139–40
Rothschild, Kurt, 93, 108–9
Rotterdam Convention, 162
Russia, transition to capitalism, 143

S&P 500 companies, 148
Samuelson, Paul, 44–5, 148, 228, 229
Save More Tomorrow programme, 24
scarcity, 10, 15–17
Scherer, F. M., 139–40
Schiller, B. R., 226
Schlosser, Eric, *Fast Food Nation*, 85
Schor, Juliet, 87; *Born to Buy*, 80, 81
Schumpeter, Joseph, 133, 134, 137, 210
second-best, theory of, 135
self-fulfilling prophecies, 68
self-interested individuals, 12
selfishness, 17; as a virtue, 13; bounded, 23–4, 25
Sen, Amartya, 89, 201
shareholder value movement, 192
shareholders, versus managers, 114–15
Sharpe, Andrew, 211
Shiller, R. J., 148, 149, 243–5, 258, 262
short-run costs, 97, 102–4
Simon, Herbert, 249
Smith, Adam, 22, 86, 94, 180, 245, 257; *The Wealth of Nations*, 13, 15
smoking of tobacco, 163; quitting of, 22
social capital, 20

social cohesion, 20–1, 26
social context, importance of, 78
social exclusion, 201
social safety net, provision of, 14
Sonnenschein-Mantel-Debreu (SMD) Theorem, 72
speculation, destabilizing, 69–70
speculators, role of, 69
spiteful egalitarians, 207
spot transactions, 141, 144, 250
Sraffa, Piero, 65–6, 104–5, 106
Stalk, G., 190
state, role of, 18–19, 196
status: as non-pecuniary benefit, 185; importance of, 185–6
Stern, Nicholas, 154–5
Stigler, George, 138
Stiglitz, Joseph, 1, 55–6, 67, 106, 143, 145, 146, 193, 245–6, 253, 260–1, 262
strategic trade policy, 222
sub-prime mortgage crisis, 70, 252, 260, 262
subsidies, 223, 231
Summers, Larry, 146
supply curve, 47–8, 62, 64, 65, 66, 118–21, 122–3, 130; of labour, 175
surplus production, 63 *see also* consumer's surplus
Sweden, child health in, 216
systematic mistakes, 22–3

tariffs, 31, 43, 45, 222–3, 231; analysis of, 225; economics of, 219–24; seen as increasing employment, 223–4
taxation, 14, 196–218; and inefficiencies, 20; based on consumption spending, 158; costs of, 52–3, 196–7; in Denmark, 210–11; international comparison of, 197–201; predictions concerning incidence of, 61–2; sales taxes, 51–2
Taylor, Lance, 166
technological change, 133, 228
technology, 93
terms of trade, changes of, 223
testing of hypotheses, 37, 38
Thaler, Richard, 24, 69
thought experiments, 38–9, 90, 101
Thucydides, 234
Thurow, Lester, 183, 192
time, scarcity of, 91
tit-for-tat strategies, 129